Library of
Davidson College

JOHN BUNYAN
CONVENTICLE AND PARNASSUS

Pencil drawing of John Bunyan, aged fifty, by Robert White, used for the engraved portrait of the Dreamer prefixed to the third edition of *The Pilgrim's Progress* in 1679. By permission of the Trustees of the British Museum.

John Bunyan
Conventicle and Parnassus

Tercentenary Essays

EDITED BY
N. H. KEEBLE

CLARENDON PRESS · OXFORD
1988

Oxford University Press, Walton Street, Oxford OX2 6DP
Oxford New York Toronto
Delhi Bombay Calcutta Madras Karachi
Petaling Jaya Singapore Hong Kong Tokyo
Nairobi Dar es Salaam Cape Town
Melbourne Auckland
and associated companies in
Beirut Berlin Ibadan Nicosia

Oxford is a trade mark of Oxford University Press

Published in the United States
by Oxford University Press, New York

© Oxford University Press 1988

All rights reserved. No part of this publication may be reproduced,
stored in a retrieval system, or transmitted, in any form or by any means,
electronic, mechanical, photocopying, recording, or otherwise, without
the prior permission of Oxford University Press

British Library Cataloguing in Publication Data
John Bunyan: Conventicle and Parnassus:
tercentenary essays.
1. Bunyan, John—Criticism and interpretation
I. Keeble, N. H.
828'.408 PR3332
ISBN 0-19-812833-9

Library of Congress Cataloging in Publication Data
John Bunyan—Conventicle and Parnassus.
Bibliography: p. Includes index.
1. Bunyan, John, 1626-1688. 2. Authors, English—Early modern,
1500-1700—Biography. 3. Puritans—England—Clergy—Biography.
4. Christian literature, English—History and criticism.
I. Keeble, N. H.
PR3331.J64 1988 828'.407[B] 87-24771
ISBN 0-19-812833-9

Set by Dobbie Typesetting Service
Printed in Great Britain
at the University Printing House, Oxford
by David Stanford
Printer to the University

Preface

IN a well-known marginal note Coleridge opined that in *The Pilgrim's Progress* 'the Bunyan of Parnassus had the better of the Bunyan of the Conventicle'. This is a strikingly trenchant formulation of one solution to the crux of Bunyan studies: whether Bunyan's literary genius was inspired by, or throve at the expense of, his religious commitment. Coleridge's words are recalled in the title to this volume of twelve original essays since they neatly define its twin concerns: Bunyan's Christian faith and his imagination. Historical and theological investigation of Bunyan's thinking must engage with dramatically and metaphorically charged sources, while the texts which literary study subjects to critical scrutiny are determinedly and relentlessly homiletic. It is consequently the relationship between Bunyan's Puritanism and his *'feigning words'* — between Conventicle and Parnassus — which, implicitly or explicitly, exercises each of the contributors to the collection. They were not asked to subscribe to Coleridge's definition of that relationship, nor does the symposium promote any particular critical, theological, or scholarly orthodoxy. Rather, it seeks to advance our understanding of Bunyan by adopting a variety of contemporary approaches to him, and to illustrate the many different kinds of interest which, after 300 years, he attracts. Contributors were, however, each invited to write on a specific topic in order that the book as a whole might, by treating the main aspects of Bunyan's life, thought, and work, offer a comprehensive summary of the present state of Bunyan scholarship and criticism. I am extremely grateful to them for accepting this editorial prescription and for the handsome way they have responded to my call upon their various kinds of expertise.

N.H.K.
University of Stirling

Contents

	Abbreviations	ix
1.	The Fellowship of Believers: Bunyan and Puritanism B. R. WHITE, Principal of Regent's Park College, Oxford	1
2.	Conscience, Liberty, and the Spirit: Bunyan and Nonconformity RICHARD L. GREAVES, Professor of History and Courtesy Professor of Religion, Florida State University	21
3.	Grace, Holiness, and the Pursuit of Happiness: Bunyan and Restoration Latitudinarianism ISABEL RIVERS, Fellow of St Hugh's College, Oxford	45
4.	'When at the first I took my Pen in hand': Bunyan and the Book ROGER SHARROCK, Emeritus Professor of English, King's College, London	71
5.	Plain and Simple: Bunyan and Style ROGER POOLEY, Lecturer in English, University of Keele	91
6.	'To be a Pilgrim': Bunyan and the Christian Life GORDON S. WAKEFIELD, formerly Principal of The Queen's College, Birmingham	111
7.	Fishing in Other Men's Waters: Bunyan and the Theologians GORDON CAMPBELL, Reader in English, University of Leicester	137
8.	'Thou must live upon my Word': Bunyan and the Bible JOHN R. KNOTT, jun., Professor of English, University of Michigan at Ann Arbor	153

9. Spiritual Discerning: Bunyan and the Mysteries of the Divine Will — 171
   U. MILO KAUFMANN, Professor of English, University of Illinois at Urbana-Champaign
10. 'With the eyes of my understanding': Bunyan, Experience, and Acts of Interpretation — 189
    VINCENT NEWEY, Senior Lecturer in English, University of Liverpool
11. Glossing and Glozing: Bunyan and Allegory — 217
    VALENTINE CUNNINGHAM, Fellow of Corpus Christi College, Oxford
12. 'Of him thousands daily Sing and talk': Bunyan and his Reputation — 241
    N. H. KEEBLE, Lecturer in English, University of Stirling

Select Bibliography — 265

Index — 271

Abbreviations

THE following abbreviations are used in the Notes. For publication details of a work cited by author and short title, see the first reference to it in the notes to that chapter. The place of publication is not given if it is London.

BDBR	Richard L. Greaves and Robert Zaller (eds.), *Biographical Dictionary of British Radicals in the Seventeenth Century*, 3 vols. (Brighton, 1982-4)
BQ	*The Baptist Quarterly*
Brown	John Brown, *John Bunyan (1628-1688): His Life, Times, and Work*, tercentenary edn., rev. Frank Mott Harrison (1928)
Casebook	Roger Sharrock (ed.), *'The Pilgrim's Progress': A Casebook* (1976)
CR	A. G. Matthews, *Calamy Revised* (Oxford, 1934)
DNB	Sir Leslie Stephen and Sir Sidney Lee (eds.), *The Dictionary of National Biography*, 22 vols. (1908-9)
ELH	*English Literary History*
ES	*English Studies*
Folio (1692)	*The Works of That Eminent Servant of Christ, Mr John Bunyan*, ed. Charles Doe (1692)
GA	John Bunyan, *Grace Abounding to the Chief of Sinners*, ed. Roger Sharrock (Oxford, 1962)
Greaves	Richard L. Greaves, *John Bunyan* (Appleford, Berks., 1969)
Harrison	Frank Mott Harrison, *A Bibliography of the Works of John Bunyan*, Supplement to *The Transactions of the Bibliographical Society*, 6 (1932)
HW	John Bunyan, *The Holy War*, ed. Roger Sharrock and James F. Forrest (Oxford, 1980)
JURCHS	*Journal of the United Reformed Church History Society*
Kaufmann	U. Milo Kaufmann, *'The Pilgrim's Progress' and Traditions in Puritan Meditation* (New Haven, 1966)
Minutes	H. G. Tibbutt (ed.), *The Minutes of the First Independent Church (now Bunyan Meeting) at Bedford, 1656-1766*, Publications of the Bedfordshire Historical Record Society, 55 (Bedford, 1976)
Misc. Wks.	*The Miscellaneous Works of John Bunyan*, gen. ed. Roger Sharrock, 12 vols. (in progress) (Oxford, 1976-)
MLN	*Modern Language Notes*

MLR	*Modern Language Review*
Newey	Vincent Newey (ed.), *'The Pilgrim's Progress': Critical and Historical Views* (Liverpool, 1980)
N & Q	*Notes and Queries*
PMLA	*Publications of the Modern Language Association of America*
PP	John Bunyan, *The Pilgrim's Progress*, ed. James Blanton Wharey, rev. Roger Sharrock, 2nd edn. (Oxford, 1960)
RES	*Review of English Studies*
Sharrock	Roger Sharrock, *John Bunyan*, corr. reissue (1968)
SP	*Studies in Philology*
Talon	Henri Talon, *John Bunyan: The Man and his Works*, trans. Barbara Wall (1951)
Works	*The Works of John Bunyan*, ed. George Offor, 3 vols. (Glasgow, Edinburgh, and London, 1860–2)

1

The Fellowship of Believers: Bunyan and Puritanism

BY B. R. WHITE

THIS essay is primarily concerned with John Bunyan's career until 1660 and with his place in the kaleidoscope of Puritan sectarianism. His experience and his writings, especially his controversies, were profoundly shaped both by the overarching Calvinism of the Puritan tradition more generally and, specifically, by his membership of the Independent Church at Bedford. The importance of the general Puritan environment and the part played in Bunyan's spiritual quest by John Gifford, the Bedford pastor, has been noted elsewhere.[1] However, the part played by Gifford and the wider Independent community in forming Bunyan's churchmanship has been given less attention. Yet to understand Bunyan's particular form of Puritanism and to locate its place within the wider tradition and the developments of the time requires more emphasis upon his experience as an Independent.

Three centuries after his death John Bunyan is mostly remembered as the author of *The Pilgrim's Progress* (1678). Yet, while in his spiritual autobiography, *Grace Abounding to the Chief of Sinners* (1666), his membership of the congregation of Independents at Bedford and their influence upon him played an important part, Christian, Bunyan's pilgrim, was essentially a lonely figure. Admittedly he had counsellors such as Evangelist and the Interpreter and, importantly, friends on the way such as Faithful and Hopeful, but the sense of the surrounding presence of a church fellowship was almost completely absent. This was not because Bunyan had in any way himself withdrawn from the Bedford congregation between 1666 and 1678 for, in fact, he had become its pastor in January 1672,[2]

---

[1] E. G. Owen Watkins, *The Puritan Experience* (1972), pp. 113-14, 106.
[2] *Minutes*, p. 71.

and remained so until his death in 1688. Partly, no doubt, the idea of a personal pilgrimage made the possibility of a community in pilgrimage difficult to handle but the strange disjunction between Bunyan's own experience and that of his pilgrim has a more fundamental explanation. It illustrates the deep cleft between the two cardinal aspects of both Calvinism itself and Puritan theology more generally, for they were both deeply concerned with the theology of individual faith and salvation and also with the nature and constitution of the visible church.

There has been a great deal of debate over the meaning of the word 'Puritanism'.[3] Yet Basil Hall made a basic contribution to the discussion near the beginning when he pointed out that it first belonged to the period 1570–1640. Contemporaries, as he said, would have applied the term to the 'restlessly critical and occasionally rebellious members of the Church of England who desired some modifications in Church government and worship, but not to those who deliberately removed themselves from that Church.'[4] Puritan ecclesiological ideals were broadly Presbyterian.

However, with the coming of the civil wars and the turning of a previously apparently secure world upside down, a new day arrived. Previously the pressure of both custom and property with a very little police work had been sufficient to discourage all but a tiny majority of Protestants from putting their convictions to any extremes of practice. In the period 1640–60, however, many men and women set to work to build, not a new Jerusalem, for that must wait for the Second Coming which many of them expected shortly, but churches which were built to the specifications of the one apostolic blueprint laid down in the New Testament. Hence, in the 1640s and 1650s, there were to be not only Presbyterians but Independents, at least four varieties of Baptists (Arminian, Calvinistic, Mixed-communion and Seventh-day), Ranters, Quakers, and a host of others. It was with the Ranters, the Quakers, and the Calvinistic Baptists with their strict communion views that John

---

[3] Cf. M. G. Finlayson, *Historians, Puritanism, and the English Revolution* (Toronto, 1983), p. 174 n. 7 lists relevant discussions. See also Richard L. Greaves's comprehensive survey of recent historical work on Puritanism, 'The Puritan-Nonconformist Tradition in England, 1560–1700: Historiographical Reflections', *Albion*, 17, no. 4 (1985), 449–86 (esp. pp. 449–52).

[4] B. Hall, 'Puritanism: The Problem of Definition', *Studies in Church History*, 2 (1965), p. 290.

Bunyan came into collision because of his mainstream Calvinistic convictions and his churchmanship learned among the Independents of John Gifford's Bedford congregation.

Hard facts about Bunyan's early life are almost as elusive as a wholly satisfying definition of 'Puritanism'. Roger Sharrock's introduction to his edition of *Grace Abounding* exemplifies many of the problems faced by a biographer when he says that the 'Bunyans must have had an accepted position in the life of the parish', that John 'for some time at least' was 'educated at a petty school or the local grammar school', that he 'presumably left early in order to earn his living', and that the school he left 'may have been the one at Houghton Conquest'. The 'must haves', 'presumablys', and 'may have beens' are part of the common stock of the candid Bunyan biographer. Nor do things immediately improve for the years after Bunyan left school. He 'probably' served in the Civil War on the parliamentary side although, as Dr Sharrock remarks, the 'John Bunyan' known to have served at Newport Pagnell in the parliamentary garrison 1644–7 is not necessarily *the* John Bunyan. Indeed, he writes, before going on to describe the various sectarian influences at work in the garrison and, therefore, possibly upon Bunyan himself, the 'surname was too common in Bedfordshire at this time for the identification to be accepted as a certainty, as it has too readily been by later biographers'. And so guesswork builds upon the shifting sands of guesswork and the building is not helped by the fact that references 'to the passage of time in *Grace Abounding* are frequent but vague.'[5]

One firm date in his biography is the birth of his blind daughter Mary, who was christened in July 1650; so his marriage must have taken place not later than the previous year. Even the name of Bunyan's first wife is unknown, although she was to bear him three more children, Elizabeth, John, and Thomas, before her death in 1658.[6]

In his Preface to *Grace Abounding* Bunyan described the book as '*a Relation of the work of God upon my own Soul, even from the very first, till now*', and as his intention in publishing that, '*if God will, others may be put in remembrance of what he hath done for their Souls, by reading his work upon me.*'[7]

Even as a child, he said, he had swung from daytime 'cursing, swearing, lying and blaspheming' to thoughts of 'the fearful torments

---

[5] *GA*, pp. xii–xvii.   [6] *GA*, p. xvi.   [7] *GA*, pp. 1–2.

of Hell-fire'. It was not, however, until his marriage to a wife 'whose Father was counted godly' that he began to think of some kind of religious commitment himself. Her dowry, such as it was, included Arthur Dent's *The Plaine Mans Path-way to Heaven* (1601), which had run to twenty-seven editions by 1650, and Lewis Bayly's even more popular *The Practise of Pietie* (1612), which had gone into about forty-seven by that date.[8] Bunyan read both with her while she frequently spoke to him of her father and 'what a strict and holy life he lived in his day, both in word and deed.' Although, Bunyan was later to confess, the books did not bring him to understand the helplessness of his situation as a sinner, they did for a while make him an enthusiastic church-goer, greatly attached to what he later came to judge the outward forms of religion.[9]

Then a sermon on sabbath-keeping pricked his conscience and 'at that time I felt what guilt was, though never before, that I can remember'. However, despairing of forgiveness, he after a while 'found a great desire to take my fill of sin' and plunged into it until rebuked by a woman, herself of bad reputation, who warned him of his ability *'to spoile all the Youth in a whole Town, if they came but in my company.'* This brought him up short and, falling into the company of 'one poor man that made profession of Religion', he began to read the Bible. Bunyan said that at the time he preferred the historical parts to the epistles of Paul, 'being as yet but ignorant either of the corruptions of my own nature, or of the want and worth of Jesus Christ to save me.' For about a year he became a reformed character and his neighbours were amazed at the change in him even though, as he himself said, he 'knew not Christ, nor Grace, nor Faith, nor Hope.'[10]

His first encounter with the Bedford Independent congregation's members was told in a famous passage:

upon a day, the good providence of God did cast me to *Bedford*, to work on my calling; and in one of the streets of that town, I came where there was three or four poor women sitting at a door in the Sun, and talking about the things of God . . . their talk was about a new birth, the work of God on their hearts, also how they were convinced of their miserable state by nature: they talked how God had visited their souls with his love in the Lord Jesus, and with what words and promises they had been refreshed, comforted

---

[8] E. H. Emerson, *English Puritanism from John Hooper to John Milton* (1968), p. 179.   [9] *GA*, §§ 4–6, 15–16.   [10] *GA*, §§ 20–1, 26–31.

and supported against the temptations of the Devil . . . they also discoursed of their own wretchedness of heart, of their unbelief, and did contemn, slight and abhor their own righteousness, as filthy and insufficient to do them any good. And me thought they spake as if joy did make them speak: they spake with such pleasantness of Scripture language, and with such appearance of grace in all they said, that they were to me as if they had found a new world.[11]

In consequence Bunyan began to spend more and more time in their company, but about the same time he also read some of the books put out by the Ranters which were 'highly in esteem by several old Professors'. He talked too with the 'poor man' who a little earlier had encouraged his Bible reading and who by then had become 'a most devilish *Ranter*'. Although Bunyan eventually turned away from him he later admitted that the man had been a source of temptation to him. Moreover, he discovered, as he carried through his work in the countryside, that several people whom he encountered 'though strict in Religion formerly' had also been swept away by the new theology. They tried to persuade him that he was in the darkness of legalism and that they had attained perfection 'and could do what they would and not sin'. This teaching, he admitted, was not without attraction, but eventually he turned from it.[12]

The depth of hostility in Bunyan to Ranter ideas is not to be judged merely from *Grace Abounding* for it helps to explain the very firm rejection by him and other leaders of the Bedford congregation of Quaker teaching a few years later. They must quickly have sensed the sharpness of the challenge which the Ranters posed. The movement had been born, apparently, in part as a consequence of the disillusionment caused by the suppression of the Levellers. From 1649–50 onwards the Ranters showed something of the considerable potential of Puritan sectarianism for producing theological, political, and even ethical revolution.[13] There was plenty, both in their teaching and practice (quite apart from the suspicions of moderate men always inclined to fear the worst), to threaten a deep-seated disturbance of traditional values and society. For the Independents in Bedford, newly formed as a congregation themselves in 1650 and without the cement to their fellowship which time itself would begin to provide, there was every reason to be uneasy.

---

[11] *GA*, §§ 37–8.   [12] *GA*, §§ 44–5.
[13] See A. L. Morton, *The World of the Ranters* (1970), chaps. 4, 5.

A number of prominent, well-publicized leaders of the Ranter way of thinking had passed from the unquestioning, if not deeply felt, episcopalianism of their parents through the various positions on the sectarian Puritan spectrum. Abiezer Coppe[14] had moved from the Presbyterians through the Baptists to the Ranters. Others, such as Laurence Clarkson,[15] Richard Coppin,[16] and Joseph Salmon,[17] had moved step by step through the Presbyterians, the Independents, and the Baptists to various forms of Ranterism. In those uncertain days a number of the Bedford Independents must have known something of such moves in their own circle and their leaders must have been deeply aware of the threat of further possible changes.

The Ranters rejected all the mainstream Calvinist theology and poured scorn on the idea that the gathered churches (whether Independent or Baptist) were likely to promote true discipleship or godliness. Furthermore, Ranters like Abiezer Coppe, who saw God himself as 'the mighty Leveller . . . to Levell the Hills with the Valleyes, and to lay the Mountaines low',[18] would be deeply disturbing to a people who, on the whole, accepted the political *status quo*, if they were allowed freedom of worship and evangelism. It is true that some may, within a few years, have had Fifth-Monarchy leanings among the Bedford Independents and that some were strong enough republicans to join in 1657 to urge Cromwell to refuse the crown, but there is not the slightest sign that, as a body, they hungered and thirsted for further revolution. If to these matters were added the widespread beliefs, shared quite evidently by Bunyan himself, that the Ranters taught and practised sexual immorality and, above all, that they replaced the guidance of the Scriptures by the appeal to the Spirit within them, then it can be seen that the Bedford men were likely to turn from Ranterism with the same horror that the London Baptists did when they published *Heart-bleedings for professors abominations*, in 1650.

As he turned against the Ranters Bunyan turned to the Bible 'with new eyes, and read as I never did before', especially the Pauline writings. But, as he continued to cry to God that he might know the truth, the way to heaven and glory, he also turned more and more towards John Gifford's congregation in Bedford. He was

---

[14] *BDBR*, i. 173-4.
[15] *BDBR*, i. 149-51.
[16] *BDBR*, i. 174-5.
[17] *BDBR*, iii. 134-5.
[18] Abiezer Coppe, *A Fiery Flying Roll* (1649; Exeter, 1973), p. 2.

drawn, he said to 'the state and happiness of these poor people at *Bedford*' and felt that they were basking in the sunshine of God while he shivered in the dark and snow outside. At last, after a period which he described as 'many months together', he explained something of his uncertainties to members of the congregation. They told their pastor, and John Gifford, who had been very largely responsible for the foundation of the church in the first place, invited Bunyan home with him to hear him 'confer with others about the dealings of God with the Soul'. As Bunyan's spiritual struggles continued he went on seeking the help of those whom he called 'the people of God' during the ups and downs of his certainties and uncertainties. During this period of at least a year of inner turmoil, while he began to struggle with the fear that perhaps he was among the lost, he continued to listen to the man whom he revered as 'holy Mr. *Gifford*, whose Doctrine, by Gods grace, was much for my stability'. It was apparently Gifford's practice to warn his people not to take any teaching on trust because some particular man or other said it was true until they found an inner personal certainty about it.[19]

Later Bunyan came to read Luther's commentary upon Galatians and asserted, 'I found my condition in his experience, so largely and profoundly handled, as if his Book had been written out of my heart', and declared that this commentary more than any other book apart from the Bible was 'most fit for a wounded Conscience'.

John Bunyan's own position, learned from his own struggles, was that:

> as God had his hand in all providences and dispensations that overtook his Elect, so he had his hand in all the temptations that they had to sin against him, not to animate them unto wickedness, but to chuse their temptations and troubles for them; and also to leave them, for a time, to such sins only as might not destroy, but humble them; as might not put them beyond, but lay them in the way of renewing his mercie.[20]

Later also he reported, as his spiritual struggles continued and he still reached no firm ground, 'I did also desire the Prayers of the people of God for me'—an evident further reference to the Bedford congregation. He obviously kept in close touch with them and mentioned, in passing, another occasion when he was 'in a Meeting of Gods People', but he was not yet actually a member of the church.

---

[19] *GA*, §§ 46, 53, 76-7, 117. [20] *GA*, §§ 129-30, 157.

Finally he reached peace on the basis of Christ's word in John 6: 37, 'Him that comes to me, I will in no wise cast out.' It was after that he felt able to join the saints at Bedford in church fellowship.[21]

Bunyan's own position over the nature of church fellowship was so evidently shaped by John Gifford's ideals that it is important to discuss them. The *Church Book* gives a very simple account of the congregation's first foundation. One day in 1650 twelve men and women 'joyntly first gave themselves to the Lord, and one to another by the will of God'. Once the church had thus been formed they unanimously appointed one of their number, John Gifford, who seems to have been the one who had brought them together in the first place, to be their pastor. Such a proceeding was characteristic of the Independent congregations of the time, but this group went one stage further and it was to be determinative for their future as a congregation and for Bunyan's own policy in later years as pastor and defender of the congregation's unity. What needs to be emphasized at this point is that the principle was John Gifford's and it was inherited from him and not initiated by Bunyan. The account of the congregation's foundation continued:

Now the principle upon which they thus entered into fellowship one with another and upon which they did afterwards receive those that were added to their body and fellowship was faith in Christ and holines of life, without respect to this or that circumstance or opinion in outward and circumstantiall things. By which meanes grace and faith was incouraged: love and amity maintained: disputings and occasion to janglings and unprofitable questions avoyded, and many that were weake in the faith confirmed in the blessing of eternall life.[22]

This principle was both most carefully maintained by Gifford and stressed in the long last letter which he despatched to the church from his death-bed and which was copied into the *Church Book*. In it he stressed the need to avoid any situations which could lead to divisions among them. Any new members should formally and solemnly agree that 'union with Christ is the foundation of all saintes' communion, and not any ordinances of Christ, or any judgement or opinion about externalls'. The specific 'externalls' he mentioned as possible causes of dispute were 'baptisme, laying on of hands, anoynting with oyle, psalmes'. These were all matters, especially the first (as Bunyan was to have good reason himself to discover) and even the last, which

[21] *GA*, §§ 179, 249, 253.   [22] *Minutes*, p. 17.

almost certainly referred to congregational singing, which had been, or were yet to be, causes of division among the sectarian congregations of the day.[23]

Disputes about baptism were apparently not in Bunyan's mind when he came to join the church: it is certainly far from clear that he was then baptized.[24] Rather, at this time was there the joy he found in the Lord's Supper, 'that blessed Ordinance of Christ' in which 'the Lord did come down upon my conscience with the discovery of his death for my sins, and as I then felt, did as if he plunged me in the vertue of the same.' It is evident that for him the term 'ordinance' rather than 'sacrament' was preferable as a biblical word and as stressing the divine authority for the rite: it was evidently not meant to imply a belief in the 'real absence' of the Lord from the Supper as it came to do for some standing in the same tradition in later generations. Nevertheless, in reaction from this joy his tortured spirit endured unease for something like 'three quarters of a year' until once more he could enjoy it and discern in it Christ's body 'as broken for my sins and that his precious blood had been shed for my transgressions'.[25]

Shortly afterwards, in another section of *Grace Abounding* Bunyan describes another aspect of Independent churchmanship. This passage, which was an account of the process which marked his formal acceptance as a preacher, was largely characteristic of the way the matter was handled in the Independent and Calvinistic Baptist congregations of the time. No member was allowed merely of his own choice to begin preaching either within the congregation or in public as an evangelist. There was a firm underlying conviction in the churches of this type that the gifts of the members were at the disposal of the body as a whole and also that the body (or rather, its male members) was responsible for testing the gifts of its members before permitting them to take a public platform.[26]

It was apparently some five or six years after his first spiritual struggle and when he had been, in his own phrase, enabled to venture his soul upon Christ, that some of the leaders of the congregation approached Bunyan and suggested that he might be willing 'to take in hand in one of the Meetings to speak a word of Exhortation unto them.' Very cautiously, and perhaps a little nervously, he agreed and

---

[23] *Minutes*, p. 19. [24] Brown, pp. 219-25. [25] GA, §§ 253, 254.
[26] Greaves, pp. 133-5.

spoke at two meetings. These occasions were, as he said, 'in private'. As would normally be expected in such a case his gift had first to be tested within the congregation before he could be encouraged to speak in public. So, after the gatherings which had almost certainly been restricted to church members, those present encouraged him with the assurance that they had been both 'affected and comforted' by what he said. The next step for him was to accompany one or two of the more experienced brethren to meetings, still of the committed, in nearby villages. Again, the reaction was very positive, with those who heard 'professing their Souls were edified thereby'. The final step in the church's recognition of his gift for preaching and the soundness of his doctrine was its formal act when, 'after some solemn prayer to the Lord, with fasting', he said, 'I was more particularly called forth, and appointed to a more ordinary and publick preaching the Word, not onely to and amongst them that believed, but also to offer the Gospel to those who had not yet received the faith thereof: about which time I did evidently find in my mind a secret pricking forward thereto'. Although the church felt able to use John Bunyan quite frequently in special disciplinary visits to church members, his preaching programme had already, by August 1657, taken him away too often on Sundays for him to serve as a deacon.[27]

Of course Bunyan's preaching was grounded firmly in the Puritan tradition: his chief themes were sin and grace and they were shaped by the Bible as understood by the English Calvinists. But his preaching was also anchored equally firmly in his own experience:

> In my preaching of the Word, I took special notice of this one thing, namely, That the Lord did lead me to begin where his Word begins with Sinners, that is, to condemn all flesh, and to open and alledge that the curse of God, by the Law, doth belong to and lay hold on all men as they come into the World, because of sin. Now this part of my work I fulfilled with great sence; for the terrours of the Law, and guilt for my transgressions, lay heavy on my Conscience. I preached what I felt, what I smartingly did feel, even that under which my poor Soul did groan and tremble in astonishment.[28]

The phrase, 'I preached what I felt, what I smartingly did feel' has often been quoted with approval and as an example to other preachers but it has less often been noted that Bunyan was himself,

[27] GA, §§ 265-8; Minutes, p. 28.   [28] GA, § 276.

at least for a while, in the themes which seemed central to him as a preacher, on pilgrimage. Two years after he had begun to preach on the sinfulness of sin he began to add another emphasis although, he claimed, 'still I preached what I saw and felt'. Having reached a further stage in his own Christian experience 'with some staid peace and comfort thorow Christ', for God, he said, 'did give me many sweet discoveries of his blessed Grace thorow him', Bunyan now laid more emphasis on God's mercy in Christ.[29] After a similar period stressing this, he said, 'God led me into something of the mystery of union with Christ: wherefore that I discovered and shewed to them also.' These three themes, he believed, amounted to the three 'chief points of the Word of God' and it was after preaching them for the space of 'five years or more' he was arrested, on 12 November 1660. His imprisonment was, in total, to last twelve years, although he was allowed out from time to time to visit friends and family and to attend meetings. He was even able to undertake a certain amount of work for the church.[30]

Bunyan admitted that the learned and professional ministry had often opposed his preaching but his own policy was not, he said, to return 'rayling for rayling' but rather to see how many 'carnal Professors I could convince of their miserable state by the Law and of the want and worth of Christ'.[31] On the other hand, turning to his fellow dissenters, he showed himself a faithful disciple of John Gifford when he claimed, several years before the public dispute with the closed communion Calvinistic Baptists came to a head:

> I never cared to meddle with things that were controverted, and in dispute amongst the Saints, especially things of the lowest nature; yet it pleased me much to contend with great earnestness for the Word of Faith; and the remission of sins by the Death and Sufferings of Jesus: but I say, as to other things, I should let them alone, because I saw they engendered strife, and because I saw they neither, in doing nor in leaving undone, did commend us to God to be his; besides, I saw my work before me did run in another channel even to carry an awakening Word; to that therefore did I stick and adhere.[32]

Issues which were, he judged, at the heart of the Gospel, were one thing, inessentials were another. Hence, he steered away from

---

[29] GA, § 278. [30] GA, § 279; *Minutes*, pp. 33, 39–42, 45–6.
[31] GA, § 283. [32] GA, § 284.

conflict over baptism, which most Calvinistic Baptists believed was involved with the heart of the Gospel and the very being of the Church but he did not hesitate, in his earliest published works, to enter directly into conflict with the Quakers.

In his own preaching he followed John Gifford's concerns closely:

> It pleased me nothing to see people drink in Opinions if they seemed ignorant of Jesus Christ, and the worth of their Salvation, sound conviction for Sin, especially for Unbelief, and an heart set on fire to be saved by Christ, with strong breathings after a truly sanctified Soul: that was it that delighted me; those were the souls I counted blessed.[33]

In an important comment about the gifts of Christian believers in general but, no doubt, about the gift of preaching in particular, Bunyan wrote in a way which underlined his commitment to the Independent tradition. The gifted believer, he said, should walk humbly with God, remembering 'that his Gifts are not his own, but the Churches; and that by them he is made a Servant to the Church, and that he must give at last an account of his Stewardship unto the Lord Jesus; and to give a good account, will be a blessed thing!'[34]

To understand the particular form of Puritanism in which Bunyan was nurtured and to which he gave his life it is necessary to see that the congregation to which he belonged was no isolated community unaware of and uncaring for any others. This was not so: the Independents generally maintained a network of relationships both locally and nationally[35] and, while they were seldom so extensively organized as the associations of the Particular Baptists in the 1650s or even Richard Baxter's Worcestershire Association, they were thoroughly aware of their need for relations with, and of their duties towards, sister congregations. In this context it is important to notice that Bunyan and his friends were accustomed to relate both to what virtually amounted to an informal national leadership in London as well as to congregations much nearer at hand.

What is not clear is just how significant it is as a guide to the convictions of the Bedford congregation that the London leaders with whom they had most to do were radicals with considerable experience of, and various degrees of commitment to, the Fifth

---

[33] *GA*, § 291.   [34] *GA*, § 304.
[35] See Geoffrey F. Nuttall, *Visible Saints: The Congregational Way* (1957), pp. 95–100.

Monarchy movement. The one congregation in London to which, over four years (1658–61), three members were commended for transfer from Bedford was that led by John Simpson[36] in St Botolph's parish church, Aldgate.[37] In 1657, Henry Jessey,[38] a close associate of Simpson who also shared his convictions about the rightness of believer's baptism and practised open communion, with others proposed a day of prayer in which the Bedford congregation joined 'with the rest of our brethren in the three nations'.[39] When the church hoped that a recalcitrant member in the capital would seek advice it was to Jessey, Simpson, and John Rogers[40] to whom they turned for help.[41] Similarly, in 1659, when the Bedford pastor John Burton was ailing and the church began to think of an assistant for him, they decided to write to Simpson, Jessey, and George Cockayne[42] asking them to recommend 'such an able godly man as may be suitable for our help'.[43] The fact that, as has been mentioned, members of the Bedford congregation wrote to London in 1657 to dissuade Cromwell from accepting the crown is a further indication that their politics generally may have been to the left of contemporary Independency.[44]

Meanwhile, locally there was concern for congregations which were much nearer. On 26 July 1656 it was agreed 'that the members of the Church of Christ in and about Steventon [*Stevington*] may breake bread with us, and we with them, as the Lord shall give opportunity'.[45] This church was probably only founded a year or so earlier and later became Baptist.[46] It may be significant that this trend was a very early one since, when there was a move at the end of October 1658 toward the drawing together of the Bedford congregation with others nearby, the Stevington church was not included. The three congregations which were to be linked with Bedford were those led by John Donne[47] at Pertenhall, William Wheeler[48] at Cranfield (these were both in Bedfordshire), and John Gibbs[49] at Newport Pagnell in Buckinghamshire. It was decided at church meeting in Bedford to appoint representatives who would

---

[36] *BDBR*, iii. 176–7. [37] *Minutes*, pp. 30, 34, 37.
[38] B. R. White, 'Henry Jessey in the Great Rebellion', in *Reformation, Conformity, and Dissent*, ed. R. Buick Knox (1977), pp. 132–53.
[39] *Minutes*, p. 28.   [40] *BDBR*, iii. 107–10.   [41] *Minutes*, p. 31.
[42] *BDBR*, i. 155–6.   [43] *Minutes*, p. 34.   [44] *GA*, p. xx.
[45] *Minutes*, p. 23.
[46] H. G. Tibbutt, *Some Early Nonconformist Church Books* (1972), pp. 23–44.
[47] *BDBR*, i. 230.   [48] *BDBR*, iii. 307–8.   [49] *BDBR*, ii. 7–8.

work for 'the continuing of unity and the preventing of differences' between the four congregations. The pastor, John Burton, and four other church members, including John Bunyan, were selected 'to consider of some things that may conduce to love and unity amongst us all'. In March the following year it was reported that, after some preparatory meetings, it had been agreed to hold a further gathering to complete drawing up the principles upon which 'unity and love' might be built. Bunyan and two others, one of them recently elected as an elder, went to represent Bedford. At church meeting next month it was decided that, because it had been agreed that 'in matters of difficulty we should advise with each other', a Bedford problem with a difficult church member should be referred to a meeting of representatives from the four congregations. It was not until the end of May, however, that it was agreed that letters should be sent inviting the representatives to come to Bedford to discuss the matter in the middle of June. The advice was given and acted upon at the June church meeting with Bunyan as one of the three to interview the problem member.[50]

It was in October 1659 that the church formally ratified the basis of association and ordered that the various proposals be 'recorded in some convenient place in our church booke and read over when occasion requireth'. Unfortunately, if this decision were followed up, the record has been lost. Nevertheless, co-operation did continue and when John Burton was ill in April 1660 the Bedford church decided, in a somewhat ambiguously worded decision, to ask the three other ministers and one of their own church members to help them by 'preaching and breaking of breade once every moneth or 3 weekes, one after another on the Lord's dayes' while their own pastor continued unwell. There seems to be no hint at this point that Burton's illness was thought particularly serious. However, at the end of August it was clear that he could not discharge his duties at all and it was decided to ask the three neighbouring ministers for assistance in finding someone to do his work. By the end of September Burton was dead and, since a further element in the agreement between the churches had been that if a pastor or teacher were removed from any one congregation the advice of all should be sought about a replacement, it was decided to arrange another representative meeting to discuss the matter. This was done but,

[50] *Minutes*, pp. 31–3.

meanwhile 'a considerable company of the brethren of our society' had decided to ask William Wheeler to leave Cranfield to come as pastor to Bedford. At the meeting Wheeler was told and he asked that the Cranfield church be told of the invitation to him and also that he should be given time to 'seek the Lord that he might see his hand leading him to us'. Wheeler eventually decided not to come (in January 1664!) and the church appointed two of its own members 'for their pastors and elders, to minister the word and ordinances of Jesus Christ to them'.[51]

After seeing Bunyan at work sharing in the building of inter-congregational fellowship it is now necessary to see him in two controversial situations, first with the Quakers and second with the Calvinistic Baptists.

His earliest published writings were aimed against the Quakers. The first was entitled, *Some Gospel-Truths Opened according to the Scriptures* (1656). The introductory note to the reader was by his then pastor John Burton. In it Burton identified the errors against which the book was written as those of the Socinians and, more particularly, 'those commonly called *Familists, Ranters, Quakers* or others'. This equation of the Quakers with the Ranters was quite common among the more orthodox Puritan sectaries and, whether accurate or not, reflected a widespread perception of the inner nature of Quaker teaching. It is clear that Bunyan shared that perception and the identification of the Quakers with the Ranters was not a mere polemical device: not only was he concerned with the resurrection of what he believed to be Ranter heresy but also with the practical antinomianism of which he believed both groups were guilty. So Bunyan asserted the Ranters' doctrine, as he understood it, to be Quaker doctrine, that *'thou mayest be saved by grace, though thou walk in the imaginations of thy own wicked heart'*. Not content with equating the Quakers with the Ranters in a marginal note he was prepared to refute Quaker teaching by emphasizing what he believed to be the central theme of the Gospel—that the one who was 'savingly convinced by the Spirit of Christ' had such 'an endless desire after Jesus Christ' that he or she could not be content with anything less than the blood of the Son of God to purge his or her conscience. Convinced as he was of the nearness of the Return of Christ and of that doctrine as a powerful motive for holy living, he

[51] *Minutes*, pp. 34-6, 38-9.

saw the contempt of 'the *Ranters, Quakers, Drunkards*, and the like' for the doctrine as a sign of the last times. In Scripture it was taught that in those days there would be scoffers and so Bunyan argued, 'if ever this Scripture was fulfilled; it is fulfilled on these men called *Quakers*'.[52]

In his second book, *A Vindication of Some Gospel-Truths Opened* (1657), Bunyan again stressed the true humanity of Christ and the distinction between the Spirit of Christ in the converted and the light of conscience which all men have. The book was once more commended by John Burton and also, on this occasion, by two other fellow church members. In it Bunyan stressed that his fundamental complaint against the Quakers was their teaching that 'every man that comes into the world hath the Spirit of Christ in him'. The generality of Quaker converts, he argued (and he could not deny that they were numerous) were either 'but light frothie professors, or else were shaken in their principles, and unstable therein'.

However, probably the most significant passage in *A Vindication* for indicating Bunyan's deep-seated distrust of the new movement came every early on when he explained why he believed that the Quakers were but new Ranters effectively teaching the same things and when he listed the points at which he believed their teaching to be virtually identical. Both groups, he believed, taught, first, that they would 'owne Christ no other waies, then only within'; second, that they could reject Scripture authority by denying 'all teaching but the teaching within'; third, that the ordinances of water baptism and the Lord's Supper could be ignored; fourth, that both taught that they were without sin—the Ranters certainly had and, Bunyan asked, 'how far short of this opinion are the Quakers?' fifth, both denied a physical resurrection of the body. On the basis of these arguments he claimed to have proved that 'the very opinions that are held at this day by the *Quakers*, are the same that long ago were held by the *Ranters*. Only the *Ranters* had made them thredbare at an Ale-house, and the *Quakers* have set a new glosse upon them again, by an outward legal holinesse'.[53]

In a real sense the issue about the truth or falsity of their teaching was settled for Bunyan before the Quakers came over his horizon: he had fought the battle with what he thought to be their doctrine

---

[52] *Misc. Wks.*, i. 7, 26, 52, 63, 85, 99.
[53] *Misc. Wks.*, i. 138–9, 148, 163–4, 211, 213.

with the Ranters and thereafter, granted he accepted the commonly held link between the Ranters and the Quakers, the Quakers were condemned.

When, in 1673, Bunyan published *Differences in Judgment about Water Baptism, No Bar to Communion*, he had a very different debate on his hands. He had been under pressure from the Calvinistic Baptists for eighteen years to adopt their closed communion position. The issue was not whether either infant's or believer's baptism was right but whether, in any case, it was worth debarring people from fellowship in a local congregation over the matter. The period of eighteen years means that the conflict had continued virtually since he first began to preach. The Baptists, he said, had endeavoured 'to persuade me to break communion with my brethren' and, indeed, 'some they did rend and dismember from us' over this period.[54] It seems that by 1676 even the church in London of which Henry Jessey had been pastor had moved over from the mixed communion to the closed communion position.[55] But, while the Baptists seem in a number of cases to have become more rigid over the matter, Bunyan, who probably had been baptized as a believer himself,[56] had grown very firm in the view that the issue of baptism was one for personal conscience rather than the one true door into church membership. His position was a faithful outworking of John Gifford's principles but it was not peculiar to the two of them: during the 1650s a number of men had held believer's baptism to be right for themselves—Jessey, Simpson, Vavasor Powell, and John Tombes among them—but had rejected the hard line which men like Henry Danvers and William Kiffin still took in making it a condition for church membership.

In *A Confession of My Faith, and a Reason of My Practice* (1672) Bunyan had outlined his view of the significance of the two ordinances of Baptism and the Lord's supper:

touching shadowish or figurative ordinances; I believe that Christ hath ordained but two in his church, viz., Water baptism and the supper of the Lord: both which are of excellent use to the church in this world; they being to us representations of the death and resurrection of Christ; and are, as God shall make them, helps to our faith therein. But I count them not the fundamentals of our Christianity, nor grounds or rule to communion with

---

[54] *Works*, ii. 618.   [55] *Minutes*, pp. 79–80.
[56] This issue is discussed in Brown, pp. 219–25.

saints: servants they are, and our mystical ministers, to teach and instruct us in the most weighty matters of the kingdom of God.[57]

So for him Baptism was *not* 'the initiating and entering ordinance into church communion'. None can be true members of a church merely because they have been baptized—by any mode or at any age. The basic qualification, Bunyan affirms (and the Baptists would agree), is to be a 'visible saint', that is, one who has been brought over to faith and holiness by the word of the Gospel and has made declaration of their 'faith and willingness to subject themselves to the lawes and government of Christ in his Church'. Should questions about baptism be likely to damage the fellowship then Bunyan was prepared to go so far as to say the ordinance should be put aside, for the edification and unity of the church are more important. If a believer were dead to sin and alive to God in Christ, and yet lacked the right light over Baptism, Bunyan would say it would not justify rejecting him or her from church membership. So he urged his Baptist critics, 'In the midst of your zeal for the Lord, remember that the visible saint is his' and that 'love which above all things we are commanded to put on, is of much more worth than to break about baptism'.[58]

His Baptist critics were unconvinced: they judged that it was a poor counterfeit of true Christian love which allowed and encouraged believers to do what they believed was contrary to the true order of a visible church, and Henry Danvers[59] pointed out that, in taking the view of baptism which Bunyan did, he was, in effect, going against the whole Christian Church and not merely against the Baptists.[60]

John Bunyan's relationship to 'Puritanism' was defined by the fact that, by the time he came to play his part in the story, there was (even if once there had been) no single manifestation of English religion which could be labelled 'Puritanism'. So, while it is true that his theology and his understanding of the Bible were largely controlled by an evangelical Calvinism which had been, arguably, characteristic of mainstream 'Puritan' preaching before the outbreak of the civil wars his church experience was limited to one of the sects into which 'Puritanism' had fractured. His experience, and none

---

[57] *Works*, ii. 604.   [58] *Works*, ii. 605, 609, 612, 615.
[59] Richard L. Greaves, *Saints and Rebels* (1985), chap. 6.
[60] Henry Danvers, *A Treatise of Baptism* (1673), p. 45.

should underestimate its richness, was shaped by the tradition of the gathered church, a fellowship of the committed, of visible saints, the Independents.

There Bunyan learned lessons about submission within the family of the local church. There he learned to preach and there he learned responsibility for his fellow members. There he learned the practice of inter-congregational co-operation. There he learned to exalt the Bible and a Calvinist tradition in resistance to a new theology. There he learned too to exalt the fellowship of 'visible saints' above even the central rites of the Christian faith.

In particular, he learned from one man, John Gifford, and from one congregation—that which, ironically, now takes its name, Bunyan Meeting, from him.

2

Conscience, Liberty, and the Spirit: Bunyan and Nonconformity

BY RICHARD L. GREAVES

Introduction

'I WAS caught in my present practice and cast into Prison,' and thus commenced 'a long and tedious Imprisonment, that thereby I might be frighted from my Service for Christ, and the World terrified, and made afraid to hear me Preach . . .'[1] Bunyan's candid reflection on his decision to pursue the path of nonconformity and the consequences of that resolution underscores the relative rapidity with which the determination was made. Unlike ministers who were ejected in August 1662 for refusing to comply with the Act of Uniformity, Bunyan had little time to ponder the ecclesiological tenets which he would subsequently adduce to justify the separatist way. Those principles were first seriously worked out in his writings only in 1671-2, in *A Confession of My Faith, and a Reason of My Practice*, though a synopsis appeared as early as 1665 in *The Holy City*. Faced with the initial outbreak of persecution that followed the election of the Convention in April and the return of the King in May 1660, Bunyan knew only that conformity would terminate his preaching and force him to worship according to the structured patterns in the *Book of Common Prayer*. Unwilling to accept either of these conditions, he consciously chose the path of passive resistance, virtually insisting upon a confrontation: 'Had I been minded to have played the coward, I could have escaped . . .'[2]

---

[1] *GA*, §§ 279, 317.
[2] *A Relation of the Imprisonment of Mr John Bunyan*, in *GA*, p. 105. For the Act of Uniformity, see Andrew Browning (ed.), *English Historical Documents 1660-1714* (1966), pp. 377-82.

Of the two considerations which persuaded Bunyan not to conform, the more important was his determination to continue preaching. 'To preach Gods word, it is so good a work, that we shall be well rewarded, if we suffer for that . . .'³ The primary goal of his ministry at this time was not the edification of the faithful but the propagation of the Gospel in 'the darkest places in the *Countrey*, even amongst those people that were furthest off of profession . . .'⁴ In this he was a true disciple of the sectarian tradition, as reflected in the 1650s, for example, in the concerted efforts of the Independents and Baptists in particular to preach in the 'dark corners' of the land.⁵ Bunyan's hortatory goal was a combination of burning personal conviction and missionary fervour. The man who preached 'as if an Angel of God had stood by at my back to encourage me' found that he inclined 'most after awakening and converting Work . . .'⁶ Conformity would abruptly terminate this preaching, since, in the eyes of the restored authorities, Bunyan had no authority to pursue such a ministry: the Act of Uniformity would recognize only episcopal orders. This Bunyan could not accept, given what he believed was the unmistakable evidence that God had blessed his efforts. There was, in fact, so much success that in these early years he battled constantly to curtail feelings of pride. It was his insistence on his right to preach that led to his arrest at Lower Samsell, Bedfordshire, on 12 November 1660, under the old Elizabethan Act against Conventicles.⁷

During the first year and a half of his imprisonment Bunyan enjoyed sufficient freedom to continue his 'wonted course of preaching', exhorting the saints to be steadfast in their faith and 'to take heed that they touched not the Common Prayer, *&c.* but to mind the word of God . . .'⁸ Here then was the second principle upon which his nonconformity was grounded, namely the refusal to worship according to the formal liturgy prescribed in the *Book of Common Prayer*. His sermons on this theme during his periods of liberty prior to April 1662 became the basis for one of his earliest prison works, *I Will Pray with the Spirit*, the first edition of which

---

³ *GA*, pp. 105-6.   ⁴ *GA*, § 289.
⁵ See Christopher Hill, *Change and Continuity in Seventeenth-century England* (Cambridge, Mass., 1975), chap. 1.   ⁶ *GA*, §§ 282, 289.
⁷ *GA*, §§ 296-302. For the Elizabethan Act, see Henry Bettenson (ed.), *Documents of the Christian Church*, 2nd edn. (1963), pp. 242-3.
⁸ *GA*, p. 129.

probably appeared in 1662. Taking as his text 1 Corinthians 14: 15, he defined true prayer as 'a sincere, sensible, affectionate pouring out of the heart or soul to God through Christ, in the strength and assistance of the holy Spirit, for such things as God hath promised, or, according to the Word, for the good of the Church, with submission, in Faith, to the Will of God'.[9] Because the enlightening work of the Spirit was the essential basis of true prayer, the *Book of Common Prayer*, which Bunyan deemed nothing more than a patchwork quilt of human inventions, was judged valueless. He even went so far as to argue that its use was expressly forbidden by Scripture, and that those who mandated its utilization were akin to the Marian Bishop of London, Edmund Bonner, 'that blood-red Persecutor'.[10] Bunyan clearly regarded the refusal of the 'godly' to accept the *Book of Common Prayer* as a fundamental basis of nonconformity. 'Look into the Goals in *England*,' he wrote *c*.1662, 'and into the Alehouses of the same: and I believe, you will find those that plead for the Spirit of Prayer in the Goal, and them that look after the Form of mens Inventions only, in the Alehouse'.[11]

When he was arrested in 1660, the magistrates were apparently interested only in Bunyan's insistence on his right to preach, but when he appeared before Sir John Kelynge (or Keeling) and other justices at the quarter sessions in January 1661, both of the principles that had led him into nonconformity were challenged. When Kelynge pressed Bunyan as to why he refused to attend services in a parish church, the latter retorted that the word of God did not command worship according to the *Book of Common Prayer*, which 'was made by other men, and not by the motions of the Holy Ghost, within our Hearts . . .'[12] Unable to shake Bunyan's conviction of the necessity of Spirit-prompted extempore prayer, the justices shifted the interrogation to the authority by which he claimed the right to preach. Bunyan retorted with references to 1 Peter 4: 10–11 and Acts 18, insisting that all who were the recipients of the Spirit-endowed gift of exhortation had the right to preach. In short, Bunyan's principal justification for nonconformity was his insistence that the ultimate authority in matters religious was the working of the Holy Spirit through the Bible and in the believer as distinct from

---

[9] *Misc. Wks.*, ii. 235.
[10] *Misc. Wks.*, ii. 249–50, 253.
[11] *Misc. Wks.*, ii. 284.
[12] *GA*, pp. 107–12, 114.

the claims of the state to govern religious behaviour. Like Martin Luther, whose commentary on Galatians had been a powerful influence in his conversion, Bunyan rested his case on the sanctity of the conscience duly enlightened by the Spirit.[13] This intensely personal approach to nonconformity was the hallmark of his first six years in prison.

It was not until the eve of his release from the county jail in 1672 that Bunyan offered a written exposition of his concept of the church as the communion of visible saints. At root these ecclesiological principles had been worked out well before 1660,[14] subsequent to which they continued to provide the foundation for most of the Nonconformist churches. Even the Presbyterians, once they were permanently ousted from the state church, embraced these ideals in practice. The true church, for Bunyan, was a fellowship of believers separated from the carnal world and gathered in freedom to pursue the holy life. The traditional concept of a parish church was unacceptable because 'visible saints by calling' could associate in 'church communion' only with those who professed faith and holiness, not with the 'open profane'.[15] To ensure the maintenance of a holy community of visible saints required both strict admission requirements and the imposition of discipline to reform wayward members and excommunicate the recalcitrant. A prospective member had to provide a 'relation' of personal faith, be examined with respect to his or her religious experience and personal conduct, and declare a willingness to be subject to the laws and government of Christ as exercised in the church. The sacrament or 'ordinance' of baptism was not a requirement for membership in the Bedford congregation.[16] While this conception of the church was manifestly at odds with the principles embodied in the restored Church of England and would have necessitated the pursuit of nonconformity, the idea of the church as the communion of visible saints, separated from the world by its profession of personal faith and holy life, was not used by Bunyan to justify his repudiation of the established church at the Restoration. More pressing to Bunyan in 1660–1 was the right of those imbued with the gifts of the Holy Spirit to preach

---

[13] *GA*, §§ 129–30, pp. 117–18.
[14] See Geoffrey F. Nuttall, *Visible Saints: The Congregational Way 1640–1660* (Oxford, 1957), and above, pp. 8, 12, 18. [15] *Works*, ii. 602–3.
[16] *Works*, ii. 604–7. See Greaves, pp. 136–44.

and of all the 'godly' to pray as the Spirit moved them. Bunyan's crisis at the Restoration was fundamentally personal, not ecclesiological.[17]

Millenarian Expectations and Spiritual Introspection

The period which extended from Bunyan's arrest in 1660 to the publication of *Grace Abounding* in 1666 was characterized both by a strongly eschatological outlook that culminated with the exposition of millenarian themes in *The Holy City* in 1665, and by a substantial amount of spiritual introspection that ranged from his assertion of the sanctity of the individual conscience to the composition of his spiritual autobiography. Apart from writing *Christian Behaviour* (1663), a practical guide to social conduct for the faithful, Bunyan devoted these years to predominantly personal concerns that were a direct outgrowth of his incarceration. Particularly after the strictness of his imprisonment increased in April 1662, his ties with the Nonconformist community were sharply curtailed. He engaged in visitation activities on behalf of the Bedford church in September and October 1661, but his name does not appear again until November 1668, though the records for these years are sparse, and in fact blank for the period between March 1664 and October 1668. Nevertheless, Bunyan's name is not mentioned in connection with either the visitation assignments of November 1661 or the selection of Samuel Fenn(e) and John Whiteman as co-pastors in January 1664.[18] Similarly, these years were essentially free of disputes with other Nonconformists. It was a time for Bunyan to ponder his own religious experience, which itself was at the root of the trouble in which he now found himself. He reflected too on God's plan for the future. For Bunyan, what Christopher Hill has called 'the experience of defeat'[19] was largely framed by these considerations.

Contemplating eschatological themes was a direct outgrowth of the fear of death which troubled Bunyan as he faced imprisonment. His first prison work, *Profitable Meditations* ([1661]), reflected

---

[17] In *GA*, § 324, Bunyan observes that as he faced imprisonment his major concern was his ability to endure if the incarceration proved to be lengthy and to face death 'should that be here my portion . . .' [18] *Minutes*, pp. 37-9.
[19] Christopher Hill, *The Experience of Defeat: Milton and Some Contemporaries* (1984).

on the Day of Judgement, though as yet his eschatological thinking was highly simplistic compared to the more mature *Holy City* published four years later. In the interval Bunyan clearly did some reading in millenarian literature, at least some of which was replete with citations from the patristics and learned language which he self-consciously lacked.[20] *Profitable Meditations* is significant as an indication of Bunyan's early success in overcoming his fear by affirming the ultimate triumph of the saints:

> I know, O Death, thou maist my body spoil,
> And bring it down: yet I do not thee fear:
> For that shall last with thee no longer while,
> Than till my JESUS in the Clouds appear.[21]

Coupled with the certainty of vindication was an assurance that those who persecuted the saints would receive their due chastisement:

> And then he will with Trumpets royal voice
> Raise up his Dead, and gather them on high;
> Then we shall live who have made Him our choice,
> When thou in fiery flames with Hell shalt lie.[22]

The *Prison Meditations* which appeared two years later (1663) reinforced the sense of spiritual well-being that stemmed from the conviction of suffering for a righteous cause. Instead of regretting the sermons that got him into trouble, Bunyan rejoiced that he had preached while he had had the opportunity.[23] Now, he reflected, I

> . . . can with very much content
> For my Profession die,

secure in the knowledge that he had a good conscience.[24] Jail had become a school in which 'we learn to dye' with the assurance of immortality.[25] The intensely personal nature of these poems is repeatedly revealed, and there is corroboration in *Grace Abounding* of the profound spiritual experience which he underwent in these years. Traditionally overlooked because of fascination with the earlier spiritual struggles that dominate most of the autobiography, the rich experience of the early prison years is no less crucial for Bunyan's

---

[20] *Works*, iii. 398
[21] *Misc. Wks.*, vi. 26, stanza CXXX.
[22] *Misc. Wks.*, vi. 26, stanza CXXXI.
[23] *Misc. Wks.*, vi. 43, stanza 8.
[24] *Misc. Wks.*, vi. 44–5, stanzas 17, 19.
[25] *Misc. Wks.*, vi. 45, 48, stanzas 24, 45.

later success as a minister. The confidence that he attained in the early 1660s was the basis for the exuberance of his subsequent ministry and writing. 'I never had in all my life so great an inlet into the Word of God as now; them Scriptures that I saw nothing in before, are made in this place and state to shine upon me; Jesus Christ also was never more real and apparent then now; here I have seen him and felt him indeed.'[26] But Bunyan offers us only a tantalizing glimpse—'a hint or two', he says—of what transpired,[27] perhaps because the experience was too mystical to be conveyed in words. From the poetic lines of the *Prison Meditations* we know that out of this experience came a conviction that those of 'true Valour' and a 'high and noble Mind' will

> . . . conquer when they thus do fall,
> They kill when they do dye:
> They overcome *then* most of all,
> And get the Victory.[28]

So for Bunyan the experience of persecution led in eschatological terms to the assurance that temporal defeat was in fact the means through which the spirit triumphed.

Thus persuaded, Bunyan pursued his millenarian studies for two more years. Although he was not inclined to speculate on a divine timetable for the inauguration of the millennium, others were, and there was mounting excitement in some Nonconformist circles as 1666 approached. This can only have reinforced Bunyan's predilection to ponder eschatological themes. Indeed, they pervade his 1665 works, including *One Thing Is Needful* and *The Resurrection of the Dead*. The former included a dramatic vision of the returning Christ, resplendent in glorious attire, who would condemn persecutors to their own 'Prison with its locks and bars.'[29] In *The Holy City* (1665) Bunyan indicated that Christ would return at the end of the millennium, an interpretation generally espoused by the Fifth Monarchists, to whom Bunyan had perhaps been attracted in the 1650s.[30] The millennium itself, which Bunyan described as a

---

[26] *GA*, § 321. [27] *GA*, § 320.
[28] *Misc. Wks.*, vi. 50, stanzas 59, 60, 62.
[29] *Misc. Wks.*, vi. 93, stanza 26. *The Resurrection of the Dead* also had an evangelical purpose; see J. Sears McGee's introduction to *Misc. Wks.*, vol. iii.
[30] Richard L. Greaves, 'John Bunyan and the Fifth Monarchists', *Albion*, 13 (1981), 84–7.

thousand-year period during which the Heavenly City—the Church—would be constructed, would be instituted when an angel confined the devil to the bottomless pit. Persecution of the Church would thereupon cease, the period of tribulation having served its purpose: 'The church in the fire of persecution is like Esther in the perfuming chamber, but making fit for the presence of the king . . .'[31] Thus in the broad context of the divine schema Bunyan visualized a purpose for the suffering of the Nonconformists. There was some consolation too in his belief that such suffering characterized the age that preceded the millennium, whose institution was seemingly imminent: 'It is now towards the end of the world . . .'[32]

As Bunyan explained his personal affliction in the context of millenarianism, he was forced to grapple with the role of governments and more precisely of monarchs in the divine plan. On the one hand, the Nonconformists obviously suffered because of state persecution, sanctioned by a sovereign who had failed to honour the promise of liberty to tender consciences made at Breda in 1660 before, and apparently as a condition of, his return. There must have been a temptation for Bunyan to castigate Charles as an agent of the Antichrist. On the other hand, the early 1660s in particular saw a recurring pattern of political activity aimed at the overthrow or substantial modification of the regime. Although the number of overt rebellious acts was few, these were years of unrelieved plotting, with the state's efforts to uncover the conspiracies enormously complicated by widespread and often unsubstantiated rumours.

Like numerous other Nonconformists, Bunyan repudiated the first attempt to overturn the Restoration government, which was launched in London by a band of Fifth Monarchists led by Thomas Venner in January 1661. 'That practice of theirs, I abhor', Bunyan insisted, adding that 'I look upon it as my duty to behave myself under the King's government, both as becomes a man and a christian . . .'[33] His profession not only rings true but accords with the general tendency of Bedfordshire Nonconformists to shun disruptive political action. An examination of the principal centres of plotting in England in the 1660s in relation to areas of Nonconformist strength reveals discontinuity rather than correlation. This suggests that apart from

---

[31] *Works*, iii. 402, 426, 431, 446.
[32] *Works*, iii. 444. The best brief introduction to *The Holy City* is by McGee in *Misc. Wks.*, vol. iii.   [33] *GA*, p. 120.

dissidents in the London area (where nonconformity was strong), the proclivity to radical political activity was greater among Dissenters in areas where they were heavily outnumbered. Thus radical activity was at least in part a response to feelings of endangerment and insecurity. In Bedfordshire the number of Nonconformists was substantial enough to undermine any government hopes of crushing them, thereby permitting Dissenters to follow a more moderate course of passive resistance. The Tong plot of 1662, the northern rebellion in 1663, and the 1665 Rathbone conspiracy, for example, did not involve Bedfordshire.[34]

In *The Holy City* Bunyan admonished monarchs for being enamoured with 'mistress Babylon, the mother of harlots,' but he judiciously cast the blame for this on the Great Whore herself. When 'this gentlewoman . . . is laid in her grave, and all her fat ones gone down to the sides of the pit, these kings will change their mind, and fall in love with the true and chaste matron, and with Christ her Lord'.[35] Rather than exhorting his readers to overthrow monarchy, Bunyan tried to teach them that sovereigns would ultimately embrace Christ, even if they were the last ones to do so. This left open the possibility that some would surely perish long before their fellow monarchs turned from their persecutorial ways. There would, in any event, be a cosmic struggle before the rulers submitted to Christ: 'They will be shaking the sharp end of their weapons against the Son of God, continually labouring to keep him out of his throne, and from having that rule in the church, and in the world, as becomes him who is the head of the body, and over all principality and power.'[36] This apparent call to arms, however, was sharply tempered by Bunyan's insistence that the Church is not a rebellious institution bent on destroying either monarchs or their wealth.[37] Interned in a Bedford jail, Bunyan perceived the struggle solely in spiritual terms.

His own spiritual battles in the 1650s were, in his mind, but a part of the greater cosmic encounter against the forces of the Antichrist. It was therefore natural for Bunyan to culminate this period of introspection by recounting his own spiritual autobiography in the hope that it might sustain others in their religious life. Of the

---

[34] Richard L. Greaves, *Deliver Us from Evil: The Radical Underground in Britain, 1660–1663* (New York, 1986), introd.
[35] *Works*, iii. 445–6.   [36] *Works*, iii. 444–5.   [37] *Works*, iii. 410.

major themes of the early 1660s, little attention is given in *Grace Abounding* to eschatological concerns apart from the immediate fate of Bunyan's own soul. However, the work not only marks the culmination of Bunyan's introspection and the affirmation of the sanctity of the individual conscience, but redirects his emphases toward the needs of others. The preface commences with a virtual apology for his recent inability to exhort the saints: '*I being taken from you in presence, and so tied up . . . I cannot perform that duty that from God doth lie upon me, to you-ward, for your further edifying and building up in Faith and Holiness . . .*'[38] Here then was a work unmistakably directed to the needs of those he had converted in the late 1650s and very early 1660s.

Exhortations to Pilgrims and Runners

The years from 1666 to 1670 are the most obscure in Bunyan's career. The 1664 Conventicle Act expired on 1 March 1669, and though some religious persecution continued in the interval prior to its re-enactment in April 1670, Nonconformists enjoyed a degree of freedom in this period, in part because of legal uncertainty concerning nonconformity.[39] In July 1669, however, a judicial opinion stated that the statutes of 13 Eliz. I, c. 12 and 14 Car. II, c. 4 concerning the qualifications of ministers who preached at religious assemblies were still in force.[40] The King thereupon issued a proclamation ordering Justices of the Peace to enforce these laws.[41] Bunyan benefited by the confusion. Although Parliament was not formally prorogued until 1 March 1669, it had last met in August 1668 without renewing the Conventicle Act. The following November Bunyan had sufficient freedom to undertake visitation and admonition responsibilities for the Bedford Church. The royal proclamation in July apparently curtailed his activities, but between October 1669 and June 1670 he was again active in the congregation's work.[42] As the magistrates began to enforce the

---

[38] *GA*, p. 1.
[39] Public Record Office, State Papers, 29/258/43. For the 1670 Conventicle Act see Bettenson (ed.), *Documents of the Christian Church*, pp. 294-5, or Browning (ed.), *English Historical Documents*, pp. 384-6.
[40] Public Record Office, State Papers, 29/262/115.
[41] Frank Bate, *The Declaration of Indulgence 1672: A Study in the Rise of Organised Dissent* (1908), pp. 64-5.   [42] *Minutes*, pp. 39-52.

1670 Conventicle Act, he apparently was more closely confined, for there is no further mention of him in the church records until April 1671. From that time until his formal release in March 1672 he enjoyed considerable liberty and was extensively involved in the congregation's affairs.[43]

A possible clue to Bunyan's activities in the late 1660s is found in the candid observation of the Bedford Church in November 1668 that many of its members had 'in these troublous times withdrawne themselves from close walking with the Church,' while others were 'guilty of more grosse miscarriages . . .'[44] *Grace Abounding* had been intended in part to shore up those who wavered, and after its completion Bunyan commenced work on a book designed to exhort Nonconformists to persevere in the 'race' for heaven. The thesis of *The Heavenly Footman* was precisely tailored for the conditions of the late 1660s: 'There are but very few that do obtain that ever-to-be-desired Glory In so much that many Eminent Professors drop short of a welcom from God into his pleasant place.'[45] The analogy of the Christian life as a race was an outgrowth of his own experience and the biblical foundations on which it rested. In his *Profitable Meditations* he had written:

> I am encourag'd in the heav'nly Race,
> Because Christ dy'd and spilt his Blood for me.[46]

The Heavenly Footman applied this theme to the conditions of nonconformity in the late 1660s. Although the work itself was not published until 1698, it was definitely composed relatively early in Bunyan's career. He refers to 'that little time which I have been a Professor' as well as to two of his earliest works, *A Few Sighs from Hell* (1658) and *The Doctrine of the Law and Grace Unfolded* (1659).[47] A reference to those who run 'a *Quaking* . . . a *Ranting* . . . after the *Baptism* . . . after the *Independency* . . . for *Free-will*, and . . . for *Presbytery*' suggests the period between the great activity of those sects in the 1650s and Bunyan's concern with sectarian issues beginning in 1671.[48] The references to Ranters in this book may have been sparked by his recollection in *Grace Abounding* of his early encounter with that group.[49] There are also allusions to persecution,

---

[43] *Minutes*, pp. 62–72.   [44] *Minutes*, p. 39.   [45] *Misc. Wks.*, v. 147.
[46] *Misc. Wks.*, vi. 9, stanza XXVIII.   [47] *Misc. Wks.*, v. 152, 178.
[48] *Misc. Wks.*, v. 152.   [49] *Misc. Wks.*, v. 153, 156; *GA*, §§ 44–5.

both past and present. Readers are exhorted to bear in mind the punishments inflicted on the saints of old, and admonished not to risk losing an eternal crown for fear of 'the loss of a few trifles'.[50] The latter was probably a reference to the penalties imposed by the 1664 Conventicle Act, which included both fines and imprisonment.[51] The evidence, then, suggests that Bunyan commenced *The Heavenly Footman* shortly after he completed *Grace Abounding*.

Before he could finish the new work, he was inspired with the idea of depicting the race for a heavenly crown in allegorical terms as a pilgrimage.

> And thus it was: I writing of the Way
> And Race of Saints in this our Gospel-Day,
> Fell suddenly into an Allegory
> About their Journey, and the way to Glory.[52]

By the time he returned to *The Heavenly Footman*, he was already thinking of the Christian life more as a challenging journey than as a race. Although he carried the race motif through to the conclusion, his new perspective is hinted at various times, as in the mixed metaphor of the closing sentence: ' . . . Run apace, and hold out to the *End*; and the Lord give thee a prosperous Journey.'[53] As Roger Sharrock has argued, 'the grand central metaphor of *The Pilgrim's Progress*'—the struggle to reach a goal by traversing arduous terrain—was already present in *The Heavenly Footman*.[54] So too were some of the physical images of the allegory: bypaths, quagmires, leaving friends and neighbours, sin as a burden which one carries, and the need of the runner to 'go close by' the cross.[55]

If, then, *The Heavenly Footman* was begun in 1666 or shortly thereafter, the first part of *The Pilgrim's Progress* belongs to the same period. Both works reflect the needs of Nonconformists at this time,

---

[50] *Misc. Wks.*, v. 164, 170.

[51] See, e.g., W. M. Wigfield, 'Recusancy and Nonconformity in Bedfordshire: Illustrated by Select Documents Between 1622 and 1842', *Publications of the Bedfordshire Historical Records Society*, 20 (1938), 167–71; *A True and Impartial Narrative of Some Illegal and Arbitrary Proceedings . . . in or near the Town of Bedford* (1670), pp. 3–9.   [52] *PP*, p. 1.

[53] *Misc. Wks.*, v. 178; cf. p. 157: 'Take heed that you have not an *Ear* open to every one that calleth after you, as you are in your Journey.' Cf. the similar passage in *PP*, p. 10. Also cf. *Misc. Wks.*, v. 164–5.   [54] Sharrock, p. 72.

[55] *Misc. Wks.*, v. 155–8, 165–6.

tempted as they were to drop out of the heavenly race or forsake the pilgrimage because of the threat of persecution. Yet Bunyan claimed he had no intention to publish the allegory, presumably because it seemed somewhat frivolous at a time when persecution was increasing: '*I did it mine own self to gratifie.*'[56] Nevertheless, the conditions facing Nonconformists in the late 1660s provided precisely the milieu that made the theme of a demanding race or a tortuous pilgrimage relevant. So too did the proximity of the completed spiritual autobiography, since *The Pilgrim's Progress* is in its most basic sense an allegorical depiction of Bunyan's spiritual struggles.

The conditions which Dissenters faced in the late 1660s coupled with internal evidence from the allegory provide the opportunity to date the first part of *The Pilgrim's Progress* more precisely. Three-fourths of the way through the allegory Bunyan wrote: 'So I awoke from my Dream. And I slept, and Dreamed again . . .'[57] Because there is no artistic or thematic reason for this break, it has been argued that the awakening signified the end of his imprisonment in 1672 and his completion of the work as a free man.[58] It is, however, more plausible that the break occurred in either the autumn of 1668 or the autumn of 1669, when Bunyan began periods of relative liberty. The initial draft of the first part must have been completed no later than April 1671, when he received considerable freedom, and possibly as early as October 1669. Two further clues in Bunyan's 'Apology' for the book support this dating: It was written, Bunyan admitted, '*to divert my self . . . from worser thoughts . . .*'[59] a probable reference to his fears of dying in prison. Moreover, his statement that he spent only '*vacant seasons*'[60] writing the allegory is compatible both with his need to make 'long Tagg'd laces' to support his family and with his involvement in the serious problems of the Bedford church beginning in 1668. Bunyan's decision to circulate the work among his friends, the time needed for probable revisions, and his reticence to publish the work account for its appearance only in 1678.[61]

---

[56] *PP*, p. 1.
[58] See, e.g., Sharrocks's commentary in *PP*, p. 333.
[60] *PP*, p. 1.
[57] *PP*, p. 123.
[59] *PP*, p. 1.
[61] *PP*, p. 2.

Nonconformist Organization and Controversy

In the period from 1670 to 1675 Bunyan's concerns shifted dramatically. At no other time in his career was he so intensely involved with Nonconformist affairs, particularly those concerning the implementation of an effective organizational structure in Bedfordshire and doctrinal and ecclesiological issues important to Dissenters.

The difficulties experienced by the Bedford Church in the late 1660s underscored the need for better organization, particularly the designation of more local units—virtually cells—and approved preachers (or 'teachers'). On Bunyan's forays from prison beginning in late 1668, he had ample opportunity to assess the problems at first hand. While he was still in prison he had the opportunity to work out an organizational structure with fellow Nonconformists. At least nine men who figured prominently in the organizational plan were in the county jail with Bunyan at some point between c.1666 and 1672: John Wright of Blunham, William Man of Stagsden, William Wheeler of Cranfield, John Donne of Pertenhall (who had a church at Keysoe), Simon Hayes, Nehemiah Coxe, Thomas Cooper, and Samuel and John Fenn(e).[62]

Subsequent to his appointment as a pastor of the Bedford congregation in January 1672 and his release from the county jail in March, Bunyan and his colleagues took advantage of the King's Declaration of Indulgence (issued on 15 March) to apply jointly for licences to preach and for places to meet. The application, which was written by Bunyan or the London tobacco merchant Thomas Taylor, included the names of such fellow former prisoners as Wright, Donne, Man, Coxe, Cooper, and the Fenn(e)s. In addition to Bedford, the application represented the interests of Nonconformist churches at Keysoe, Cranfield, Stevington, and Newport Pagnell, including twenty-one satellite meetings (twelve of which were connected with the Bedford Church). The application included the names of twenty-seven men in twenty-six towns and villages in six counties. In addition to providing closer supervision of and support for church members, such meticulous organization made it extremely unlikely that the revival of persecution could stamp out nonconformity in Bedfordshire and the contiguous counties.[63]

---

[62] Richard L. Greaves, 'The Organizational Response of Nonconformity to Repression and Indulgence: The Case of Bedfordshire', *Church History*, 44 (1975), 472–4.

[63] Greaves, 'Organizational Response', pp. 474–84.

The organizational efforts brought to the fore such crucial ecclesiological questions as the requirements for Church-membership and the role of baptism. About 1671 Bunyan dealt with these issues in *A Confession of My Faith*, which was published the following year. Amplifying what he had written in *The Holy City* (1665), he argued, as we have seen, for a Church constituted solely of visible saints, without baptism as a condition of membership. Bunyan was thereupon attacked by the General Baptist John Denne in *Truth Outweighing Error* (1673) and the Particular Baptist Thomas Paul in *Some Serious Reflections* (1673), which included an epistle by William Kiffin. Bunyan retorted in *Differences in Judgment About Water-Baptism, No Bar to Communion* (1673), which carried a supportive statement by Henry Jessey, another advocate of open-membership views. Bunyan was in turn repudiated by the Particular Baptist Henry Danvers in a postscript to his *Treatise of Baptism* (1673), to which Bunyan replied in *Peaceable Principles and True* (1674). In the mean time Danvers' *Treatise* sparked off an enormous pamphlet war between paedobaptists such as Richard Baxter and Obadiah Wills and Baptists such as John Tombes and Thomas Delaune. Bunyan, however, was not involved in the wider dispute.[64]

In practical terms Bunyan's position on baptism and Church membership affected his Church's relations with London Nonconformists. When Bedford members desired to transfer to a London congregation, the Church took special care to recommend a congregation with compatible views. Those which met their standards included the churches of Henry Jessey, George Griffith, Anthony Palmer, George Cokayne, and John Owen.[65] Of these men, only Jessey considered himself—like Bunyan—to be fundamentally a Baptist. Although Bunyan is rightly regarded as an open-membership Baptist, his closest relations in the Nonconformist community were with the Congregationalists. There was, however,

---

[64] See Richard L. Greaves, *Saints and Rebels: Seven Nonconformists in Stuart England* (Macon, Ga., 1984), chap. 6. For Denne, Paul, Kiffin, Jessey, and Tombes see *BDBR*, s. vv.

[65] *Minutes*, pp. 66, 71, 79. Cf. p. 92 for a 1690 letter concerning relations with Matthew Mead's Church. For all these men see *BDBR*, s. vv. For Owen see also Peter Toon, *God's Statesman: The Life and Work of John Owen* (Exeter, 1971), and for Griffith see Greaves, *Saints and Rebels*, chap. 3. Cokayne, Griffith, Palmer, and Owen probably were the inspiration for Captains Boanerges, Conviction, Judgment, and Execution in *The Holy War*. See Greaves, 'John Bunyan's "Holy War" and London Nonconformity'. *BQ* 26 (1975), 158–68.

a rupture with the Congregationalist Church of Francis Holcroft in Cambridge c.1670 when the Bedford congregation insisted on admitting John Waite of Toft, who had been excommunicated by Holcroft's group.[66]

While Bunyan was sorting out his relations with other Nonconformists, he became embroiled in a doctrinal controversy with the ex-Puritan Edward Fowler. Regarded by Bunyan as a man who could, 'as to religion, turn and twist like an eel on the angle; or rather like the weather-cock that stands on the steeple,' the Latitudinarian Fowler had provoked Bunyan's ire by his book, *The Design of Christianity* (1671). Its thesis—that Christ's work was intended to reform people's lives and restore the righteousness they once possessed in Adam—repudiated the doctrine of justification solely by the imputed righteousness of Christ. Bunyan asserted his position in *A Defence of the Doctrine of Justification, by Faith* (1672), in which he also castigated the Quaker William Penn. Fowler or his curate responded in the vituperative tract, *Dirt Wip't Off* (1672).[67] This, the most argumentative phase of Bunyan's career, came to an end with some parting but oblique shots against Fowler and Penn in *Light for Them That Sit in Darkness* (1675).[68] These doctrinal controversies left him convinced of 'the Accursed Condition of those among the Religious in these Nations whose notions put them far off from Jesus . . .'[69]

The Pastoral Era

With the passing of the period of bitter doctrinal and ecclesiological disputes in 1675, Bunyan moved into a serener phase of his career in which his dominant concerns were pastoral in nature. His writings in this period reflect the evangelical themes of his ministry. *The Strait Gate* (1676), an exposition of Matthew 7: 13-14, not only recapitulated the theme of *The Pilgrim's Progress* about the difficulty of attaining heaven, but also underscored the reorientation of

---

[66] Richard L. Greaves, 'John Bunyan and Nonconformity in the Midlands and East Anglia', *JURCHS* 1 (1976), 191-2. The historical controversy over Bunyan's denominational affiliation is surveyed by Joseph D. Ban, 'Was John Bunyan a Baptist? A Case Study in Historiography', *BQ* 30 (1984), 367-76.
[67] Greaves, pp. 82-5. See further below, pp. 55-62.
[68] *Misc. Wks.*, viii. 86, 91, 94, 101, 108, 133 ff.
[69] *Misc. Wks.*, viii. 160.

Bunyan's efforts: 'Now we discourse not about things controverted among the godly, but directly about the saving or damning of the soul . . .'[70] In this work he insisted that few would be saved, a theme to which he returned in *Saved by Grace* (1676), where attention shifted primarily to the elect and the basis of their redemption. Despite the fact that Bunyan thought the number of the elect was relatively small, the warmth of the Gospel message triumphed over the logical implications of the Calvinist doctrine of predestination in his most popular sermon, the evangelical *Come, & Welcome, to Jesus Christ* (1678). His pastoral preoccupations were similarly reflected in the catechism he wrote for the saints, *Instruction for the Ignorant* (1675). At times reflecting the personal and experiential qualities that are the hallmark of Bunyan's writing, the catechism is unusual in the emphasis it places on self-denial.[71]

Despite the challenges and rewards of the pastoral ministry and opportunities to preach in London to sizeable crowds,[72] these were not trouble-free years for Bunyan. Undoubtedly jealous of his popularity, ecclesiastical officials prosecuted him. Following the revocation of the 1672 licences to preach early in 1675, a warrant for Bunyan's arrest was issued on 4 March on the grounds that he had illegally preached at a conventicle. What effect this had on him is not known; he may have gone into hiding or been fined and even briefly imprisoned under the terms of the 1670 Conventicle Act. By April his name had been presented by the churchwardens for refusing to attend the parish church and he was excommunicated. When he refused to appear in the Archdeacon's court to answer for his conduct, a writ was issued for his arrest. About December 1676 he again entered prison and remained there until the following June. The renewed persecution appears to have prompted him to dust off the manuscript of *The Pilgrim's Progress*, perhaps make some final revisions, and submit it to the printer Nathaniel Ponder. It was entered in the Stationers' Register on 22 December.[73]

The most sensational event in England in 1678 was not the publication of *The Pilgrim's Progress* but the revelations of the Popish Plot. In the climate of fear that ensued, Bunyan—like any good pastor—utilized the concerns of the day as a setting for his religious

---

[70] *Misc. Wks.*, v. 69.
[71] *Misc. Wks.*, viii. xxx–xlii.   [72] *Folio* (1692), pp. 873–4.
[73] *Misc. Wks.*, viii. xix–xxiv. For Ponder see *BDBR*, s. vv.

message. The result, a sermon on Revelation 14: 7, was expanded and published as *A Treatise of the Fear of God* (1679); it contained a particularly scathing attack on hypocrites. *Israel's Hope Encouraged*, posthumously published in Charles Doe's 1692 folio edition of Bunyan's *Works*, probably belongs to this period too, for it refers to the time after the disclosure of the Popish Plot as one when people feared their throats would be cut and their children slaughtered.[74] The time was therefore propitious to ponder the lot of the wicked. Already basking in the success of *The Pilgrim's Progress*, Bunyan set about to describe 'the life and death of the ungodly, and of their travel from this world to hell'.[75] The result was *The Life and Death of Mr Badman* (1680), a work which must be placed in the historical context of the Popish Plot and the recriminations and concerns which it sparked off. Those circumstances were clearly in Bunyan's mind as he wrote: 'England shakes and totters already, by reason of the burden that Mr. Badman and his friends have wickedly laid upon it.'[76]

Political Crisis, Evangelical Concerns, and the Nonconformist Community

As Bunyan moved into the 1680s his evangelical, pastoral interests remained strong, as reflected in such publications as *The Greatness of the Soul* (1682), *A Holy Life* (advertised in 1683; first edition dated 1684), and *A Discourse Concerning the Pharisee and the Publican* (1685). A successful author, he was confronted not only with readers who clamoured for more allegorical works but with imitators anxious to exploit his popularity. Out of these circumstances came Part II of *The Pilgrim's Progress* (1684), with its reflections on Nonconformist life and principles. There are echoes, for example, of Bunyan's earlier controversies with traditional Baptists such as Danvers, Paul, and Denne. As Roger Sharrock has suggested, the characters of Fearing and Feeble-mind represented persons of tender conscience for whom the open-membership churches were particularly appealing.[77]

Bunyan's trips to London in this period rekindled his old flame for doctrinal controversy. His final work in this genre, *Questions*

---

[74] *Works*, i. 585.   [75] *Works*, iii. 590.   [76] *Works*, iii. 590.
[77] Sharrock, p. 141.

About the Nature and Perpetuity of the Seventh-Day Sabbath, was published in 1685. The principal object of Bunyan's attack was Francis Bampfield, whose congregation of Seventh-day Baptists shared Pinners' Hall, Broad Street, with the Congregationalist church of Richard Wavel. Bunyan had preached to Wavel's flock in 1682, and the expanded version of that sermon had been published as *The Greatness of the Soul* (1682). Although Bampfield himself was arrested in February 1682, his congregation continued to meet and survived his death two years later. Bunyan found sabbatarian views sufficiently objectionable to attack them in his tract. His tone, however, was moderate, befitting his desire that sabbatarian Baptists not 'take it ill at my hand that I thus freely speak my mind.'[78]

London Nonconformists were likewise the occasion of Bunyan's foray into the seventeenth-century disputes concerning the role of women in religious affairs. There was some precedent in Baptist circles for women to meet separately for spiritual exercises. The ladies of Thomas Lamb's General Baptist church had done so as early as the 1640s, and in 1645 they convened for lectures on Tuesday afternoons at Bell Alley, Coleman Street. One of those who spoke to them was the infamous sectary Mrs Attaway. In the early 1680s a 'Mr. K.' (possibly Benjamin Keach, William Kiffin, Daniel King, or Hanserd Knollys) supported the right of women to meet together for prayer.[79] When they learned of Bunyan's opposition to this practice and pressed him for his reasons, he responded with *A Case of Conscience Resolved* (1683). Such meetings, he argued, contravened biblical principles, were unnecessary because there were enough men to convene and direct worship, and were blemishes on the church because they manifested female 'unruliness'. Women must 'keep their places'.[80] Part II of *The Pilgrim's Progress*, which followed a year later, does not indicate that Bunyan retreated from the traditional role of male superiority, and should not be interpreted as an attempt by Bunyan to place women on a plane equal to that of men.

The most striking change that marks this period of Bunyan's life concerns his political outlook. The bitter struggle over the exclusion

---

[78] *Works*, ii. 385. See Greaves, *Saints and Rebels*, chap. 7.
[79] For all these people, including Mrs Attaway, see *BDBR*, s. vv. See also Dorothy Ludlow, 'Shaking Patriarchy's Foundations: Sectarian Women in England, 1641-1700', in *Triumph Over Silence: Women in Protestant History*, ed. Richard L. Greaves (Westport, Conn., 1986), chap. 3. [80] *Works*, ii. 673-4.

of the Duke of York from the line of succession, the campaign to remodel the corporations, the renewal of persecution, and the execution in 1681 of the Whig martyr Stephen College, a supporter of the Earl of Shaftesbury,[81] boded ill for the Nonconformists. Against this background Bunyan returned to matters of state in *The Holy War* (1682), a technically sophisticated but not altogether satisfying allegory. The relative obliquity of the allegory was a necessity ordained by the trying political conditions, while the multiple levels of meaning provided Bunyan with the opportunity to address levels of need ranging from the concerns of the individual soul to the endangered Dissenting community. As king of Mansoul, Diabolus clearly was a reminder of Charles II, even as such new burgesses and aldermen as Mr Atheism and Mr False Peace were caricatures of the Tory-Anglicans who ruled the land. In contrast, Bunyan's expectations of good governors were reflected in his account of Emanuel's work after he gained control of Mansoul. Despite the persecution of the early 1680s, Bunyan did not include a call to arms in *The Holy War*. Instead, in the critical supplement to the allegory, *Seasonable Counsel: or, Advice to Sufferers* (1684)—a work regularly overlooked by students of Bunyan—he made it clear that in times of persecution the saints could do no more than patiently suffer and pray to God for deliverance from evil rulers. In this tract Bunyan expressed one of his profoundest insights: the necessity for Christians to suffer *actively* for righteousness by *willingly* embracing affliction.[82]

The posthumous work *Of Antichrist and His Ruin* (1692) probably also dates from this period, for it espouses the doctrine of Christian suffering enunciated in *Seasonable Counsel* and deals with some of the same political issues found in *The Holy War*. Although Charles II was implicitly but forcefully denounced in the allegory, in *Of Antichrist* Bunyan cautiously expressed loyalty to the King and attributed a special apocalyptic function to monarchs in general. When Antichrist was overthrown, it would be at the hand of earthly sovereigns divinely ordained for that task. Before that could transpire, Bunyan contended, the church would have to undergo much severer persecution, even to the point that few visible churches would be left in the

---

[81] BDBR, s. v.   [82] *Works*, ii. 707-8, 710-11, 725.

world.[83] Thus Bunyan's outlook in the early 1680s was heavily influenced by the conviction that massive suffering was imminent for the Nonconformists. Yet as a minister he not only warned of impending persecution but encouraged the godly to remain steadfast in their convictions. Perhaps the quieter tone of the second part of *The Pilgrim's Progress* was in part an attempt to calm Dissenters in the face of suffering: 'Be ye watchful, and cast away Fear; be sober, and hope to the End.'[84]

The Final Years: Relations with a Catholic King

The last phase of Bunyan's career commenced in the summer of 1686 when James II adopted a policy of co-operation with Nonconformists as part of his scheme to provide offices and other opportunities to Catholics. In addition to issuing a new Declaration of Indulgence in April 1687, the King determined to remodel the corporations and commissions of the peace, thereby making way for Nonconformists and Catholics and thus undoing the Tory–Anglican dominance Charles had imposed. The story that Bunyan was offered 'a Place of Publick Trust'[85] cannot be corroborated, but he certainly was not opposed to some co-operation with the King, for at least six members of his church accepted positions in the remodelled Bedford Corporation in the spring of 1688.[86] Bunyan's position *vis-à-vis* James is consistent with the views expressed in *Of Antichrist and His Ruin* about the role of sovereigns in toppling Satan. Bunyan's unfinished commentary on Genesis, on which he was probably at work in these last years, did not espouse tyrannicide but called on the saints to 'stand their ground', pray for their rulers, and accept persecution as a divine means to purge the church.[87] But Bunyan must have been chary of the general drift of James's policies, for the commentary unmistakably opposes absolute monarchy.[88]

Bunyan's final years were incredibly busy because of his preaching and writing. The strongly evangelistic emphasis that commenced

---

[83] *Works.*, ii. 61, 66, 74, 88. For a full discussion of Bunyan's views on church–state relations, see Richard L. Greaves, 'The Spirit and the Sword: Bunyan and the Stuart State', in *John Bunyan in Our Time*, ed. Robert G. Collmer (forthcoming). For views of Antichrist by Bunyan's contemporaries, see Christopher Hill, *Antichrist in Seventeenth-century England* (1971). [84] *PP*, p. 306.
[85] 'A Continuation of Mr Bunyan's Life', ad cal. *GA*, p. 163.
[86] *Misc. Wks.*, xi. xvi–xviii. [87] *Works*, ii. 456.
[88] *Works*, ii. 497–8; William York Tindall, *John Bunyan: Mechanick Preacher* (New York, 1934), p. 266.

without abatement to the end. The publications of these years—such as *Good News for the Vilest of Men* (1688), *The Work of Jesus Christ as an Advocate* (1688), *The Water of Life* (1688), and *The Acceptable Sacrifice* (1689)—are of a piece with *The Strait Gate* (1676) and *Come, & Welcome* (1678). Nor did Bunyan the pastor forget the needs of children, for whom he wrote his emblem collection, *A Book for Boys and Girls* (1686). This work, suggests Graham Midgley, 'shows Bunyan at his best and most adventurous as a poet, and expresses more completely the many sides of his personality . . . '[89] It was probably compiled over a period of years and thus reflects the changing circumstances of his later life.

Bunyan's relations with other Nonconformists in these last years were peaceful. His popularity in London remained high and undoubtedly contributed to the demand for his printed sermons. The posthumous *Desires of the Righteous Granted* (1692) was preached in 1685 or 1686 to the open-membership congregation of Stephen More in Southwark, while his *Last Sermon* (1689) was delivered in John Gammon's church in Boar's Head Yard, off Petticoat Lane. *Good News* (1688), an invitation to the most immoral persons to convert, may also have been preached in London. Bunyan never retreated from his conviction that baptism must not be a necessary condition of church membership, but in these last years his tone was more conciliatory, perhaps because he was more mature or possibly because he had come to recognize the greater dangers that stemmed from Catholicism and the drift toward an arbitrary monarchy. In his poetic work *A Discourse of the Building, Nature, Excellency and Government of the House of God* (1688) he insisted on a reasonable degree of toleration within the church:

> For those that have *private* opinions too
> We must *make* room, or shall the Church undo;
> Provided they be *such* as don't impair
> Faith, Holiness, nor with good Conscience jarr.[90]

The sacraments have their symbolic value, but strife abounds when

> . . . *Moles* are *Mountains* made, or fault is found,
> With every *little, trivial, petty* thing.[91]

[89] *Misc. Wks.*, vi. lvii. [90] *Misc. Wks.*, vi. 311
[91] *Misc. Wks.*, vi. 310.

The only requirement for fellowship with the church was 'a *Certificate,*/To shew thou seest thy self most *desolate.*'[92]

Here was the core of the Christian life—the experiential basis of faith, without which religious profession was barren and lifeless. For Bunyan this experience of living faith was possible only through the agency of the Spirit. It was the conviction of the Spirit's inner work—in preaching and in prayer—that had initially persuaded him to choose the path of nonconformity, and it was the same conviction that sustained him throughout his ministry. Although the various periods in Bunyan's career must be distinguished if we are to understand his development and the proper historical context of his works, his belief in the inner working of the Spirit and its implications for the Christian pilgrimage provided a unifying theme for his life as a Nonconformist.

[92] *Misc. Wks.*, vi. 281.

3

Grace, Holiness, and the Pursuit of Happiness: Bunyan and Restoration Latitudinarianism

BY ISABEL RIVERS

The Religion of Grace and the Religion of Reason

IT is one of the ironies of religious and cultural history that *The Pilgrim's Progress*, which has consistently been one of the world's religious best sellers (perhaps only Thomas à Kempis's *The Imitation of Christ* has outstripped it in popularity), was written partly as a polemical work in order to define the crucial religious conflict of late seventeenth-century England and to defend the position that lost.[1] Bunyan was unable to avert the shift that was taking place during his lifetime from what can loosely be called the religion of grace (the descendant of Reformation protestantism, represented by the majority of the Nonconformists) to the religion of reason (usually termed by contemporaries 'latitudinarian' or 'moral religion' and by modern historians 'Anglican rationalism' or 'moralism').[2] This shift involved by the end of the century the virtual eclipse of Calvinism, a reassertion of the capacities of ordinary human nature, and a much more accommodating view of the relationship between religion and the world.

---

[1] The argument and some of the material in this chapter is taken from my forthcoming book, *Reason, Grace, and Sentiment: Studies in the Language of Religion and Ethics in England, 1660–1780*.

[2] For Anglicanism see esp. H. R. McAdoo, *The Spirit of Anglicanism* (1965); Irène Simon, *Three Restoration Divines: Barrow, South, Tillotson*, vol. i (Paris, 1967); Norman Sykes, *From Sheldon to Secker* (Cambridge, 1959), chap. v. See also Martin I. J. Griffin jun., 'Latitudinarianism in the Seventeenth-century Church of England', Ph.D. thesis (Yale, 1962). C. F. Allison, *The Rise of Moralism* (1966), gives a hostile account of the beginnings of the shift.

The nature of this shift can partly be gauged by comparing the two popular Puritan devotional and practical handbooks of the early seventeenth century that Bunyan's first wife brought him on their marriage, Arthur Dent's *The Plaine Mans Path-way to Heaven* (1601) and Lewis Bayly's *The Practise of Pietie* (1612), with the book that effectively replaced them to become the most popular and influential religious work in the late seventeenth century and throughout the eighteenth, *The Practice of Christian Graces* (1658) by the royalist and High-Churchman Richard Allestree, better known by its subtitle of *The Whole Duty of Man*.[3] Both Dent and Bayly are concerned to give practical guidance for Christian conduct only within the framework of predestinarian theology: both stress the worthlessness and corruption of natural man, the irrelevance of good works to justification, the necessity of regeneration, the small number of the saved, the importance of fear in awakening sinners to an awareness of their condition; and both also emphasize that good works are the necessary fruits of regeneration even though they count for nothing in achieving salvation. They are agreed that far from predestinarian theology inhibiting human action or making the cultivation of good works or the practice of piety irrelevant,[4] it is only in the framework of this theology that the importance of works or piety can be understood. The regenerate performs good works, according to Bayly, to glorify God, to show himself thankful for his redemption, to make sure his election (good works being one of the signs of election, not the reason for it), and to win others to Christian profession.[5] *The Whole Duty of Man*, on the other hand,

---

[3] *GA*, § 15. On Dent see Maurice Hussey, 'John Bunyan and Arthur Dent', *Theology*, 52 (1949), 459–63, and 'Arthur Dent's *Plaine Mans Path-Way to Heaven*', *MLR* 44 (1949), 26–34; J. B. Wharey, 'Bunyan's *Mr Badman*', *MLN* 36 (1921), 65–79. On Bayly see J. E. Bailey, 'Bishop Lewis Bayly and his *Practice of Piety*', *Manchester Quarterly*, 2 (1883), 201–19; C. J. Stranks, *Anglican Devotion* (1961), chap. ii. On *The Whole Duty of Man* see Stranks, chap. v. It was always published anonymously; for Allestree's authorship see *DNB*, s.v. Dorothy, Lady Pakington; P. Elmen, 'Richard Allestree and *The Whole Duty of Man*', *The Library*, 5th ser., 6 (1951), 19–27. C. John Sommerville, *Popular Religion in Restoration England* (Gainesville, Fla., 1977), provides a very interesting comparison of Nonconformist and Anglican literature. Other accounts of Anglican, Puritan, and Nonconformist devotion are Horton Davies, *Worship and Theology in England from Andrewes to Baxter and Fox, 1603–1690* (Princeton, 1975), chap. iii; H. R. McAdoo, *The Structure of Caroline Moral Theology* (1949); Gordon Wakefield, *Puritan Devotion* (1957).

[4] Arthur Dent, *The Plaine Mans Pathway* (1601), pp. 297–312, interestingly allows Antilegon the caviller to voice the obvious objections to predestinarianism.

[5] Lewis Bayly, *The Practise of Pietie* (1643 edn.), pp. 401–2.

not only devotes very little space to doctrinal exposition, but is also in its theological assumptions fundamentally opposed to Dent and Bayly. The Christian, before he can have the benefit of the scriptural promises, must perform the condition, which is to fulfil his duty as summed up in Titus 2:12, 'where the word *Soberly* contains our *duty* to our *selves*: *Righteously*, our duty to our *neighbour*, and *Godly*, our *Duty* to *God*.'[6] Where Dent and Bayly stress election and regeneration (and the fruits that follow), Allestree stresses fulfilment of duty and holiness of life as the condition on which the promises are given.[7] The object of *The Whole Duty of Man* is to show the nature of the Christian's duties and how they may be fulfilled, and the pleasure that is to be derived from them. To the Calvinist this is preaching up the works of the law or legal preaching: it was to become the dominant Anglican mode after the Restoration.

Bunyan defined the conflict between the religion of grace and the religion of reason, between the culture and values of Nonconformity and those of conformity, as turning on two main issues: first, the problem of the status of 'mere morality', the nature of holiness, and the relationship between divine grace and the human heart or conscience as motivating forces to action; and second, the problem of happiness and the world, the opposition between the view that it is necessary to suffer in this world in pursuit of happiness in the next and the view that there is a close connection between the practice of religion and the enjoyment of happiness in this world. Bunyan dramatized these issues in the first part of *The Pilgrim's Progress* in the confrontations between Christian and those characters who together embody the range of attitudes he found so wrong-headed and indeed dangerous in the conformists to the established Church: Mr Worldly-Wiseman, Mr By-ends and his companions, and Ignorance. Bunyan gave careful attention both to his opponents' doctrines (though his version of them is a caricature) and to their characteristic terminology, and he clarified his own position in relation to theirs. This essay is concerned with the significant development of Anglican thought in the 1660s and 1670s known as latitude or latitudinarianism, especially as represented by its leading figure, John Wilkins, with Bunyan's hostile response to one

---

[6] [Richard Allestree], *The Whole Duty of Man* (1659 edn.), p. 4. See n. 25 below.
[7] [Allestree], *Whole Duty*, p. 8.

particular latitudinarian, Edward Fowler, and with his attempt to demolish the latitudinarian view of holiness and happiness and to strengthen by contrast his own view of the nature of the Christian life. It suggests that to understand Bunyan more fully we must study him in relation not only to the embattled Nonconformist culture to which he belonged, but to the dominant Anglican culture which he denounced.

Latitudinarianism

Three very illuminating accounts of the principles and adherents of latitude were published in the 1660s and 1670s: *A Brief Account of the New Sect of Latitude-Men* (1662), by S. P. (usually attributed to Simon Patrick);[8] *The Principles and Practices, of Certain Moderate Divines of the Church of England, (greatly mis-understood) Truly Represented and Defended* (1670), by Edward Fowler (*Abusively called Latitudinarians* is added to the title of the second edition of 1671); and 'Anti-fanatical Religion, and Free Philosophy', Essay VII of *Essays on Several Important Subjects in Philosophy and Religion* (1676), by Joseph Glanvill.[9] In addition Gilbert Burnet gave a sympathetic account of the origins of the movement in the first volume of his *History of his Own Time* (published posthumously in 1724, though he began writing it in the 1680s).[10] Latitude was originally a university movement; it developed as a response to the Calvinist theological climate especially at Cambridge in the 1640s and 1650s, and was transmitted from the first generation of latitude-men, who were students before the Civil War and fellows and heads of colleges during the Interregnum, to the second, who were students in the late 1640s and 1650s. The key figures of the first generation were Benjamin Whichcote and John Wilkins.[11] Whichcote had a powerful influence at Cambridge (as

---

[8] See introd. by T. A. Birrell, The Augustan Reprint Society (Los Angeles, 1963).
[9] An abbreviated version of 'Bensalem being a Description of A Catholick & Free Spirit both in Religion & Learning', first published by J. I. Cope in '"The Cupri-Cosmits": Glanvill on Latitudinarian Anti-Enthusiasm', *Huntington Library Quarterly*, 17 (1954), 269-86.
[10] Gilbert Burnet, *History of His Own Time*, 2 vols. (1724-34), i. 186-91.
[11] Whichcote and his Cambridge associates, among them John Smith and Ralph Cudworth, are usually called the Cambridge Platonists, a label which is for various reasons unsatisfactory, one of them being that it obscures the link with Wilkins. C. A. Patrides (ed.), *The Cambridge Platonists* (1969; repr. Cambridge, 1980), provides a very useful bibliography. *DNB* gives details of all the latitude-men named.

Fellow of Emmanuel, Provost of King's, and especially as lecturer at Trinity Church). During the same period Wilkins was at Oxford, as Warden of Wadham; he was then for a short time before the Restoration Master of Trinity College, Cambridge. Important members of the second generation were John Tillotson, Simon Patrick, and Isaac Barrow at Cambridge and Edward Fowler and Joseph Glanvill at Oxford. In terms of doctrine the latitude-men wanted to reduce the Christian religion to a few plain and largely moral fundamentals; in terms of discipline they were prepared to accommodate themselves to the church government of the day. They found no difficulty in holding office during the Interregnum, when the episcopal Church had been abolished; similarly, after the Restoration, when several of them, including Whichcote and Wilkins, lost their university posts, they found conformity to the re-established Church an obvious step to take. (Fowler seems to have hesitated for some time.) One consequence was that London became the focal point of latitudinarian influence: the majority of latitude-men, including Whichcote, Wilkins, Tillotson, Patrick, and Fowler, held livings or lectureships in the City in the 1660s or 1670s, so that city pulpits now became the main source of latitudinarian ideas.[12]

Though they remained on the whole friendly to the Nonconformists, and anxious to broaden the base of the Church of England so that it might comprehend as many as possible of those who found the requirements for conformity too stringent (an attitude that made them unpopular among stricter churchmen), the latitude-men were critical of the Nonconformists' methods, language, and doctrine. The terms they repeatedly used to characterize their own position were moderation and sobriety,[13] and they laid particular stress on social demeanour and the tone of religious discourse. They thought that preaching should appeal to the understanding rather than the

---

[12] The most important pulpit was that of St Lawrence Jewry, with which the principal latitude-men were associated: Tillotson was Tuesday lecturer there from 1661; Wilkins was Vicar from 1662 until the Great Fire of 1666 when the church was burnt down, and on one occasion employed Barrow as guest preacher; when Wilkins became Bishop of Chester in 1668 he suggested that Whichcote should succeed him as Vicar, and Whichcote held the living until his death in 1683 (he was obliged to use the Guildhall Chapel for seven years until St Lawrence was rebuilt).

[13] See, e.g., Edward Fowler, *The Principles and Practices of Certain Moderate Divines* (1670), pp. x–xi; S[imon] P[atrick], *A Brief Account of the . . . Latitude-men* (1662), p. 12.

affections, or move the affections through the understanding.[14] The language of preaching should be plain and simple, and unnecessary terms, phrases, notions, and speculations beloved of the Nonconformists should be avoided.[15] They regarded a hundred years of English Calvinism as in many ways a wrong turning for the church. Their own intellectual forebears were the classical moralists, the early fathers of the church, Aquinas, the Dutch Remonstrants, and among English divines William Chillingworth, Jeremy Taylor, and Henry Hammond.[16] Their doctrinal positions include the following: natural religion is the foundation of revealed religion; faith is an act of reason; human beings must choose to co-operate with grace for it to be effective; repentance and obedience are the necessary conditions of justification.[17] Terms which are antithetical to traditional Protestants—grace and virtue, faith and works—mean essentially the same thing to the latitude-men.[18] The tone and emphasis of latitudinarian religion can be gauged from some of their favourite biblical quotations: 'Let your moderation be known unto

---

[14] See, e.g., John Beardmore's account of Tillotson as a preacher: 'his arguments of persuasion were strong and nervous, and tended to gain the affections by the understanding: and those, that heard him with attention, must either be persuaded to become good, or else they must do violence to their best faculties, and notoriously act contrary to their own reason' (*Some Memorials of . . . Tillotson*, in Thomas Birch, *The Life of the Most Reverend Dr John Tillotson*, 2nd edn. (1753), p. 409). The most important account of the method of latitudinarian preaching is in the rev. edn. of Wilkins's *Ecclesiastes* (1669), sect. ii, 'Concerning Method' (see n. 31 below).

[15] See, e.g., Patrick, *A Friendly Debate betwixt . . . a Conformist [and] a Non-Conformist* (1668), in *Works*, ed. A. Taylor, 9 vols. (Oxford, 1858), vol. v; Glanvill, *Essays* (1676) vii; Tillotson, Sermon ccxxvii, 'Of justifying faith', in *Works*, 12 vols. (1742-3), vol. x. Beardmore summarizes the latitudinarian view in his account of Tillotson's language: 'His composures were no jargon, or cant; did not consist of phrases or forms of words suited to any sect, or party of men, or that had little real matter in them. It was one thing, that he disliked in the Nonconformists, that they used divers distinctive phrases and expressions, that seemed to have some sublime meaning; when, if search'd to the bottom, they were scarce sense, or however might be better expressed in more plain and intelligible words' (Birch, *Life of Tillotson*, p. 406). See further below, pp. 93-7.

[16] McAdoo, *The Spirit of Anglicanism*, is particularly useful on their intellectual origins.

[17] See, e.g., Tillotson, Sermon ciii, 'Instituted religion not intended to undermine natural', Sermons cvi-cx, 'Of the nature of regeneration', in *Works*, vol. vi; Glanvill, *Essays*, vii.

[18] See, e.g., Tillotson, Sermon ccii, 'The fruits of the SPIRIT, the same with moral virtues', *Works*, vol. x; Whichcote, *Select Sermons*, ed. [Shaftesbury] (1698), Part II, Sermon i, p. 256; Fowler, *Principles and Practices*, pp. 114, 157; id., *The Design of Christianity* (1671), p. 221.

all men' (Philippians 4: 5);[19] 'The spirit of man is the candle of the Lord' (Proverbs 20: 27);[20] 'Fear God, and keep his commandments: for this is the whole duty of man' (Ecclesiastes 12: 13);[21] 'Her ways [*those of wisdom*] are ways of pleasantness, and all her paths are peace' (Proverbs 3: 17);[22] 'For my yoke is easy, and my burden is light' (Matthew 11: 30);[23] 'his commandments are not grievous' (1 John 5: 3);[24] 'we should live soberly, righteously, and godly, in this present world' (Titus 2: 12).[25] The latitudinarian view of morality ('nineteen parts in twenty, of all Religion' in Whichcote's phrase)[26] may be summarized as follows: men are by nature sociable and disposed to act well; sin is an unnatural deviation from this disposition; men naturally pursue happiness, though they often miscalculate the method of attaining it; happiness is achieved through holiness, and understood properly is in fact the same thing; the religious life is the most advantageous because religion enables men to act according to their true nature and in their own best interest by choosing the path that will make them holy and therefore happy. It is therefore the task of the religious moralist to channel men's innate desire for happiness by appealing to their prudence and self-interest and demonstrating that the rewards of the religious life easily outweigh any others. The truly religious man will be

[19] See, e.g., Wilkins, Sermon xiii (on this text), in *Sermons Preached upon Several Occasions* (1682).
[20] See, e.g., Whichcote, *Several Discourses*, ed. J. Jeffery, 4 vols., 2nd edn. (1702), no. xi, i. 294.
[21] See, e.g., Wilkins, *Of the Principles and Duties of Natural Religion*, 6th edn. (1710), where the phrase 'the whole duty of man', which should read 'the whole of man', since 'duty' is not in the Hebrew, is glossed as 'the *Essence*, the *Happiness*, the *Business* of Man' (pp. 286-7). McAdoo, *The Spirit of Anglicanism*, p. 224, suggests that Wilkins's use of Proverbs and Ecclesiastes is 'in part the origin of the Latitudinarian stress on prudence, practicality, moderateness and happiness'.
[22] See, e.g., Barrow's Sermon i (on this text), 'The Pleasantness of Religion', in *Theological Works*, 7 vols. (Oxford, 1830), vol. i.
[23] See, e.g., Fowler, *Design*, p. 305: 'Every good man feels that Christ's yoke is not less *Pleasant* than it is *Easie*, nor his Burthen more *Light* than it is *Delightful*'. Cf. [Allestree], *Whole Duty*, p. 384: '*Christs yoke is an easy*, nay a *pleasant yoke*, his *burden a light, yea a gracious burden*'.
[24] See, e.g., Tillotson, Sermon vi, 'The precepts of Christianity not grievous', *Works*, vol. i.
[25] This is perhaps the most widely cited text. See, e.g., Fowler's analysis, *Principles and Practices*, Part I, pp. 75-8.
[26] Whichcote, *Moral and Religious Aphorisms*, ed. S. Salter (1753), no. 586.

happy and holy, prudent and wise, and rewarded here as well as hereafter.[27]

A clear sense of the prudential and hedonistic tendency of latitudinarian thought can be gained from the work of Wilkins, the dominant figure in the group in the decade following the Restoration and the Act of Uniformity.[28] Whichcote's sermons did not appear in print until the end of the century, though his influence as a preacher was considerable.[29] Tillotson's first important publication in the 1660s was the sermon appropriately entitled 'The Wisdom of Being Religious' (1664), though again the bulk of his work did not appear until the end of the century. His significant role as a publicist for latitudinarian ideas in the reign of Charles II lay in his editing of the work of Wilkins and Barrow.[30] Wilkins had published a number of popular scientific and religious works from the late 1630s to the early 1650s, the most important from the point of view of the development of latitude being *Ecclesiastes*, a handbook for preachers, first published in 1646. This was reprinted many times in the course of the century and at the beginning of the next, and revised three times; the revisions themselves tell us a good deal about the growing importance of latitude.[31] As the moving spirit behind the Royal Society and its first Secretary, Wilkins has been of particular interest to historians of science, and his major scientific work was his attempt to create a universal language and system of classification, his *Essay towards a Real Character, and a Philosophical Language* (1668). According to Burnet, Tillotson worked with Wilkins on this book and was much influenced by its emphasis on the need for simplicity in language.[32]

---

[27] This necessarily brief summary of latitudinarian ethics is based on the work of the principal preachers, Whichcote, Wilkins, Tillotson, and Barrow, and that of the apologists for latitude, Patrick, Fowler, Glanvill, and Burnet.

[28] For Wilkins's intellectual leadership see Barbara J. Shapiro, *John Wilkins 1614–1672: An Intellectual Biography* (Berkeley and Los Angeles, 1969), chap. vi; for his thought see McAdoo, *The Spirit of Anglicanism*, pp. 207–30.

[29] See James Deotis Roberts, 'A Critical Examination of Whichcote's Writings', Appendix to *From Puritanism to Platonism in Seventeenth-century England* (The Hague, 1968).

[30] See Simon, *Three Restoration Divines*, chap. iv, and 'Note on the Text of Barrow's Sermons'.

[31] Wilkins considerably revised the text of the 5th edn. of 1669, presenting central latitudinarian principles in a simple and convenient form, and enlarged the book lists. At Tillotson's request John Williams brought out the 7th edn. in 1693, enlarging the lists further, and the 8th edn. of 1704 was again enlarged.

[32] Burnet, *A Sermon Preached at the Funeral of . . . John . . . Lord Archbishop of Canterbury* (1694), p. 13.

On his death in 1672, Wilkins left his papers to his friend, colleague, and son-in-law Tillotson: these included the manuscripts of sermons and of what is arguably his most important book, *Of the Principles and Duties of Natural Religion*, which Tillotson edited and brought out in 1675. It went through many editions until the 1720s and was much venerated by latitude-men: Burnet thought candidates for holy orders should almost know it by heart.[33]

Tillotson in his Preface describes the threefold design of the work as, first, to establish the principles of religion, the being of God, and a future state; second, to convince men of the obligation of moral duties; and third (and most interesting from the point of view of the issues dividing Anglican from Nonconformist),

To persuade Men to the *Practice* of *Religion*, and the *Virtues* of a good Life, by shewing how natural and direct an Influence they have, not only upon our *future* Blessedness in another World, but even upon the Happiness and Prosperity of this *present* Life. And surely nothing is more likely to prevail with wise and considerate Men to become Religious, than to be throughly convinced, that *Religion* and *Happiness*, our *Duty* and our *Interest*, are really but one and the same thing considered under several Notions.[34]

The first book, entitled 'Shewing the Reasonableness of the Principles and Duties of Natural Religion', will not be considered in detail here as its emphasis is largely epistemological, though it is worth noting that Wilkins describes himself as writing against the contemporary 'Humour of Scepticism and Infidelity' and arranging his argument so as to be sufficient to convince anyone with 'an *ordinary capacity*, and an *honest mind*'.[35] It is the fundamental assumption of Wilkins's moral philosophy that the end of human life is happiness, and that its pursuit is a natural principle, a necessity, with regard to which human beings do not have a liberty of acting. However, they do have a liberty as to which means they choose to effect this end, and the correct means Wilkins calls moral duties.[36] The object of Wilkins's argument in the second book, which is entitled 'Of the Wisdom of practising the Duties of Natural Religion', is to show the relationship

---

[33] Burnet, *A Discourse of the Pastoral Care*, 3rd edn. (1713) (1st pub. 1692), p. 149.
[34] Wilkins, *Of . . . Natural Religion* (1675), sig. A6.
[35] Wilkins, *Of . . . Natural Religion*, Book I, chap. i, pp. 1–2.
[36] Wilkins, *Of . . . Natural Religion*, Book I, chap. xiv, pp. 213–14. Cf. the same argument in *Ecclesiastes*, 6th edn. (1675), sect. iv, pp. 118–21, and *Sermons*, i, pp. 11–12.

between these two, the necessary pursuit of happiness and its actual achievement through the voluntary performance of moral duties. This whole process is included in the term 'religion'. The 'great Advantage of Religion', argues Wilkins, is that 'besides the principal work which it doth for us, in securing our Future Estates in the other World, it is likewise the most effectual means to promote our Happiness in this World.'[37] Having set out in tabular form the scope of human happiness in this world and the next, Wilkins proceeds to explain systematically how religion conduces to our outward happiness in this world in respect of health, liberty, safety, quiet, riches, pleasure, honour, and reputation,[38] and to our inward happiness in respect of regulation of the faculties and peace and tranquillity of mind.[39] His method is to make general assertions and then to consider some objections and exceptions which in his view do not alter the validity of the rule. An example which is especially relevant to the situation of Bunyan and the Nonconformists comes in the chapter showing 'How Religion conduces to the Happiness of the Outward-Man, in respect of Liberty, Safety, and Quiet'. Wilkins observes: 'There is one Objection that lies very obvious against what I have been proving; and that is from those *Scriptures* where 'tis said, that *whoever will live godly in Christ Jesus, must suffer persecution.*'[40] Wilkins makes two answers to this objection. The first blames the individual for choosing persecution unnecessarily: 'Some Persons who for the main may be truly religious, may yet by their own Follies and Imprudence, expose themselves to needless Sufferings. And in such cases, Religion is not to be charged as being the cause of their Suffering, but their defect in it, and mistakes about it.'[41] The second answer blames particular times of persecution, such as the early history of the church to which the biblical texts about persecution apply. These texts 'are not equally applicable to such other times and places, when and where the true Religion is publickly professed and encouraged ... because in such times and places, the profession of Religion will be so far from hindring, that it will rather promote

---

[37] Wilkins, *Of . . . Natural Religion*, Book II, chap. i, p. 306.
[38] Wilkins, *Of . . . Natural Religion*, Book II, chaps. ii–vi.
[39] Wilkins, *Of . . . Natural Religion*, Book II, chap. vii.
[40] Wilkins, *Of . . . Natural Religion*, Book II, chap. iii, p. 327. Cf. 2 Tim. 3: 12; also Matt. 5: 11.
[41] Wilkins, *Of . . . Natural Religion*, Book II, chap. iii, p. 328.

a Man's Secular Advantage.'[42] Though Wilkins consistently opposed the persecution of Nonconformists, this argument suggests that he regarded their sufferings as partly self-inflicted.

What kind of secular advantage does Wilkins imply? In the chapter showing 'How Religion conduces to the Happiness of the Outward-man in respect of Riches' he defines riches to mean sufficiency of possessions and acquiescence of mind in what is really sufficient,[43] but it is clear that he also means the growth of material wealth. The most able and wealthy men are usually the most religious: 'such places, where Men have the Opportunity of being instructed in, and excited to the Duties of Religion, do thereupon thrive and flourish most; it being one property of Religion to civilize Men, and make them more inquisitive in Learning, and more diligent in practising their several Professions.'[44] He grants that there are 'particular exempt Cases' of good men who suffer poverty. However, some good men 'may sometimes be defective in several of those Duties which Religion doth oblige them to, Diligence, Caution, &c. And the Poverty of such may justly be ascribed to their Defect in Religion.'[45] Again, the exceptions prove the rule. After he has considered the worldly advantages of religion one by one, Wilkins concludes this central part of his argument by urging his readers to verify his doctrine empirically: 'I appeal to the Experience of all considering Men, whether this doth not appear to them, that the generality of those who live most pleasantly in the World, are the most religious and virtuous part of mankind.'[46]

Edward Fowler's *Design of Christianity*

How much knowledge did Bunyan have of contemporary Anglican and especially latitudinarian thought? His own work, as will be suggested below, reflects informed if hostile consciousness of

---

[42] Wilkins, *Of . . . Natural Religion*, Book II, chap. iii, p. 329. Cf. the same argument in Tillotson, Sermon vi, 'The precepts of Christianity not grievous', *Works*, i. 164–5.
[43] Wilkins, *Of . . . Natural Religion*, Book II, chap. iv, p. 333.
[44] Wilkins, *Of . . . Natural Religion*, Book II, chap. iv, p. 338.
[45] Wilkins, *Of . . . Natural Religion*, Book II, chap. iv, p. 342.
[46] Wilkins, *Of . . . Natural Religion*, Book II, chap. vii, p. 383. In his last two chaps. Wilkins turns to happiness in the next world, and the superiority of revelation to the light of nature, but the emphasis of the work as a whole is deliberately on natural religion and this world.

characteristic latitudinarian ideas and terms. It seems reasonable to assume that during the 1670s he became more familiar with the moralist and prudential tendency of Anglican preaching in the City, perhaps as a result of his own visits to London to preach and his growing friendship with London Nonconformist ministers and congregations.[47] He could easily have learned about the ideas of Wilkins or the younger generation of latitude-men through his friendship with John Owen, the leading London Congregationalist after the Restoration.[48] Owen and Wilkins had worked together during the 1650s when Owen was Vice-chancellor of the University of Oxford and Wilkins Warden of Wadham College; they acted as two of the five Commissioners in charge of the University. After the Act of Uniformity Wilkins kept up his contacts with Nonconformists, doing his best to bring them into the established Church by rational persuasion and to mitigate the effects of the legislation against them. However, with one exception there is no direct external evidence that Bunyan was familiar with the work of the latitudinarians. The exception is Edward Fowler. In 1671 Fowler published a sequel to *Principles and Practices*, his apology for latitude, with the following title: *The Design of Christianity: or, A plain Demonstration and Improvement of this Proposition, viz. That the enduing men with Inward Real Righteousness or True Holiness, was the Ultimate End of our Saviour's Coming into the World, and is the Great Intendment of His Blessed Gospel*. At the time of writing it Fowler was Vicar of Northill, Bedfordshire (he obtained a London living in 1673, apparently as a reward for these two works), and it was presumably because of geographical proximity that Bunyan read it while still in prison (though he does not seem to have read *Principles and Practices*). The *Design* was reprinted twice in Fowler's lifetime (1676 and 1699) and twice in the eighteenth century (1760 and in Richard Watson's *A Collection of Theological Tracts*, 1785, volume vi), and Fowler also published a continuation, *Libertas Evangelica: or, A Discourse of Christian Liberty. Being a farther Pursuance of the*

---

[47] On Bunyan's London connections see 'A Continuation of Mr Bunyan's Life', *GA*, p. 171; Charles Doe, 'The Struggler', in *Works*, iii. 766-7; Brown, pp. 366-7; William York Tindall, *John Bunyan Mechanick Preacher* (New York, 1934), p. 211; Richard L. Greaves, 'John Bunyan's *Holy War* and London Nonconformity', *BQ* 26 (1975), 158-68; *HW*, pp. ix-xii; *Misc. Wks.*, ix. xvii.

[48] Sharrock, *HW*, p. 254, suggests Owen as a source for Bunyan's apparent knowledge of Wilkins's scientific speculations.

Argument of the Design of Christianity (1680). Watson on the title page of his edition expressed surprise that the *Design* had not been reprinted more often, associating it with *The Whole Duty of Man*, Taylor's *Holy Living and Dying*, and à Kempis's *The Imitation of Christ* among others as 'works of a similar tendency'. In other words, Watson identified the *Design* as a valuable contribution to the tradition of moral Christianity that was to predominate in the late seventeenth and eighteenth centuries.

Three aspects of the *Design* are particularly relevant to the dispute between Nonconformists and Conformists about the relationship between grace and morality: Fowler's definition of holiness (in chapter i), his view of Christ's role as essentially exemplary (in chapter v), and his account of justifying faith (in chapter xix). (The last of these recapitulates part of the argument of *Principles and Practices*.)[49] In his account of holiness Fowler emphasizes the qualities inherent in human nature. Since his terminology and its implications are important (and are seized on by Bunyan) his definition is quoted at length:

> *It is so sound and healthful a Complexion of Soul, as maintains in life and vigour whatsoever is Essential to it, and suffers not any thing unnatural to mix with that which is so; by the force and power whereof a man is enabled to behave himself as becometh a Creature indued with a principle of Reason; keeps his Supreme Faculty in its Throne, brings into due Subjection all his Inferiour ones, his sensual Imagination, his Brutish Passions and Affections.*
>
> *It is the Purity of the Humane Nature, engaging those in whom it resides, to demean themselves sutably to that state in which God hath placed them, and not to act disbecomingly in any Condition, Circumstance, or Relation.*
>
> *It is a Divine or God-like Nature, causing an hearty approbation of, and an affectionate compliance with the Eternal Laws of Righteousness; and a behaviour agreeable to the Essential and Immutable differences of Good and Evil.*[50]

Fowler perceives the process of achieving holiness as the perfection or restoration of innate human qualities in the light of rationally

---

[49] Fowler, *Principles and Practices*, Part I, pp. 114 ff.
[50] Edward Fowler, *The Design of Christianity* (1671), chap. i, p. 6. Fowler assumes the existence of eternal and immutable morality (cf. Cudworth's *A Treatise concerning Eternal and Immutable Morality*, not published until 1731), and that there are self-evident first principles in morals just as in mathematics, a favourite latitudinarian maxim (Fowler, *Design*, p. 8; cf. Whichcote, *Aphorisms*, no. 298).

observed laws; there is a direct relationship between reason or knowledge and action. The main function of the Incarnation was to provide a pattern for this process: 'The Promoting of Holiness was *the* Design of our Saviour's *Whole Life, and Conversation among Men.*'⁵¹ In a fascinating passage Fowler presents Christ for the reader's emulation in terms that portray him as the model gentleman:

His whole Life was one Continued Lecture of the most Excellent *Morals*, the most Sublime and exact Vertue.

For instance; He was a Person of the Greatest *Freedom*, *Affability*, and *Courtesie*, there was nothing in his Conversation that was at all Austere, Crabbed or Unpleasant. Though he was always *serious*, yet was he never *sowr*, sullenly Grave, Morose or Cynical; but of a marvellously conversable, sociable and benign temper.⁵²

And Fowler goes on to refer to 'the *Candour* also and *Ingenuity* of his Spirit'.⁵³ In addition to these exemplary characteristics of temper and behaviour, Fowler stresses Christ's prudence, a crucial virtue for Anglicans:

Nor was the *Wisdom of the Serpent* less Conspicuous in him, than was the *Innocence of the Dove. Prudence* is the first of the Primitive vertues, or of those from whence all other take their Original, and are derived: She is the chief Governess of humane actions; and those which are performed without her direction, do want a main circumstance that is necessary to give them the denomination of truly vertuous.⁵⁴

---

⁵¹ Fowler, *Design*, chap. v, pp. 36–7. J. S. McGee sees stress on the imitation of Christ as a characteristically Anglican as opposed to Puritan position in the 1640s, *The Godly Man in Stuart England* (New Haven, 1976), pp. 107–11.

⁵² Fowler, *Design*, chap. v, p. 39.

⁵³ Fowler, *Design*, chap. v, p. 41. Ingenuity, candour (in the sense of generosity) and benignity are among the favourite latitudinarian terms for describing human nature. See, e.g., Barrow, Sermon xxvi, 'Of the Love of our Neighbour': 'Man having received his soul from the breath of God, and being framed after the image of his most benign parent, there do yet abide in him some features resembling God, and relics of the divine original; there are in us seeds of ingenuity, of equity, of pity, of benignity, which being cultivated by sober consideration and good use, under the conduct and aid of heavenly grace, will produce noble fruits of charity' (*Works*, ii, 36); Whichcote, *Select Sermons*, Part II, Sermon vi: '*Religion* produceth a sweet and gracious Temper of Mind; *calm* in its self, and *loving to Men*. It causeth a *Universal Benevolence* and *Kindness* to Mankind. For, these are the Things of which it doth consist; *Love, Candour, Ingenuity, Clemency, Patience, Mildness, Gentleness*, and all other Instances of *GOOD-NATURE*' (p. 431). On the term 'ingenuity' see Robert A. Greene, 'Whichcote, Wilkins, 'Ingenuity', and the Reasonableness of Christianity', *Journal of the History of Ideas*, 42 (1981), 227–52.

⁵⁴ Fowler, *Design*, p. 63, referring to Matthew 10: 16. Cf. Wilkins, Sermon vii, which analyses carnal policy, moral prudence, and spiritual wisdom.

These virtues and qualities are all imitable by mortals: 'it is impossible we should not have the *Design of Christianity* accomplished in us . . . if we make *our Saviour's most Excellent Life* . . . the *Pattern of our Lives.*'[55]

Fowler's definition of justifying faith is such that holiness is not, as for Calvinists, its consequence but its essential component: '*it is such a belief of the Truth of the Gospel, as includes a sincere resolution of Obedience unto all its Precepts*; or (which is the same thing) includes *true Holiness* in the nature of it.'[56] He defines the doctrine of imputed righteousness (a phrase he does not much care for) to include inherent righteousness:

> it consists in dealing with *sincerely* righteous persons, as if they were *perfectly* so, for the sake and upon the account of Christ's Righteousness. The *grand* intent of the Gospel being to make us partakers of an *Inward* and *Real* Righteousness, and it being but a *secondary* one that we should be *accepted* and rewarded as if we were *completely* righteous; it is not possible that any other notion of this Doctrine should have truth in it.[57]

He regards the doctrine of justification by faith alone as necessarily antinomian.[58] Despite his insistence in chapter xiv of the *Design* on the superiority of the gospel to classical ethics, there is little doubt that he is far more sympathetic to classical moralists, whom he repeatedly cites (Hierocles in particular), than to Reformation theologians, whom he ignores (of the moderns he cites Patrick and John Smith). Like Wilkins, he regards pleasure as the natural consequence of the practice of religion. In the Conclusion he writes: 'There is no true Christian that needs to be told, That the more careful he is to *obey God*, the more sweetly he enjoys himself: Nor, That a Vertuous and Holy Life doth several ways bring in a constant Revenue of Peace and Pleasure'.[59]

Bunyan obtained a copy of the *Design* on 13 February 1672 and by 27 March had completed his reply.[60] It was the last work

---

[55] Fowler, *Design*, chap. xxvii, p. 296.
[56] Fowler, *Design*, chap. xix, p. 221.
[57] Fowler, *Design*, chap. xix, pp. 225–6. Cf. *Principles and Practices*, Part I, pp. 114–15, 126–7.
[58] Fowler, *Design*, chap. xx; cf. *Principles and Practices*, Part I, pp. 128 ff.
[59] Fowler, *Design*, p. 305.
[60] His 'Premonition to the Reader' is dated 'From Prison, the 27th of the 12th Month, 1671' (Old Style), and he informs Fowler that he obtained the book on the 13th of the 11th month (*Works*, ii. 281). On the dispute between Fowler and Bunyan

he wrote before his release from prison in May 1672.[61] The title reads in part: *A Defence of the Doctrine of Justification, by Faith in Jesus Christ; shewing, True Gospel-Holiness flows from Thence; or, Mr. Fowler's Pretended Design of Christianity, Proved to be nothing more than to trample under Foot the Blood of the Son of God; and the Idolizing of Man's own Righteousness.* Bunyan's method is to attack Fowler's doctrine as heathen or 'naturalist',[62] to supply the correct doctrine in its place, and to impugn Fowler's motives as self-seeking, temporizing, and mercenary. Bunyan takes particular exception to Fowler's opening definition of holiness; he repeats again and again Fowler's terms 'the sound complexion of soul', 'the purity of the human nature', 'the divine or God-like nature'. For Bunyan these are only words without meaning, since the condition they purport to describe does not exist.[63] He is hostile to the suppositions underlying Fowler's remarks about the 'supreme faculty'—that the soul can be free from sin and hence the conscience free from guilt and 'perfectly clear and light'.[64] His evidence, constantly repeated, is from the Bible, especially the Pauline epistles (he has nothing but contempt for Fowler's citations from the classical moralists and John Smith), and he summarizes his long attack on Fowler's original premisses thus: 'I conclude then upon the whole, that the gospel hath cast out man's righteousness to the dogs; and conclude that there is no such thing as a purity of human nature, as a principle in us, thereby to work righteousness withal.'[65] Bunyan argues that there are three things essential to inward gospel holiness of which Fowler's description is 'utterly destitute': '1. *The Holy Ghost.* 2. *Faith in Christ.* 3. *A new heart, and a new spirit.*'[66] Citing Paul's distinction between the spirit of the world and the spirit of God (1 Corinthians 2: 12), he identifies the former with Fowler's principles, and with the 'candle of the Lord' (Proverbs 20: 27—one of the favourite latitudinarian texts): it represents 'human principles, good motions to moral duties, workings of reason, dictates of nature to obey God as Creator. . . . They that preach, or speak by this spirit, they preach or speak of the world, of the virtues of the world . . . Now when this spirit is received, embraced, and followed, as the

---

see Tindall, *John Bunyan,* pp. 50-2, 60-3; Greaves, p. 80 ff; *Misc. Wks.,* viii. xxxiii, xxxvii.

[61] Brown, pp. 176-7 (but see *PP,* p. xxv, and above p. 34).
[62] *Works,* ii. 288.   [63] *Works,* ii. 282.   [64] *Works,* ii. 283.
[65] *Works,* ii. 296-7.   [66] *Works,* ii. 288.

spirit that is of God, then it must be branded with the mark of the spirit of error, and of antichrist'.[67] For Bunyan there can be no connection between the holiness Fowler describes as 'the purity of the human nature' and holiness that is consequent on faith and a new spirit. Fowler erroneously tries to make holiness and works 'the very radicals of Christianity' whereas they are 'only remote, and after conclusions'.[68] Interestingly, in the counter-attack on Bunyan entitled *Dirt Wip't Off* (written either by Fowler or his curate), with the subtitle *A manifest Discovery of the Gross Ignorance, Erroneousness and most Unchristian and Wicked Spirit of one John Bunyan*, this distinction, essential to Bunyan's argument, is itself perceived as consisting merely of words: 'And then for *a new heart and a new spirit*, What difference is there between *these* and *Purity of nature*, and *a Sound Complexion of Soul*, and *a Divine or Godlike nature*? doth not every body know that these are but several expressions of the very same thing?'[69]

Bunyan is contemptuous of Fowler's account of the life of Christ: it is 'none other than heathenish'; his fifth chapter consists of 'words spoken to the air.'[70] From Bunyan's point of view, Fowler completely misunderstands Christ's essential function, which is that of mediator, saviour, sacrifice, not example. Bunyan grants that Christ has an exemplary function, but his interpretation of this function is utterly different from Fowler's: it is a subordinate function, it is relevant only to those justified by faith, and the virtues it promotes are not Fowler's benign and sociable ones:

Indeed in some things he was an example to us to follow him; but mark, it was not as he was Mediator, not as he was under the law to God, not as he died for sin, nor as he maketh reconciliation for iniquity. But in these things consist the life of our soul, and the beginning of our happiness. He was then exemplary to us, as he carried it meekly and patiently, and

---

[67] *Works*, ii. 289. Bunyan's account of the separate functions of Mr Conscience (erstwhile Recorder of Mansoul, promoted by Emanuel to Minister) and the Lord High Secretary (the Holy Spirit) is relevant here: the subordinate Conscience must confine himself to 'the teaching of Moral Vertues, to Civil and Natural duties', whereas his superior the Secretary teaches 'all high and sublime Mysteries'. Conscience 'must not look for life from that which he himself revealeth, his dependance for that must be founded in the Doctrine of the other Preacher' (*HW*, pp. 140–2). Bunyan thought that Fowler, like the Quakers, could not understand this crucial distinction. On the Quaker view of conscience, see *Misc. Wks.*, i. 56, 147, 163. On the inadequacy of the 'candle' of understanding, judgement, and conscience, see *Misc. Wks.*, ix. 286.
[68] *Works*, ii. 285. [69] *Dirt Wip't Off* (1672), p. 33.
[70] *Works*, ii. 300, 302.

self-denyingly towards the world: But yet not so neither to any but such to whom he first offered justification by the means of his own righteousness.[71]

These terms are very different from Fowler's, as Bunyan notes. Fowler makes Christ 'instead of a saviour, by his blood, the instructor, and schoolmaster only of human nature'; 'faith, with you, must be turned into a cheerful and generous complying with the dictates of the human nature'.[72] Bunyan objects to Fowler's list of Christ's virtues to be imitated (above, p. 58) that the reason Christ perfectly fulfilled the law was to be acceptable to God as sacrifice; therefore, argues Bunyan, 'it is blasphemy for any to presume to imitate him'.[73]

The only motives Bunyan can ascribe to Fowler for adopting these antichristian principles are sheer greed and self-interest: many conformist ministers are men 'that have done violence to their former light', 'persons whose lives are debauched, and who in the face of the world, after seeming serious detestings of wickedness, have for the love of filthy lucre, and the pampering their idle carcasses, made shipwreck of their former faith'.[74] Fowler's principles would enable him to turn Mahometan in Turkey without difficulty. And Bunyan holds up to the reader 'a glorious Latitudinarian, that can, as to religion, turn and twist like an eel on the angle; or rather like the weather-cock that stands on the steeple.'[75] He can find nothing to say in Fowler's favour: 'Your book, Sir, is begun in ignorance, managed with error, and ended in blasphemy.'[76]

---

[71] *Works*, ii. 302.   [72] *Works*, ii. 312.   [73] *Works*, ii. 329.
[74] *Works*, ii. 313.
[75] *Works*, ii. 322. Cf. the portrait of the 'temporizing latitudinarian' in *The Strait Gate* (1676): 'he is a man that hath no God but his belly, nor any religion but that by which his belly is worshiped, his religion is always like the times, turning this way and that way, like the cock on the steeple, neither hath he any conscience but a benumned or seared one, and is next door to a downright athiest' (*Misc. Wks.*, v. 126).
[76] *Works*, ii. 332. Bunyan's outright condemnation should be compared with Richard Baxter's much more sympathetic response in *How Far Holiness is the Design of Christianity* (1671). Baxter is concerned to provide his own definition of holiness rather than to assess Fowler's, but interestingly he sees Fowler's work as a natural response to antinomianism: 'He knoweth not the hurtful miscarriages of our times, who knoweth not . . . how the Gospel hath been supplanted, by an erroneous crying up the Gospel, and crying down the Law; and how Justification hath been abused, by mens seeming to extol it, and sanctification injured by such pretexts: And he that with one eye looks on that disease and its effects, and with the other looks on the Book you tell me of [*i.e. the* Design] . . . will quickly see what Sore this Plaster was

The Pilgrim's Progress and Anglicanism

In *The Pilgrim's Progress* Part I Bunyan clearly set out his differences from his opponents on the subjects of grace, morality, holiness, suffering, and the worldly advantages of religion. The crucial episodes are those containing Christian's meeting with Mr Worldly-Wiseman, the pilgrims' sufferings in Vanity Fair, the discussion Mr By-ends and his companions have among themselves and with Christian, Hopeful's account of his conversion, and Christian's dispute with Ignorance. It is striking that the episodes containing Mr Worldly-Wiseman, Evangelist's warnings about Vanity Fair, and Mr By-ends' companions were additions; this suggests that Bunyan thought it necessary to strengthen his case against the dangerous tendencies of moral and prudential religion.[77]

Christian meets Mr Worldly-Wiseman early in his journey, after he has been directed to the wicket gate (representing the essential experience of conversion) by Evangelist.[78] Mr Worldly-Wiseman,

---

provided for, and how much excellent matter there is in it, which the foresaid persons and diseases need' (p. 20). F. M. Powicke has some interesting speculations about Baxter, Bunyan, and Fowler in *The Reverent Richard Baxter under the Cross* (1927), pp. 53–9. Baxter commented on the reception of the *Design* in *Reliquiae Baxterianae* (1696), Part III, p. 85, and in 'A Defence of Christ', in *The Scripture Gospel Defended* (1690), p. 49. In the latter, partly on the strength of Bunyan's attack on Fowler, Baxter described Bunyan as 'an unlearned Antinomian-Anabaptist', though Baxter believed him to be 'an honest Godly man' 'who attained the design of Christianity'. Cf. N. H. Keeble, *Richard Baxter: Puritan Man of Letters* (Oxford, 1982), p. 24.

[77] *PP*, pp. xlii, xliv, xlvi. The Worldly-Wiseman episode (added to the 2nd edn.) is over eight pages long (*PP*, pp. 16–25); that of By-ends' companions (added to the 3rd edn.) is over five pages (pp. 100–6) and is 'the last addition of any consequence Bunyan made to the text' (p. xlvi).

[78] Bunyan may have taken some hints from R[ichard] B[ernard], *The Isle of Man* (1626), where the enemies to virtue include Mr Out-side, 'a carnall Securitan', Sir Worldly-wise, Sir Lukewarm, and Sir Plausible Civill (9th edn. (1634), pp. 15–18). In turn, Bunyan influenced B[enjamin] K[each], *The Travels of True Godliness* (1683), where Sir Worldly Wiseman, a divine, asks 'what is Religion, but to live an honest and sober life, to fear God, honour the King, say our Prayers, and pay our Debts' (3rd edn. (1684), pp. 24, 26). Mr Legalist, who lives near Mount Sinai, mistakes Godliness for Morality; Godliness explains that though they are alike in some things, they differ in many others: 'He teaches you to seek for Justification by doing, but I only by believing; he by keeping the Law, or by living a sober and honest Life, I by Gods Free Grace, through the Merits of Christ', and he warns Legalist against the thundering of Sinai (pp. 82–7). In the sequel, *The Progress of Sin* (1684), the dwellers in the town Morality are Deists and Quakers; both 'basely wrong and miscall Morality, and make a Christ of it' (4th edn. (1707), pp. 143–4). Sharrock associates the Worldly-Wiseman episode with Bunyan's early legalist period, *GA*, p. 136, and esp. with Fowler, *PP*, pp. 314–15.

a dweller in the town of Carnal-Policy, advises Christian to rid himself of his burden speedily, and warns him against the road pointed out to him by Evangelist: '*thou art like to meet with in the way which thou goest, Wearisomness, Painfulness, Hunger, Perils, Nakedness, Sword, Lions, Dragons, Darkness; and in a word, death, and what not?*' Instead, he offers Christian a road without dangers: if he goes to the village of Morality a gentleman called Legality or his son Civility will help him off with his burden.[79] Christian is persuaded, and makes his way towards Mr Legality's house; but he is terrified by the high hill overhanging his way, Mount Sinai, which flashes fire, and he now finds his burden heavier than before. He is rescued by Evangelist, who explains Mr Worldly-Wiseman's doctrinal errors. He is rightly named, says Evangelist, 'partly, because he favoureth only the Doctrine of this World (therefore he always goes to the Town of *Morality* to Church) and partly because he loveth that Doctrine best, for it saveth him from the Cross'. And Evangelist objects specifically that Mr Worldly-Wiseman has tried to turn Christian out of the way, to make the cross odious to him, and to lead him to damnation by teaching him justification by works of the law. But 'by the deeds of the Law no man living can be rid of his burden: therefore Mr. *Worldly-Wiseman* is an alien, and Mr. *Legality* a cheat'.[80]

Evangelist's advice is vindicated when Christian's burden falls off at the cross.[81] But the cross is not only the doctrine of justification by faith alone and of imputed righteousness; it is also the unavoidable dangers and sufferings the pilgrims must go through on their journey, and Evangelist is careful to prepare them for what will happen to them in Vanity Fair.[82] Christian and Faithful outrage the inhabitants because in every way they are aliens in the world (whereas Mr Worldly-Wiseman was an alien to the true way): they wear strange clothing, which prompts the people to call them 'Fools', 'Bedlams', or 'Outlandish-men'; they speak a strange language, 'the

[79] *PP*, pp. 17–19.   [80] *PP*, pp. 20–3.   [81] *PP*, pp. 38.
[82] *PP*, p. 87. On suffering cf., e.g., *GA*, § 279; *The Strait Gate, Misc. Wks.*, v. 84; *A Holy Life, Misc. Wks.*, ix. 296; *Seasonable Counsel: or, Advice to Sufferers, Works*, ii. 691–741; *HW*, p. 230 (the Bloodmen), Bunyan's 'Dying Sayings': 'I have often thought that the best of Christians are found in the worst of times', *Works*, i. 66 (cf. ii. 707). The fullest accounts of Nonconformist suffering are Gerald R. Cragg, *Puritanism in the Period of the Great Persecution 1660–1688* (Cambridge, 1957) and N. H. Keeble, *The Literary Culture of Nonconformity in Later Seventeenth-century England* (Leicester, 1987).

Language of *Canaan*; and they refuse the wares that are on sale, because 'their Trade and Traffick [is] in Heaven.' It is in this episode that Bunyan makes explicit the metaphor from Hebrews 11: 13 on which the whole allegory is based: when the pilgrims are asked at their examination 'whence they came, whither they went, and what they did there in such an unusual Garb' they reply that they are 'Pilgrims and Strangers in the world . . . going to their own Countrey . . . the Heavenly *Jerusalem*'.[83] The trial and execution of Faithful is one kind of fulfilment of Evangelist's warning that 'you must through many tribulations enter into the Kingdom of Heaven.'[84]

It is therefore ironically appropriate that the first person Christian meets after he escapes from Vanity Fair, accompanied by Hopeful, is Mr By-ends, who epitomizes what Bunyan saw as the cowardice, self-seeking, and material worldliness of the conformists, as distinct from their doctrinal errors.[85] Mr By-ends explains that he and his wife 'somewhat differ in Religion from those of the stricter sort, yet but in two small points: First, we never strive against Wind and Tide. Secondly, we are always most zealous when Religion goes in his Silver Slippers; we love much to walk with him in the Street, if the Sun shines, and the people applaud it.' To this Christian retorts: '*If you will go with us, you must go against Wind and Tide . . . You must also own Religion in his Rags, as well as when in his Silver Slippers, and stand by him too, when bound in Irons, as well as when he walketh the Streets with applause.*'[86] Mr By-ends and his three companions, Mr Hold-the-world, Mr Mony-love, and Mr Save-all, subsequently together debate and agree the essential compatibility of the pursuit of material advantage with the religious life. Mr Hold-the-world's argument is particularly interesting, in that it reads like a provocative caricature of latitudinarian preaching:

---

[83] *PP*, p. 90.
[84] *PP*, p. 87.
[85] See Tindall, *John Bunyan*, pp. 60–3, 116; Sharrock, *PP*, p. 328. According to Tindall, By-ends' name was probably suggested by Fowler's observation that most professors think that if the promoting of holiness 'was at all a Design of [Christ's] coming into the world . . . yet it was at best but a Bye-one' (Fowler, *Design*, p. 2; Tindall, *John Bunyan*, p. 60). However, Bunyan used the term in a similar sense to that in *Pilgrim's Progress* in *A Few Sighs from Hell* (1658): 'O thou that for by-ends dost carry on an hypocrites profession, because thou wouldest be counted some body among the children of God, but art an enemy to the things of Christ in thine heart . . .' (*Misc. Wks.*, i. 301; cf. ix. 68).
[86] *PP*, pp. 99, 100.

Let us be wise *as Serpents*, 'tis best to make hay when the Sun shines; you see how the Bee lieth still all winter and bestirs her then only when she can have profit with pleasure.... For my part I like that Religion best, that will stand with the security of Gods good blessings unto us; for who can imagin that is ruled by his reason, since God has bestowed upon us the good things of this life, but that he would have us keep them for his sake. *Abraham* and *Solomon* grew rich in Religion.[87]

Mr Mony-love gives a materialist answer to a casuistical question, which involves confusing different meanings of 'good'. A tradesman who gets a rich wife or more custom in his shop by becoming religious, 'gets that which is good, of them that are good, by becoming good himself; so then here is a good wife, and good customers, and good gaine, and all these by becoming religious, which is good. Therefore to become religious to get all these is a good and profitable design.' The others conclude this answer to be 'most wholsome and advantagious'.[88] When the same question is put to Christian, he urges how abominable it is 'to make of ... religion a stalking horse to get and enjoy the world' (which is exactly the implication of By-ends' name).[89] Christian adds, 'that man that takes up Religion for the world, will throw away Religion for the world', which shortly proves to be the case: By-ends and his companions turn aside at the call of the worldly Demas to explore the silver mine in the dangerous hill Lucre, and, comments the narrator, 'I observed, that they never was seen again in the way.'[90]

The last character who embodies Bunyan's hostility to Anglicanism is Ignorance, whom Christian and Hopeful meet in the final stages of their journey.[91] In the portrait of Ignorance Bunyan is concerned not with the materialism of Mr By-ends but with the moralism of Mr Worldly-Wiseman. In addition to the confidence in works which he shares with Mr Wiseman, Ignorance further represents the

---

[87] *PP*, p. 102.   [88] *PP*, p. 104.
[89] *PP*, p. 105. Cf. Mr Badman's wooing: 'he knew that he made use of the name of God, of religion, good men, and good books, but as a stalking-horse, thereby the better to catch his game' (*Works*, iii. 619).   [90] *PP*, pp. 106–8.
[91] See Tindall, *John Bunyan*, p. 62; Sharrock, *PP*, p. 337. Sharrock also suggests a resemblance to Dent's Antilegon (*PP*, p. 333); see *The Plaine Mans Path-way*, pp. 271, 346–55. Cf. Mistress Heart in *The Isle of Man*, who urges in her defence the country people's claim to have 'a good *Heart* towards God'; she represents, however, the natural and corrupt, not the sanctified heart (pp. 134–6). *Contra* Sharrock, it is not unreasonable to associate Ignorance with the Quakers, since Bunyan thought Fowler and the Quakers guilty of similar errors.

latitudinarians' optimistic view of human nature and their co-operative view of justification. It is important that Ignorance's account of his views follows Hopeful's detailed history of his conversion: this juxtaposition of two rival creeds represents the most carefully worked out theological statement in *The Pilgrim's Progress*. Hopeful learns the irrelevance of his own works to justification and the impossibility of satisfying the demands of the moral law: 'notwithstanding my former fond conceits of my self and duties, I have committed sin enough in one duty to send me to Hell, though my former life had been faultless.' When he understands that grace and faith are all that are needed for justification, this revelation confounds him 'with the sence of [his] own Ignorance'.[92] By contrast, the 'very brisk Lad' called Ignorance has come into the way by 'a little crooked Lane' from 'the Countrey of *Conceit*'.[93] Ignorance insists that he is 'full of good motions', that his heart and life are good, and that he will be justified through God's acceptance of his obedience to the law: 'Christ makes my Duties that are Religious, acceptable to his Father by vertue of his Merits; and so shall I be justified.'[94] In response to Christian's explanation of justifying faith, Ignorance accuses him of loosening the reins of lust (i.e. of antinomianism), of distracted brains, and whimsies; and the talk breaks up. Christian and Hopeful express their pity for Ignorance, and for the abundance of those who think like him; but the concluding note of the narrative, when Ignorance is bound hand and foot and put through the door in the side of the hill to hell, is not pity but condemnation.[95]

Faith and Holiness

It seemed obvious to Fowler that adherents of strict Calvinism and of the doctrine of imputed righteousness must be antinomians, just as it seemed obvious to Bunyan that latitudinarians, Quakers, and Catholics must be heathens. But Bunyan was as opposed to 'libertine' antinomians as he was to legalists or mere moralists. Each group misrepresented the Gospel and chose the path that led to destruction. He held this position consistently. Thus he writes in *A Few Sighs*

---

[92] *PP*, pp. 140, 144.   [93] *PP*, p. 123.
[94] *PP*, pp. 144–7. Ignorance's mixing of inherent and imputed righteousness is similar to Fowler's (see above, p. 59).   [95] *PP*, pp. 148–50, 163.

from Hell (1658): 'unlesse you have the true and saving work of the Faith and Grace of the Gospel in your hearts, you will either go on in a legall Holiness according to the tenour of the Law; or else through a notion of the Gospel (the Devil bewitching, and beguiling thy understanding, will, and affections) thou wilt Ranter-like turn the Grace of God into wantonness'.[96] This position is put more simply in *The Strait Gate* (1676): 'There are two errors in the world about the law, one is, when men think to enter in *at the strait gate by the righteousness of the law*, the other is, when men think, *they may enter into heaven without the leave of the law.*'[97] In *A Holy Life* (1684) he describes more charitably the difficulty in balancing the doctrines of faith and holiness:

If faith be preached as that which is absolutely necessary to *Justification*; then faith-fantastical, and loosness and remisness in life (with some) are joyned therewith. If holiness of life be preached, as necessary to *salvation*, then faith is undervalued, and set below its place; and works as to justification with God set up and made co-partners with Christs merits in the remission of sins.[98]

The crucial question for Bunyan is to establish this balance. He is not opposed to morality as such; Christians must be well acquainted with the moral law, 'not as it comes from *Moses*, but from Christ'; it must be a rule for their 'conversation [*i.e. behaviour*] in the world.'[99] Faithful explains to Talkative that a work of grace in the soul is discovered by '*a life of holiness; heart-holiness, family-holiness . . . and by Conversation-holiness in the world*'.[100] 'In a word,' Bunyan writes in his domestic handbook, *Christian Behaviour* (1663), 'a life of Holiness and Godliness in this world, doth so inseparably follow a principle of Faith, that it is both monstrous and ridiculous to suppose the contrary.'[101] And he acknowledges with

---

[96] *Misc. Wks.*, i. 381–2. [97] *Misc. Wks.*, v. 79.
[98] *Misc. Wks.*, ix. 326. Cf. Baxter, *Holiness*: 'If any say too much in making our Holiness Gods *only End*, it ill beseemeth those to be their censurers, who have tempted them to it, by erring more on the contrary extream. And it is not to be denied or hid, that more than downright *Antinomians*, have so ill expounded the points of Christs suretiship, and of the Imputation of his Righteousness to us, as hath proved the great occasion of some mens running into the contrary errour' (p. 14); see also his *The Judgment of Non-Conformists About the Difference between Grace and Morality* (1676).
[99] *Misc. Wks.*, ix. 331.   [100] *PP*, p. 83.   [101] *Misc. Wks.*, iii. 15.

a certain irony in the conclusion to *A Holy Life* that men cast dirt at those who tell them of practical holiness as 'legal preachers'.[102]

But though Bunyan undoubtedly stressed the importance of holiness, just as the latitude-men stressed the importance of faith, this does not mean that the differences between them are more apparent than real. For Bunyan religious language and religious narrative involve drawing distinctions, defining opposites, and identifying enemies. The tendency in the writing of the latitude-men, on the other hand, is to conflate terms: grace and virtue, faith and works, religion and happiness—these are but one and the same thing, to use a favourite latitudinarian phrase. For Bunyan religion is about salvation to glory in the next world. The consequence of justification by faith is a life of holiness in this world, but holiness has nothing to do with rewards, in this world or the next. It may bring content, but it is more likely to bring suffering; the religious man will more often go in rags than in silver slippers, be bound in irons than walk the streets with applause. For the latitude-men religion is about two things, reason and morality. To understand the relation of man to God and to live the morally good life in the light of that understanding will bring about happiness in this world as well as the next. Those who choose to suffer mistake the nature of religion. The assumptions of these two different versions of Christianity were incomprehensible to each other.

[102] *Misc. Wks.*, ix. 351.

4

'When at the first I took my Pen in hand': Bunyan and the Book

BY ROGER SHARROCK

THIS essay attempts to describe Bunyan's material activity as an author, the production of his books, the transmission of his texts, and his relations with both the booksellers and the contemporary public. Inevitably the account will not be restricted to consideration of his books as physical objects, and will pass over at some points to examine his motive for writing and his authorial relationship with his readers.

Sermons and Fictions

The descriptive bibliographer finds himself facing the same problem as the literary critic of Bunyan: the relation of the sermons and controversial treatises which constitute the bulk of his production to the book which sold most copies, *The Pilgrim's Progress* (1678), to the other two fictions, and to the spiritual autobiography. It is a problem created for the modern reader for whom there is a great gulf fixed between the two groups: he can, with varying degrees of effort, read the fictions, but he can hardly read the other group at all; it is as simple as that. Nor will any of the likely modern models for the career of a best-selling author be applicable; nor, indeed, will models apply for the self-discovery of a creative artist. There is no simple transition from preacher to allegorist: it is not a case of Bunyan, having once struck the vein of narrative imagination, continuing to mine it. *Mr Badman* (1680), *The Holy War* (1682), and Part II (1684) do succeed *The Pilgrim's Progress*, but two years before his death Bunyan essayed a new genre in the emblem book *A Book for Boys and Girls* (1686) and the sermon treatises continue throughout these years, no fewer than ten of them appearing in the last year of Bunyan's life. Charles Doe, Bunyan's first editor, in 1692 made no special mention of *The Pilgrim's Progress* and referred to the works as a whole: 'Here's Sixty Pieces of his Labours and he was Sixty Years of Age'.[1] Since copyright difficulties seem to have prevented Doe from including the allegories in the one volume of his collected edition to appear, it may be inferred that he calculated on the theological and pastoral works exercising sufficient appeal on their own, at any rate to a Nonconformist public. But the Anglican Anthony à Wood, writing about the same time, could speak of Bunyan as 'the author of several useful and practical books'.[2] Doe was certainly deeply stirred by Bunyan the awakening preacher; he describes in his autobiography how terrified he was by an account of the eternal nature of the torments of Hell in *A Few Sighs from Hell* (1658); he goes on to tell of first hearing Bunyan preach in a Southwark meeting-house a sermon which must have been the substance of *The Desires of the Righteous Granted* (1692); finally he pays the highest possible tribute to one of the pastoral sermon treatises: 'March 1686, as I was reading Mr. *Bunyan*'s Book, *Saved by Grace*, I thought certainly this is the best Book that ever was writ or I read, except the *Bible*, and then I remembered I had received a great deal of Comfort in all of his Books.[3] Charles Doe does not say anything about *The Pilgrim's Progress*, but if we try to see with his eyes and imagine a reader who could enjoy *Saved by Grace* (1676) approaching the allegory, we begin to realize how much in the latter, in the dialogue portions where the action halts, is like the sermon treatises. Christian's discourse to Hopeful, under numbered heads, on the 'suddain backsliding' of Temporary and others, would provide a fair example. Bunyan lived in an age when the idea of the universe as a book of the creatures to be read in terms of complex similitudes was giving way after Hobbes to a preference for restricted *trompe-l'œil* effects and one-to-one likenesses. He can hardly have been aware of the powerfully archaizing tendency in *The Pilgrim's Progress* or the emblems of *A Book for Boys and Girls* (1686).[4]

---

[1] *Folio* (1692), sig. 5T1 (in *Works*, iii. 763).
[2] The comment comes in his memoir of Bunyan's Latitudinarian opponent Edward Fowler: Anthony à Wood, *Athenae Oxonienses*, ed. Philip Bliss, 4 vols. (1820), iv. 613.
[3] Charles Doe, *A Collection of Experience* (1700), pp. 52, 57.
[4] Cf. Michel Foucault, *The Order of Things: An Archaeology of the Human Sciences* (1970), p. 51: 'The age of resemblance is drawing to a close. It is leaving

This unitary Bunyan, a famous preacher who publishes his sermons and writes allegorical fiction as well, has a writing life roughly coterminous with the reign of Charles II. However, his earliest published works preceded the Restoration: these are the two controversial tracts against the Quaker Edward Burrough, *Some Gospel-Truths Opened* (1656) and *A Vindication of Some Gospel-Truths Opened* (1657), *A Few Sighs from Hell* (1658), and *The Doctrine of the Law and Grace Unfolded* (1659), his most ambitious and elaborate theological work. These first works of Bunyan have their place in that ferment of radical and experimental religious publication which characterized the Interregnum; but also these books like Bunyan's later ones belong to a larger seventeenth-century development, the response to the rapid increase in literacy and the consequent dissemination in print of material belonging to the old oral culture. The fearsome denunciation of the sinner in *A Few Sighs*, for instance, in its highly coloured rhetoric, its appeal to the poor by branding the more fortunate and the materially extravagant, and its implied offer of other-worldly compensation for present suffering, is closer to traditional homily than to Gerrard Winstanley or the Levellers:

O thou that dost spend whole nights in carding and dicing, in rioting and wantonness, thou that countest it a brave thing to swear as fast as the bravest, to spend with the greatest spend-thrift (as we call them) in the countrey: O thou that lovest to sin in a corner when nobody sees thee! O thou that for by-ends dost carry on an hypocrites profession, because thou wouldest be counted some body among the children of God, but art an enemy to the things of Christ in thine heart: . . . thy soul will fall into extreme torment, and anguish so soon as ever thou dost depart this world, and there thou shalt be weeping and gnashing thy teeth, *Matth.* 8.11,12. *And besides all this*, thou art likely never to have any ease or remedy, never look for any deliverance, if thou die out of Christ; thou shalt die in thy sins; and be tormented as many years as there are stars in the firmament, or sands on the sea-shore; *and besides all this*, thou must abide it for ever.[5]

---

nothing behind it but games. Games whose powers of enchantment grow out of the new kinship between resemblance and illusion; the chimeras of illusion loom up on all sides, but they are recognized as chimeras; it is the privileged age of *trompe-l'œil* painting, of the comic illusion, of the play that duplicates itself by representing another play, of the *quid pro quo*, of dreams and visions; it is the age of the deceiving senses; it is the age in which the poetic dimension of language is defined by metaphor'.

[5] *Misc. Wks.*, i. 301. Bunyan's stress in *A Few Sighs* and elsewhere on the physical torments of hell reveals him as an extreme conservative voice in the

Bunyan's education, which may have been for a time at a grammar school (like Vavasor Powell), enabled him from the start of his writing to construct grammatical and coherent sentences and paragraphs. Provincial forms are on the whole excluded from the non-fictional works, but they make their way into the allegories (for example, the non-emphatic forms of 'have' in the first edition of *The Pilgrim's Progress*, scrupulously regularized by the printer in subsequent editions apparently without the author's protest.[6]) This, like his mistake in thinking 'spendthrift' to be a non-literary word, marks an important staging-post in the transition from an oral to a print culture. Even the secular folk-tales of his unregenerate boyhood, 'George on horseback and Bevis of Southampton', were not heard at the chimney-corner but read by him in chap-books, probably versions of Richard Johnson's *Seven Champions of Christendom*.[7] The position of Bunyan as a highly self-conscious reader is reflected in his delighted reverence for the few books he knew; it is illustrated by his memorializing in *Grace Abounding* the two books brought to him as his first wife's dowry, Arthur Dent's *The Plaine Mans Path-way to Heaven* (1601) and Lewis Bayly's *The Practise of Pietie* (1612). The drama and raciness of Dent's dialogue entered deeply into Bunyan's mind and it is one of the few books, apart from the Bible, of which one can say that *The Pilgrim's Progress*, or *Mr Badman*, would not have been the same without it. But Dent's title tells the whole story. His plain man, ancestor of many an Everyman, and intelligent man or woman, stands at the threshold of an era of vulgarization. All Bunyan's works from this aspect represent a vulgarization of reformed and covenant theology. An outstanding example of this new literate man's awed feeling for the book from the past that bears the knowledge of former days to a new generation is the beautifully evoked reminiscence of his first encounter with Luther's *Commentary on Galatians*:

---

contemporary debate reviewed in D. P. Walker, *The Decline of Hell: Seventeenth-century Discussions of Eternal Torment* (1964). Bunyan's Nonconformist contemporary Richard Baxter, always a moderate voice, pays much more attention to the mental sufferings of the damned. For Winstanley, see *BDBR* and *DNB*, s.v.

[6] Cf. the discussions of the changes of idiom from the 1st edn. texts in *GA*, p. xxxviii, and *PP*, p. xciv.

[7] *Misc. Wks.*, i. 133. For the transition to literacy as marked by the growth of a public for the chap-books, see Margaret Spufford, *Small Books and Pleasant Histories* (1981), esp. pp. 19–82.

Well, after many such longings in my mind, the God in whose hands are all our days and ways, did cast into my hand, one day, a book of *Martin Luther*, his comment on the *Galathians*, so old that it was ready to fall piece from piece, if I did but turn it over. Now I was pleased much that such an old book had fallen into my hand; the which, when I had but a little way perused, I found my condition in his experience, so largely and profoundly handled, as if his Book had been written out of my heart . . .[8]

With his characteristic power to suggest concrete presence Bunyan describes the old book as a physical thing. But if we turn to his own writings before *Grace Abounding* and *The Pilgrim's Progress* it is impossible to find any *mystique* of the book as defined separate object, exercising its peculiar gift of communicating meaning and therefore, as repository of wisdom, sharing in the truth which it asserts. On the contrary, in the early works particularly, one meets a total unselfconsciousness in regard to the function of the writer. This is because the book is treated simply as an extension of the oral sermon. Bunyan's line of division, because of his experience of censorship and restrictive power, is drawn between freedom to speak and compulsory silence, not between speaking and writing. Luther's book is a free action, a gift. Bunyan's own words and phrases remain those of speech. He begins a book abruptly like one in the course of addressing an audience: 'I shall not trouble you with long preambles, or fore-speech to the matter, nor shall I here so much as meddle with the context, but shall immediately fall upon the words themselves, and briefly treat of the *Fear of God*.'[9] Admittedly, in *Some Gospel-Truths Opened* (1656), amid tedium and repetition, the reader is made aware of Bunyan's repulsion by the Friends' concept of an inward working of the Spirit as something amorphous and chaotic, his reliance on the firm, plain ground of 'a Christ crucified without the gates of Jerusalem.' Likewise in *The Doctrine of the Law and Grace* (1659) the formal structure of debt, surety, and redemption is coloured by examples and insights from the writer's personal experience of the temptation to despair.[10] The reader is put in possession of that main constituent of a modern book, its provision of knowledge of a writer's personality, even though Bunyan ignores this literary element except as a homiletic device; when it does become at all prominent, as in the autobiographical

---

[8] *GA*, § 129.   [9] *A Treatise of the Fear of God* (1679), *Misc. Wks.*, ix. 5.
[10] *Misc. Wks.*, ii. 159–60.

interventions, Bunyan is concerned to keep it strictly under control: nothing must divert the mainstream of Biblical testimony leading to the passionate proclamation of free grace.

Thus, when Bunyan commences as writer, and in his works up to his spiritual autobiography and *The Pilgrim's Progress*, literature is necessarily subordinated to the total claims of saving truth; 'One thing is needful'. But, in his own terms, grace accepted, and the beginning of the gradual process of sanctification, cannot waive individual desire for one particular means rather than another to strengthen conviction. So Bunyan had 'longed' to share 'some ancient Godly man's Experience' who had gone down himself into the deep. In spite of restraint, the early works follow the inner life of his conversion as it was reflected in his preaching: first, the sheer terrors of the law projected into the appalling punishments of *A Few Sighs from Hell* (1658); then the joyful reliance on the person and attributes of Christ (*Law and Grace*). The intimate relation of the pattern of preaching to inner history is thus described in *Grace Abounding*:

> now I altered in my preaching (for still I preached what I saw and felt;) now therefore I did much labour to hold forth Jesus Christ in all his Offices, Relations, and Benefits unto the World, and did strive also to discover, to condemn, and remove those false supports and props on which the World doth both lean, and by them fall and perish.[11]

The 'terrours of the Law' had been reflected in *A Few Sighs* and now the change to an approach stressing the intercessory function of Christ is shown in the sermons which became the material for *Law and Grace*.

Bunyan's literary production supplied the new literacy of yeomen, artisans, and small tradesmen. In its immediate origins it belongs to the publishing upsurge of the period of the civil wars and Commonwealth. The purchases of the publisher and book collector George Thomason averaged three new books a day from the outbreak of the war down to 1660. Bunyan's early tracts were a part of 'the enormous and variegated production of books after the suspension of any effective censorship by the government in 1640'.[12] Christopher Hill has reminded us how rigorous the

---

[11] *GA*, § 278.
[12] Keith Wrightson, *English Society 1580–1680* (1982), p. 199; [G. K. Fortescue], *Catalogue of the Pamphlets . . . Collected by George Thomason*, 2 vols. (1908).

Laudian censorship was:[13] if Nicholas Ferrar had difficulties over the publication of Herbert's *The Temple*, it seems unlikely that the avowed covenant theology of *Law and Grace* would have found a publisher. Also it is important to note that after 1660 even the vigilance of Roger L'Estrange (who became official licenser in November 1663) could not restore the press to its earlier subjection. Bunyan published steadily down to his death and his works included the open and violent attack on the Anglican Edward Fowler, later to be Bishop of Gloucester, *A Defence of the Doctrine of Justification by Faith* (1672). But two books were printed on Bunyan's responsibility and without the intervention of a bookseller, *I Will Pray with the Spirit* ([1662?]) and *The Holy City* (1665); the former defended conventicles against the Common Prayer and the latter, though politically innocuous, might have had Fifth Monarchy overtones read into it: it is not surprising if booksellers would not handle them, though 'J. Dover' was responsible for some copies of the first edition of *The Holy City*.

Yet Bunyan's relation to radical Puritanism is ambiguous, at least on the evidence of publication. It must be recognized to start with that before toleration and even long after 1689 any statement of a particular ecclesiastical position had direct political implications. Further, many of Bunyan's brethren, the London Baptists, had been involved in Fifth Monarchy plots and in intrigues concerning a post-Protectorate settlement; within a year of the publication of his first book they had addressed to Charles II in Holland 'The Humble Address of the Subscribers' offering their support against Cromwell.[14] Bunyan's name, together with that of another member of the Bedford Church, Richard Spencly (or Spensely), is found as early as 1653 attached with thirty-four others to the 'Letter from the people of Bedfordshire to the Lord General Cromwell, the councell of the army' (13 May 1653);[15] John Fenn(e), an elder of the Church associated with Bunyan in visiting sick or disaffected

---

[13] Christopher Hill, 'Radical Prose in Seventeenth-century England: From Marprelate to the Levellers', *Essays in Criticism*, 32 (1982), 95–8 (repr. in id., *Writing and Revolution in Seventeenth-century England* (Brighton, 1985), where see also the essay 'Censorship and English Literature').

[14] The address is given at length in Clarendon, *History of the Rebellion and Civil Wars in England* (Oxford, 1707), iii. 625–34.

[15] *Original Letters and Papers of State Addressed to Oliver Cromwell*, ed. John Nickalls (1743), p. 92.

members, was one of those who signed 'The Humble and Serious Testimony' (1657) which opposed the suggestion that Cromwell should assume the title of monarch as a 'change in Government from a Commonwealth, whereby we conceive a foundation is laid for a new, most bloody, and desolating War.'[16] But there is no evidence that Bunyan was politically radical in the manner of some of his fellow-Baptists who wished to overturn the social order. The test case is his millenarianism. All the sectaries believed in Christ's reign with his saints as the completion of history; so did probably a majority of the adherents of the establishment. Revolutionary aims are associated with those who would attach the prophecies of Revelation to present personalities and events immediately expected. This kind of millenarianism is absent from Bunyan's two commentaries on the Apocalypse, *The Holy City* and *Of Antichrist and his Ruin* (1692). The introductory epistle to the former denounces Rome in a manner acceptable to any Protestant Englishman; in the latter there is the far from revolutionary suggestion that the reign of the saints might be inaugurated by an alliance of Protestant princes.[17] Bunyan condemned Venner's Fifth Monarchy uprising of 1661; that was at the beginning of his first imprisonment, and nothing can be more uncompromising than the statement of loyalty he made to the magistrates' clerk Ralph Cobb on that occasion: 'I look upon it to behave under the King's government, both as becomes a man and a christian; and if an occasion was offered me, I should willingly manifest my loyalty to my Prince, both by word and deed.'[18]

Similarly, though there are violently class-conscious attacks on the rich in *A Few Sighs from Hell* these do not spring from an egalitarian political position like that of the Levellers. The rich refuse Lazarus and his kind 'because they are not Gentlemen, because they cannot with *Pontius Pilate* speak Hebrew, Greek, and Latine.'[19] The attitude is traditional, looking back to medieval homiletic: the poor are more likely to be among the saved; the Christian must be content with few of this world's goods. Likewise, though Bunyan's theology has been considered by Richard Greaves to exhibit some antinomian

---

[16] *A Collection of the State Papers of John Thurloe*, ed. Thomas Birch (1742), vi. 228-30.   [17] *Of Antichrist and His Ruine*, *Works*, ii. 72-4.
[18] *GA*, p. 120; cf. *Holy City* (1669 edn.), p. 55, and *Seasonable Counsel* (1684), *Works*, ii. 706-9.   [19] *Misc. Wks.*, i. 304.

features, he was always emphatic in his rejection of the ethical radicalism of the Familists and Ranters, their ecstatic pantheism and advocacy of sexual promiscuity. Like the bitterness of his opposition to the Quakers, the frequency of his denunciations demonstrates awareness of the direct competition in evangelism offered by Ranter preachers to the same Bedfordshire or Southwark congregations with which Bunyan was involved.[20]

Yet the question of his debt to the radicalism of 'the good old cause' is not wholly a simple one; What did he mean when he wrote that he hoped 'that my imprisonment might be an awakening to the Saints in the Country'? Probably, a strengthening of communal resolution in the Baptist churches in Bedfordshire. But the intense excitement of his seed-time in the 1650s might have led him still to hanker after a more favourable public settlement. After all, this was before the Act of Uniformity came into force on St Bartholomew's Day, 1662 and the initiation of wholesale persecution. Though he would not, like Baxter, have been ready to accept any imposed form of worship, however moderate, adaptable, and varied, he might have felt like him in the period of the Savoy Conference that the nature of the ecclesiastical settlement still hung in the balance: 'This was yet to be done, and till this were done we were uncertain of the Issue of all our Treaty: but if that were done, and all settled by Law, our Divisions were at an end.'[21] When disillusion came he may have recalled the old cause of liberty of conscience more nostalgically. Emanuel's troops and their captains in *The Holy War* reflect the dash and discipline of the godly regiments of the New Model which he had seen, marching and counter-marching, when he was a raw adolescent recruit in a county levy at Newport Pagnell. Many passages in the later writings, and one whole work, *Seasonable Counsel; or, Advice to Sufferers* (1684), deal with the problem of living under persecution:

I speak not these things, as knowing any that are disaffected to the government; for I love to be alone, if not with godly men, in things that are convenient. But because I appear thus in public, and know not into whose hands these lines may come, therefore thus I write. I speak it also to show my loyalty to the king, and my love to my fellow-subjects; and my desire that all Christians should walk in ways of peace and truth.[22]

---

[20] *Some Gospel-Truths Opened* (1656), *Misc. Wks.*, i. 7, 26; *GA*, § 44.
[21] Richard Baxter, *Reliquiae Baxterianae* (1696), Lib. I, Part ii, p. 303.
[22] *Seasonable Counsel, Works*, ii. 709.

If this sounds quietistic, there is one really rebellious note struck in Bunyan's writings and that is in *I Will Pray with the Spirit* ([1662?]) published at the moment when a period of uneasy hope was turning into an age of persecution. There is no compromise in his proclamation of the freedom of the Spirit against any imposed liturgy:

> For, he that advanceth the *Book of Common-Prayer*, above the *Spirit of Prayer*, he doth advance a Form of mens making above it.
>
> But this do all those who banish, or desire to banish them that pray with the Spirit of Prayer, while they hug and imbrace them that pray by that Form onely, and that because they do it.
>
> Therefore they love and advance the Form of their own, or others inventing, before the Spirit of Prayer, which is God's special and gracious Appointment. . . .
>
> If you desire the clearing of the *Minor*, look into the Goals in *England*, and into the Alehouses of the same: and I believe, you will find those that believe in the Spirit of Prayer in the Goal, and them that look after the Form of mens Inventions only, in the Alehouse.[23]

It is significant that the work was printed for Bunyan: it was too hot for a bookseller to handle. Copies of the first edition of *The Holy City* (1665) also appear without a bookseller's name on the title-page. It seems likely that it was the millenarian theme with its inevitable political overtones which made the book unattractive to cautious publishers a year after the Yorkshire Fifth Monarchy outbreak.[24]

The Books and their Publishers

The booksellers who published Bunyan's other works were generally those associated with Nonconformist authors, some of them notoriously. He published through thirteen booksellers in all, but three of these were responsible for twenty-three of the titles of his sixty books. These were Nathaniel Ponder,[25] ever famous for

---

[23] *Misc. Wks.*, ii, 284.

[24] On the nature of post-Restoration censorship see Ronald Hutton, *The Restoration: A Political and Religious History of England and Wales 1658–1667* (Oxford, 1985), pp. 155–6, and on the violent reaction of L'Estrange's press to events in Yorkshire, ibid., p. 206. There is a chapter on censorship as it affected Nonconformists in N. H. Keeble, *The Literary Culture of Nonconformity in Later Seventeenth-century England* (Leicester, 1987).

[25] The principal account is in Frank Mott Harrison, 'Nathaniel Ponder: the Publisher of *The Pilgrim's Progress*', *The Library*, 4th ser., 15 (1934), 257–94.

issuing *The Pilgrim's Progress*; Francis Smith,[26] the one most in trouble with the authorities and a prominent Whig propagandist at the time of the Popish Plot; and George Larkin[27] who published *Grace Abounding to the Chief of Sinners*. No clear explanation can be given why Bunyan turned from one bookseller to another, but certain patterns of activity may be detected. It was natural that after the overwhelming success of *The Pilgrim's Progress* Ponder should have accepted other books by Bunyan, from *A Treatise of the Fear of God* (1679) onwards, including Part II of the allegory (1684); also natural that these should include more books of pious fiction and entertainment like *Mr Badman* and *A Book for Boys and Girls* (1686). Likewise it is understandable that Benjamin Alsop, who had been jointly responsible with Dorman Newman for *The Holy War* in 1682, should wish to publish four further works by Bunyan in the ensuing two years. It is less easy to guess why his colleague Dorman Newman should have waited six years to publish *The Advocateship of Jesus Christ* (1688); one might also ask why he, and not Nathaniel Ponder, should have handled the work, since the latter, as well as publishing godly fiction, seems to have had an interest in religious treatises describing the divine gifts under a single unified metaphor (he had published *The Water of Life* in the same year as *The Advocateship* appeared). But in any age the question why authors choose publishers or publishers authors is not entirely capable of rational solution. In his last years Bunyan appears to have accumulated a number of manuscripts some of which were held back for fear of the censorship since these were the dangerous years of the Tory revenge against Shaftesbury and his Nonconformist supporters. In 1687-8 many of these were released to the public, the author and the booksellers encouraged by the comparative freedom of utterance and worship which Protestant Nonconformists shared with Catholics after James II's Declaration of Indulgence. Others, ten of them, had to wait until the Folio of 1692. Its editor Charles Doe, in his promotional essay on Bunyan's works *The*

---

[26] Accounts of his career in the period he was connected with Bunyan are in his own *Account of the Injurious Proceedings against Francis Smith* (1680) and J. G. Muddiman, *The King's Journalist 1659-1689: Studies in the Reign of Charles II* (1923), pp. 153-61.

[27] See H. R. Plomer, *A Dictionary of the Printers and Booksellers who were at Work in England, Scotland, and Ireland from 1668 to 1725* (1922; repr. Oxford, 1968), pp. 183-4; Plomer also carries a brief notice of Ponder, pp. 240-1.

Struggler, is able to say, 'By the late Act for Liberty of Conscience [*the Act of Toleration of 1689*], it is Lawful now to Print the Works of Dissenters, though it was not formerly.[28] But always with the men through whom Bunyan published before 1688 there was the threat of prosecution causing them either to go out of business for a time or to have qualms about a particular book. Francis Smith, known from his sign as 'Elephant' Smith, was thrown into the Gatehouse for printing *Annus Mirabilis* with its vaguely seditious portents and lost his shop and trade for a time; in 1666 his stock, 'as many books as two porters could stand under', was carried away by agents acting for L'Estrange; and there were similar incidents throughout his chequered career.

Bunyan's first four books, all before 1660, constitute his pre-imprisonment phase of publication. For a few years as author he enjoyed the wide freedom of the press existing under the Commonwealth. He also began, as he was not to continue, by adhering to one publishing house, that is if M. Wright who issued the last two works was the widow and successor of J. Wright who issued the first two. Certainly the second Wright continued to publish 'at the King's Head in the *Old Bailey*'. It seems at first surprising that *Some Gospel-Truths Opened* (1656) and the following *Vindication* (1657), salvoes in a purely local dispute with the Bedfordshire Quakers, should find a London publisher. But apart from the university presses there were few provincial printers or publishers until the end of the seventeenth century. All these early works except *A Few Sighs from Hell* (1658) survive in copies which show the Newport Pagnell imprint of Matthias Cowley as well as the London one of John Wright the Younger.[29] It may be inferred that Cowley was a bookseller in the narrow sense who had been enlisted to ensure distribution of the work in the region where the author was known and where his controversy with Edward Burrough and his fellow Quakers was in progress. There was no bookshop in Bedford. It is a fair presumption that *A Few Sighs* also had some copies printed with the Newport title-page none of which has survived. In this matter of the advertisement of Bunyan's works it is interesting to note that in the period extra copies of title-pages were run off to serve for this purpose; in both the British Library and

---

[28] Charles Doe, *The Struggler*, in *Folio* (1692), sig. 5T1ᵛ (*Works*, iii. 764).
[29] Harrison, pp. 3–10; *Misc. Wks.*, i. 223.

Bodleian copies of the second edition of *I Will Pray with the Spirit* (1663) such pages have been bound into the book, perhaps inadvertently, and the second (1684) and third (1686) editions of *Come, & Welcome to Jesus Christ* in the British Library likewise have two title-pages. It can be seen that the Newport title-pages could have provided advertising sheets in the immediate neighbourhood. If they were distributed by packmen, J. Wright probably had regular commercial dealings with them, since he and his father, the elder John Wright, had large holdings in the ballad stock of the Stationers' Company.[30]

John Burton, Gifford's successor as pastor of the Bedford Church, wrote a long epistle to the reader for *Some Gospel-Truths* in which he dwelt on the meanness of the author's condition and his lack of education; this manner of speaking in regard to the writing of 'mechanicks' was becoming conventional: it strongly resembles the *humilitas-sublimitas* antithesis as it is found in Augustine and Bernard of Clairvaux.[31] In the short preface recommending *A Vindication* Burton is joined by two other church members, Richard Spencly and John Child. Child later apostasized, defended submission to the Church of England, and hanged himself in a fit of remorse. The 'I.G.' who signs the epistle to the reader before *A Few Sighs* is probably John Gibbs, the Baptist minister who was vicar of Newport Pagnell under the Cromwellian establishment. He could not have been John Gifford, as George Offor thought, since the latter died in 1655; Gibbs was one of those ejected in 1662.[32]

Bunyan's imprisonment from early 1660 did not interrupt his publications. Francis Smith, who had also endured imprisonment in the early Restoration years for his pamphlets, now became his regular publisher, until he gave *The Pilgrim's Progress* to Nathaniel Ponder, but there were always others. The only noticeable effect of confinement is that some of the books appearing in the years immediately following 1660 are slight, two short volumes of verse, for instance, and none is so long or so ambitious as *The Doctrine of the Law and Grace Unfolded* (1659). During the last half of the

---

[30] H. R. Plomer, *A Dictionary of the Booksellers and Printers . . . 1641 to 1667* (1907; repr. Oxford, 1968), p. 198).
[31] See Erich Auerbach, *Mimesis: The Representation of Reality in Western Literature* (Princeton, 1953), pp. 151–5, referring particularly to Bernard's commentary on S. of S. 1: 5.
[32] *Misc. Wk.*, i. xxv–xxvi, 398; *Works*, iii. 667; CR, s.v. Gibbs.

twelve-year imprisonment no books appeared at all. It is unlikely that this was because Bunyan was held under stricter conditions; if anything, conditions were mitigated after the fall of Clarendon, the chief author of penal legislation, in November 1667. Vavasor Powell, like Bunyan an early victim under the old Elizabeth Conventicle Act, was released at this time,[33] and from October 1668, after a seven-year interval, Bunyan's name begins to appear again in the Bedford *Church Book* as being present at meetings of the congregation.[34] The reason for the interval between 1666 and 1672 in his prolific publishing career is more likely to be connected with the composition of Part I of *The Pilgrim's Progress*. There are independent statements by Doe and Cokayne, men who knew him well, that the work was written at this time, and there seems no good reason to reject them:

> Whilst he was thus twelve years and a half in prison, he writ several of his published Books (as by many of their Epistles appears) as Pray by the Spirit, Holy City, Resurrection, Grace abounding, and others; also the Pilgrim's Progress, as himself and many others have said.

> During these confinements he wrote these following books, viz.: *Of Prayer by the Spirit*; *The Holy City*; *Resurrection*; *Grace Abounding*; *Pilgrim's Progress, 1st part.*[35]

The long time that elapsed before the book was sent to the printer may be explained by doubts whether it should be printed at all, and the anxious consultations with friends who were brought in as readers, described in the prefatory verses. The theory of composition during the short second imprisonment, promulgated by John Brown when the date of that imprisonment was still uncertain, only grew up to satisfy the unnecessary demand that the dates of imprisonment and of publication should come close together.[36] 'And I slept, and Dreamed again' applies better to 1672 than to 1677; the latter date would leave less than a year for the whole work to be written, read and criticized by several people, seen through the press, and published. It would also involve the unlikelihood of Bunyan adding in the same year considerable episodes to a second edition of a work he had only just completed.

---

[33] *DNB*, s.v. Vavasor Powell; also *Dictionary of Welsh Biography*, s.v.
[34] *Minutes*, p. 39.
[35] *Works*, iii. 765-6; *A Continuation of Mr Bunyan's Life* (1692), p. 185, in *GA*, p. 172.   [36] Brown, pp. 246-8

There are then persuasive, if negative grounds for accepting 1666–72: there are difficulties about any later date. But the positive argument for composition in the later years of the first imprisonment is the direct and intimate relation of the allegory to the autobiography; as I have argued elsewhere, the narrative of *The Pilgrim's Progress* represents the translation of Bunyan's own interior conflicts into dramatic and symbolic form.[37] The relation of episodes and characters to the process of sanctification charted in *Grace Abounding*, especially to Bunyan's lapses during that process into the sin of despair, are close and detailed. The additions to Part I in the second and third editions (in 1678 and 1679) are more external and critical; the interest turns from the struggles of conversion to failures in Christian practice, hypocrisy, and greed. This is particularly so in the conversation of By-ends and his companions (1679): 'Nor is it unlawful to get a riche wife, or more custome to my shop.'[38] Bunyan is developing from the dramatized conversion narrative to the observed, objective manner of *The Life and Death of Mr Badman* (1680). New pressures were at work to modify both his radical origins and his religious individualism; by 1679 he had years of pastoral experience behind him: from being driven in on his own spiritual pathology he passed to taking stock of the outer world in Bedford and beyond.

The prefatory verses to *The Pilgrim's Progress* embody the idea of inspiration: 'Still as I pull'd it came.' Thus even while Bunyan is defending his use of similitudes to a pious public accustomed to be on their guard against any divagation from simple truth, he is demonstrating an easy confidence in his powers. This confidence grows with success and the verses before Part II gleefully celebrate his new characters, the scrupulous and fearful 'professors' with whom he feels a special bond on account of his early suffering, and the resolution that emerged from it. Most significantly this confidence extends to conscious acknowledgement of the colloquial manner as the cornerstone of his success:

> ... *thine own native Language, which no man*
> *Now useth, nor with ease dissemble can.*[39]

The same note of assurance is struck in the verse introduction to *The Holy War* (1682) where truth of personal vision is claimed to

---

[37] Sharrock, pp. 73–89.   [38] *PP*, p. 104.   [39] *PP*, p. 168.

justify the allegory: 'I saw the Princes armed men . . .', 'I was there when the Gates were broken ope.'[40] There is perhaps only one place in the non-fictional works which proclaims the fact of vision and immediacy like this; it comes in the introduction to *The Holy City* (1665), not surprisingly, since that work is more vision than discourse. He speaks of how in a period of blankness and sterility, when his fellows in prison expected 'something out of the Word for our mutual edification', an idea of the heavenly city formed in his mind like the image of jasper in Revelation:

> wherefore having got in my eye some dim glimmerings thereof, and finding also in my heart a desire to see farther thereinto, I with a few groans did carry my meditations to the Lord Jesus for a blessing, which he did forthwith grant according to his grace; and helping me to set before my brethren, we did all eat, and were well refreshed . . . Methought the more I cast mine eye upon the whole discourse, the more I saw lie in it.[41]

Like the metaphor of spinning flax in *The Pilgrim's Progress* introduction, this image comes from nothing, shines out of darkness, in fact, but when it has come it multiplies and is drawn out in increasing concreteness and accumulation of detail. The sense of a special experience, a sort of waking dream, is reinforced by one of the revisions in the third edition of *Grace Abounding*. The visual image of passing through a little door in a mountain to reach the fellowship of the Bedford gathered church had been seen 'in a Dream or Vision' in the first edition. In the third it has become 'a kind of Vision.'[42] Bunyan feels the need to define his experience more scrupulously than the too biological 'dream' or the too claim-pressing 'vision' will. Wordsworth felt a similar scruple in speaking of the workings of the lonely mind. In *The Prelude* he describes how he felt on Salisbury Plain, recalling the supposed human sacrifices of the Druids. Wordsworth uses the fairly modest word 'reverie':

> by the solitude o'ercome,
> I had a reverie and saw the past.[43]

What solitude calls up for Wordsworth is supplied for Bunyan by the biblical text in front of him, and the bright images circling out from the one word 'jasper'; for both writers the transfer to word and book came after a preparatory period of emptiness and silence.

[40] HW, pp. 2-3.   [41] *Works*, iii. 397-8.   [42] GA, § 53.
[43] Wordsworth, *The Prelude* (1805), xii. 319-20.

Both Wordsworth and Bunyan have access to these moods of reverie and are anxious to report them faithfully. Bunyan directs his attention to the content of the vision which can be objectively validated by Scripture; Wordsworth hardly attempts to separate the content from the shaping of his imagination. But both share a more purely bibliographical characteristic: they are inveterate revisers of their own work. As Wordsworth expanded, added to, and altered *The Prelude*, so Bunyan treated his works. For instance, in *Grace Abounding* the three sections on his contacts with the Ranters are added in the third edition; so is the story of his meeting with Luther's *Commentary on Galatians*, and a section on the errors of the Quakers which expands an earlier one; the long defence of his personal conduct against slander is added in the fifth. In *The Pilgrim's Progress*, the Worldly-Wiseman episode, Charity's talk with Christian about his family, the monument to Lot's wife, Giant Despair's wife, and the trumpeters who welcome the pilgrims to the Celestial City, are all added in the second edition. By-ends' conversation with his three friends is added in the third. Phrases, marginal notes, and scripture references continue to be introduced in the other editions published during Bunyan's lifetime.

Printing and Press Revision

The substantive additions to both the autobiography and the allegory help us to frame an answer to the most important bibliographical question concerning Bunyan's works. How far was he responsible for his text after delivering his manuscript to the printer? For spelling and punctuation there is the evidence of Joseph Moxon, writing his manual of the printer's craft within the period of Bunyan's authorship, that these were the printer's responsibility.[44] The same applied to the other accidental features, capitalization and italicization; the frequent use of the latter for emphasis or to mark off contrasting clauses, phrases, or words within the sentence, is amply demonstrated by Bunyan's printers. It would be difficult to be sure that any great number of Bunyan's own spellings were retained in the first editions of his works; there are several forms common to the earliest editions of *The Pilgrim's Progress* and *Mr Badman*, but that may be because

[44] Joseph Moxon, *Mechanick Exercises*, ed. Herbert Davies and Henry Carter (1962), pp. 215–17; see also James Thorpe, *Principles of Textual Criticism* (San Marino, 1972), p. 152.

Ponder was employing the same printer in 1678 and 1680: that some of the same forms occur in the portions of the Bedford *Church Book* believed to be written by Bunyan may be coincidental, and the manuscript specimen is too small to be decisive. But the additional passages and substantive changes in the reprintings are sufficiently characteristic to establish that Bunyan had marked up a copy of the first edition, or, in the case of longer passages, had presented the printer with new manuscript copy. The evidence here is in the surviving editions of *Grace Abounding* after the first (the third, fifth, and sixth) and in the second and third editions of the original *The Pilgrim's Progress*. As for Bunyan's hand, the pages of the *Church Book* recording meetings under Bunyan's pastorate are written in a medium-sized, angular, rather sprawling mixed hand with a few secretary forms. The deed of gift to his second wife (1685) is written in a larger and more careless version of this hand. But like other seventeenth-century writers he may have used a more modern smaller book hand for his sermon abstracts and literary manuscripts. This possibility is strengthened by an intriguing statement of Doe in the Folio. He says that the ten posthumous manuscripts there printed took more sheets than he had estimated on account of the smallness of Bunyan's hand.[45] This evidence can be supplemented by that provided in a mistake common to all the editions of *The Pilgrim's Progress*, Part II, where Madam Bubble offers her slaves 'Cheating' and 'Good' instead of 'Feasting' and 'Food'.[46] The error is based on a confusion of the capital F and G of the secretary hand, which suggests that however small the hand in which Bunyan wrote his copy for the printer it was still a mixed hand retaining some secretary forms.[47]

Bunyan is clearly responsible for the substantive revisions in these editions. But this does not mean that he supervised the editions as a whole. For, among the new authorial matter, there are passages where colloquialisms and loose grammar, undoubtedly Bunyan's, have been regularized or softened. The treatment of such features in later editions of *Grace Abounding* may serve as an example:

---

[45] *Folio* (1692), title-page.   [46] *PP*, p. 302, and p. 352 n.
[47] On Bunyan's hand see also Anthony G. Petti, *English Literary Hands from Chaucer to Dryden* (1977), p. 123, and T. J. Brown, 'English Literary Autographs XXXIII', *Book Collector*, ix (1960), 53–5.

as it made my heart to ake 1	that it made 3,5,6
I was a going 1	a *om*. 6
took up under her apron 1	in her arms 3,5,6
was brought those sayings 1	were brought 3,5,6
scrabling shift 1	scrambling 3,5,6
stounded 3,5	stunned 6
witch 3,5	Wizzard 6

The effort to make Bunyan's English more genteel was part of a general movement to greater regularity of forms by printers in the last decades of the seventeenth century. It was certainly not resisted by Bunyan. Proofs were still read by the author in the printing house.[48] Bunyan was hindered by his periods of imprisonment, when visits to London during spells of parole must have been rare and perhaps dangerous. Then there are suggestions that his pastoral duties after 1672 prevented him from overlooking his works with any care. 'Reader, thou art desired to mend these Erratas with thy pen, and bear with some mispointings that have hapned by reason of the Authors absence from the Press.' These words are prefixed to fourteen lines of corrections in *A Defence of the Doctrine of Justification by Faith* (1672). But there are similar apologies accompanying the errata in *A Treatise of the Fear of God* (1679) and in *A Holy Life the Beauty of Christianity* (1684), where there is no errata list.

Bunyan's passion for developing what he had already written did not, therefore, imply concern with the form of his text: spelling and minor points of grammar could be left to the printer. Yet he could be interested in adding quite small details, like the number of appended phrases and Scripture references in *A Few Sighs from Hell* (1658), or the numerous minor changes in the later editions of *Come, & Welcome to Jesus Christ* (1678).

Bunyan, like his lesser contemporary Vavasor Powell, was a preacher and evangelist who rushed into print as an extension of his pulpit. Then, unlike Powell, he found himself as a writer, both as introspective autobiographer and story-teller. One can only speculate on how he was affected by his friends in high places, John Owen and Thomas Barlow, Bishop of Lincoln.[49] They may have

---

[48] Philip Gaskell, *A New Introduction to Bibliography* (Oxford, 1972), pp. 110–16.

[49] William Orme, *Memoirs of the Life and Writings of John Owen, DD* (1826), i. 304–5.

had something to do with the postponement of publication of the allegory to consider criticisms. Probably he was influenced towards a more purely rhetorical and instrumental view of literature, and was drawn away from that sense of the book as a living thing, like Luther's old book, embodying a living self. Certainly the later works are more proficiently organized than the earlier; the careful tables of contents in *Good News for the Vilest of Men* (1688) and *The Advocateship of Jesus Christ* (1692) bear witness to this.[50] From this rhetorical point of view it could be argued that Part II of *The Pilgrim's Progress* has more dramatic ease than the first and represents the climax of Bunyan's achievement if we look to him for conscious art.[51] But always, as in the crossing of the river in Part II, he is drawn away from rhetorical organization by a less definable and more poetic strain. When Dispondencie's daughter 'went thorow the River singing, but none could understand what she said',[52] we are returned from the print culture to the ballad. Bunyan's broadsheets belong to a category outside the polite Restoration limits for literature;[53] and towards the end of his life he published an emblem book (*A Book for Boys and Girls* (1686)) where one-to-one resemblances have to be extracted from the complex mystery of the book of the creatures. Four years before his death *The Pilgrim's Progress* appeared reduced to a round dozen pages as a 'Penny Godliness.'[54] So on the fringes of the public he had found another hardly literate public returned him to the borders of literacy and to the primitive essentials of the story of an encounter which is the basic encounter with a story.

[50] *Misc. Wks.*, xi. 9–11, 101–8.
[51] It has been by Charles W. Baird, *John Bunyan: A Study in Narrative Technique* (Port Washington, New York, 1977), pp. 57–93.   [52] *PP*, p. 308.
[53] *A Mapp Shewing the Order and Causes of Salvation and Damnation* ([c.1664]), included in *Folio* (1692) as a folded sheet; *One Thing is Needful*, 3rd. edn. (1683). *Prison Meditations* is also listed by Doe as a broadsheet but no copy of this has survived; the *Meditations* are known only from their inclusion in later works by Bunyan (*Misc. Wks.*, vi. 39).
[54] Published by Thomas Passinger in 1684; on the copy in the Pepys Collection in Magdalene College, Cambridge, see Spufford, *Small Books*, p. 198.

5

Plain and Simple: Bunyan and Style

BY ROGER POOLEY

I could also have stepped into a stile much higher then this in which I have here discoursed, and could have adorned all things more then here I have seemed to do: but I dare not: God *did not play in convincing of me: the* Devil *did not play in tempting of me; neither did I play when I sunk as into a bottomless pit, when* the pangs of hell caught hold upon me: *wherefore I may not play in my relating of them, but be plain and simple, and lay down the thing as it was.*[1]

THIS statement of intent in the Preface to *Grace Abounding* represents one strand in Bunyan's sense of style, and our own sense of the Puritan programme; that there can be no playing about with matters of eternal consequence. Compare this with his defence of his authorship of *The Pilgrim's Progress*, in a poem appended to *The Holy War*:

> It came from mine own heart, so to my head,
> And thence into my fingers trickled;
> Then to my Pen, from whence immediately
> On Paper I did dribble it daintily.
> Manner and matter too was all mine own . . .[2]

It's not exactly Cavalier abandon, but 'dribble it daintily' is very different from the austere fierceness of *Grace Abounding*. Does Bunyan's attitude change over those twenty years, not least as a result of the experience of composing his masterpiece? And if there is a change, what effect does it have on his practice as a writer? Answers to these questions need closer analysis, but also an appreciation of

---

[1] 'A Preface', GA, pp. 3-4. [2] HW, p. 251.

the wider contexts; a sense of the changing historical context in which Bunyan wrote, changes in Nonconformity in particular, but also rapid changes in other Christians' sense of the appropriate language for religious discourse.

Contexts for Bunyan's Style

Puritan Arguments About Rhetoric

William Perkins, one of the founding fathers of English Puritanism, wrote *The Arte of Prophecying* in 1592, and its precepts are as good a guide to Puritan habits of preaching as we have. In preaching, he argues, 'two things are required: the hiding of humane wisdom, and the demonstration (or shewing) of the spirit.'[3] For a university-educated man like Perkins, and indeed for most who read his treatise in its original Latin, hiding learning needed a positive effort, and one which went against some of the fashions for 'metaphysical' preaching with its Greek and Latin quotations. *Ars celare artem* was not a Puritan invention, of course; but the Puritans did more than take over the classical 'low style', they tightened its limits and suggested that straying from it produced impiety, not just indecorum. So Perkins on the images which were needed as part of a technique for memorizing the discourse: 'the animation of the image, which is the key of memorie, is impious; because it requireth absurd, insolent, and prodigious cogitations, and those especially, which set an edge upon and kindle the most corrupt affections of the flesh.'[4] And it wasn't just a question of unadorned exposition of the Scripture text; plain and forceful application was advised, too. The final point of Perkins's summary is advice 'To apply (if he have the gift) the doctrines rightly collected, to the life and manners of men in a *simple and plaine speech*.'[5]

This was enough to set the Puritans apart from their university-educated fellows; but it was also the beginning of a sense that 'humane learning', i.e. a degree, was not necessary for preaching. 'There were those who didn't have any learning to hide, and in books like Samuel How's *Sufficiency of the Spirit's Teaching without Humane Learning: Or a Treatise tending to Prove Humane Learning*

---

[3] William Perkins, *Works*, 3 vols. (Cambridge, 1616), ii. 670.
[4] Perkins, *Works*, ii. 670.
[5] Perkins, *Works*, ii. 673; original italics.

to be no help to the Spirituall Understanding of the Word of God (1639) we can see something of the charismatic populism that developed in the Civil War and Commonwealth period and opened the way for such as Bunyan to exercise their gift. How was a cobbler, who preached the sermon that became the book at the prompting of John Goodwin, a leading Independent. Some of How's sentences are very long and rambling, but the main argument is clear enough: that education is no help in understanding the Scriptures. Knowledge of languages, he concedes, is helpful for translation, but no good for discerning spiritual meaning. How stresses that the message of the Gospel is simplicity itself, not arcane; spiritual transformation as it affects style is a simplification. He has a little trouble with Apollo, who in Acts 18: 24 is described as 'an eloquent man'. But then, How reflects, 'as he came to be taught further in the knowledge of Christ, he then became more and more suitable to the rudenesse and simplicity of the gospel'.[6] What's interesting here is that How cannot conceive of someone staying 'eloquent', at any rate in his understanding of the term, and being a spiritually minded Christian. 'By fair words and flatteries they deceived the simple'; that's how 'eloquent' men work.[7] That kind of thinking is why Bunyan, certainly in his early writings, regarded simplicity of expression as crucial. After all, he could have stepped into a higher style, he writes, and there are times when he does.

Restoration Arguments About Plain Style

After 1660 many of the rules changed. In religious terms, it wasn't simply a Restoration; for while the Church of England reverted to Laudian practice, it didn't have a Lancelot Andrewes or a John Donne in the pulpit. When Perkins wrote and preached, you could tell a Puritan by the lack of decoration, and Greek and Latin, in his sermons. By the time Bunyan was able to preach again, in the 1670s, it was the new Anglican fashion to be plain and virtually image-free in sermons; and they accused the Nonconformists (as the heirs of the Puritans should by then be called) of being over-elaborate. Samuel Parker, for example, later Bishop of Oxford, writing in 1670:

---

[6] Samuel How, *The Sufficiency of the Spirits Teaching* (1655 edn.), p. 31 For How (d. 1640) see J. F. Maclean in *BDBR*, ii. 114–15; for Goodwin, see J. C. Spalding in *BDBR*, ii. 15–17; *DNB*; and *CR*, s.v.   [7] How, *Suffiency*, p. 9.

And herein lies the most material difference between the sober Christians of the Church of England, and our modern sectaries, that we express the Precepts and Duties of the Gospel in plain and intelligent terms, whilst they trifle them away by childish Metaphors and Allegories, and will not talk of Religion but in barbarous and uncouth similitudes.[8]

What is behind this attack is a new variation on the old Puritan/Anglican argument. The issue of learning is still there ('barbarous and uncouth') but the argument for clarity appears to have swapped sides; plainness is now the sign of intelligence. And there is a new sense of religion, as an exercise in virtue and obedience ('Precepts and Duties'), as opposed to the essentially metaphoric doctrines of the Reformation, like justification by faith, which were still at the centre of Nonconformist preaching.[9] There comes a point when talking of God stretches language beyond bare statement. That was argued against Parker by John Owen, former chaplain to Cromwell's army, the leading congregationalist after the Restoration, and one of Bunyan's contacts in London; and Richard Baxter writes in the same period, 'Talk not . . . against all Allegorical expressions about God, till you would forbid Mortals to talk of God at all'.[10] More eirenic Anglicans, like Herbert Croft, the Bishop of Hereford, suggested in 1675 that there was still an excess of learning displayed in some preaching:

So that the sermon is rather a banquet for the wantons that are full, than instruction to those that are even starved for want of spiritual food, the plain and saving word of Christ, not the nice conceited word of Man, which may nourish Camelions, never make solid sound Christians.[11]

Comparisons between Bunyan's sermons and those of his counterparts in the Restoration Established Church are a little difficult to make, because Bunyan did not publish his sermons as such, but tended to work them up into 'sermon treatises', clearly too long for delivery in one session, even for the extended aural appetites

[8] Samuel Parker, *A Discourse of Ecclesiastical Politie* (1670), p. 75.
[9] I argue this in more detail in 'Language and Loyalty: Plain Style at the Restoration', *Literature and History*, 6 (1980), 2–18.
[10] Richard Baxter, Preface to John Bryan *Dwelling with God* (1670); quoted in N. H. Keeble, *Richard Baxter: Puritan Man of Letters* (Oxford, 1982), p. 54.
[11] [Herbert Croft], *The Naked Truth* (1675), p. 26. Croft was accused of an 'Enthusiastik' style by Francis Turner in *Animadversions upon a late Pamphlet Entituled The Naked Truth* (1676). Turner goes on to criticize some of Croft's metaphors, so my point holds.

of the seventeenth century. The title-page of *The Greatness of the Soul* (1682) is instructive: 'First Preached at *Pinners-Hall*, and now Enlarged'. By contrast, the published sermons of the episcopalian divines John Tillotson, Robert South, and Isaac Barrow are much shorter and, we must assume, closer to their spoken form. However, Tillotson's watchword, 'plainly and briefly', may indicate that they were preaching shorter sermons anyway. Audiences were different, too; it may be unfair to judge Tillotson's sermons preached at Lincoln's Inn and the Court with Bunyan's, occasionally preached to City audiences but just as likely to come from Toft's barn in Bedford. But that contrast, of class and education, is part of the story. Tillotson became Archbishop of Canterbury, and was a member of the Royal Society. But unlike many of his Anglican establishment contemporaries, he seems less anxious about nonconformity than about 'Atheism, and . . . scoffing at Religion.' His theological emphasis is clearly different from Bunyan's, though; of his fifty-four printed sermons, only seven have texts from St Paul, and none from Romans or Galatians. However, here, in a sermon on the causeless doubts of good men, we have him dealing with a subject, and a text, close to Bunyan's concerns:

Another cause of these doubts is, that men expect more than ordinary and reasonable assurance of their good condition; some particular revelation from God, an extraordinary impression upon their minds to that purpose, which they think the Scripture means by the *testimony* and *seal* and *earnest of the Spirit*, is to my apprehension no more but this, That the Holy Spirit which God bestowed upon Christians in so powerful and sensible a manner was a seal and earnest of their resurrection to eternal life, according to that plain text. Rom. 8. 11 . . . But then, who they are that have the Spirit of God is only to be known by the real fruits and effects of it. If we be *led by the Spirit* and *walk in the Spirit*, and *do not fulfil the lusts of the flesh*, then *the Spirit of God dwelleth in us*. But this is very far from an immediate and extraordinary revelation from the Spirit of God to the minds of good men telling them in particular that they are the children of God. I know not what peculiar favour God may shew to some, but I know no such thing, nor ever yet met with any wise and good man that did affirm it of himself: And I fear that in most of those who pretend to it, it is either mere fancy, or gross delusion.[12]

---

[12] *The Works of the Most Reverend Dr John Tillotson*, 3rd edn. (1701), pp. 168-9. The sermon (no. XV) is not dated, but from other dated material in the volume and its arrangement, we might assume a date in the early 1680s.

Compare this with Bunyan in his early treatise *The Doctrine of the Law and Grace Unfolded* (1659), answering an objection, and heading towards the same chapter in Romans:

First, to think that your condition is good, because there is some change in you from a loose profane life, to a more close, honest, and civil life and conversation; I say to think this testimony sufficient for to ground the stress of thy salvation upon, is very dangerous. First, because such a soul doth not onely lay the stress of its salvation besides the man Christ Jesus that dyed upon the Cross: But secondly, because that his confidence is not grounded upon the Saviour of sinners; but upon his turning from gross sins, to a more refined life (and it may be to the performance of some good duties), which is no Saviour: I say this is very dangerous; therefore read it, and the Lord help you to understand it; for unless you lay the whole stress of the salvation of your souls upon the merits of another man (namely Jesus) and that by what he did do, and is a doing without you; for certain, as sure as God is in heaven, your souls will perish: And this must not be notionally neither, as with an assenting of the understanding onely: but it must be by the wonderful, invisible, invincible power, of the Almighty God, working in your souls by his Spirit, such a real, saving, holy faith, that can through the operation of the same Spirit by which it is wrought, lay hold on, and apply these most heavenly, most excellent, most meritorious benefits of the man Christ Jesus, not onely to your heads and fancies, but to your very souls, and consciences, so effectually, that you may be able by the same faith to challenge the power, madness, malice, rage, and destroying nature, either of sin, the Law, death, the Devil, together with hell, and all other evils, throwing your souls upon the death, burial, resurrection, and intercession of that man Jesus without sin. *Rom.* 8. 32 . . . .[13]

Apart from the differing exegetical emphases, the stylistic contrast is quite marked—sentence structure, balancing, and climaxing in particular. The vocabulary is not dissimilar, although words like Tillotson's 'apprehension' are more Latinate and abstract than Bunyan's 'I say this is very dangerous', and this goes with the whole difference in tone between Tillotson's calming, cooling third-person assurances and Bunyan's urgent, second-person warnings. Both tones can be found in the English translation of Romans 8, interestingly; reasoned oppositions and climactic lists in different parts of the chapter. When we come to syntax, the basic sentence models are not all that different. Tillotson's are shorter, but we could shorten

---

[13] *Misc. Wks.*, ii. 66–7.

Bunyan's by no more than different punctuation, until we get to the start of the climax at 'And this must not be notionally . . .', when the elementary rhetorical balancing of threes and twos ('wonderful, invisible, invincible'/'real, saving, holy', e.g. 'heads and fancies'/ 'souls, and consciences') introduce another level of sentence organization, leading to the three extended lists at the end of the sentence where five, six, and four items don't exactly balance or correspond to each other, but do take the weight of emphasis on the great opposition that Bunyan is stressing. Tillotson's balancing doublet, 'mere fancy, or gross delusion', is a climax, or at least a neat closure, but isn't so striking, and, of course, would be distruptive of the whole, reasonable approach if it were.

'Plainness' is a contested term in the Restoration period, and a contrast such as this shows at least one reason why. An Anglican like Tillotson might point to the rhetorical strenuousness of a passage like that of Bunyan's and argue that his own preaching was the plainer, in the sense of being refined and restrained in style; and with his lack of mystery in discussing spiritual matters. But Bunyan might equally well argue that there was little decoration in his style (even counting 'invisible, invincible' as word-play); and he was certainly being plain, in the sense of a forthright, unmistakable laying out of the options. The new Restoration plainness, a reaction against 'strong lines' metaphysical preaching, revolutionary Puritanism, and redundancy in scientific and philosophical writing, was hardly likely to appeal to Bunyan, and probably made his preaching and writing sound increasingly old-fashioned. But the roots of Bunyan's plainness, particularly colloquial English, folktale, and the Bible, did not disappear with the Commonwealth, and nor did his audience. Contesting arguments about style are usually indices of something more—in this case, class, doctrine, politics, and spirituality.

The Argument from Biblical Style

The authority and fearfulness of the Bible were paramount for Bunyan in all aspects of the Christian life; so we might expect its authority in matters of style to be important, too. However, it might be more accurate to talk of the Bible's styles, plural rather than singular, even if Bunyan's habit of using the concordance would have pressed him towards thinking of the Bible as a single text rather than a collection of discrete books with different authors. How did his contemporaries deal with the question?

Robert Boyle's *Some Considerations touching the Style of the Holy Scriptures* (1661) is interesting for a number of reasons. Here is one of the founder members of the Royal Society, itself the instigator of a programme of stylistic reform in scientific discourse, defending the style of the Bible against its classically learned detractors; the dedication to his brother encourages him to imitate Cowley's biblical epic *Davideis*; and he is critical of what he sees as the excess, even affected literalness of the English translation.[14] So, we might think, an educated man speaking to educated men, a long way from Bunyan's concerns. Not so. In the first place, his dedication to 'the Grand Fundamental' that the Scripture is the word of God, and his opposition to 'the Predominant and Contagious Profanenesse of the Times' suggest they have much in common.[15] Secondly, his awareness of the diversity of Biblical style may help us to see something of Bunyan's own, complex indebtedness to biblical style. Boyle's argument is that many passages in the Bible are put 'in a plain and familiar way' for the benefit of unlearned members of the church; whereas others have a degree of obscurity, to excite 'elevated wits' and to remind us that digging for the truth is good for us.[16] In the same way, Bunyan's style veers between the openness of plain declaration and the mysterious suggestiveness of allegory, and he can find biblical source and warrant for both. 'I have used similitudes', he announces from Hosea on the title-pages of *The Pilgrim's Progress* and *The Holy War*; and, showing a sense of metaphor in his first published work, argues 'Heaven in Scripture, is taken sometimes metaphorically, and sometimes properly'.[17] He also notes '*It was the great care of the Apostle* Paul *to deliver his Gospel to the Churches* in its own simplicity, *because*, SO *it is the Power of God unto Salvation to every one that believeth*'.[18]

In terms of the seventeenth-century debate, and indeed Bunyan's own perceptions, the Bible is an appeal court in stylistic matters; yet there is both plainness and hiddenness there. Auerbach, drawing on the *Christian Doctrine* of St Augustine which contains one of the

---

[14] Gerald Hammond, one of the most acute contemporary apologists for the Authorized Version, regards this as one of its virtues. See his *The Making of the English Bible* (Manchester, 1982).
[15] Robert Boyle, *Some Considerations Touching the Style of the Holy Scriptures* (1661), pp. 77–8, 146–7.   [16] Robert Boyle, *Considerations*, pp. 25, 38.
[17] *Some Gospel-Truths Opened, Misc. Wks.*, i. 77.
[18] *Light for them that sit in Darkness, Misc. Wks.*, viii. 49.

earliest Christian discussions of rhetoric, argues that the Gospels dissolved the distinctions of high, middle, and low style into one, because if a cup of water (Matthew 25, and a low-style image) can affect one's eternal salvation (a matter of epic proportions), what is left of the classical standards of decorum?[19] The consequence for Christian writing is that a mixture of styles becomes possible without being ridiculous, not that everything is collapsed into plain style. So, for Bunyan, even in his most elevated vein, in *The Holy War*, for example, there is always the possibility of mixing the styles, of introducing the everyday and the humorous into the epic momentousness.

In what sense can we say that Bunyan's style is biblical, though? So much Scripture is embedded in his works; and yet C. S. Lewis's judgement, that the language of the Authorized Version and the language of Bunyan's works are quite distinct, has not been successfully challenged.[20] But which biblical style are we to look for? The Psalms? Old Testament or Gospel narrative? Apocalyptic? All of them have their impact, but we must begin where the Reformation began, with St Paul; and here the literalism of the English translators, beginning with Tyndale, gives us an identifiable Pauline style. Janel M. Mueller's study of what she calls Scripturalism in English prose up to the end of the sixteenth century is particularly helpful here. She argues that Tyndale's own prose style is consciously taken over from his translations of St Paul as a 'sharp challenge' to the received features of vernacular prose at the time he was writing. Her whole book, especially chapters 5 and 6, is of great interest to this discussion; the following sentences are taken from the heart of her section on Tyndale's Scripturalism:

It is not difficult . . . to recognize in the strategic placement of the NP [*noun phrase*] catalogues an effectual alternative to word pairs as means for maximal articulation of meaning, or delineating a universe of values, or projecting the energy intrinsic in 'strong forms' of language. To the extent that NP catalogues can substitute with equal or greater semantic and rhetorical effectiveness for word pairs [*seen as the signature of aureate style earlier in Mueller's argument*], to that extent they call for a corresponding adjustment in the all but exclusive standing associations of the latter with

---

[19] Eric Auerbach, 'Sermo humilis', in *Literary Language and its Public in Late Latin Antiquity and the Middle Ages*, trans. Ralph Manheim, Bollingen Series, LXXIV (New York, 1965); see also the first two chaps. of *Mimesis*.

[20] C. S. Lewis, *The Literary Impact of the Authorized Version* (1950), pp. 18–20.

authoritative utterance. But the matter of word pairs and catalogues is minor compared with the implications stemming from the insistent binary responsions in sentence form which Tyndale, emulating Paul, infused in a wide scale into the writing of English prose . . . In the Apostle's conception of the meaning of Scripture, the affectivity of the saving word arises from the complementary working of the two great halves of the message, the Law that condemns and the Gospel that saves, within the believer's heart. Then binary responses of Pauline sentence forms recurrently mirror this specific apprehension of Biblical meaning, and with sustained insistence in the fifth and sixth chapters of Romans . . . Tyndale himself absorbed the thrust of the great Pauline oppositions, which at the same time were complementarities, registering them as the core of the Scriptural message and at the same time projecting them as the dynamic of his own prose style.[21]

This points to a theological dynamic which Bunyan shares; does his style respond in the same way as Tyndale's? In *The Doctrine of the Law and Grace Unfolded* (1659), as might be expected, it is not difficult to find this kind of Pauline sentence:

If thou wouldest know the authority and power of the Gospel, labour first to know the power and authority of the Law; for I am verily perswaded that the want of this one thing, namely, the knowledge of the Law, is one cause why so many are ignorant of the other.[22]

But when we turn to the more likely moments of *The Pilgrim's Progress*, the structure is less insistent. The words of Evangelist after Christian's fright at Mount Sinai are full of Pauline doctrine, but much more loosely paratactic in sentence structure. Only this sentence about the bondwoman comes close to the binary response: 'Now if she with her children are in bondage, how canst thou expect by them to be made free?'[23] The rest of Evangelist's words are strongly argumentative; but two sentences later he is out of St Paul's style, though not his sentiments:

No man was as yet ever rid of his burden by him, no, nor is like to be: ye cannot be justified by the Works of the Law; for by the deeds of the Law no man living can be rid of his burden: therefore Mr. *Worldly-Wiseman* is an alien, and Mr. *Legality* a cheat: and for his son *Civility*, notwithstanding his simpering looks, he is but an hypocrite, and cannot help thee.

---

[21] Janel M. Mueller, *The Native Tongue and The Word: Developments in English Prose Style 1380-1580* (Chicago, 1984), pp. 196-7.
[22] *Misc. Wks*, ii. 13.   [23] *PP*, p. 23.

The phrase beginning 'ye cannot' is almost a paraphrase of Galatians 3: 11, translated into the terms of the allegory (and those terms themselves are derived from the Bible); but by 'simpering' Bunyan has gone beyond even St Paul's plain speaking. It is as if even the plain style of the Bible needed to be brought home through the colloquial expressions and sentence structure of Bunyan's own characters, without assuming anything about the audience for the moment. The binary responsion, for example, is sufficiently constructed, rhetorically, to count as a high point, a climax, from which the descent into plain speaking can be accomplished.

Similarly, we can see Bunyan's characteristically dialogic framework, the question and answer technique that informs the controversial works as well as *The Pilgrim's Progress*, as part of a Pauline approach, even if it were as likely to have its immediate source in Arthur Dent's *The Plaine Mans Path-way to Heaven* as the rhetorical questions of the Epistles.

We must conclude, then, that one of Bunyan's styles, or part of Bunyan's style, is biblical; but that he often surrounds that kind of sentence form with others. The Bible is a point of reference, a store of images and styles for Bunyan as a writer; but there is a work of assimilation to another style comparable to the exegetical need of making the plain sense plainer.

'The language of Canaan' v 'Satanical Rhetoric'

Discernment is one of the ways that Christian grows in *The Pilgrim's Progress*; discerning the false from the true pilgrim, learning from his mistakes when he has travelled out of the way, remembering what he has been taught so he can deal with the present crisis. Part of the discernment he attains is stylistic, particularly in the way that he learns to see through deception.

The Worldly-Wiseman episode makes this point particularly clearly. Worldly-Wiseman is a Restoration moralist. His keywords — Civility, Legality, 'credit and good fashion' — invite Christian to abandon the risky road of faith for the reassurance of good deeds.[24] The Worldly-Wiseman episode is interesting as a type of the kind of stylistic discernment we are called on to make a number of times in *The Pilgrim's Progress*. Words are weapons: not just when

---

[24] *PP*, p. 19. Cf. above, pp. 63–4.

they are Bible texts, as in Christian's battle with Apollyon, but in many of the encounters with the opponents and false pilgrims. And there are times when excess of words—Talkative's, for example—is a sure guide to unreliability. Worldly-Wiseman has the kind of verbal tics, 'I will add', 'as I said', 'to speak on', which denote awareness of prolixity and inability to cure it. Christian's interventions are little more than prompts after he has explained why he is on the road and how terrible his burden is.

The parallel we are invited to draw is with Evangelist. Worldly-Wiseman 'beshrews' him for his advice and preaches the alternative gospel of 'Legality' for the relief of Christian's burden. How do the two differ, stylistically? To begin with, Evangelist's technique is more catechetical, prompting Christian's response with a series of questions. I've already suggested that Evangelist's words contain a hint of Pauline language beyond the actual quotation; Worldly-Wiseman doesn't quote or allude to Scripture at all. And Evangelist avoids abstract nouns. In his little three-point sermon he advises Christian to abhor:

1. His turning thee out of the way.
2. His labouring to render the Cross odious to thee.
3. And his setting thy feet in that way that leadeth unto the administration of Death.[25]

In describing the temptations of Worldly-Wiseman, Evangelist uses more active words than his opponent—'turning', 'labouring', and 'setting' are immediately less abstract, more directly related to the language of pilgrimage. They function, too, as a kind of exposé of Worldly-Wiseman's promises of ease, which are too strenuously put. And they point to a class perception: Worldly-Wiseman is a gentleman, whose habit is to cover things with fine words, 'noise', which cannot help the poor pilgrim to get rid of his burden, which is spiritual, not the lack of social 'credit and good fashion'.

In a way this is a point about characterization, a point that is virtually impossible to make in Part II because the opposition is so rarely allowed a voice. In *The Holy War*, the position becomes different again, because of Bunyan's habit of using characters in series—four captains in a row delivering parallel messages, for example. But there is a call to the reader, especially in the early part

[25] *PP*, p. 22.

of the book, and often delivered through the marginal notes, to discern between 'Satanical Rhetorick' and the true promises of Emanuel and his spokesmen. Here, the discernment has to operate at two levels, because Bunyan has given us Diabolus and Emanuel, Satan and Christ, as well as their allegorized followers. It is not just a question of seeing that Pityless is lying when he says his name is Chear-Up, or of recognizing the wisdom of Mr Godlyfear's advice. The reader of *The Holy War* has to follow the twists and turns of Diabolus's speeches as well as recognizing the justice and mercy of Emanuel's. Unusually in Bunyan, it is Diabolus who gets the lower style, desperate, cajoling, and angry by turns; whereas Emanuel is almost always formal, even in his condescension (a word that had none of the pejorative associations it now has when Bunyan wrote). The central question in *The Holy War* is, who is telling lies? The consistency of Emanuel's style, along with the variations in Diabolus's, is thus a necessary feature of the interpretation, as well as the characterization, of the allegory.

Polemic and Humour

Bunyan began his writing career in controversy. His inexperience as a writer does show up in the sometimes repetitive and rambling structure of *Some Gospel-Truths Opened* (1656); but when it is compared with the writings of Edward Burrough, his Quaker opponent, it becomes clear that the differences between the two in doctrine and spirituality result in differences in language. Once again we observe that 'plainness' is the contested term. Quaker plainness was even more radical than that of the Independent congregations Bunyan knew at this time. Their commitment to silence, and their sense of godly, honest speech arising out of God speaking into silence, was seen by many of their opponents as wilful idiosyncracy, but, as Richard Bauman argues, reflected their sense of the pivotal Christian experience as well as a metaphor for suppressing the flesh.[26] As we know from *Grace Abounding*, hearing the voice of God was a key experience for Bunyan, too, but with a different effect: recognizing the implacable demands of the Law, and needing a sense of the forgiveness and release of the Gospel of justification by faith

---

[26] Richard Bauman, *Let Your Words Be Few: Symbolism of Speaking and Silence Among Seventeenth-century Quakers* (Cambridge, 1983), pp. 22, 30.

before peace with God could ensue. Both Burrough and Bunyan lay claim to 'plain' texts of the Bible, but they do so in very different kinds of sentences. This is particularly noticeable when they are not involved in the hand-to-hand combat of taking issue with particular sentences of each other's, but attempting to hit some higher, more general tone. Burrough's works tend to open in the Quaker 'incantatory' style.[27] That this is a conscious style he steps into is clear from the opening of *The True Faith of the Gospel of Peace . . .* (1656), his reply to *Some Gospel-Truths Opened*. The address to the Reader asserts his 'simplicity of heart' and his rejection of 'Mastery by multitude of words' in fairly straightforward sentences; then the text proper begins: 'How long yee crafty fowlers will yee prey upon the Innocent, and shoot at him secretly; how long shall the righteous be a prey to your Teeth, yee subtill Foxes, who seekes [*sic*] to devour . . .'[28] and so on for two pages until the tumbling, paratactic period comes to an end. The structure of this kind of sentence owes something to biblical parallelism and the small range of connectives in English biblical narrative, echoing the Hebrew; but it is much more chaotic. A better example of this comes in a similarly long invocation to another tract of 1656:

therefore in Judgement is the Lord appearing, to work the purpose of his heart, and to fullfill the intent of his mind; and will not spare to punish the transgression of the wicked upon his own head; and is already clothed with the garment of vengeance, and clad with zeal as a cloak . . .[29]

It is not difficult to see how these sentences can be generated by a series of repetitive increments; or to see how impressive they might be in the oral situation.

Bunyan is no less impassioned at times, but his high-flown, climactic sentences appear more consciously constructed with their precision of opposites, and often bear the force of the argument in a summary way, instead of being an invocation for it:

The new and false Christ, is a Christ crucified within, dead within, risen againe within, and ascended within in opposition to the Son of Mary, *who*

---

[27] Described by Jackson Cope in 'Seventeenth-century Quaker Style', *PMLA* 76 (1956), 725-54.
[28] E[dward] B[urrough], *The True Faith of the Gospel of Peace contended for, in the Spirit of Meekness* (1656), p. 1.
[29] Edward Burrough, *Stablishing against Quaking, Thrown down, and overturned, and no defence found against it* (1656), p. 3.

was crucified without, dead without, risen againe without, and ascended in a cloud away from his Disciples into heaven without them.[30]

This is an early example of the forcefulness of Bunyan's style in presenting irreconcilable oppositions, confronting the mystic inwardness of the Quakers with a defence of the incarnation. We can see the affinities with the Pauline Scripturalism mentioned above; and remember that the master-texts for Bunyan's theological understanding come from Galatians, whereas the Quaker teaching of the inner light derives from a verse in John's gospel. This is not the point to enlarge on the differences between Burrough and Bunyan, or to adjudicate in the controversy; simply to say that Bunyan's writing career began in conscious opposition to a writer for whom a kind of plainness (especially as explicitness and honesty) was an article of faith, and that the problem of objectivity and solidity to spiritual matters, in a word, incarnation, preoccupies him from the first.[31] Spiritual words are not the same, necessarily, as spiritual substance; which is the point of the Talkative episode.

One of the techniques that Bunyan picked up early for this kind of writing was the dialogue form, if not as an organizing principle, then certainly as a way of dramatizing and dealing with objections. In *The Pilgrim's Progress*, he sometimes manages to get his opponents to condemn themselves and make the rebuttal easier. This is particularly the case with the religious hypocrites, regularly the butts of Bunyan's humour.[32] By-ends from Fair-Speech, for example, claims to have become a Gentleman of good quality (always grounds for suspicion in *The Pilgrim's Progress* — compare Demas as well as Worldly-Wiseman): 'yet my Great Grand-father was but a Waterman, looking one way, and Rowing another: and I got most of my estate by the same occupation.'[33]

Trial scenes concentrate the dialogue form in a particularly formal and intense way. Apart from the general Puritan sense of the Christian life as trial, one familiar to readers of Milton, Bunyan had been on trial himself. His account of it, in the posthumously published *A Relation of The Imprisonment* (1765), contains a number of fascinating exchanges. In his appearance at the Bedford Quarter

---

[30] *Some Gospel-Truths Opened*, Misc. Wks., i. 19–20.
[31] Cf. S. J. Newman, 'Bunyan's Solidness', in Newey, pp. 225–50.
[32] A point made by Elizabeth Adeney in 'Bunyan: A Unified Vision?', *Critical Review*, 17 (1974), 97–109. [33] *PP*, p. 99.

Sessions, there was a long argument about the *Book of Common Prayer*. At one point, one of the Justices, fearing that Bunyan would do them harm by speaking, sought to stop him speaking; whereupon Justice Keelin (usually referred to as Kelynge) said, 'No, no, never fear him, we are better established than so; he can do no harm, we know the Common Prayer-book hath been ever since the Apostles time.'[34] As presented by Bunyan, most of the proceedings seem to be more like debates about the meaning of Scripture than points of law. The trials in his allegories take on something of that quality, but they are more compressed, and recognize the nature of the opposition far more. So in the trial of Christian and Faithful in Vanity Fair, a lot of the work is done by the naming; the blazing self-confidence of Justice Hategood and the false witnesses may recall Kelynge's classic mistake, but the imaginative impact is from the loading of the jury, grimly humorous about their delivery of the appropriate verdicts—'*A sorry Scrub*, said Mr. *High-mind*'[35]—and so to the torture and execution. At that point the tone changes quite markedly, and here we might detect the influence of the martyrdoms in Foxe's *Acts and Monuments*, a copy of which Bunyan had in prison with him.[36] The description of Faithful's death does seem to lean on the selection of deaths in the woodcuts in Foxe, though with an echo of Hebrews 11 as well:

They therefore brought him out, to do to him according to their law; and first they Scourged him, then they Buffetted him, then they Lanced his flesh with Knives; after that they Stoned him with Stones, then prickt him with their Swords, and last of all they burned him to Ashes at the Stake.[37]

Compare this with the death of Richard Gibson and two other Protestant martyrs of Mary's reign in Foxe:

And being brought thither to the stake, after their prayer made, they were bound thereunto with chains, and wood set unto them, and after wood, fire, in the which being compassed about, and the fiery flames consuming their flesh, at the last they yielded gloriously and joyfully their souls and lives into the holy hands of the Lord . . .[38]

Sometimes Foxe is more detailed than this, with the sort of famous last words that might have inspired the great conclusion to Part II

---

[34] *GA*, pp. 116–17.   [35] *PP*, p. 97.
[36] The copy supposed to be Bunyan's is now in New York; it is the three-vol. 1641 edn. See Brown, pp. 153–4 and *GA*, p. 153.
[37] *PP*, p. 97.   [38] John Foxe, *Acts and Monuments* (1641 edn.), iii. 859.

of *The Pilgrim's Progress*; Mr Great-Heart's last words, 'Welcome Life', coincide with those of Laurence Sanders, one of the Marian martyrs in Foxe.[39] It is difficult to be definitive about Foxe's style, because he is often simply compiling rather than retelling stories. But it is noticeable that he goes in for more realistic detail than Bunyan, and tends to maintain a more even tone. Part of the impact of Faithful's death lies in its contrast to what's gone before; and Bunyan emphasizes the change with stylistic markers, particularly the biblical doubling—'stoned with stones', for example. He doesn't comment on the cruelty, as Foxe sometimes does. The contrast with the closed minds of the judge and jury is all the comment he wants. Once again, we are aware that Bunyan is in control of a number of levels of style; but that even the highest is a mode of reticence.

Colloquialism and Popular Art

The critical theory of our own time, deriving from a Symbolist aesthetic, has made a sharp distinction between literary language and ordinary language, the multivalence and mystery of one versus the flat utilitarianism of the other. It is not a distinction that is very easy to make in practice, not least because of the inventive qualities of colloquial English.[40] Bunyan's own debt to the power of colloquial English is considerable; but it is not undiscerning. It is not that he is an unconscious artist, whose rude untutored English issued in a masterpiece because of some inherent vitality in colloquial language. It is because he had another sense of language deriving from the Bible that we get a sense of two language worlds in the major works, sometimes colliding, sometimes cohering. Here is an example of the collision, from Mr Hold-the-World:

Let us be wise *as Serpents*, 'tis best to make hay while the Sun shines; you see how the Bee lieth still all winter and bestirs her then only when she can have profit with pleasure. God sends sometimes Rain, and sometimes Sunshine; if they be such fools to go through the first, yet let us be content to take fair weather along with us.[41]

---

[39] Foxe, *Acts and Monuments*, iii. 139; PP, p. 307. Sanders says 'Welcome Life' from the flames in the woodcut; 'Welcome the crosse of Christ, welcome eternal life' in the body of the text.
[40] A position argued convincingly at length by Mary Louise Pratt in *Towards a Speech Act Theory of Literary Discourse* (Bloomington, 1977), chaps. 1-3.
[41] PP, p. 102.

Worldly wisdom is here dramatized through popular proverbs; the irony is that Mr Hold-the-World doesn't see how the biblical proverbs ('Let us be wise as serpents') undermine his position. The Interpreter in Part II, by contrast, coins a whole series of profitable proverbs, for example, 'One leak will sink a Ship, and one Sin will destroy a Sinner'.[42]

Colloquialism can also be the demonstration of audacity in matters of faith; confidence and intimacy with God as well as the audience expressed in a close, oral mode rather than a distant, abstract, written mode of communication.[43] There are a number of examples in *The Pilgrim's Progress*—'have a pluck with Gyant Dispair', 'that Lock went *damnable* hard', 'This River has been a Terror to many, yea the thoughts of it also have often frighted me. But now methinks I stand easie . . .'[44] Bunyan's more elevated style in *The Holy War* shows a similar easiness, an almost defiant humour, especially where the Diabolonians are concerned:

> they presently call a Councel to contrive yet further what was to be done against the famous Town of *Mansoul*; for their yawning panches could not wait to see the result of their Lord *Lucifers*, and their Lord *Apollyons* counsel that they had given before, (for their raging gorge thought every day even as long as a *short-for-ever*) until they were filled with the body and soul, with the flesh and bones, and with all the delicates of *Mansoul*.[45]

The town has fallen to Emanuel, to Mansoul's delight; and the colloquial mockery of the tyrants is an expression of that joy just a much as the more formal expressions of loyalty and gratitude elsewhere. The present tense 'call' is part of that drawing in of the audience characteristic of oral story-telling.[46] But it's the vocabulary that really establishes the tone of confident mockery—'panches' and

---

[42] PP, p. 203.

[43] This characterization of oral features in writing derives from Wallace Chafe, 'Integration and Involvement in Speaking, Writing, and Oral Literature', chap. 3 of Deborah Tannen (ed.), *Spoken and Written Language: Exploring Orality and Literacy*, Advances in Discourse Processes IX (Norwood, NJ, 1982), pp. 35–53.

[44] PP, pp. 281 mg., 118, 310. Charles Firth, in *Essays Historical and Literary* (Oxford, 1938), p. 150–1, suggests that 'damnable' is actually a drop into unregenerate language; but I wonder if it's not a pun, as they are escaping from damnation at the hands of Giant Despair at the time. The fact that it's italicized may indicate irony as well as emphasis, too. Cf. Sharrock's note in PP, p. 332.

[45] HW, p. 227.

[46] See Livia Polanyi, 'Literary Complexity in Everyday Storytelling', in Tannen, *Spoken and Written Language*, pp. 155–170.

'delicates' reduce the devils to fee-fi-fo-fum giants. As with the giants of Part II of *The Pilgrim's Progress*, the folk-art connection is exploited for purposes of ridicule. These are childish, or out-of-date horrors. This is different to Part I, where the folk-tale connection is a source of numinous power as well.[47]

Conclusions: 'The Thing as it was'

Graham Midgley's recent edition of Bunyan's *Poems* has established, in that form at least, a sense of Bunyan's stylistic development, learning to use words more easily and less clumsily, moving away from earlier models, establishing a personal vision.[48] In the prose works, there is an increasingly confident structural control, and, from 1678, a great expansion of its imaginative resources. So is the awed plainness of the Preface to *Grace Abounding* modified, if not abandoned, by the time we get to some of the epic speeches of *The Holy War*? In the extract quoted at the beginning of this essay, Bunyan states that he could have stepped into a higher style, not later when he came to write *The Holy War*, but then. Perhaps he already had, in *A Few Sighs From Hell* (1658), for example. We need to read the Preface to *Grace Abounding* as, precisely, a preface to that work, rather than to the collected works.[49] It is really very different in style to anything else that he wrote, even though echoes from the experience crop up constantly in Bunyan's work. In it he tracks the movement of his mind, back and forth, too uncertain of its direction to construct a sentence except as a switchback narrative, arguing with itself:

And as I was thus before the Lord, that Scripture fastned on my heart, *O man, great is thy Faith*, Matt. 15. 28 even as if one had clapt me on the back, as I lay on my knees before *God*; yet I was not able to believe this, that this was a prayer of Faith, till almost six months after; for I could not think that I had Faith, or that there should be a word for me to act Faith

---

[47] See Roger Sharrock in Newey pp. 55–67; and the present writer in 'The Structure of *The Pilgrim's Progress*', *Essays in Poetics*, 6 (1979), 59–70.
[48] *Misc. Wks.* vi. xlvii.
[49] Ebenezer Chandler and John Wilson, in their preface to *Folio* (1692), the nearest thing to a Collected Works in the seventeenth century, remark that Bunyan '*had a peculiar Phrase to himself in expressing the Conceptions of his Mind*', and that his works feature '*deep things brought into a familiar Phrase*' (sigs. A1, A2ᵛ).

on; therefore I should still be as sticking in the jaws of desparation, and went mourning up and down in a sad condition, crying, *Is his mercy clean gone? is his mercy gone for ever?* And I thought sometimes, even while I was groaning in these expressions, they did seem to make a question whether it was or no; yet I greatly feared it was.[50]

The physical, colloquial intensity—clapped on the back, stuck in the jaws—is localized. This is a prose of moments, each dilemma real because both parts can dominate the imagination for the moment. It is not artless, because Bunyan is so concerned to convey the force of each moment. But it is like nothing else in his work; there is a disturbing lack of distance between the writer and the event.

Bunyan never really moved away from that first commitment to incarnation, that central problem of Christian writing—giving the spiritual material reference, in the steps of 'the man Christ Jesus', as Bunyan referred to him. But towards the end of his career, in such high spots as the conclusion to Part II of *The Pilgrim's Progress* and the final speech of Emanuel in *The Holy War*, he shows that he can stand back from the immediacy of spiritual experience, the need to 'close with Christ' now, and see it in the confident perspective of death and eternity. There are glories which are inexpressible, as the dreamer confesses at the gate of heaven; but to get in, you have to keep truth.[51]

[50] *GA*, § 201.   [51] *PP*, p. 161.

6

'To be a Pilgrim':
Bunyan and the Christian Life

BY GORDON S. WAKEFIELD

IN terms of theological ideas and schemes, Bunyan must be called Calvinist; but his understanding and interpretation of the Christian life come from his own humanity and experience not from bloodless categories; from his desire for the living God and his fascination with people not from iron, pre-mundane decrees. Their somewhat prudish audiences thought it daring when popular Victorian expositors described *The Pilgrim's Progress* as a novel, but about Bunyan as a whole there is more than a moralist's interest in men and women, even though the condemnation of the unrighteous is without remission and those who trust in their own works and knowledge rather than in Christ, though virtuous, are, like Ignorance, consigned to hell even from the gate of heaven.

Underlying all is compassion: Bunyan's pastoral care excludes none. Austerity does not become Ministers of the Gospel, 'neither in Doctrine nor in Conversation: We ourselves live by Grace: Let us give as we receive, and labour to perswade our fellow-sinners which God has left behind us, to follow after, that they may partake with us of Grace. We are saved by Grace, let us live like them that are *gracious*'.[1] Even those condemned at the last will recognize the sweet reasonableness of the Divine justice:

I have often thought of the day of Judgment, and how God will deal with sinners at that day: And I believe it will be managed with that sweetness, with that equitableness, with that excellent Righteousness as to every sin, and circumstance, and agravation thereof, that men that are damned, before the Judgment is over, shall receive such conviction of the righteous Judgment

---

[1] *Misc. Wks.*, xi. 80.

of God upon them, and of their deserts of Hell-fire, that they shall in themselves, conclude that there is all the reason in the world that they should be shut out of Heaven and go to Hell-fire; *These shall go away into everlasting fire*, Matt. 25.46.[2]

Bunyan observes and loves human life as does the poet or artist, who, according to that master of many distinguished Methodists and others, W. R. Maltby (1865–1951), 'cannot in the end help loving a thing so strange, piteous and enthralling as the story of every human soul must be'.[3]

There is no doubt that Bunyan's own spiritual struggles recorded in *Grace Abounding* and elsewhere gave him a tender and merciful heart. He is in his travail one with Martin Luther and a signal example of Lutheran influence on English Protestantism, tempering Calvinism.[4] Apart from this there is an earthiness, at times a coarseness, in Bunyan, expressed in his vigorous yet musical Anglo-Saxon prose, which, though on a heavenward journey, keeps him close to 'man, the heart of man and human life'. He uses the things around him in the world to describe eternal realities. Conversion comes upon him in roadways, doorways, shops, and fields. 'Walking brought him closer to heaven'.[5] In his moods of joy and assurance he could have spoken of God's love and mercy 'even to the very Crows that sat upon the plow'd lands before me, had they been capable to have understood me'.[6] The Interpreter's House in *The Pilgrim's Progress* is full of the phenomena of Bedford town and countryside. An ordinary farmyard bonfire does duty for the mystic flame.[7] And although he condemned the destructive sensuality of worldly pleasure, there was music and dancing in the Father's house and rapturous joy in the presence of the angels of God.

Throughout his spiritual struggles of the 1650s, Bunyan was no recluse. By the time he was confined to jail many of his worst spiritual

---

[2] *Misc. Wks.*, xi. 52.

[3] W. R. Maltby, quoted R. Newton Flew, *The Idea of Perfection in Christian Theology* (Oxford 1934), pp. 340–1.

[4] Cf. *GA*, § 129. Gordon Rupp in *Luther's Progress to the Diet of Worms 1521* (1950) made *The Pilgrim's Progress* the framework for his account of the young Luther's career.

[5] See Patricia Caldwell, *The Puritan Conversion Narrative* (Cambridge, 1983), p. 24. Joan Webber: 'Donne and Bunyan: The Styles of Two Faiths', in Stanley E. Fish (ed.). *Seventeenth-century Prose: Modern Essays in Criticism* (Oxford, 1971), pp. 489–532.   [6] *GA* § 92.

[7] See Roger Sharrock, 'Bunyan and the English Emblem Writers', *RES* 21 (1945), 111.

agonies and conflicts were over. In the period described retrospectively in *Grace Abounding* he was engaged not only in his trade of a tinker but in preaching, disputing (with Quakers, Ranters, and others), writing, and the Church life of the Bedford Independents. 'I preached what I felt, what I smartingly did feel',[8] but what he felt and saw[9] compassed a whole universe of experience, temporal and eternal; the roughness and brutality of soldiers, the seductive vices of the fairground, the precedents and prejudices of the lawcourts, advocates, judges, juries, the penalties meted out alike by the civil arm and Christians to one another, drunkenness and debauchery, shrewish wives and henpecked husbands, the poor women of Bedford talking theology and speaking 'as if joy did make them speak'.[10] All this and the inner and outer realities of heaven and hell, depression leading to the iron cage or Doubting Castle of Despair, joy transporting to the marriage supper of the Lamb.

He had the gift Péguy ascribed to Victor Hugo 'de voir la création comme si elle sortait ce matin des mains du Créateur'.[11] He had 'an intuitive contemporaneity with the events he proclaimed from the pulpit':[12]

. . . me thought I was as if I had seen him born, as if I had seen him grow up, as if I had seen him walk thorow this world, from the Cradle to his Cross; to which, also, when he came, I saw how gently he gave himself to be hanged and nailed on it for my sins and wicked doings; also as I was musing on this his progress, that droped on my spirit, *He was ordained for the slaughter*, I Pet. 1.19.20.

When I have considered also the truth of his resurrection, and have remembered that word, *Touch me not Mary* &c., I have seen as if he leaped at the Graves mouth for joy that he was risen again, and had got the conquest over our dreadful foes, *John* 20.17. I have also in the spirit seen him a man on the right hand of God the Father for me, and have seen the manner of his comming from Heaven to judge the world with glory . . .[13]

'Thy righteousness is in Heaven'

There is, therefore, in Bunyan's temperament, talents, and life, that which modifies the Calvinist scholasticism which was his theological

---

[8] GA, § 276.   [9] GA, § 278.   [10] GA, § 38
[11] Charles Péguy, *Victor Marie, Comte Hugo*, Œuvres complètes de Charles Péguy (Paris, 1916–55), xi. 121, quoted Talon, pp. 118–9.
[12] Richard L. Greaves, 'The Nature of the Puritan Tradition', in R. Buick Knox (ed.), *Reformation, Conformity, and Dissent: Essays in Honour of Geoffrey Nuttall* (1977), p. 262.   [13] GA, §§ 120, 121.

milieu. None the less, the Christian life for him begins not in human faith or decision but in the Covenant of Grace which was made between the Father and the Son before first creation. Bunyan argues this with typically Puritan ratiocination, supported by quotations mostly from later books of the New Testament, in an early work, *The Doctrine of the Law and Grace Unfolded* (1659): '... this Covenant or Bargain was made indeed and in truth before man was in being. Oh! God thought of the salvation of man before there was any transgression of man ... the price was agreed upon before the world began ... *The precious Blood of Christ*'. Similarly the promise of eternal life, and the choice of us, his saints, his people: the transaction is but secondarily with the Patriarchs, or with the House of Israel and Judah (Jeremiah 31:33).[14] It does not rest on weak human wills, the inconsistencies even of the saints, the contingencies of the passing ages of mankind. It is founded on the unity of the Godhead, on the eternal love of the Father and the Son. Bunyan himself, both in *The Doctrine of the Law and Grace Unfolded* and in *Grace Abounding* tells of the comfort he received when the sentence fell upon his soul, *Thy righteousness is in Heaven*.[15] His righteousness did not depend upon his own moods, nor even on his feelings towards goodness or evil, but on 'Jesus Christ, the same yesterday, today and forever'.

The necessary response to the eternal covenant in the very heart of the Godhead is that we trust no more in the Covenant of Works, in our own efforts to be good and one with God. Such trust is not only vain and futile; it is the sin which may damn a person at the very end. The fate of Ignorance in Part I of *The Pilgrim's Progress* seems perplexingly severe. It almost dims the glories of the pilgrims' entry into the Celestial City. True, Ignorance is a brash and irritating fellow, so self-assured and over-confident, 'a very brisk lad' from the Country of Conceit. One has met him often, not always in theological encounters; but does he deserve utter damnation? Would Dante have consigned him to hell? Bunyan is inexorable. There is no hope of salvation if one goes to Christ in a 'Legal and Old-Covenant Spirit', with a long ledger of self-improvement and a tally of deeds well done, sacraments received, prayers said. This is hypocrisy and self-deceit, a

---

[14] *Misc. Wks.*, ii. 90-2. Cf. Milton, *Paradise Lost*, iii. 80-260, on which for comments on ll. 131-49 see Christopher Ricks, *The Force of Poetry* (Oxford, 1984), pp. 68-70.   [15] *Misc. Wks.*, ii. 147; GA, § 229.

total failure to recognize what one is really like; it is a trifling with God and with grace, a making of Christ 'a painted Saviour or a Cipher':

> Thou must therefore, if thou wilt so lay hold of Christ, as not to be rejected by him, I say thou must come to him as the basest in the world, more fitter to be damned, if thou hadst thy right, then to have the least smile, hope, or comfort from him: come with the fire of hell in thy conscience; come with thy heart hard, dead, cold, full of wickedness and madness against thine own salvation; come as renouncing all thy tears, prayers, watchings, fastings; come as a blood-red sinner, do not stay from Christ, till thou hast a greater sense of thy own misery, nor of the reality of Gods mercy; do not stay while thy heart is softer, and thy spirit in a better frame, but go against thy minde, and against the minde of the devil, and sin, throw thyself down at the foot of Christ with a halter about thy neck, and say, Lord Jesus, hear a sinner, a hard-hearted sinner, a sinner that deserveth to be damned, to be cast to hell; and resolve never to return, or to give over crying unto him, till thou do finde, that he hath washed thy conscience from dead works with his blood vertually, and clothed thee with his own righteousness, and made thee compleat in himself, this is the way to come to Christ.[16]

Conversion is necessary, a turning to God in Christ out of an utter hopelessness, a near suicidal despair. There must be depths before there are heights. Deep calls to deep; depth of sin to depth of mercy.

The Venture of Faith

In spite of this fearsome self-abnegation in which one goes to Christ, this almost pathological humility, the Christian life is a venture, a joyful abandon to Divine Providence, to use the term of Bunyan's French contemporaries, notably Jean-Pierre de Caussade. Not that there must be forced comparisons with a very different spirituality.[17] But the Bunyan who has been plunged into self-despair, summons all the strength of his will with exultant courage, whatever God's purpose for him:

> I thought also, that God might chuse whether he would give me comfort now, or at the hour of death; but I might not therefore chuse whether I would hold my profession or no: I was bound, but he was free: yea it was my dutie to stand to his Word, whether he would ever look upon me or no, or save me at the last: Wherefore, thought I, the point being thus, I am for going on, and venturing my eternal state with Christ, whether I have

---

[16] *Misc. Wks.*, ii. 184-5.
[17] See J. Neville Ward's articles on 'Abandon' and 'de Caussade' in Gordon S. Wakefield (ed.), *A Dictionary of Christian Spirituality* (1983).

comfort here or no: if God doth not come in, thought I, I will leap off the Ladder even blindfold into Eternitie, sink or swim, come heaven, come hell; Lord Jesus, if thou wilt catch me, do; if not, I will venture for thy Name.[18]

God saves the vilest of sinners; the preaching of the Gospel by the command of the Risen Christ must, according to Luke 24: 27, begin at Jerusalem, the very stronghold of Christ's enemies, the place which crucified the Lord of Glory. The 'Jerusalem-sinner' must be so bold as 'to venture himself upon this Grace':[19]

Let us therefore upon the sight of our wretchedness, fly and venturously leap into the Arms of Christ, which are now as open to receive us into his Bosom, as they were when nailed to the Cross.

Where canst thou find that God was ever false to his Promise, or that he ever deceived the Soul that ventured it self upon him?[20]

The Christian life is therefore a venture, a pilgrimage, a journey, with risks and hazards. As Bunyan makes plain in *The Heavenly Footman* (1698) there is a sense of running for one's life, and yet the way must be studied, mused over; there must be an athlete's stripping, discipline, and realism, not a wild, frantic unheeding dash towards a mirage. Bunyan was all too well aware of the many competing ways which offered salvation to the Christian. The seventeenth century was the last in European history in which signposts to secular and political ambition as well as to hopes beyond this world were largely painted in religious colours and there was a variety of daubs from the dun to the garish. Quakers and Ranters had nearly led him, so he believed, to destruction, and although he counted himself an anabaptist, since he could not accept infant baptism—he also described himself as a Congregationalist as late as 1672[21]—he warns his readers against having too much company with some of them.[22] Christ is the way; not any other name or sect.

---

[18] *GA*, § 337. [19] *Misc. Wks.*, xi. 69.
[20] *Misc. Wks.*, xi. 69, 65. Cf. *Misc. Wks.*, viii. 51, ll. 12-14; 174, ll. 1-2; 339, ll. 22-3. See also Richard L. Greaves, *Misc. Wks.*, xi. xxx-xxxi.
[21] See Christopher Hill in R. Buick Knox (ed.), *Reformation, Conformity, and Dissent*, p. 212 with reference to J. Waddington, *Congregational History 1587-1700* (1874), p. 426. See Hill's essay also for the relief at which some of the dispossessed after 1662 hailed the settlement, for, cruel as it was, it was better than the previous 'Munsterian anarchy' (p. 214).   [22] *Works*, iii. 383.

The School of the Cross

The Christian life is full of hazards. God's chosen are most likely to be afflicted by temptation, most tested and tried. They must not be daunted, many as are the discouragements. The burden of guilt rolls from their backs at the Cross, but the Cross does not disappear from their view. 'Take heed of being offended at the cross that thou must go by, before thou come to heaven.'[23] The Cross, on which the Son of God offered himself once for all for our sins, is the sign of our salvation, but it also points the way along which we must follow him:

> The cross is the standing way-mark by which all they that go to glory must pass by . . . Christ is the way . . . if thou art in him, thou wilt presently see the cross, thou must go close by it, thou must touch it, nay, thou must take it up, or else thou wilt quickly go out of the way that leads to heaven.[24]

The Cross may be recognized in six things—in justification, by which we repudiate our own righteousness, our pious exercises and self-centred efforts to acquire virtue, and throw ourselves wholly on Christ; in mortification, our death to self and 'to the world and all its toys';[25] in perseverance, a holding out to the end for all the thousands of miles of the journey, 'briars and quagmires and all other incumbrances'; in self-denial; in patience; and in giving to the poor, that ancient mark of Christianity, not in remote and detached benevolence but in communion and genuine fellowship with them.

Vicissitudes are indeed conditions of the pilgrim way. This is a theme of *The Pilgrim's Progress*, in which the pilgrim, among much else, must endure what corresponds in another spirituality to 'the dark night of the soul'. Bunyan, ever interpreting the Christian life in the terms and images of Scripture, calls this 'the valley of the shadow of death'.[26] In these ecumenical times when comparative spirituality is an interest, it is inevitable that it should be asked whether there is any similarity here to the experience described by St John of the Cross.[27] It is doubtful if there was any direct

---

[23] *Works*, iii. 386.
[24] *Works*, iii. 386.
[25] The phrase is Charles Wesley's.
[26] Ps. 23: 4.
[27] See, *The Complete Works of St John of the Cross*, trans. E. Allison Peers 3 vols., rev. edn (1953); also E. Allison Peers, *Flame of Love* (1943; repr. 1979) and *Studies in the Spanish Mystics I*, 2nd edn (1951), pp. 183–235; Rowan Williams, *The Wound of Knowledge* (1979), chap. 8; Gerald Brenan, *John of the Cross, His Life and Poetry* (Cambridge, 1973); Hans Urs von Balthasar, *The Glory of the Lord: A Theological Aesthetics*, III (Edinburgh, 1986), pp. 105–71.

Dionysian influence on Bunyan, though such mystical theology was in the mid-seventeenth-century air, witness John Everard[28] and others who belong to the Protestant underworld; but Bunyan's is a different ethos. It is notable that Bunyan's valley has two parts, the second far more dangerous, but there is too little detail in his few paragraphs alongside the Spanish mystic's lengthy treatment to establish any correspondence with St John's night of the senses and night of the spirit. For both, however, God is all and to be desired above all, and the soul's journey is to lead to the beatitude of the Divine love. Both knew agonizing spiritual struggles, a Lutheran *anfechtung* (dereliction), and persecution from fellow-Christians; their great works came out of imprisonment, though the Carmelite's was at once shorter and more harsh; both were steeped in Scripture, though they did not dwell equally on the same passages; both were insistent on faith and a stripping of the confidence of the natural man and the conventional exercises and achievements of devotion, which may be the deepest of pitfalls; both insisted that Christ could not be sought without the Cross, and for both darkness is at once the most terrifyingly dangerous and the most illuminating of experiences. Bunyan quotes Job 12: 22 that God 'discovereth deep things out of darkness and bringeth out to light the shadow of death.' There is more clutter of snares, gins, traps in Bunyan's dark valley. His is the way one might have to tread on a foul night in Bedfordshire woods and fields. For John of the Cross the way is the ascent of a pitiless Spanish mountain, the desolation is the appalling absence of God. But Bunyan's Christian knows mental confusion even as John of the Cross's pilgrim may feel vacant of mind and incapable of coherence.

As Christian goes on, the day breaks and there is light enough at the last to see him safely through. Even then as he journeys, he will be assailed at times by melancholy and imprisoned by despair; but there is joy too, strengthening companionship, the beauty now and then of the way itself, the vision of God and of glory, and, above all, the promises which assure him that these very tribulations are the tokens that he is set on course for the kingdom of God.

Some similarities may be discerned between Bunyan's spirituality and that of the Desert Fathers and its influence on Western

---

[28] For Everard see Wakefield, *A Dictionary of Christian Spirituality*, and *DNB*, s.v.

Christianity through Gregory the Great. There is, in Bunyan, what Gregory called 'Compunction', the Divine piercing and goading and 'the gift of tears'. Bunyan would have understood better than modern Methodists a verse of Charles Wesley's which also represents one aspect of Orthodox piety:

> Deepen the wound thy hands have made
> In this weak, helpless soul;
> Till mercy with its kindly aid,
> Descends to make me whole.

He might not have been so happy with the implied perfectionism of the following stanzas:

> The sharpness of thy two-edged sword
> Enable me to endure;
> Till bold to say: My hallowing Lord
> Hath wrought a perfect cure.
>
> I see the exceeding broad command
> Which all contains in one:
> Enlarge my heart to understand
> The mystery unknown.
>
> O that with all thy saints I might
> By sweet experience prove
> What is the length, and breadth, and height,
> And depth of perfect love!

Bunyan's pilgrims in spite of their joyous dances are always in some sense the walking wounded. There is no 'perfect cure' in this world; yet the mystery may be known, as Bunyan makes plain in his posthumously published exposition of Ephesians 3: 18-19. The difference here between Bunyan and Wesley is not vast. Certainly for Bunyan the soul must be wounded, the heart enlarged to breaking-point before mercy can do its perfect work. And there are tears. They are necessary to repentance. They should be induced in young children. Before they are taught forms of prayer, which without repentance will make them hypocrites, they should be taught of their 'wretched state and condition': 'tell them of hell fire, and their sins, of damnation and salvation: the way to escape the one, and enjoy the other (if you know it your selves) and this will make tears run down your sweet babes eyes, and hearty groans flow from their hearts. . . .'²⁹ The water often stands in Christian's eyes. There is no *apatheia* as he considers the way he has been led, the perils from which he has been delivered, the sins and weaknesses and lack of faith to which he has been prone all along, and, above all, the infinite mercy which saves sinners—the vilest sinners—at such tremendous cost. There are tears of joy as well as of grieving. Says Hopeful, in the account of his conversion:

And then I saw from that saying, [*He that cometh to me shall never hunger, and he that believeth on me shall never thirst*] That believing and coming was all one, and that he that came, that is run out in his heart and affections after Salvation by Christ, he indeed believed in Christ. Then the water stood in mine eyes, and I asked further, But Lord, may such a great sinner as I am, be indeed accepted of thee, and be saved by thee? And I heard him say, *And him that cometh to me, I will in no wise cast out.*[30]

And Bunyan himself, in the conclusion of *Grace Abounding* writes most movingly:

Of all tears, they are the best that are made by the Blood of Christ; and of all joy, that is the sweetest that is mixt with mourning over Christ: O 'tis a goodly thing to be on our knees, with Christ in our arms, before God: I hope I know something of these things.[31]

There is also reference in Bunyan to Enlightment. He derives this from Hebrews 6: 5 and 10: 32, but it is Justin Martyr's term for entry into the Christian life sealed by Baptism, and an element in the spirituality of the desert.[32] In *The Heavenly Footman* (1698), the reader is told to 'Beg of God' that he will *'enlighten thine Understanding'*. This is in order to see the glories of the other world. The unsaved Gentiles walk in darkness 'having the understanding darkened being alienated from the life of God through the ignorance that is in them because of the blindness of their heart' (Ephesians 4: 17–18).[33] 'The School of the Cross is the School of Light'.[34]

Sin in Believers

The Christian is never wholly free from sin in this life. He must never be complacent, never relax, never depart from Christ for an instant.

---

[29] *Misc. Wks.*, ii. 269.   [30] *PP*, p. 143.   [31] *GA*, p. 102.
[32] Justin Martyr, *The First Apology* (various trans. and edns), 61. Cf. also Alan Jones, *Soul Making: The Desert Way of Spirituality* (1986), p. 86.
[33] *Misc. Wks.*, v. 162.
[34] 'Mr John Bunyan's Dying Sayings', *Works*, i. 65.

The allegory of *The Holy War* shows dramatically how the repelled diabolical invaders may return and recapture the city of Mansoul; how there are forever plots and stratagems on the part of the evil agents; how Mansoul may be worsted through being over-bold and rash in the conflict.

It is essential that we know our faults, above all that particular sin to which we are constitutionally prone, our 'darling sin'. We must especially be aware of the iniquities of our times, those sins which assail us because we live in a certain age. It is tempting to expatiate on this and to ask what are the sins of the twentieth century as compared with those of the seventeenth, or to notice how the virtues of an age may also create its sins—Victorian respectability and high moral standards leading, for example, to hypocrisy and harsh judgements. Bunyan knew well that situations produce their own sins. There are sins of which those who live in families are in danger, as well as 'closet sins', which attack us in the secret place, the results of self-indulgence in imagination, or our desperate desire to justify ourselves and present ourselves as formally good.

There is a problem here. Why does God allow sin to persist in those who are his chosen and converted? Emanuel touches on this in his farewell address to Mansoul in *The Holy War*:

Nothing can hurt *thee but sin; nothing can* grieve *me but sin; nothing can make thee base before thy foes but sin; Take heed of sin my* Mansoul. *And dost thou know why I at first, and do still suffer* Diabolonians *to dwell in thy walls, O* Mansoul? *it is to keep thee wakening, to try thy love, to make thee watchful, and to cause thee yet to prize my noble* Captains, *their Souldiers and my mercy.*
It is also that yet thou maiest be made to remember what a deplorable condition thou wast once in. I mean when, not some, but all did dwell, not in thy walls, but in thy Castle, and in thy stronghold, O Mansoul!

Were the city of the soul completely free from its enemies, it might be so much off guard as to let in the whole host from outside. The enemies may do the soul good if they keep it watchful and warring and drive it nearer to God for strength and reliance on him and not on its own resources.

. . . let the sight of a Diabolian *heighten thy love to me. I came once and twice and thrice to save thee from the poyson of those arrows that would have wrought thy death; stand for me, thy friend, my* Mansoul, *against the* Diabolonians, *and I will stand for thee before my Father and all his Court.*

Love me against temptation, and I will love thee notwithstanding thine infirmities.

The continuing presence of sin must also make the soul have regard to Emanuel's 'Captains'. These are the means of grace and the good faculties of the soul which grace implants. As we shall see, later, they belong to Bunyan's understanding of the Church.[35]

This constant conflict with sin gave rise to many cases of conscience. The Puritans used gallons of ink in trying to resolve these. Bunyan was not a casuist of the rank of William Perkins or William Ames, but he was aware, above all others, that the very strength of the promises together with the hazards of the journey through the world, caused doubts. 'Is it not all too good to be true? There is this great salvation reserved for me, sinner as I am. But is my calling and election sure? Can it possibly be that I shall attain this beatitude with God? May I not, without knowing it have fallen into sin, even that unforgiveable sin against the Holy Spirit, of which Christ speaks?'

Bunyan writes shrewdly of Conscience in *The Holy War*. Conscience is a minister in Mansoul but has a humble role as a scholar of the Holy Spirit, who must confine himself to the teaching of virtue, of Christian morality and duty, but 'must not attempt to presume to pretend to be a revealer of those high Mysteries' which are kept close in the bosom of Shaddai, Emanuel's Father,[36] and which only the Holy Spirit can declare. Conscience is old—one of Bunyan's innumerable senior citizens—and has been much abused and needs the constant refreshment, strengthening, and purifying of the new wine of the Kingdom. He is in the Christian life subordinate to the Gospel. He warns the unconverted of the wrath to come, but he may torture through the proliferation of scruples, or deceive through assurances which simply have not reckoned with the sinfulness of sin. He may also become hardened; he needs above all to be kept tender, especially in believers, who yet are not content to rest in his approval but to the end cast themselves on the mercy of Christ.

But what of the most agonizing case of conscience, the sin against the Spirit? Bunyan treats of this in his early work, *The Doctrine of the Law and Grace Unfolded* (1659) and in one of his last, *Good News for the Vilest of Men* (1688), better known as *The Jerusalem-Sinner Saved*. In these works, he argues by question and answer and logic; in *Grace Abounding* he writes of his own terrible conflict.

[35] *HW*, pp. 249–50.   [36] *HW*, p. 142.

Bunyan is as much haunted by the rigorism of the letter to the Hebrews as by the words of Christ.[37] He is also impaled on the dilemma implicit in Scripture itself. There is so much of mercy. '*And him that cometh to Christ he will in no wise cast out*'.[38] Peter is restored after his denial and made chief of the Apostles; yet it would seem that there is a sin which cannot be forgiven.

In his own torment, Bunyan could find no comfort in any of the pardons of Scripture. David was forgiven adultery and murder, of which Bunyan was not guilty, but these were sins against the Law of Moses whereas he had transgressed the Gospel. Peter was forgiven but he had denied Christ, whereas Bunyan felt that he might, though unwittingly, have sold him, and deserved the horrendous fate of Iscariot. 'I thought with myself that there might be more ways than one to commit the unpardonable sin'. To read and think of God's infinite love and mercy for sinners increased his torment for had he not slighted these? At times hope dawned upon him and the promises prevailed. His soul hung as in a pair of scales 'sometimes one end would be uppermost, and sometimes again the other', now in 'peace' and then in 'trouble'.[39]

Writing in a cool hour for the help of others, healed of his own bruised conscience, Bunyan finds it difficult to see that the sin against the Spirit is not a sin against Christ. Not all sins against the Spirit are unpardonable, witness Jonah, who went deliberately in a direction other than that bidden by the Spirit, and yet was received to mercy out of the belly of hell.

He concludes that the sin against the Spirit is the total and deliberate rejection of Christ, the trampling underfoot of the Son of God, the profaning of the blood of the Covenant. It is the sin against the Holy Spirit because by saying that Christ's works are those of the Devil, it denies the Spirit of God in him; and it is also a sin against the Spirit which has enlightened us and a sin which resists all motions of the Spirit of goodness within our hearts and 'all its gentle intreatings of the soul'.[40] It repudiates the teachings of the

---

[37] It is interesting to consider the effect of Hebrews on Bunyan. The passage which most distressed him was the condemnation of Esau 'who found no place of repentance though he sought it with many tears' (12: 16-17) (*GA, passim*), added to the terrible strictures against those who apostasize. Yet at the last it was Heb. 12: 22-4 which completed his release (*GA*, §§ 262-4).
[38] *Misc. Wks.*, xi. 89; quoted often in *Grace Abounding* and *The Pilgrim's Progress* (see, e.g., n. 30).
[39] *GA*, § 205.   [40] *Misc. Wks.*, ii. 206.

Apostles and Prophets. But, above all, it is wilful. If there is the least vestige in our heart of desire for Christ, of opposition to sin, of longing for goodness, then we cannot have committed the unpardonable sin. Thus Bunyan himself in the end read salvation out of the sternest of the epistles, for the word which came into his heart, 'I must go to Jesus', and illumined his soul with the assurance that he in spite of everything wanted Christ, took him to that most numinous passage about coming, not to the Sinai of bondage, but to Mount Zion, to the whole company of heaven, to God, and to Jesus, *'the Mediator of the New Testament, and to the blood of sprinkling, that speaketh better things than that of Abel . . .'* (Hebrews 12: 24).

Thus, for Bunyan himself (in spite of the heights and depths within his own soul), and for those he sought to counsel, the case was resolved and salvation realized in the Church.

The Church and the Ordinances

To the superficial and unsympathetic reader there may seem to be an almost terrifying individualism about the Christian life according to Bunyan. Other people would seem often to be more hindrances than helpers on the way. Yet it is no lone journey.[41] There are many good companions, as in *The Pilgrim's Progess* (both parts). In the dark valley, Christian hears a human voice going before him and reciting the words of the Psalm '*Though I walk through the valley of the shaddow of death, I will fear none ill, for thou art with me*'. He then knew 'that some who feared God were in this Valley as well as himself', and 'he hoped [*could he overtake them*] to have company by and by.'[42] Throughout Bunyan's writings there is a very clear doctrine of the Church, the communion of saints, who are the apple of God's eye. Misunderstanding may occur on the part of post-Tridentine Catholics because the Church is no hierarchical institution; it is the fellowship of believers, but it is everywhere and inescapable. Christ and his Church are one. 'For God, and Christ, and his People are so linked together, that if the Good of one be prayed for, to wit, the Church, the glory of God, and advancement

---

[41] Fr. Hubert Northcote, *The Venture of Prayer* (1948), p. 44 is guilty of this misunderstanding. [42] *PP*, p. 64.

of Christ must needs be included.'[43] 'Church fellowship rightly managed is the glory of the world.'[44]

The Palace Beautiful in *The Pilgrim's Progress* is Bunyan's picture of the Church, where the pilgrim is received with courtesy and given rest in the chamber called Peace, though not without enquiry as to his credentials. He talks over his Christian life with the virtuous girls who live there—Discretion, Piety, Charity, and Prudence—it is notable that women are in charge—and he has supper at a table 'furnished with fat things and with Wine that was well refined; and all their talk at the Table was about the Lord of the Hill; As namely, about what he had done and wherefore he did what he did . . .'[45]

Beautiful is the repository of the holy and living tradition, the records of the past, and the promise and hope of the future. It gives a vision of the Delectable Mountains, from which, when the pilgrims get there, the Celestial City may be seen. It is a museum of the heroes of old, but also the armoury where the pilgrim is equipped for the warfare ahead. And he leaves with a viaticum of bread and wine and raisins.

The young are catechized at Palace Beautiful. And there is further sacramental allusion in the pills which are given to cure certain distempers—*ex Carne et Sanguine Christi*—which echoes the tradition going back to Ignatius of Antioch, who, within a generation of the New Testament, refers to the Eucharist as 'the medicine of immortality'.[46]

The ordinances of the Church are the pledges of God's presence, 'his love-letters and love-tokens too'. The true Christian loves to be at the breaking of the bread where Christ as at Emmaus, makes himself known. Here is feasting 'made for mirth'. There is rapture at the Lord's Table. When Bunyan was admitted to fellowship with the people of God in Bedford, 'while I thought of that blessed Ordinance of Christ, which was his last Supper with his Disciples before his death, that Scripture, *Do this in rememberance of me*, Luke. 22. 19, was made a very precious word unto me; for by it the Lord did come down upon my conscience with the discovery of his death for my sins, and, as I then felt, did as if he plunged me in the vertue of the same.' The exaltation did not last and soon the Sacrament became a means of the vilest temptations to blasphemy

---

[43] *Misc. Wks.*, ii. 244.   [44] *Works*, i. 758.   [45] *PP*, p. 52
[46] Ignatius, *To the Ephesians*, xx. 2, in *The Apostolic Fathers*, trans. Francis Glimm, Joseph Marique, and Gerald Welsh (New York, 1947; repr. 1969), p. 95.

'and to wish some deadly thing to those that then did eat thereof'. But this forced Bunyan to 'bend' himself to pray to be kept from such profanations; 'and also to cry to God to bless the Bread and Cup to them as it went from mouth to mouth'. He blamed the temptation on his lack of reverence in his first partaking; but after nine months the power of the Dominical command reasserted itself and Bunyan remained 'usually very well and comfortable in partaking of that blessed Ordinance' and able to discern the Lord's Body 'as broken for [*his*] sins and that his precious Blood has been shed for [*his*] transgressions.'[47] He may well, like Agnes Beaumont who rhapsodized about the joys of the Lord's table at the Gamlingay meeting to which Bunyan had taken her in 1674, have not infrequently found not calm and serene assurance only but sublime rapture in the Sacrament.[48]

The Sacraments are obligations and very precious, conveyances of Christ in his fullness; but they do not themselves save us. 'Baptism and the Lord's Supper both, were made for us, not we for them'.[49] 'I count them not the fundamentals of our Christianity, nor grounds or rule to communion with saints: servants they are and our mystical ministers, to teach and instruct us in the most weighty matters of the kingdom of God'.[50]

Bunyan opposed the exclusiveness of Baptists, who would have made a new law out of Baptism. The 'one baptism' of Ephesians 4: 5 is no liturgy, but the baptism of the Spirit and this is what is vital. As the title of Bunyan's treatise has it, 'Differences in judgment about water-baptism' should be 'no bar to communion'. Love and not baptism is the badge of Christ and love is more discovered when we receive for the sake of Christ than when we refuse his children for want of water. Behind Bunyan's tolerance and charity, lie bitter and divisive controversies, arguments 'mixed with gall', between Protestant Christians, which have bid fair to destroy, not to edify.

The Supper, for Bunyan, is the greater Sacrament about which Scripture is more explicit. 'The Church as a Church is much more concerned in that than in water-baptism both as to her faith and comfort; both as to her union and communion'.[51]

---

[47] *GA*, §§ 253-4.
[48] Cf. Gordon Rupp, 'A Devotion of Rapture in English Puritanism', in R. Buick Knox (ed.), *Reformation, Conformity, and Dissent*, p. 129. Agnes Beaumont's riding pillion to and from the meeting with John Bunyan was an occasion of scandal: see *GA*, pp. 155-6, 176-80.
[49] *Works*, ii. 630.
[50] *Works*, ii. 604.
[51] *Works*, ii. 630.

The Church is a gathered Church. And communion—by which Bunyan means more than receiving of the Supper, though that is implied—must be with 'visible saints', those who are converted, and separated in their manner of life from the profane. There is no scorn, nor contempt towards the carnal and profane 'as men'. But no more than iron can be mixed with miry clay can the saints mix with them 'in the worship of God and the fellowship of the Gospel'.[52]

There is a ministry in the Church, as we have seen above in what Emanuel says about his captains in *The Holy War*. Bunyan himself owed much to John Gifford at Bedford. In Part II of *The Pilgrim's Progress* there is no more noble figure than Great-heart: the magnanimous man in the sense of τὸ ἐπιεικές of Philippians 4: 5; the soldier who fights against giants on behalf of his pilgrim band; the exemplar of patient endurance, who leads his people to the gate of heaven, and returns again and again to fetch more; the expositor, able to unravel the knottiest theological problem or case of conscience, and who proceeds by conversation, discourse, not just monologue. Alexander Whyte (1836–1921), the Minister of Free St George's, Edinburgh, for half a century, who lived much of the time in Bunyan, compared the discussion of Great-heart with Christiana to the 'question-day' at Highland communions when 'questions that have arisen in the minds of "the men" in connection with doctrine and with experience are on that day set forth, debated out, and solved by much meditation and prayer; age, saintliness, doctrinal and experimental reading and personal experience all making their contribution to the solution of the question in hand.'[53] The reasoning out of how we have pardon by Word and Deed is stiff and the distinctions of such evangelical scholasticism not natural to our times, but the end is the individual's appropriation of the Church's praise of the Divine Love in the great tradition of affective piety:

Chris. *True, methinks it makes my Heart bleed to think that he should bleed for me. Oh! thou loving one, Oh! thou Blessed one. Thou deservest to have me, thou hast bought me: Thou deservest to have me all, thou hast paid for me ten thousand times more than I am worth. No marvel that this made the water stand in my Husbands Eyes, and that it made him trudge so nimbly on . . .*[54]

---

[52] *Works*, ii. 616.
[53] Alexander Whyte, *Bunyan Characters* 2nd ser. (Edinburgh and London, 1894), p. 179.
[54] *PP*, p. 212.

For Bunyan there is no better way to good works than constantly to affirm to others within the fellowship the doctrine of justification by grace. In his tract on *Christian Behaviour* (1663), he has similes from the garden and the boudoir:

> Christians are like the several flowers in a garden, that have upon each of them the dew of heaven, which being shaken with the wind, they let fall their dew at each other's roots, whereby they are jointly nourished and become nourishers of one another. For Christians to commune savourly of God's matters one with another, it is as if they opened to each other's nostrils boxes of perfume.

'God's matters' are supremely of his saving grace, and as Christians talk together of these they speak like the women of Bedford, 'as though joy did make them speak', and are brought to Christiana's overwhelming emotion and a communion which has the sweet smell of Christ's own sacrifice.[55]

'Prayer is an Ordinance of God' and Bunyan discourses on it in an exposition of 1 Corinthians 14: 15, 'I will pray with the Spirit and I will pray with the understanding also'. 'Prayer', he says, 'is a sincere, sensible, affectionate pouring out of the heart or soul to God through Christ in the strength and assistance of the holy Spirit, for such things as God hath promised, or, according to the Word, for the good of the Church, with submission, in Faith, to the Will of God'.[56]

Such a definition confines Prayer to petition, rather more than do those accounts from the Catholic tradition, which regard prayer more essentially as communion with God within which our petitions have their place but as part of the relationship of prayer rather than its primary purpose. Prayer also seems to be confined, as on Calvinist understanding it must be, to the Church. Is it possible to pray for those who, by unalterable decree, are outside the Covenant of Grace, who cannot receive the benefits of Christ or the influences of Grace, because their hearts are eternally hardened? They form 'the world' in the Johannine sense. They are those for whom Christ does not pray in John 17, which, together with the prayers of Paul, is Bunyan's model.

Such Prayer cannot be any other than in the Spirit. Bunyan's exposition is an attack on set or stinted forms of Prayer, on the use

---

[55] *Works*, ii. 570; *GA*, § 38; *PP*, p. 212.
[56] *Misc. Wks.*, ii. 235.

of books, the *Book of Common Prayer* in particular, and on the Christian Calendar. In *The Holy War* Bunyan tells how as the end of the season of Lent approaches in Mansoul, Harmless-mirth is hired to bring good cheer after so long a fast. But Harmless-mirth is in fact Lord Lascivious and the relief from fasting produces an orgy.[57] In *I Will Pray with the Spirit* ([1662?]), Bunyan sneers at his contemporaries who have:

both the *Manner* and *Matter* of their Prayers at their finger ends; setting such a Prayer for such a day, and that twenty years before it comes. One for *Christmass*, another for *Easter*, and six dayes after that. They have also bounded how many syllables must be said in every one of them at their publick Exercises. For each Saints day also, they have them ready for the generations yet unborn to say. They can tell you also, when you shall kneel, when you should stand, when you should abide in your seats, when you should go up into the Chancel, and what you should do when you come there. All which the Apostles came short of, as not being able to compose so profound a matter.[58]

St Paul says that we do not know how we ought to pray or what to pray for; we need the Spirit to help us, so prayers cannot be prescribed in advance. And prayer without the Spirit is blasphemy. By nature we are infirm, yet cannot truly know our misery for we are cold and dead. Yet once we are enlightened as to our true state, we would fly from God without the Spirit, who gives us confidence even in our wretchedness, shows us the right way of coming to God through Christ and enables us to be bold to call God 'Father' as the born-again children of God. To babble the Lord's Prayer is no salvation. 'No, here is the life of Prayer, when in, or with the Spirit, a man being made sensible of sin, and how to come to the Lord for mercy; he comes, I say in the strength of the Spirit, and cryeth *Father*.'[59]

But Prayer must be with the understanding also. The Corinthians made their spiritual gifts an occasion for boasting and their prayers were more a display of their extraordinary powers than an edifying of the Church. Understanding means prayer in our mother-tongue. Bunyan does not expound this; it could exclude both the Latin Mass and enthusiastic *glossolalia* alike. Understanding means also to pray *experimentally*—to know our wants, to know God's willingness to save sinners, to marshall our arguments, for prayer is not without

---

[57] *HW*, p. 168.   [58] *Misc. Wks.*, ii. 247–8.   [59] *Misc. Wks.*, ii. 252.

disputation; it is even a wrestling with God. It is, as George Herbert said, an 'engine against the Almighty', though the Almighty himself has devised it for us, for he has destined us not for mystical absorption in the Infinite but for a dynamic relationship of living beings with a living God.

This is a bald summary of Bunyan's usual plethora of expository points. He goes on to deal with cases, but the essence of prayer is 'a detestation to sin and the things of this life' and 'a longing desire after Communion with God, in a holy and undefiled state and inheritance'. Nothing should discourage us from prayer, not our senselessness, nor fear, nor the temptations which steal in to pervert and pollute our holy desires. In all we must remember that God hears us from the Mercy-seat, sprinkled with the Blood of Jesus to stop the course of Divine Justice. He concludes with twelve Words of Advice to all God's people, telling them *inter alia* to expect temptations which are to be looked for the first day that they enter into Christ, 'his Congregation', to 'be jealous' of the deceits of the heart in the evidences for heaven, to beware flatteries, and to take heed of little sins.[60]

The End of the Journey

Bunyan himself testified that 'God led me into something of the mystery of union with Christ'.[61] This is not the union of the contemplative, the mystery into which the mystic enters. It is the union which is the 'focal theme' of Calvinist spirituality; the union which comes through faith, which is complementary to the love of God in the Catholic tradition. This union marks the beginning of the Christian life, what Bunyan's contemporary, the ejected Presbyterian minister Walter Marshall, closely following Calvin, called 'the first work of saving grace in our hearts'.[62] Yet it is described in Scripture in metaphors of the utmost intimacy—vine and branches, bread and eater. But this spirituality would hesitate to use the language of Deification in spite of the safeguards.[63] The distinction

---

[60] *Misc. Wks.*, ii. 285–6.   [61] *GA*, § 279.
[62] Walter Marshall, *The Gospel Mystery of Sanctification* (1692), pp. 51, 69. For Marshall see *DNB* and *CR*, s.v.
[63] See Vladimir Lossky, *The Mystical Theology of the Eastern Church* (1957) *passim*. For a Protestant critique see Ben Drewery's 'Deification' in Peter Brooks (ed.), *Christian Spirituality: Essays in Honour of Gordon Rupp* (1975), pp. 35–62.

between creature and Creator is always maintained. And the union never ignores the Church, the goodly fellowship of God's chosen people who, though saved individually through an intensity of personal conflict, travel together and reach the heaven which is a Celestial City, a glorified society of the saints.

Bunyan preached the Calvinist doctrine of the final perseverance of the saints rather than Catholic perfection. So much of his writing deals with sin of which the soul is always in danger. It has been questioned whether there is any real pilgrims' *progress*. There are different stages of the journey, there is at last the calm of Beulah land, corresponding perhaps to the greater serenity of Bunyan's own later years. (He does not face the problems of geriatrics, of senility, and the appalling distresses which some experience in years of dying.) But is there what Catholics would call an 'ontological' change through the work of Divine grace? Is it not a matter of imputed righteousness to the end, so that all the Christian can plead to the last is the righteousness of Christ and he remains a sinner, albeit a forgiven sinner, even as he goes into the presence of his God?

Many Evangelicals would be content to leave it like that. When Charles Simeon, the Cambridge preacher of the late eighteenth and early nineteenth centuries, deplored the vogue of ostentatious and triumphant deathbeds, he expressed his own desire in almost these words.[64] There is grave danger in perfectionism and nothing can so lead back into the self-preoccupation of sin as an attempt to measure one's own state of grace. John Wesley used some unguarded language in his eagerness to claim that because faith should make a difference to the kind of people we are and because we should set no limits to what God in Christ can do for us, we may judge ourselves to have attained perfect love in this life.[65] Did he take sufficient account of the corporate nature of sin and of the fact that in spite of our personal holiness we are 'involved in all mankind'?[66]

If, following Gregory of Nyssa and the Greek fathers, perfection is understood not as a state so much as a continual advance towards a transcendent glory which we attain only as we see that it beckons

---

[64] See Charles Smyth, *Simeon and Church Order* (Cambridge, 1940), p. 312. For Simeon see *DNB*, s.v.
[65] John Wesley, *Works*, 14 vols. (Wesleyan Conference Office, undated), xi. 401–2.
[66] The discussion by R. Newton Flew, *The Idea of Perfection*, pp. 313–41, is still an excellent appraisal and critique of Wesley's teaching.

us to heights we have yet to scale, it may be more compatible with Bunyan's analogy of pilgrimage.[67] Perseverance amid all temptations and hazards may not be so very different from it, though there is a difference of *ethos*, which must not be ignored.[68]

It must not be thought that the notion of imputed righteousness rules out a real transformation. This is notably expressed in George Herbert's 'Aaron'—and Herbert be it remembered was a Calvinist.[69] He implies a priestly vesting and Laudian ceremonial Bunyan would have eschewed; but in truth he is clad in profaneness, defects, and passion:

> Onely another head
> I have, another heart and breast,
> Another musick making live not dead,
>   Without whom I could have no rest:
>   In him I am well drest.
>
> Christ is my onely head
> My alone onely heart and breast,
> My onely musick, striking me ev'n dead;
>   That to the old man I may rest,
>   And be in him new drest.
>
> So holy in my head,
> Perfect and light in my deare breast,
> My doctrine tun'd by Christ, (who is not dead,

---

[67] See, e.g., Gregory of Nyssa, *The Life of Moses*, trans. and ed. Abraham J. Malherbe and Eeverett Ferguson (New York, 1978), esp. p. 116.

[68] No more succinct an account has been given of this than in Nathanial Micklem, *Prayers and Praises*, 2nd edn (1954), p. 13. 'The real significance of the Reformation is, I think, to be seen, not so much in formulation of doctrine or simplification of rite, as in a new religious apprehension of that which hitherto had been muffled or overlaid, though never quite denied, a new apprehension of reconciling grace; it was a change of emphasis, a deepening of religious experience in normal persons who laid no claim to being "mystics"; it was a resetting of an old picture with new perspectives and new outlines. It is true that the Roman Church practises the solemn rite of absolution and thereby brings to present experience the sense of sins forgiven, but typically and normally it points to the discipline of santification as the way to forgiveness and bliss at the last end of the journey, and not till then. The Reformed Church, in its turn, laid much stress upon sanctification through the discipline of God imposed by the duties and experiences of life (rather than by the regulation of a spiritual director); but primarily and typically it rejoiced in the experience of sins forgiven, and put first as the basis and presupposition of the Christian life that which the Roman Church in its distinctive emphasis puts last. . . . For my part, I venerate and love the solemn and sacred devotional discipline of other traditions, and would gladly learn from them, but our music, to be authentic and acceptable, must be written in a different mode or key.'

[69] See Joseph Summers, *George Herbert: His Religion and Art* (London and Cambridge, 1954), *passim*.

But lives in me while I do rest)
Come people; Aaron's drest.[70]

Max Beerbohm's often-quoted story of 'The Happy Hypocrite' is a secular illustration of the same truth. Lord George Hell falls in love with a chorus girl of sweetest innocence and purity and buys a mask to conceal his ravaged features and woo and win her as a handsome man. One day the mask melts. Lord George Hell confesses his deceit as the wax drips down, but the girl looks at him in amazement. The beauty of the mask was as nothing to that of the face which has become beautiful through wearing it.

Imputed righteousness, our putting on of Christ, our mystical union with him by faith does change us, but we may not be so conscious of it as to claim perfection or be dispensed from constant vigilance and clinging to the one with whose righteousness our sinful selves are clothed.

For Bunyan there is heightened joy because of the destruction from which we have been delivered and the grace which is rescuing us all the time from 'the perils and dangers of this life'. There are many glimpses of heaven from the pilgrim way. At the last there is the dark river, which is not a folk-memory of Styx, but rather the Jordan of Scripture.[71] Each pilgrim receives a different summons and finds the waters at a different temperature and depth. Christian comes near to sinking at one point, but all in the end reach the happy shore. There is no Gerontius-like revulsion from the sight of God, no Purgatory. Mr Stand-fast has the easiest passage of all, but his final words of a calm death and the joy set before him speak the hopes of all:

This River has been a Terror to many, yea the thoughts of it also have often frighted me. But now methinks I stand easie, my Foot is fixed upon that, upon which the Feet of the Priests that bare the Ark of the Covenant stood while *Israel* went over this *Jordan*. The Waters indeed are to the Palate bitter, and to the Stomack cold; yet the thoughts of what I am going to, and of the Conduct that waits me on the other side, doth lie as a glowing Coal at my Heart.

I see myself now at the *end* of my Journey, my *toilsom* Days are ended. I am going now to see *that* Head that was Crowned with Thorns, and *that* Face that was spit upon, for me.

[70] *The Works of George Herbert*, ed. F. E. Hutchinson (Oxford, 1941), p. 174.

[71] I do not reckon this to be a baptizing of the Charon myth, *pace* John A. T. Robinson, *On Being the Church in the World* (1960), p. 131.

I have formerly lived by Hear-say, and Faith, but now I go where I shall live by sight, and shall be with him, in whose Company I delight myself.[72]

Questions From Another Age

Revived interest in 'spirituality' these past twenty years has not meant a return to Bunyan as it has, for example, to Julian of Norwich. The decline and transmutation of English Dissent may have something to do with it, but there has been a shift over many decades in our understanding of sin. The analysts' consulting rooms may be full of men and women like Bunyan in his doubts and dreads yet without his sense of God, who is both a just God and a Saviour, but in the Churches there has been an increased preoccupation with social rather than individual sins, a Marxist belief that evil is in 'the system' rather than in personal deviations from accepted morality. Some of the present-day saints of popular Christian canonization have not always kept the commandments, but have protested with prophetic heroism against the evils of racism, inequality, poverty. Bunyan was in fact in opposition to the State and suffered for his nonconformity. He shows great compassion for the state of the poor and anger against the greed of the exploiting rich.[73] But he thinks within an economic philosophy already outmoded and could have no premonition of the industrial civilization yet to come, or of the aspirations and the problems of democracy in an over-populated world made small by technology.

The whole world is now, literally, a City of Destruction, on which annihilating fire may rain down at the press of a button. From this wrath to come no flight is possible. Its relation to the judgement of God foretold in Scripture is hard to determine. Those who see in it the promised end may be in danger of a fatalism which will hasten nuclear winter. Faith in God demands resistance to man's self-destructive folly and wickedness, not acquiescence in Armageddon as the Divine will in which the chosen will be safe.

Whether Bunyan's account of the Christian life has value for our time depends on whether we are able in any sense to believe in his God, to accept that our business in this world is mostly with God.

---

[72] *PP*, pp. 310–11.
[73] There is a fine study of Bunyan's 'Political and Social Thought' in Talon, pp. 282–304.

His God is the God of the Bible and of the Christian myth, not of the philosophers and scientists. There are those who feel that this God speaks to them and to their condition both in judgement and in mercy. The pilgrim image seems relevant not only as committed Christians meditate upon their lives and on the grace they need[74] but because so many of the world's poor and homeless have no abiding city and are menaced by giants of all kinds, from oppressive governments, of both Right and Left, to multinational corporations. The hymn sung by Mr Valiant-for-Truth no longer needs an editor of *The English Hymnal* to demythologize it.[75] And the faith, which like that of Abraham, ventures out at God's injunction, not knowing whither, seems intellectually, institutionally, and spiritually to be demanded in this age.

Are we finished with the Calvinist/Arminian controversy? No one would want a form of Christianity which creates such scruples about election, or seems to elevate human arbitrariness and vindictiveness to the throne of heaven, or limits the offer of Divine Grace for every sinner free, or restricts the scope of our prayers. Yet we need a faith beyond universalist optimism, which will not be at a loss when Christians are in a minority, nor expect easy and inevitable success; a faith which accepts hazards and vicissitudes as a proof of God's choice of us and which sings:

> Fear him ye saints and you will then
> Have nothing else to fear;

a faith which relies on a love which was before the foundation of the world and a mercy which sustains us from a Cross eternal in the heart of God.

---

[74] Cf. e.g. Basil, Cardinal Hume, *To Be a Pilgrim* (1984).
[75] PP, p. 295. Cf. *The English Hymnal* (1924; repr. 1933), no. 402.

7

Fishing in Other Men's Waters: Bunyan and the Theologians

BY GORDON CAMPBELL

IN common with other writers in the Puritan tradition Bunyan believed that his theological beliefs derived solely from the Bible. The preface to *Light for Them that Sit in Darkness* (1675) contains a characteristic statement of his position:

I have not . . . borrowed my Doctrine from Libraries. I depend upon the sayings of no man: I found it in the Scriptures of Truth, among the true sayings of God.[1]

This is a universal conviction among adherents of religions based on a sacred book. Its corollary is a denial of the historical development of doctrine in favour of an affirmation of its eternal truth. Bunyan's Roman Catholic contemporaries acknowledged that doctrines had developed through the accumulated theological wisdom of the centuries, and some Anglicans took a similar view, though they tended to truncate the canon of theologians on whose wisdom they would draw, preferring to look to the Church fathers rather than to medieval theologians. Other Anglicans argued, with William Chillingworth, that 'the Bible is the only religion of Protestants',[2] and Puritans enthusiastically concurred. Puritanism was professedly a religion of the Book, and Puritans deemed the Bible to be the sole and sufficient source of doctrine. In practice, however, the process of exegesis did not consist in teasing doctrines out of the Bible, but rather in reading doctrines in which they already believed into the Bible. The Bible is not, after all, a theological work, but rather a

---

[1] *Misc. Wks.*, viii. 51.
[2] See William Chillingworth, *The Religion of Protestants, A Safe Way to Salvation* (1638).

collection of narratives and epistles from which, at best, doctrines can be inferred; even the relatively explicit teaching of the apostle Paul stands in need of strenuous explication if it is to be transformed into the dogmas of the Christian faith. Most of the doctrines championed by Bunyan and his contemporaries were first expounded not in the Bible but in the writings of the theologians of late antiquity. In *Some Gospel-Truths Opened according to the Scriptures* (1656), for example, Bunyan poses a question to an imaginary interlocutor who is wondering whether he has been born again: 'when didst thou see . . . in the light of the spirit of Christ . . . that thou wert under the wrath of God because of original sin? Nay, dost thou know what original sin means?'[3] In the margin Bunyan prints a reference to Romans 5:12, in the belief that that verse demonstrates the authenticity of the doctrine of original sin, by which he means that the sin of Adam had been transmitted to all of Adam's descendants, and had thus corrupted the entire human race. But the origin of this doctrine is not to be found in the Greek text of the closing phrase of this verse, but rather in a mistranslation of that phrase by Ambrosiaster which was endorsed by Augustine, whose command of Greek was imperfect: both followed an Old Latin version in translating $\dot{\epsilon}\phi'\tilde{\omega}$ as *in quo* ('in whom'; it actually means 'because'), and construed it as a reference to Adam, 'in whom all sinned'.[4] The fact that the doctrine of original sin rested on a mistranslation did not impede its influence, and it became a central doctrine of the faith. Bunyan believed it, and believed it to be biblical.

To some extent the formulations of Bunyan's theology were shaped by the Bible which he read. His Bible was not the Latin (Junius–Tremellius), Greek, Hebrew, and Syriac versions favoured by learned Puritans. Bunyan could read no language other than English, and his Bible had of necessity to be an English Bible. It is not entirely clear which English translation he used, as the problem has not attracted scholarly investigation. My impression is that in his early works he relied on a sixteenth-century translation, probably the Geneva version; departures from that translation may be due to Bunyan's habit of quoting from memory, or he may have used one of the related translations. Sometimes his quotations from memory

---

[3] *Misc. Wks.*, i. 93.
[4] See J. N. D. Kelly, *Early Christian Doctrines*, 5th rev. edn. (1977), pp. 354, 363.

contain echoes of the Authorized (*King James*) Version, which he would have heard read in church, even if, in common with many Puritans and sectaries, he regarded it as an Anglican translation. Puritan distrust of the Authorized Version was deeply rooted. One manifestation of these misgivings was a bill presented to the Long Parliament in 1653; the bill, which was designed to enable revision of the Authorized Version, spoke darkly of its inaccuracies and 'prelatical language'. In his later works, on the other hand, Bunyan seems to have turned to the Authorized Version; sectarian misgivings about the Authorized Version were receding, and the new enemy was the *Book of Common Prayer*.

Bunyan's inability to read the Bible in its original languages made him vulnerable to attack from educated theologians, but Bunyan characteristically presented this limitation as a virtue. In a memorable exchange recorded by his friend Charles Doe, Bunyan's right to preach was once challenged by a scholar (probably Thomas Smith, Professor of Arabic at Cambridge) on the grounds that Bunyan did not have a Bible written in the original languages:

Then said Mr Bunyan, Have you the original? Yes, said the scholar. Nay, but, said Mr Bunyan, have you the very self-same original copies that were written by the penmen of the scriptures, prophets and apostles? No, said the scholar, but we have the true copies of those originals. How do you know that? said Mr Bunyan. How? said the scholar. Why, we believe what we have is a true copy of the original. Then, said Mr Bunyan, so I do believe our English Bible is a true copy of the original. Then away rid the scholar.[5]

In some book-centred religions adherents are obliged to study and recite the holy book in its original language, and translations into the vernacular are forbidden. Seventeenth-century sectarians were unusual in their elevation of an English translation to the status of a holy book. Bunyan never felt the need to learn the biblical languages, and never attempted to refer to the Greek or Hebrew text when formulating his theological views. In Bunyan's account of his examination before the Justices in November 1660, he records that William Foster, a Bedford lawyer, accused him of ignorance of the Bible in that he knew no Greek. Bunyan replied:

that if that was his opinion, that none could understand the Scriptures, but those that had the original Greek, &c. then but a very few of the poorest

[5] *Works*, iii. 767; cf. Brown, pp. 114–17.

sort should be saved, (this is harsh) yet the Scripture saith, *That God hides his things from the wise and prudent*, (that is from the learned of the world) *and reveals them to babes and sucklings*.[6]

Bunyan saw his religion as the faith of the poor. As the study of Greek was restricted to the wealthy educated classes to whom God denied access to his wisdom, the poor who could not study Greek had a privileged access to the wisdom of the Bible. In *A Few Sighs from Hell* (1658) he poured scorn on those who would not honour the '*Lazarus's*' of Jesus because 'they are not Gentlemen, because they cannot, with *Pontius Pilate*, speak Hebrew, Greek, and Latine';[7] he viewed competence in the biblical languages not merely with suspicion, but with contempt.

Alongside the Bible Bunyan used a second book which for Puritans assumed the status of a holy book. As he explained in the preface to *Solomon's Temple Spiritualized* (1688), 'my Bible and Concordance are my only library in my writings'.[8] The concordance was a powerful weapon, because it enabled Bunyan to assemble pieces of evidence in support of a doctrine, in much the same way that some modern historians 'lump' evidence together to illustrate their points.[9] Unfortunately we do not know which concordance Bunyan used for his early writings, but his signature on a 1673 edition of the radical Vavasor Powell's *Concordance* (now in the library of the Baptist College in Bristol) suggests that in later life he used the concordance of a man with whom he had in common a long experience of incarceration.

Bunyan's insistence that he used only a Bible and a concordance is coupled with a disclaimer to the effect that he had not 'fished in other men's waters'. An investigation of Bunyan's theology must inevitably have as its starting-point an assertion that Bunyan was a piscatory poacher. Some of the doctrines which Bunyan adopted were currently fashionable, while others were nearing the end of their history. Bunyan seems, for example, to have been one of the last prominent Christians to have believed in the medieval notion that one of the delights of heaven will be the contemplation of the torture being undergone by those in hell: 'when the godly think of hell, it will

---

[6] *A Relation of the Imprisonment of Mr John Bunyan*, in *GA*, p. 111.
[7] *Misc. Wks.*, i. 304.   [8] *Works*, iii. 464.
[9] J. H. Hexter charges Christopher Hill with 'lumping' in *TLS* 3841 (24 Oct. 1975), 1250–2.

increase their comfort'.¹⁰ The blood-chilling enthusiasm which Bunyan brings to his lurid descriptions of the tortures of hell in tracts such as *A Few Sighs from Hell* reflects a gusto for the suffering of one's fellow men that was becoming less acceptable as the doctrine of hell declined in popularity.¹¹

The ultimate origins of Bunyan's theology lie in the formulations of the Latin fathers, but my concern in this essay will be to outline more immediate origins in Protestant theology. Unlike his Anglican contemporaries, Bunyan did not study theology at one of the ancient universities. Indeed, he boasted of his lack of formal education—'I never went to School to *Aristotle* or *Plato*'¹²—and at times, as we have seen, endorsed the radical view that knowledge is an impediment for the Christian. The Holy Spirit was deemed a better teacher than Oxford or Cambridge. In the epigram of a fellow radical, Samuel How,

> The Spirit's teaching in a cobbler's shop,
> Doth Oxford and Cambridge o'retop.¹³

Bunyan did, however, draw furtively on the writings of a few university theologians. I have argued elsewhere¹⁴ that Bunyan's *Mapp of Salvation* ([1664?]), a diagrammatic exposition of his theology, derives directly from a diagram in William Perkins's *Golden Chain*. Similarly, Richard Greaves, the best student of Bunyan's theology, has traced Bunyan's covenant theology to the covenantal teachings of Perkins and his student William Ames.¹⁵

Some of Bunyan's doctrines can be traced to learned sources, but the main source of his theological doctrines, and his sense of whether adherence to any particular doctrine was essential to salvation, must have derived from the collective beliefs of the Independent Bedford Church which he attended, and of which in due course he became

---

¹⁰ *The Resurrection of the Dead*, in *Works*, ii. 127. The humane Richard Baxter shared this view: see *The Saints Everlasting Rest*, 2nd edn. (1651), i. 96.

¹¹ See D. P. Walker, *The Decline of Hell* (1964).

¹² *The Doctrine of the Law and Grace Unfolded*, in *Misc. Wks.*, ii. 16.

¹³ Cit. *Works*, ii. 278. For How see *BDBR*, s.v. and above, pp. 92-3.

¹⁴ See 'The Source of Bunyan's *Mapp of Salvation*', *Journal of the Warburg and Courtauld Institutes*, 44 (1981), 240-1, pl. 38-9, in which the date is misprinted as 1646 instead of 1664.

¹⁵ See three discussions of Bunyan and covenant theology by Richard L. Greaves: Greaves, pp. 97-121, *Misc. Wks.*, ii. xxi-xxxii, and 'John Bunyan and Covenant Thought in the Seventeenth Century', *Church History*, 36 (1967), 151-69.

pastor. Baptism is a good example. The question of whether baptism was essential to salvation or merely an emblem of salvation was in Bunyan's time a subject of violent controversy. Bunyan's position on this issue was markedly tolerant, but he none the less entered into this debate with all the acerbity and vituperation which characterized seventeenth-century theological debate. Similarly, arguments about the correct mode—immersion, submersion, or infusion—and the correct time—in infancy (paedobaptism) or on conversion (believer's baptism) or on the deathbed (clinical baptism)—had raged since at least the time of the *Didache* in late antiquity through Church fathers such as Tertullian and Augustine up to the Reformers and thence to Bunyan's time.

The minutes of the *Church Book* of the Bedford Church confirm that baptism was still a contentious issue. At the meeting on 'the 28th of the 3rd moneth' (i.e. 28 June 1656), for example, it was recorded that 'our brother Cromp desires to stay still upon the account of baptisme' and that 'our sister Linford having upon the account of baptisme, (as shee pretended) withdrawne from the congregation was required to be at this meeting to render a reason for her so doing.'[16] Thirty-five years later (and several years after Bunyan's death) the congregation was still arguing about the matter; Ebenezer Chandler records that:

with respect to baptisme, I have my liberty to baptise infants without making it my bisiness to promote it amonst others, and every member to have his liberty in beleivers' baptisme, onely to forebare discourse and debates on it that may have a tendency to break the peace of the Church . . . we doe not designe to make baptisme, whether of belivers' or infants, any bar to communion.[17]

The final phrase echoes the title of Bunyan's *Differences in Judgment about Water-Baptism, No Bar to Communion* (1673). Bunyan felt strongly that baptism was not a means of grace, and was therefore a matter for individual conscience. He affirmed as much in his *Confession of My Faith* (1672), in which he had argued against the view that baptism 'is the initiating and entering ordinance into church communion'.[18] This tolerant view provoked Baptist controversialists into challenging Bunyan to a public debate in London, and (when Bunyan declined) writing a tract attacking his

[16] *Minutes*, pp. 23, 22. [17] *Minutes*, pp. 93–4. [18] *Works*, ii. 605.

view. This attack hardened Bunyan's position, and clarified his views. He replied with *Differences in Judgment*, which begins with a withering attack on his opponents and then confronts their fourteen arguments, declaring that he will 'impartially consider them'. This assertion of impartiality may seem surprising to anyone who samples this strident polemic, but it should be realized that Bunyan was not merely scoring a debating point: religious belief is in its nature partisan, and Bunyan was defending a belief which he already held, not impartially examining the views of his opponents. This attack on the Baptist view that the baptism of conscious believers was a prerequisite for communion is not of course an attack on the baptism of believers, of which Bunyan was an advocate. Believer's baptism was the only form of baptism available in the Bedford Church until Chandler became pastor, and in Part II of *The Pilgrim's Progress* Christiana and her children profess their faith at the House of the Interpreter and then immerse themselves in 'The Bath Sanctification', as Bunyan calls it in his marginal note.[19]

Despite this advocacy of believer's baptism, Bunyan arranged for his three children to be baptized as infants. The parish register of Elstow records the baptism of his daughter Mary on 20 July 1650 (before Bunyan joined the Bedford Church) and the 'birth' (i.e. baptism)[20] of his daughter Elizabeth on 14 April 1654 (within a year of Bunyan's admission into the Bedford Church), and the register of St Cuthbert's (Bedford) records the baptism of his son Joseph on 16 November 1672, the year in which Bunyan wrote his *Confession of my Faith*, in which he attacked benighted creatures who rely on the efficacy of christening.[21] The christening of his own children may have been no more than a form of spiritual fire insurance, but it may reflect a private conviction at odds with the public stance which Bunyan was forced to adopt in the face of an onslaught from closed-communion Baptists in competition with his own church for the hearts of believers. When reproached by the Baptists for using 'the arguments of the paedobaptist', Bunyan replies 'I ingenuously tell you, I know not what paedo means'[22].

---

[19] *Works*, ii. 635; *PP*, p. 207.
[20] An Act of Parliament of 1653 had ordered that 'births' rather than 'baptisms' be recorded in parish registers. In the Bishop's transcript of the Elstow parish for 1653 Elizabeth is again recorded as having been 'borne', as are the other twenty-two children listed s.v. 'christenings'.
[21] *Works*, ii. 615.   [22] *Works*, ii. 654.

In common with all except the most radical of Christians, Bunyan believed in the doctrine of the Trinity. His affirmation of the Trinity is a good example of a belief which cannot be traced to the Bible for the simple reason that there is no biblical doctrine of the Trinity. It is possible on biblical evidence to mount an argument of some respectability for the divinity of Jesus, but it is a long step from that doctrine to a belief in a triune godhead. The doctrine of the Trinity was first articulated by Theophilus of Antioch late in the second century; Theophilus discerned a divine triad ($\tau\varrho\iota\alpha s$) of God and his word and his wisdom, though his sense of the two latter terms distinguishes his Trinity from later versions.[23] The notion of one god existing in three equal persons was not hardened into dogma until the Council of Constantinople in 381, although various Trinitarian theories had been championed in the preceding centuries as monotheistic Judaic Christianity absorbed the Trinitarian formulations of Neoplatonism. Trinitarianism has always had its detractors; in the early Church various manifestations of subordinationism had to be dealt with, and a radical strain in Reformation theology survived in Bunyan's time in the form of Socinianism and Unitarianism;[24] even Bunyan's older contemporary Milton thought the doctrine of the Trinity unbiblical, and therefore rejected it.[25]

The doctrine of the Trinity was central to Bunyan's theoretical sense of his faith. In *The House of the Forest of Lebanon* (1692) he proclaimed 'The Doctrine of the Trinity! that is the substance, that is the ground and fundamental of all. For by this doctrine, and by this only, the man is made a Christian; and he that has not this doctrine, his profession is not worth a button.'[26] It seems odd that in his profuse writings Bunyan only once attempted a theological exposition of the doctrine of the Trinity. This exposition is contained in his *Exposition on the First Ten Chapters of Genesis* (1692). He begins, as is his habit, with a quotation from the Bible, seizing on 1 John 5: 7 ('the Father, the Word, and the Holy Ghost: and these three are one').[27] It is hard to believe that Bunyan did not know that

---

[23] On Theophilus's holy triad see Kelly, *Early Christian Doctrines*, pp. 99–104.

[24] See H. J. MacLachlan, *Socinianism in Seventeenth-century England* (1951); Alexander Gordon, *Heads of English Unitarian History* (1895); and E. M. Wilbur, *A History of Unitarianism* (Cambridge, Mass., 1952).

[25] See Maurice Kelley, '*Antitrinitarianism*', in *Complete Prose Works of John Milton*, ed. Don M. Wolfe, 8 vols. (New Haven, 1953–82), vi. 47–73.

[26] *Works*, iii. 520.   [27] *Works*, ii. 415.

this verse had been widely recognized as a spurious seventh-century insertion into the text of the Bible; it seems more likely that he was aware of the challenge to its authenticity, and chose to ignore it on the grounds that his English Bible, which included the verse, was 'a true copy of the original'. Initially Bunyan tries to resist the scholastic terminology around which debates about the nature of the Trinity had revolved:

> Now the godly in former ages have called these three, thus in the Godhead, Persons or Subsistances; the which, though I condemn not, yet choose rather to abide by scripture phrase, knowing, though the other may be good and sound, yet the adversary must needs more shamelessly spurn and reject, when he doth it against the evident text.[28]

The nervous admission that the terms of traditional Trinitarian debate 'may be good and sound' amounts to an admission that Bunyan is out of his depth. The 'scripture phrase' on which he rests his case consists of one word: 'three'. He goes on to affirm the version of the Trinity which was current in the western Church, insisting on the coequality of the three persons. The extent to which Bunyan failed to grasp the finer points of the doctrine of the Trinity is illustrated visually in his diagrammatic *Mapp of Salvation*.[29] The doctrine of the double procession of the Holy Spirit, according to which the Spirit had proceeded conjointly from the Father and the Son, had made the equilateral triangle a popular symbol of God in the western Church (in the east inter-Trinitarian procession, the belief that the Son was generated by the Father and that the Spirit proceeded from the Son, encouraged the use of a line rather than a triangle), and, accordingly, Bunyan placed a triangle at the top of his chart. Traditionally the three corners of the triangle represented the Father, Son, and Holy Spirit, and the centre of the triangle was occupied by an appropriate symbol of godhead, such as an eye. But Bunyan placed 'God' at the vertex of his triangle, 'Father' on the lower left, and 'Spirit' on the lower right. In the centre, in defiance of orthodox Christian theology, he placed the 'Son', and accentuated his position by printing underneath the name of the Son the phrase 'he is Lord of all'. This gaffe provides the clearest possible illustration of Bunyan's conviction that the Son is the most important figure in the

---

[28] *Works*, ii. 415. [29] *Works*, iii, between pp. 348 and 349.

godhead. In an earlier century he could have been burnt for this aberration, but in the sectarian thought of the late seventeenth century (and its twentieth-century successors), the Son is the central figure of the Christian faith. Bunyan subscribed to a version of the Trinitarian doctrine which he shared with his Anglican and Roman Catholic contempories, but his theological works exalt the Son to a degree which would have offended those contemporaries.

The reason for this elevation of the Son is that Bunyan's faith centred on the quest for salvation rather than the worship of God, and that salvation was deemed to derive from the Son. In Anglican and Catholic theology soteriology (the doctrine of salvation) was not a central concern, because it was assumed that salvation was available to all who grew up in a Christian country. In the view of Bunyan and his fellow sectarians, however, salvation was reserved for a tiny minority of committed Christians who would be snatched from the eternal bonfires which awaited most of their countrymen, and the ascertaining of whether one was on the list of those exempted from eternal torment was the central concern of their lives as believers. Accordingly, *The Pilgrim's Progress* is a soterial journey, and *Grace Abounding to the Chief of Sinners*, Bunyan's spiritual autobiography, is the record of a search for assurance that Bunyan is one of the elect. Soteriology is the focal point of Bunyan's theology, and it is the background to that doctrine to which I should now like to turn.

Bunyan subscribed to the doctrine known as double predestination, according to which God not only chose those who were to be saved, but also those who were to be condemned to an eternity in hell. Double predestination has a long history. Its first formulation may tentatively be attributed to Gottschalk, a ninth-century Saxon monk who based his doctrine on an elaboration of doctrines taught by Augustine and his follower, the North African bishop, Fulgentius. Gottschalk's doctrine was condemned by the Church as a denial of the universal saving will of God, and he was accordingly imprisoned for the rest of his life. His doctrine was condemned at the Synod of Mainz in 848. A doctrine which privileges a minority has considerable appeal for minorities, and double predestination continued to find advocates. At the Reformation its chief exponent was John Calvin, who openly denied the universal saving will of God, and argued that the Son died only for the elect. Those who were to be damned had been condemned by God for reasons known only to himself, and not because of any particular fault on the part of the victim.

Bunyan's soteriology, like his affirmation of the Trinity, has a public face which is slightly at odds with his private convictions and practices. Although Bunyan never wrote an analytical theological treatise on the subject (unless he was the author of *Reprobation Asserted* ([1674?])),[30] he did write a polemical treatise on justification directed against the Anglican divine, Edward Fowler, and he often commented on predestination and reprobation in the course of his writings. He insisted that 'this decree, choice or election was before the foundation of the world, and so before the elect themselves, had being in themselves';[31] elsewhere he argues that 'grace signifies that God still acts in this as a free agent, not being wrought upon by misery of the creature, as a procuring cause; but of his own princely mind'.[32] These statements suggest that Bunyan subscribed to the subspecies of Calvinism known as supralapsarianism (or ante-lapsarianism), according to which God selected individuals for salvation before the fall of man, and without being motivated by the plight of fallen man.[33] In adopting this hardline position, he was inevitably in opposition to moderate Calvinists (sub-, infra-, or post-lapsarians) who attempted to make God's act seem more reasonable by asserting that he did not determine the fate of individuals until after the Fall. Proponents of these views, and of the opposing Arminian doctrines in which predestination was rejected in favour of a theology emphasizing freedom of the human will, could all prove the correctness of their own positions by selective quotation from the Bible, and this is precisely what Bunyan did. In the tradition which Bunyan championed, God was deemed to have chosen candidates for salvation and damnation without reference to their relative merits and for reasons known only to himself, and to have sent his Son to die for the former group; this denial that Christ died for all mankind is the central tenet of the doctrine of limited atonement. When God chose by his grace to elect an individual to salvation, that grace was irresistible and inadmissible. That view left no room for man's exercise of his free will, but Bunyan did not

---

[30] Richard L. Greaves disputes Bunyan's authorship in 'John Bunyan and the Authorship of *Reprobation Asserted*', *BQ* 21 (1965), 126-31; Paul Helm reasserts the claim for Bunyan's authorship in 'John Bunyan and *Reprobation Asserted*', *BQ* 28 (1979), 87-93.
[31] *Works*, ii, 598.   [32] *Works*, i. 644.
[33] For an opposing view which claims Bunyan as an infra-lapsarian, see Greaves, p. 52.

flinch from this consequence: he insisted that 'there is no such thing in man by nature, as liberty of will, or a principle of freedom, in the saving things of the kingdom of God'.[34] Even if man did wish to be saved, he insisted on various occasions, he did not want to be saved in the way that God wanted to save him.

This doctrine had a counterpart in spiritual autobiography, one of the conventions of which (for those of Bunyan's persuasion) was that one did not seek salvation by means of personal reformation, but rather looked inwards for signs of the operation of God's grace, with a view to establishing whether or not one had been elected to salvation. In *Grace Abounding* Bunyan explains that what he doubts is 'whether I was elected', having grasped that:

> unless the great God of his infinite grace and bounty, had voluntarily chosen me to be a vessel of mercy, though I should desire, and long, and labour untill my heart did break, no good could come of it. Therefore, this would still stick with me, How can you tell if you are Elected? and what if you should not? how then?[35]

Bunyan's sentiments were shaped by the Calvinist doctrines of the congregation into which he had been converted, and the language of the *Church Book* uses the same theological vocabulary. It was not sufficient to declare that one wished to join the congregation on the grounds that one subscribed to the principles of the faith. At a meeting on 'the 25th of the 10th moneth' (i.e. 25 January 1657) it was agreed:

> that such persons as desire to joyne in fellowship, if upon the conference of our friends with them, who shall be sent for that purpose, our saide friends be satisfyed of the truth of the worke of grace in their heartes, then they shall desire them to come to the next church-meeting, and to waite near the place assigned for the meeting, that they may be called in.[36]

The congregation required a detailed account of the work of grace; such an account is presented when Christian is accepted into the Palace Beautiful.

Clearly the discovery that one has been elected to salvation is a happy one. But 'what if you should not? how then?' The theological

---

[34] *A Defence of the Doctrine of Justification*, in *Works*, ii. 312. For the controversies between Calvinists and Arminians, see Alan P. Sell, *The Great Debate: Calvinism, Arminianism, and Salvation* (Worthing, 1982).

[35] *GA*, § 59   [36] *Minutes*, p. 24.

answer to the question exposes the harsh face of Calvinism; nothing can be done if one happens not to have been chosen, and despite the best efforts of the penitent he will be justly condemned for his sins to an eternity of torment. Bunyan's theological attitude to those who have not been chosen is one of resignation. Discussing the fate of Pliable in *The Pilgrim's Progress*, Faithful says, 'But who can hinder that which will be?' and Christian proposes that Pliable be abandoned: 'let us leave him, and talk of things that more immediately concern ourselves'. The Christian's own spiritual welfare is his primary responsibility. That is why Christian must desert his family in his quest for salvation: 'the Man began to run; Now he had not run far from his own door, but his Wife and Children perceiving it, began to cry after him to return: but the man put his fingers in his Ears, and ran on crying Life, Life, Eternal Life: so he looked not behind him, but fled'. Those passed over for election, in Bunyan's view, are justly condemned for their sins. The position is clearly different if the person who has not been elected is oneself. The anguish of *Grace Abounding* on this point occasions a search for signs of grace. The problem for the practising Christian who suffers doubts, Bunyan explains in a Biblical commentary, is that 'the Holy Ghost doth not use to confirm us by new revelations of grace and justification'.[37]

A system according to which individuals have their fate determined aeons before they are born clearly leaves little room for the free exercise of human will. And because free will was associated with Arminians and other hell-bound heretics, Bunyan was determined to dissociate himself from its taint. In his last sermon he was still insisting that 'I am not a free-willer, I do abhor it'.[38] It is in this aspect of Bunyan's soteriology that a discrepancy arises between the theological position which he had inherited from the Bedford congregation and his practical private beliefs. Although he insisted in theory that the human will could play no part in salvation, in practice he never ceased to exhort his congregation and his readers to repent of their sins. And in allegorical works such as *Mr Badman* and *The Holy War*, the insistence on the need for repentance is so strong, and the will so important, that did one not know

---

[37] *An Exposition on the First Ten Chapters of Genesis*, in *Works*, ii. 481; *PP*, pp. 10, 68.
[38] *Mr Bunyan's Last Sermon*, in *Works*, ii. 756.

otherwise one would suspect that they had been written by a 'free-willer'.

Bunyan's soteriology, according to which most of mankind is condemned to eternal torment by the whim of God, is bound to seem repugnant to many twentieth-century readers. It is one of the paradoxes of the English literary tradition that such an apparently abhorrent theology should have given rise to a work of the imaginative greatness of *The Pilgrim's Progress*. A sympathetic understanding of that theology is much more difficult to achieve than is a comparable sympathy with the theology which informs the poems of writers such as Homer, because the process of deconversion from Christianity is not yet complete, whereas no one believes any longer in the capricious gods who populate Homer's poems. The study of Homer's theology may be hampered by our inability to engage with the beliefs of a culture so remote from our own, but we are at least spared emotional entanglement with that theology. Bunyan presents the opposite problem, for his religion is still alive, and the response of the modern student to his theology is complicated by the degree of belief or disbelief which the student brings to that theology. The problem is particularly acute in Bunyan's doctrinal and expository works, but it also impinges on popular perceptions of his allegories. Because Bunyan's theology impinges to some extent on *The Pilgrim's Progress*, students of literature too often dismiss it as a book which champions a faith to which they feel hostile, if they are non-believers, or which they find distastefully evangelical, if they subscribe quiescently to a liberal form of Christianity. But the redeeming literary quality of *The Pilgrim's Progress* resides in the fact that Bunyan's imagination transcends his theological convictions, in much the same way that his energetic pursuit of souls shows a compassion for the fate of the dispossessed which rises above his cold theological conviction that an overwhelming proportion of humanity has been consigned irrevocably to hell. *The Pilgrim's Progress* is not in its essentials an allegorical presentation of Bunyan's theology.[39] Indeed, his cruel God does not even appear in the narrative. It pictures Christian in a world without God, and is only unattractive in those rare instances in which God intervenes in Christian's life, such as the occasion when the narrative is disrupted by Christian's

---

[39] I develop this view in 'The Theology of *The Pilgrim's Progress*', in Newey, pp. 251–62.

improbable discovery of the Key of Promise in his bosom. The doctrine of election which was so central to Bunyan's theological beliefs does not inform Christian's progress, and the related doctrine of reprobation impinges only by way of an explanation for Christian's resigned attitude to the fate of Pliable. Such moments are rare in *The Pilgrim's Progress*, most of which is concerned with Christian's struggle to find his way to his destiny with no supernatural support. And although Christian meets others on his journey, that journey is essentially solitary. This motif is a powerful theme in English literature, and Bunyan's imaginative and sympathetic presentation of Christian's journey makes *The Pilgrim's Progress* attractive even to those readers who cannot subscribe to Bunyan's theology.

8

'Thou must live upon my Word': Bunyan and the Bible

BY JOHN R. KNOTT, jun.

Interpreting and Applying the Word

WHEN Bunyan was arrested for preaching in November of 1660, he took his stand upon the biblical injunction: '*As every man hath received the gift, even so let him minister the same unto another*'.[1] If God's imperatives clashed with man's, in this case an Elizabethan act against Nonconformists, Bunyan's choice was clear, even though his refusal to submit to the law meant prison and the possibility of banishment. Like the Protestant martyrs whose cases he knew from John Foxe's *Acts and Monuments*, Bunyan insisted upon taking God's Word as the arbiter of truth, meeting with Scripture the accusations of his judges and the exhortations to submit of the seeming friends who counselled him. The justices saw Bunyan as 'a breaker of the peace',[2] who stubbornly refused every opportunity, informal as well as formal, to indicate that he would return to his parish church and give up preaching in conformity with the law. Bunyan saw himself as a potential martyr in the line of Paul and all those whose constancy in the face of persecution was celebrated by Foxe: 'I am willing to lie down, and to suffer what they shall do to me.'[3]

The series of pastoral letters that make up *A Relation of The Imprisonment* (1765) offers a particularly dramatic demonstration of how thoroughly the Bible had come to condition Bunyan's thinking and behaviour in the early years of his preaching.[4] Rather than

---

[1] 1 Pet. 4: 10; *GA*, pp. 108, 117.   [2] *GA*, p. 127.   [3] *GA*, p. 125.
[4] See Roger Sharrock, 'The Origin of *A Relation of the Imprisonment of Mr John Bunyan*,' *RES*, new ser. 10 (1959), 250-6. Sharrock discusses the circumstances

avoid arrest, as friends counselled him, he saw it as a test of his loyalty to the Gospel and his trust in the will of God; he thought that his imprisonment, in the early days of persecution under the Restoration, might prove 'an awakening to the Saints in the country'.[5] In prison Bunyan counted on Scripture to strengthen him against temptation and to supply him with arguments. At one point during his examination he imagined God sending him the appropriate text to respond to the interrogating justice, 'as if the Scripture had said, Take me, take me'.[6]

The foundation of Bunyan's resistance, to ostensibly friendly counsellors as well as to threatening Justices, was his insistence upon understanding the Bible literally, even when the truth contradicted the world's wisdom. Thus he took biblical exhortations to pray with the Spirit as making it impossible for him to accept the set forms of the *Book of Common Prayer* urged upon him by the Justices. He found himself before his examiners in the first place because he understood the injunction to minister according to one's gift as a command to preach the Gospel rather than, as his chief examiner patronizingly suggested, to follow his calling as a tinker. Bunyan shook off the argument of the Clerk of the Peace that the Bible was subject to differing interpretations. He insisted that Scripture would 'open itself' to one who knew how to read it, and he was confident of his own grasp of God's truth.

Bunyan's first two published works, *Some Gospel-Truths Opened* (1656) and *A Vindication of Some Gospel-Truths Opened* (1657), show him defining his understanding of Scripture and demonstrating the intensity of his commitment to its 'truths' in response to the challenge of Quakers active in Bedfordshire. In Bunyan's view the Quaker insistence upon a Christ *'crucified within . . . risen again within'*[7] corrupted Scripture by failing to distinguish between 'justification wrought by the man Christ without, and sanctification wrought by the Spirit of Christ, within'.[8] By spiritualizing the life of Christ the Quakers threatened the very basis of Bunyan's sense of scriptural truth. In response he insisted upon the necessity of believing in the 'blood of the Son' and assembled texts to prove the

---

surrounding the eventual publication of the work and speculates that it originated in letters from Bunyan to his congregation.

[5] *GA*, p. 113. [6] *GA*, p. 115. [7] *Misc. Wks.*, i. 20.
[8] *Misc. Wks.*, i. 156.

reality of the crucifixion and the resurrection. It was crucial to Bunyan that one believe in the literal truth of the events of Christ's life and accept the fact that 'the very man Christ' would return in judgement. The Quakers were to him 'false prophets,' no better than the Ranters, because they turned the core of the New Testament into an allegory of the action of the Holy Spirit in man. Bunyan's visualization of the scene in which the risen Christ appears to the disciples, elaborating it in such a way as to draw out its dramatic potential, gives a good indication of the character of his literalism: 'what, doe you thinke that I am a spirit? Do you think your eyes dazle? *behold my hands and my feet*. Look well upon me, and see my hands, and the holes in them; and likewise my feet, and the holes in them, and know that it is I myself, and not a spirit, as you suppose.'[9] The empathy that Bunyan demonstrates here suggests how he was able to enter into the life of biblical events and make them as real for his audience as they were for him.

When, in Bunyan's earliest published sermon, *A Few Sighs from Hell* (1658), a damned soul confesses with what stubbornness he had rejected the 'gentle and blessed profers of the Gospel', we perhaps catch a glimpse of the indifference to Scripture Bunyan had had himself to overcome. The preacher threatened hell and alleged 'many a Scripture', but he might as well have been speaking to a post: 'The Scriptures, thought I, what are they? a dead letter, a little ink and paper, of three or four shillings price. Alas, what is the Scripture, give me a Ballad, a Newsbook, *George* on horseback, or *Bevis* of *Southampton* . . . but for the holy Scriptures I cared not.'[10] This picture of impiety lends force to Bunyan the preacher's call to ground one's life in the Word of God:

Would thou know what thou art, and what is in thy heart, then search the Scriptures . . . The Scriptures I say, they are able to give a man perfect instruction into any of the things of God necessary to faith and godliness, if he have but an honest heart, seriously to weigh and ponder the several things contained in them.[11]

Bunyan follows his assertion with four pages of questions keyed to scriptural texts that answer them. Like Puritans generally, Bunyan saw Scripture as providing the answers to all questions about how

---

[9] *Misc. Wks.*, i. 72.   [10] *Misc. Wks.*, i, 333.
[11] *Misc. Wks.*, i. 324–5.

one should live. The 'rule of the Word' was the key to the godliness that should flow naturally from faith. Bunyan showed how to apply this rule to the particulars of daily life, as in *Christian Behaviour* (1663), where he derives the duties of the master of the family, wife, children, and servants from Scripture. He made the dangers of ignoring the 'rule' vividly apparent in *Mr Badman*, which illustrates the desperate consequences of a neglect of Scripture that hardens into rejection. Mr Badman's progressive degeneration can be traced to his refusal to admit the influence of the Word. Bunyan judges all his actions, even sharp business practices, by applying the 'rule of the Word'.

The Bible could become a manual of godly living for the faithful, a source of instruction in such matters as how to conduct a Christian household. Yet it also functioned as a touchstone by which to test one's spiritual condition. It was necessary to 'search the Scriptures', as Puritan preachers frequently urged, to achieve the faith that made true godliness possible. In the catechism he wrote for his Bedford Church, *Instruction for the Ignorant* (1675), Bunyan refers his hypothetical questioner repeatedly to Scripture. If one seeks to know God: 'Let him apply his heart unto the Scriptures, as unto a light that shineth in a dark place (even this World) until the day dawn, and the day-Star arise in his heart'.[12] If he wants to know his sins in order to confess them, he 'must then search and try [*his*] ways by the holy Word of God'.[13] In his sermons Bunyan frequently urges his audience to apply a particular doctrine to themselves, to test themselves by the Word. Such testing was critical to the continuing struggle to establish a secure and deepening faith.

It was not enough, however, to accept the necessity for consulting the Bible and applying it to the spiritual and practical questions of one's life. A deep and persistent concern with *how* one should experience Scripture runs through Bunyan's works. In *A Holy Life* (1684), written near the end of his career, Bunyan makes a favourite distinction between those to whom the Gospel comes 'in word only' and those to whom it comes in power.[14] The former may be so taken with the 'sound of the word' that they are willing to profess it, but they are merely 'wordy Professors', or 'notionists', as Bunyan calls them elsewhere. At their worst these are blatant hypocrites such

---

[12] *Misc. Wks.*, viii. 21. [13] *Misc. Wks.*, viii. 22.
[14] *Misc. Wks.*, ix. 285.

as Talkative or By-ends in *The Pilgrim's Progress*, types that Bunyan was quick to detect among those who claimed the name of Christian. These false professors abound in his writings, testimony to the severity of the standards of faith and holiness that he applied and the seriousness with which he took the problem of distinguishing a genuine from a merely superficial grasp of Scripture.

Bunyan gave frequent indications of what he believed it meant to experience the power of the Word. One has to 'Tremble at the Word of God',[15] in Bunyan's view, to be able to feel in the heart the 'threatnings' of the Law and the 'promises' of the Gospel. The first step toward salvation is to experience what Bunyan called 'the condemning, killing, and destroying power of the law'[16] to convict one of sin; then one is ready to experience the power of the Gospel to 'comfort, quicken, and revive' the soul.[17] Only thus, Bunyan shows at length in *The Doctrine of the Law and Grace Unfolded* (1659), can one learn to speak of the things of the Law and the Gospel 'experimentally', and move from the 'Legal Spirit' of confidence in one's own righteousness to the 'Gospel Spirit' of trust in the embracing love of God. Bunyan's almost physical sense of the force of Scripture comes through again and again in his works, in his accounts of the 'terrible words' of judgement and their opposite, the 'sweet' and 'warm' words embodying the promise of grace, often compared with the 'comfortable' beams of sunlight.[18]

Bunyan's account of his own early encounters with Scripture in *Grace Abounding* offers the most compelling evidence of his sense of the power of the Word. There he traces the process by which he awakened to the truth of Scripture, from insensibility, to hypersensitivity to its apparently conflicting messages, to assurance of his own salvation. Critics have commented on the way disembodied texts take hold of Bunyan's imagination, at one moment seeming to damn him and at the next offering the prospect of grace.[19] Recent commentary has shown how much Bunyan's conception of opposing forces of law and grace, acting through

---

[15] *Misc. Wks.*, viii. 25.   [16] *Misc. Wks.*, i. 354.
[17] *Misc. Wks.*, i. 356.   [18] *Misc. Wks.*, viii. 267.
[19] See, e.g., Sharrock, pp. 60 ff.; Talon, pp. 62, 135. Peter J. Carlton, 'Bunyan: Language, Convention, Authority,' *ELH* 51 (1984), 17–32, has argued more recently that in talking about biblical passages as falling upon him Bunyan was using 'disclaiming locutions' to attribute to God, or the devil, responsibility for his own thoughts.

individual texts, owes to Luther's *Commentary on Galatians*, one of the few works other than the Bible that he knew well.[20] In both Luther's *Commentary* and Bunyan's autobiography one is struck by the sense of the aloneness, and vulnerability, of the individual before the Word. Luther insists that 'God will have us fix our eies and to rest wholy upon the word it selfe'[21] and describes his helplessness before the 'horrible terrours' stirred up by the Law, from which he can be freed only by the restorative powers of the Gospel.

Both Bunyan and Luther open themselves to the influence of the Word, with the sense that it must determine their spiritual fates, but Bunyan appears more completely at the mercy of texts that act upon him in unpredictable ways. At one point he imagines his soul 'like a broken Vessel, driven, as with the Winds'[22] into despair. At another he is calmed by a consoling text that comes to him like a 'sudden rushing Wind', suggesting the mysterious influence of the Holy Spirit. Bunyan personalizes the divine and demonic forces that he perceives as contending for his soul, imagining a literal tug of war with Satan over a verse or an act of intervention by Christ, 'as though I had seen the Lord Jesus look down from Heaven through the Tiles upon me, and direct these words unto me'.[23] There is little hope that this conflict will be resolved as long as isolated texts, alternately arousing hopes and fears, continue to displace each other in his consciousness. Bunyan gains some measure of control over his 'tumultuous thoughts' only when he learns to understand Scripture as a coherent whole.

The key moment in Bunyan's understanding of Scripture comes when he can perceive the text that has most troubled him, one describing Esau as denied his father's blessing because of having sold his birthright,[24] as not in fact signalling his exclusion from grace. He reaches this conclusion by comparing Old and New Testament texts to ascertain 'what might be the mind of God in a New-Testament stile and sence concerning *Esau*'s sin',[25] and concluding that Esau's rejection of his birthright can be understood typologically

---

[20] See John R. Knott, jun., *The Sword of the Spirit* (Chicago, 1980), pp. 132 ff.; Dayton Haskin, 'Bunyan, Luther, and the struggle with Belatedness in *Grace Abounding*', *University of Toronto Quarterly*, 50 (1981), 300–13, *passim*.

[21] *A Commentarie of Master Doctor Martin Luther upon the Epistle of S. Paul to the Galatians*, 9th edn. (1635), p. 49ᵛ.

[22] GA, § 186.   [23] GA, § 207.   [24] Heb. 12: 16–17.
[25] GA, § 226.

as a rejection of the beginnings of regeneration. On this basis he can distinguish his case from Esau's and free himself from his obsessive fears.[26] What Bunyan does here, drawing in other texts as well, is find a way to achieve that 'concurrance and agreement in the Scriptures'[27] that he perceived to be necessary for his hold on the promises to be secure. Texts no longer cancel each other out when he finds a principle of interpretation, essentially the 'analogy of faith' recommended by the Elizabethan Puritan William Perkins and others, by which he can make them agree.

Grace Abounding shows Bunyan attaining a spiritual calm after extraordinary turbulence and also making space for himself in what he imagined as a world defined by Scripture and opposed to the everyday world of life in Bedfordshire. Two visionary scenes suggest how starkly Bunyan saw this opposition and how urgently he felt the need to break through into what he thought of as 'the reality of the Word'. In the first Bunyan imagines himself squeezing through a gap in the wall, representing the Word, that separates him from the godly poor of Bedford visible on the sunny side of a mountain.[28] In the second he escapes the 'avenger of blood' to gain sanctuary in Joshua's City of Refuge, joining the elders of the city, understood as the apostles.[29] One was decisively in or out of the spiritual life generated by the experience of Scripture, in Bunyan's view, and to be truly in was to enjoy the refreshing favour of God and the company of the faithful.

The preface of *Grace Abounding*, in which he writes as a minister encouraging his flock, reveals Bunyan securely established in the scripturally defined world that in the autobiography itself he shows himself struggling to enter. He would have thought of the language he uses there as 'Scripture language'; the Justices who examined him upon his arrest would have called it canting: '*I now once again, as before from the top of* Shenir *and* Hermon, *so now from* the Lions Dens, and from the Mountains of the Leopards (Song 4. 8), *do look yet after you all, greatly longing to see your safe arrival into* THE *desired haven.*'[30] In his sermons and in his imaginative works Bunyan moves easily into such scripturally based discourse, which

---

[26] On Bunyan's reinterpretation of the Esau story see Felicity Nussbaum, ' "By These Words I was Sustained": Bunyan's *Grace Abounding*', *ELH* 49 (1982), pp. 25-6; Elizabeth Bruss, *Autobiographical Acts* (Baltimore, 1976), p. 48.
[27] *GA*, § 195.   [28] *GA*, § 54.   [29] *GA*, § 210.
[30] *GA*, p. 1.

he thought of as the languge of truth. Here it is intended to authenticate the experience he goes on to describe and to reinforce his injunction to remember '*the Word that first laid hold upon you*'.[31] He would convince his readers of the efficacy of the Word and plant them firmly in the spiritual world established by it.

In his sermons and the treatises based upon them Bunyan loosely followed the common Puritan practice of deriving doctrines from the text, justifying these with a series of reasons, and applying them to the condition of his audience in uses.[32] In one of his most popular sermons, *Come, & Welcome, to Jesus Christ* (1678), Bunyan painstakingly explicates each significant word of his text ('All that the Father giveth me, shall come to me; and him that cometh to me, I will in no wise cast out') and then elaborates his message of assurance by introducing a series of observations that speak to common failings and concerns before concluding with uses of 'Examination' and 'Encouragement'. Bunyan's vigorous preaching style—with its colloquialism, homely imagery, and liberal use of anecdote and exemplum—shows the influence of the medieval popular style of preaching traced by G. R. Owst.[33] It is distinguished by the powerful dramatic sense that Bunyan brought to the task of explaining Scripture to his audience and giving it urgency and immediacy for them.

In *Come, & Welcome* Bunyan turns key words of his text into a character in the drama of conversion, showing '*shall-come*' taking the rebellious Paul by the hand: 'behold he is over-mastered, astonished, and with trembling, and reverence, in a Moment becomes *willing* to be obedient to the Heavenly call, Acts 9.'[34] Here the device of personifying the words makes their force seem irresistible. Elsewhere Bunyan brings his auditor into the spiritual drama that he creates, seeking to overcome his imagined doubts by the richness of the promises: 'Coming-Sinner, Christ inviteth thee to Dine and Sup with him. . . . But I doubt it, sayes the Sinner: But 'tis answer'd; He calls thee, invites thee to his Banquet, to his Flaggons, Apples;

---

[31] *GA*, p. 3.

[32] For commentary on the structure and variety of Bunyan's sermon-treatises see Talon, pp. 94–130 and E. Beatrice Batson, *John Bunyan: Allegory and Imagination* (London and Totowa, NJ, 1984), chap. 7.

[33] See G. R. Owst, *Literature and Pulpit in Medieval England*, 2nd edn. (Oxford, 1961), pp. 97–109, for a discussion of Bunyan's relationship to the English tradition of popular preaching.   [34] *Misc. Wks.*, viii. 280.

to his Wine, and to the Juyce of his Pomgranate.'³⁵ The traditional device of listing questions or objections and supplying answers frequently turns into a living dialogue in Bunyan's sermons.

Bunyan was particularly attracted to the dramatic potential of biblical stories and showed a striking gift for elaborating these in such a way as to make them homely and immediate. In *A Few Sighs from Hell* (1658) he enters into the character of the rich man Dives, who in the parable turns Lazarus away from his table and later finds himself barred from entering heaven: 'What, shall I regard *Lazarus*? Scrubbed, beggarly *Lazarus*? what shall I so far dishonour my fair sumptuous and gay house, with such a scabbed creep-hedge as he; no, I scorne he should be entertained under my roof.'³⁶ In a much later work, *Seasonable Counsel* (1684), Bunyan includes the story of the beheading of John the Baptist among a host of accounts of the suffering of the faithful:

The executioner comes to John; now, whether he was at dinner, or asleep, or whatever he was about, the bloody man bolts in upon him, and the first word he salutes him with is, Sir, strip, lay down your neck, for I am come to take away your head. But hold, stay; wherefore? pray, let me commit my soul to God. No, I must not stay; I am in haste: slap, says his sword, and off falls the good man's head.³⁷

In this instance Bunyan creates a scene that takes place off-stage in the biblical story, giving it a startling reality by his simple, brisk narrative. Both examples show Bunyan's readiness to improvise upon biblical texts, following his instinct for the dramatic scene and the telling phrase.

Like many Puritans, Bunyan stressed the simplicity of the Gospel message of salvation and its availability to anyone, even those without university educations. In his own preaching and writing he sought to emulate what he described as '*the great care of the Apostle Paul to deliver his Gospel to the Churches* in its own simplicity'.³⁸ Yet Bunyan also speaks of 'glorious mysteries of the Gospel' that invite explanation. He was powerfully drawn to the figurative language of the Bible and took this as warrant for his own use of metaphoric language and the kind of 'feigning' he indulged in *The Pilgrim's Progress* and *The Holy War*:

---

³⁵ *Misc. Wks.*, viii. 344–5.   ³⁶ *Misc. Wks.*, i, 304.
³⁷ *Works*, ii. 702.   ³⁸ *Misc. Wks.*, viii. 49.

> Was not Gods Laws,
> His Gospel-laws in olden time held forth
> By Types, Shadows and Metaphors?[39]

One sees Bunyan's attraction to the figurative in sermons based upon parables (*The Barren Fig Tree* (1682)) or important biblical metaphors (*The Water of Life* (1688)) as well as in his more sustained efforts at biblical exegesis (including *The Holy City* (1665), *Solomon's Temple Spiritualized* (1688), and *Of Antichrist and His Ruin* (1692)). At its best this can be an imaginative play of the mind upon configurations of text, at its worst a wringing out of metaphors to produce lists of doctrines.[40]

Bunyan would have seen no inconsistency between his strong commitment to the literal truth of biblical narrative and his increasing interest in the 'spiritual' or 'mystical' sense of Scripture. He operated within the Protestant tradition that acknowledged only one, literal sense and saw 'spiritual' interpretations as, in the words of the Elizabethan Puritan William Whitaker, 'not various senses, but various collections from one sense, or various applications and accommodations of that one meaning'.[41] Bunyan absorbed this tradition, as he did the common practice of reading the Old Testament typologically, without the kind of education most commentators brought to the Bible. From the beginning Bunyan was confident of his ability to understand Scripture, with the aid of the Holy Spirit, despite his lack of education. In *Some Gospel-Truths Opened* (1656) he asserted that 'though I am not skilled in the Hebrew tongue, yet through grace, I am enlightned into the Scriptures'.[42] In a prefatory comment to the learned reader Bunyan reveals his self-consciousness about not using the language of the learned, with its 'cloud of sentences' from the fathers, as he asserts the sufficiency of relying upon Scripture alone. He would do this more boldly in the preface to *Solomon's Temple Spiritualized* (1688):

---

[39] *PP*, p. 4.
[40] As in *The Barren Fig Tree*. See Kaufmann, pp. 54–5.
[41] William Whitaker, *A Disputation on Holy Scripture*, ed. William Fitzgerald, Parker Society (Cambridge, 1849), p. 404. On Protestant efforts to unify the literal and spiritual senses of Scripture see Janel M. Mueller (ed.), *Donne's Prebend Sermons* (Cambridge, Mass., 1971), p. 930; William Madsen, *From Shadowy Types to Truth* (New Haven, 1968), pp. 18–48. For Whitaker see *DNB*, s.v.
[42] *Misc. Wks.*, i, 39.

'I have not for these things fished in other men's waters; my Bible and my Concordance are my only library in my writings'.[43] Needless to say, Bunyan was untouched by the nascent 'critical' interpretation of the Bible, which scrutinized the historical and linguistic context of biblical passages and questioned the validity of figural interpretation.[44]

Bunyan's early meditation on two chapters of Revelation, *The Holy City* (1665), an outgrowth of his efforts to expound the Word to his prison companions, shows an appealing sense of wonder and delight at the mysterious way Scripture unfolds its meanings to him. These multiply, he suggests, like the inexhaustible loaves and fishes with which Jesus fed the multitude.[45] The freedom with which Bunyan ranges over Old Testament as well as New Testaments texts in *The Holy City*, developing a coherent vision of the promised restoration of the primitive church of God, shows no lack of confidence in his ability to understand the mysteries of Revelation. Bunyan's insistent allegorizing of the detail of the New Jerusalem, with its walls and gates and jewels, may strain the patience of a modern reader, yet it is hard not to respond to his striking vision of the recovery of the purity of apostolic doctrine and the unity of the primitive church through the agency of the Word. When Antichrist falls, and the Gospel 'breaks out in its primitive glory',[46] Bunyan insists, 'all shall be recovered and brought into order again by the golden reed of the word of God.'[47]

Bunyan saw the New Jerusalem of Revelation as the fulfilment of Old Testament prophesies, such as Jeremiah's,[48] that God would gather together the scattered sheep of Israel. He read Scripture typologically throughout his work, occasionally commenting on this practice or illustrating it at some length, as in his discussion of different kinds of types of Christ in *Light for Them That Sit in Darkness* (1675).[49] Bunyan's most sustained and flexible typological interpretations appear in such late works as *Solomon's Temple*

---

[43] *Works*, iii. 464; cf. above, p. 140.
[44] See Hans Frei, *The Eclipse of Biblical Narrative* (New Haven, 1974), chaps. 1 and 2.
[45] *Works*, iii. 398.
[46] *Works*, iii. 433.　　[47] *Works*, iii. 421.　　[48] Jer. 31: 10-12.
[49] See *Misc. Wks.*, viii. xliii-1, for a discussion by Richard L. Greaves of Bunyan's typology in relation to that of the period. For a more comprehensive discussion of typology in the period, with some reference to Bunyan, see Paul J. Korshin, *Typologies in England: 1650-1820* (Princeton, 1982).

Spiritualized (1688) and *The House of the Forest of Lebanon* and *An Exposition on the First Ten Chapters of Genesis*, both published posthumously in Charles Doe's 1692 edition of the *Works*. Bunyan found a feast of 'similitudes' in the divine directions for the building of the temple reported in Ezekiel. In *Solomon's Temple Spiritualized* its windows become figures of the Word, the altar a type of Christ, the golden candlesticks types of the churches of the New Testament. The 'net-work' ornamenting the capitals of the temple's pillars was for Bunyan a figure of the net of the Gospel by which apostles caught men: 'See therefore the mystery of God in these things.'[50] The 'types, figures, and similitudes' that Bunyan found in descriptions of the temple and the ceremonial law revealed to him 'how the New and Old Testament, as to the spiritualness of the worship, was as one and the same'.[51] Yet for all his delight in the intricacy of the typological correspondences he discovered, he did not pretend, any more than he had in *The Holy City*, that his explanations could exhaust the 'mystery of God'.

Allegorizing the Word

We read Bunyan now not because he could produce ingenious typological readings of Scripture, like many of his contemporaries, but because he had a genius for using biblical metaphor and biblical language to create lasting works of the imagination, most notably *The Pilgrim's Progress* and *The Holy War*. In the Apology to Part I of *The Pilgrim's Progress* Bunyan defends his use of 'feigning' and 'similitudes' by appealing to the example of Scripture and at the same time asserts that *'Dark figures'* and *'Allegories'* in Scripture yield *'those rayes / Of light that turns our darkest nights to days'*.[52] He embraces the paradox that the brightest truths may be found in 'dark' words, or in 'riddles', to cite another favourite term. Bunyan claimed that his work contained *'Nothing but sound and honest Gospel-strains'*,[53] as if to insist upon the purity of his materials and his intentions, yet the real thrust of the Apology is to defend his rendering of these *'Gospel-strains'*, with an eye to the mysteries embodied in the figures of Scripture.

The Bible gave Bunyan the basic scheme of *The Pilgrim's Progress*, the idea for many of its characters, and the descriptive and

[50] *Works*, iii. 472. [51] *Works*, iii. 464. [52] *PP*, p. 4.
[53] *PP*, p. 7.

metaphoric language that he elaborated into the landscapes that define the spiritual condition of Christian and the other pilgrims. Hebrews was a particularly decisive influence, serving to establish the idea of life as a pilgrimage to a 'heavenly' country, along with texts from Genesis and Exodus describing Abraham as a pilgrim.[54] One can trace many other significant biblical sources, including Old Testament passages describing the experience of the Israelites, Pauline epistles, and such rich sources of figurative language as the Song of Songs and Revelation. In fact, the influence of the Bible upon *The Pilgrim's Progress* is so pervasive that one must be alert to it continuously even when Bunyan does not point to specific biblical passages with citations in the margin.

Bunyan's real talent lay in adapting biblical materials to the experience of his readers by fusing biblical and colloquial language and creating a narrative that is realistic enough to be entirely credible and yet at the same time uncannily surreal. *The Pilgrim's Progress* works in part because of the tension Bunyan set up between the expectations of everyday experience, dominated by practical wisdom about surviving in the world, and the imperatives and promises of Scripture. The decisive action with which the work begins, Christian's flight from the familiar surroundings he has come to see as the City of Destruction, dramatizes the need to break with expected patterns of experience and pursue a way defined by faith. Christian must reject the sensible suggestions of Worldly-Wiseman about providing for himself and his family and set himself against the way of the world typified by Vanity Fair. Evangelist, exhorting Christian and Faithful as they are about to enter Vanity Fair, sets forth most plainly what the pilgrim must do: 'let the Kingdom be always before you, and believe stedfastly concerning things that are invisible'.[55] Christian is moved to leave home by his experience 'of the Powers, and Terrours of what is yet unseen'[56] and sustained in his journey by the promise of gaining the heavenly country promised by Scripture. Bunyan's great accomplishment in *The Pilgrim's Progress* was to give substance to this unseen world and to make it seem, by the end of the work, more real than the Bedfordshire setting from which Christian and those he encounters emerge.

---

[54] Brainerd P. Stranahan has documented this influence persuasively and discussed a number of other important biblical sources for *The Pilgrim's Progress*. See 'Bunyan and the Epistle to the Hebrews: His Source for the Idea of Pilgrimage in *The Pilgrim's Progress*, SP 79 (1982), 279-96.   [55] PP, 86-7.   [56] PP, p. 12.

Christian's progress can be seen as a matter of growth in understanding Scripture and in becoming capable of visualizing the kingdom that lies beyond the wilderness of this world for the truly faithful. The opening scene of *The Pilgrim's Progress*, in which we see a solitary Christian reading the Bible, recalls Bunyan's rendering of his own situation in *Grace Abounding* and at the same time suggests the condition of all Protestants, charged to try their souls by searching the Scriptures. The character of Christian's response, marked by weeping and trembling as he experiences the power of the Word to convince him of his sinfulness, is as important as the fact of his reading. Once he has responded to the threat of judgement under the Law, he is ready to be instructed in the promises of salvation and the nature of faith.

The three major places in which he receives instruction—the Interpreter's House, Palace Beautiful, and the Delectable Mountains—mark stages in his understanding of Scripture and his ability to relate his experience to it. In the first of these Christian receives instruction in interpreting biblical texts by means of a series of emblematic scenes expounded by the Interpreter, understood by Bunyan as the Holy Spirit.[57] Palace Beautiful offers a different kind of instruction, chiefly in the scriptural and extra-scriptural tradition of heroism in the name of faith and what Christian must do to become a part of it, beginning with putting on the Pauline armour of the Christian soldier. Prudence, Piety, and Charity draw Christian into the invisible church of the elect, with an emphasis upon the trials of the warfaring Christian. (In Part II of *The Pilgrim's Progress* the emphasis of Palace Beautiful has shifted to the education and support in godly living provided by the Church.) By the time Christian has reached the Delectable Mountains he and Hopeful are spiritually ready for the vision of the gate of the Celestial City from the Hill Clear that the shepherds offer through their 'Perspective Glass'. The pilgrims' parting song ('*Come to the* Shepherds *then, if you would see / Things deep, things hid, and that mysterious be*')[58] reflects a sense that the mysteries of Scripture are revealed to the faithful by divine agency that appears elsewhere in Bunyan's work, as in lines

---

[57] Dayton Haskin sees Christian as learning how to interpret for himself in the Interpreter's House and finds it significant that Christian loses his burden immediately after this episode. See 'The Burden of Interpretation in *The Pilgrim's Progress*', *SP* 79 (1982), 271-2. See also Kaufmann, pp. 62 ff., for an extended discussion of the Interpreter's House. [58] *PP*, p. 123.

on the Holy Spirit in a late poem: 'Dark *Riddles* he doth here to us unfold, / Yea makes us things *Invisible* behold'.[59] Christian and Hopeful here *see* things 'invisible' as they will more clearly when they reach Beulah ('within sight of the City') and will with perfect clarity when they ascend to the New Jerusalem where they will enjoy the 'perpetual sight' of God. The fact that the shepherds offer warnings as well as revelations testifies to Bunyan's sense that faith must be dynamic, strengthening itself in response to continuing trials, especially for those far enough advanced in their spiritual progress to be subject to over-confidence.

The shepherds' initial questions ('Whence came you?' 'How got you into the way?'), like those put to Christian when he arrives at the Interpreter's House and at Palace Beautiful, are of a sort that might be put to any 'way-faring men' but in the context of *The Pilgrim's Progress* they require a particular kind of confirmation of identity. Christian must demonstrate that he is acting upon the Word of God, as he does when he describes himself at the Interpreter's House as 'a Man that am come from the City of *Destruction*, and am going to the Mount *Zion*'[60] and when he recapitulates his experience of the way in response to more extensive questioning at Palace Beautiful.[61] Talkative fails an analogous kind of testing when he is questioned by Faithful, because he does not demonstrate the '*practical Subjection in Faith, and Love, to the power of the word*'[62] that Faithful takes as the mark of a true Christian.

The interrogations that Christian undergoes, particularly the sustained one at Palace Beautiful, have the effect of exercising his memory as well as trying his faith. Bunyan saw remembering Scripture, and one's experience of acting upon it, as critical to spiritual progress. Much of Christian's experience, and the reader's experience of *The Pilgrim's Progress*, is designed to train the memory, from an emblematic episode such as the encounter with the pillar of salt ('*Remember Lot's wife*') to the extended dialogues of Christian and his companions. Many of Christian's lapses can be seen as failures of memory. Near the beginning of his journey he forgets the roll that signals his election. The Valley of Humiliation where he nearly succumbs to Apollyon lies just beyond '*Forgetful-Green*', we

---

[59] *Misc. Wks.*, vi. 282.   [60] *PP*, p. 28.
[61] Kaufmann, pp. 217–31, relates this kind of recapitulation of experience, including Hopeful's extended account of how he came to be in the way, to the Puritan tradition of meditation upon experience.   [62] *PP*, p. 83.

learn in Part II. Christian and Hopeful languish in the dungeon of Doubting Castle, with Hopeful exhorting Christian to recall his valiant deeds and be patient, until Christian remembers that he has a key called *'Promise'*. The resolution of this episode, troubling to modern readers because it seems so improbably delayed, offered Bunyan a dramatic way of underscoring the importance of remembering the Gospel promises. The suddenness with which Christian remembers, like the suddenness with which he thinks of the biblical verse with which he defeats Apollyon, suggests the miraculous intervention of grace. Texts pop into the mind at critical moments, 'as God would have it', not unlike the way they do in *Grace Abounding*. The manner of Christian's escapes reflects Bunyan's confidence that the Holy Spirit would prompt the memory of the faithful.

Christian's final trial, crossing the river of death, makes plain the importance of memory in sustaining the faithful. The 'great darkness and horror' that fall upon Christian, 'so that he could not see before him', recalls the psychic disorder of the Valley of the Shadow of Death. Bunyan shows fear, 'horror of mind', threatening to overwhelm the assurance that his experience in the way and his sense of Scripture ought to give him: 'he could neither remember nor orderly talk of any of those sweet refreshments that he had met with in the way of his Pilgrimage.' To revive Christian Hopeful must recall the passage from the psalms ('My Brother, you have quite forgot the Text') that contrasts his state of mind with that of the wicked at death. The turning-point comes, as it does in the Valley of the Shadow of Death, when Christian is able to recall and confidently proclaim a text that promises deliverance. The recovery of vision, 'Oh I see him [*Christ*] again', naturally accompanies this renewed grasp of Scripture.[63] Bunyan uses imagery of sight throughout *The Pilgrim's Progress*, and especially at the end, to suggest the growth of spiritual vision that accompanies a faith based in the Word. For the successful pilgrim the invisible world becomes gloriously visible.

Bunyan's attempt at epic, *The Holy War*, gave him new ways of representing the role of the Bible in spiritual life. He could suggest the power of the Word in the form of the army of Emanuel besieging the town of Mansoul, with its battering rams and slings and its thundering captains representing the assault of the Law. The figure

[63] *PP*, pp. 157–8.

of a besieged town allowed Bunyan to emphasize the obduracy of sinful mankind under satanic influences. Emanuel himself must appear before Eargate can be breached and the town new modelled before the hold of Diabolus can be broken. Bunyan has Emanuel validate the truth of the scriptural message and confirm its salvational purpose as well as its power: 'All my words are true, I am mighty to save, and will deliver my *Mansoul* out of his [*Diabolus's*] hand'.[64] Diabolus, by contrast, relies upon 'Lying language' and strategies based upon deceit, recognizing that recourse to fraud is the only hope of defeating the truth represented by Emanuel.

Bunyan's fable gave him a vehicle for showing the interaction of Law and Gospel, in the relationship between Emanuel and his captains and in the two faces of Emanuel himself: the stern conqueror who will accept nothing less than unconditional surrender and the embodiment of divine mercy and love who forgives the inhabitants of Mansoul and feasts them. It also enabled him to represent more concretely than before the agency of the Holy Spirit in the process of understanding and acting upon the Word. The Spirit, in the person of the 'Lord chief *Secretary*,' plays a key role in *The Holy War*: ''tis he, and he only that can teach you clearly in all high and supernatural things'.[65] After the town of Mansoul has fallen to Diabolus and his army of Doubters, the godly remnant can succeed in their petition to Emanuel for help only with the aid of the Lord Secretary. The incident of the petition illustrates Bunyan's view that one must pray with the Spirit. It also demonstrates that one must trust in the promises. The Lord Mayor cites a passage that forms part of Bunyan's text for *Come, & Welcome, to Jesus Christ*: 'And him that cometh to me I will in no wise cast out'.[66] Emanuel's response is to send his army to deliver Mansoul, with the 'word', or battle-cry: '*The Sword of the Prince* Emanuel, *and the Shield of Captain Credence*', [67] explained as '*The word of God and faith*'. The conjunction is significant, since it requires faith, evidenced by a properly framed petition, to summon the power of the Word.

Perhaps the best example in all Bunyan's work of the nurturing and consoling properties of Scripture occurs in *The Holy War*, in the scene of feasting that follows Emanuel's first triumphal entry into Mansoul. In a treatise that appeared the same year as *The Holy War*,

[64] *HW*, p. 77.   [65] *HW*, p. 139.   [66] *HW*, p. 211.
[67] *HW*, pp. 219–20.

The Greatness of Soul (1682), Bunyan drew upon several biblical metaphors in characterizing the soul's experience of Scripture: 'the Soul of a Saint can Tast and Relish Gods word, and doth oft-times find it *sweeter* than Honey, *nourishing* as Milk, and *strengthening* like to strong Meat'.[68] On their 'Feasting-day' the people of Mansoul are treated by Emanuel to 'outlandish food' from 'his Fathers court', glossed by Bunyan as 'Promise after promise'. Musicians play and wine flows at this marvellous banquet. Bunyan makes the scene credible and delightful by showing the naïve wonder of the 'Townsfolk': 'But still when a fresh dish was set before them, they would whisperingly say to each other, *What is it?* for they wist not what to call it'.[69] Emanuel provides appropriate entertainment by explaining the 'Riddles' of scriptural metaphors that portray him ('the way'), with a gesture of love removing all anxiety about the mystery of Scripture.

This scene and others celebrating the triumphs of Emanuel—with psalm-singing, dancing, bell-ringing, strewing of the streets with flowers and branches—are characterized by a holy joy that suggests Bunyan's descriptions of Beulah in *The Pilgrim's Progress*. Yet despite the strongly biblical colouring of the scenes, with their suggestions of Christ's entry into Jerusalem and of Old Testament celebrations, they remain rooted in this world. The most extraordinary thing about them is that Bunyan daringly brings Emanuel into the urban setting of Mansoul, dissolving the distance between human and divine. Bunyan gives his readers a dazzling preview of the heavenly bliss of the saints and at the same time reminds them that Diabolus and his followers, like Spenser's Blatant Beast, remain at large in their world. In his final speech Emanuel distinguishes this world with its dangers and anxieties from the world to come, where Mansoul will be remodelled in an altogether new way and its inhabitants will experience such communion with divinity 'as is not possible here to be enjoyed'.[70] Emanuel's parting advice, 'thou must live upon my Word',[71] puts simply and powerfully the essence of Bunyan's message about Scripture. His *Relation* and *Grace Abounding* show him trying to live upon the Word, and his didactic and his imaginative works attempt in their diverse ways to persuade his readers to do the same.

[68] *Misc. Wks.*, ix, 149–50.   [69] *HW*, p. 115.   [70] *HW*, p. 247.
[71] *HW*, p. 250.

9

Spiritual Discerning: Bunyan and the Mysteries of the Divine Will

BY U. MILO KAUFMANN

Introduction

THE influence of Calvinist thinking upon Bunyan's allegories is evident in the attention Bunyan gives to those two great mysteries of the divine will, election and providence. The mystery of election Bunyan treats at length in the two parts of *The Pilgrim's Progress*, developing his conviction by way of a remarkable assortment of false as well as true pilgrims. The mystery of providence is a central concern of *The Life and Death of Mr Badman*.

For Calvin, nature, history, and the individual human life are at the same time wholly meaningful and profoundly mysterious. No arguments have been more rigorous than Calvin's for a sovereign divine will which achieves its ends in every precinct of time and space. Yet to insist, as Calvin did, upon the providential reading of nature and history is not to make plain how divine purpose is to be understood in each apparent evil and apparent good. Moreover, while every human career is utterly meaningful by virtue of the eternal decree of God, the mystery of the divine will in election is enduringly problematic.

'Single acts', says Calvin, 'are so regulated by God, and all events so proceed from His determinate counsel that nothing happens fortuitously.'[1] William Perkins (1558–1602), the greatest of the early English expounders of Calvin, concurs altogether:

Considering that God is King over heaven and earth . . . it must needs be that hee hath determined how all things shall come to passe in his kingdome,

---

[1] John Calvin, *The Institutes of the Christian Religion*, trans. Henry Beveridge, 2 vols. (Grand Rapids, 1957), i. 176.

with all their circumstances, time, place, causes, &c. in such particular manner, that the very least thing that may bee, is not left unappointed and undisposed.²

This divine will which governs the finest details of the universe is beholden to no other will. God can, in Bunyan's words, 'do whatsoever his soul desireth'. This freedom extends to the saving and damning of individual soul, for he has not only made all things but 'for his pleasure they both were and are created. Rev. 4.11.'³ We cannot wonder that such an utterly efficacious will is a lodestar for Bunyan's interest throughout his allegories.

The two sections of the discussion which follows respect a natural division in Bunyan's own treatment of the matter. The two parts of *The Pilgrim's Progress*, we shall notice, develop two complementary approaches to the implications of divine election for the Christian pilgrim. *The Life and Death of Mr Badman* addresses the question of how honesty can be reconciled with pastoral expedience in interpreting the mystery of providence.

Pilgrims and Hypocrites

For readers of Bunyan's time the scene which opens the narrator's dream in *The Pilgrim's Progress*—i.e. the man standing in a field, book in hand, and crying *'what shall I do?'*—might be expected to present irony of two kinds. If, as we must suppose, the book is the Bible, then on the common Calvinist understanding, the book was no more and no less than the detailed answer to the ragged man's question. But to hold the book and to understand it are of course two distinct things. Illumination by grace is required for the book to speak anything to its possessor. A further irony attends the state of the inquirer after he has had the book illuminated so that he may begin his course. If not of the elect, he may pursue to the end the way outlined in the book, only to find himself damned at the last.

Christian, shortly after his entering upon the way to life, encounters two travellers, aptly named Formalist and Hypocrisie, who are on the road by virtue of having tumbled over the wall 'on the left hand of the narrow way'. A heated dialogue ensues in which Christian wonders at their inauspicious access. What is more, their wish to

---

² William Perkins, *The Workes*, 3 vols. (1617-18, 1626), i. 140.
³ *Works*, ii. 340.

travel to Mt. Sion for praise makes their motives as suspect as their origins. Still, they advise Christian, 'as to *Laws and Ordinances*' they can observe them as conscientiously as Christian himself. 'We see not wherein thou differest from us, but by the Coat that is on thy back'.[4]

Now these two are representative of a host of false pilgrims in *The Pilgrim's Progress*, characters who, unlike the figures at wayside, are actively involved in travelling the way to life and who, thereby, pose in sundry forms the question of what in fact *does* constitute taking the Christian way. If we consider only those false pilgrims who appear after Christian is admitted through the little wicket gate, we still have something like fifteen to explain. Formalist and Hypocrisie at the opening, and Ignorance at the close, respectively announce and then sum up the terrifying possibility of wayfaring without effectual grace. In between we meet Mistrust and Timorous, who are in retrograde flight, as are also the children of the spies who attended Caleb and Joshua, as well as Discontent, who has been turned back by the Valley of Humiliation. Then there are Talkative, By-ends, Mr Hold-the World, Mr Money-love, and Mr Save-all. Since these last three all hail from '*Coveting* in the North', they may be, as J. W. Draper has proposed, Bunyan's slap at the Scotch Presbyterians.[5] Later apostates encountered are Turn-away and that boisterous renegade Atheist.

Ignorance is the false pilgrim who has received the most attention from scholars, in a dialectic of articles stretching back at least to Draper's discussion of 1927. This most unsettling of Bunyan's false pilgrims has been seen to represent the incipient Deism of the century to come, Quakerism, and prideful unbelief.[6] Without doubt Maurice Hussey has been the most circumspect of the commentators, simply claiming as he does that Ignorance, much like Antilegon in Arthur Dent's *The Plaine Mans Pathway to Heaven*, is to be seen as a hypocrite in the seventeenth-century understanding.[7] I shall be considering the complexity of that understanding, expecting that in

---

[4] *PP*, p. 40.
[5] J. W. Draper, 'Bunyan's Mr Ignorance', *MLR* 22 (1927), 14–21.
[6] The suggestions are made in the following articles, respectively: Draper (see n. 3 above); Richard R. Harden, 'Bunyan, Mr Ignorance, and the Quakers', *SP* 69 (1972), 496–508; James F. Forrest, 'Bunyan's Ignorance and the Flatterer', *SP* 60 (1963), 12–22.
[7] Maurice Hussey, 'Bunyan's Mr Ignorance', *MLR* 44 (1949), 483–9.

the process an important difference in the way the two parts of *The Pilgrim's Progress* address the mystery of election will become apparent.

In modern usage 'hypocrite' denotes a person who misrepresents himself to others in an attempt to deceive. In seventeenth-century Calvinist usage this meaning was only one of three with wide currency, and the least important of the three, at that. Calvin's doctrine of the perseverance of the elect rendered especially troublesome the case of the apparent believer who did not persevere. Such a lapsed one plainly experienced only 'temporary faith', a state which testified to momentary but ineffectual calling. In the language of the time, he was designated a 'formal hypocrite', one who deceived others as well as himself about his true state of grace. Yet a third category included those persons who, without the intent of deceiving others, yet, through inadvertency, carelessness, or sloth, contrived to remain ignorant of their own true state.

In the terminology of the Puritan Robert Bolton, the three kinds were: 'Privie', 'Grosse', and 'Formal'. The first deceived only himself. The second deceived others, but not himself. The third deceived both himself and others. Be it noted that both 'Privie' and 'Formal' hypocrites would not, by modern standards, be considered hypocrites at all, since they were sincere in their representations to others. Bunyan's century was less forbearing than ours, since the mystery of election was at issue.

I shall let the words of Robert Bolton expand this matter. In his *Discourse about the State of True Happinesse* (1611) Bolton gives considerable attention to 'formall hypocrisie'. By that term he denotes a frame of heart in which 'a man doth not onely deceive others with a show of piety and outward forme of Religion; but also his owne heart, with a false conceit and perswasion that hee is in a happie state. . . .'[8] A bit later he takes up the vexatious matter of 'temporary faith'. Such a formal hypocrite 'may be made partaker of some measure of inward illumination, of a shadow of true regeneration; there being no grace effectually wrought in the faithfull, whereof a resemblance may not be found in the unregenerate.' He goes on to describe the hearer in Jesus's parable of the sower (Luke 8) who is likened to stony soil. Such a man, says Bolton,

---

[8] Robert Bolton, *A Discourse of True Happiness* (1611), p. 34. For Bolton see *DNB*, s.v.

'is the formall hypocrite; who is there said, to beleeve for a time'. By the inward 'though more generall and inferiour working of the Spirit' he may have a 'temporary faith begot in him'.

This pointed association of the formal hypocrite with temporary faith, together with the metaphor which follows, must make us wonder if Bolton does not provide the source for Bunyan's episode alluded to above. 'Nay, and besides all these, that which nailes him fast unto formalitie . . . is a persuasion that he is already in the way of life, when as yet he never entered, no not the very step unto it.'[9]

If the term 'formal hypocrite' designated one who observed the forms of the Christian Life by virtue of the preliminary stirrings of the Holy Spirit in temporary faith, the term 'atheist' in the seventeenth-century Calvinist understanding was apt to describe that species of hypocrite whose atheism was nothing more than his allowing of genuine, if inferior, goods to crowd God from his reckoning. A Bedfordshire antecedent of John Bunyan's, Thomas Adams, whose works we have every reason to believe Bunyan knew, published two notable sermons on hypocrisy, one titled 'The Black Devill' and the other 'The White Devill'. James Forrest has proposed the latter as a possible source for Bunyan's Mr Ignorance.[10] That may be, but I am here interested in the work as it illuminates Bunyan's laughing Atheist. Mr Honest's reference to those travellers to Heaven 'who when they have been almost there, have come back again, and said there is none' certainly is illustrated in the person of Atheist, though we might not at first regard him as a hypocrite. Late in their journey Christian and Hopeful glimpse a pilgrim 'with his back toward *Sion*'. When he has reached them he asks them whither they are going.

Chr. *We are going to the Mount* Sion.
Then *Atheist* fell into a very great Laughter.
Chr. *What is the meaning of your Laughter?*
Atheist. *I laugh to see what ignorant persons you are, to take upon you so tedious a Journey; and yet are like to have nothing but your travel for your paines.*[11]

Atheist then explains how he set out to find the Celestial City twenty years before, but he has found no more of it 'then I did the first day I set out'.

---

[9] Bolton, *Discourse*, p. 37.
[10] James F. Forrest, 'Ignorance as White Devil: A Bunyan Debt to Thomas Adams?', *Canadian Journal of Theology*, 8 (1962), 49–50.   [11] *PP*, p. 135.

Thomas Adams describes the hypocrite in strikingly similar language:

> An hypocrite is a kind of honest Atheist: for his owne *Good* is his *God*; his heaven is upon earth, and that not the *Peace of his conscience*, or that kingdome of heaven, which may be in a soule living on earth, but the secure peace of a worldly estate; he stands in awe of no Judge, but mans eye; that he observes with as great respect, as *David* did the *eyes of God*; if man takes notice, hee cares not, yet laughs at him for that notice, and kills his Soule by that laughter. . . .[12]

The hypocrisy of such an atheist is, plainly, that of a person altogether genuine and complete in his self-deception, whether or not we see in Adams's description the evidence of temporary faith. Bunyan's pilgrim is one who has lost his first vision, whatever its source, and he, for certain, together with those other of his sort mentioned by Mr Honest, has experienced a calling inadequate to the stringencies of the journey.

What then does Bunyan seem to be commending to his readers in his juxtaposing of pilgrims and 'hypocrites'? Surely it is the closest possible scrutiny of the personal will. If the divine will must remain incorrigibly mysterious, at least one can examine one's own. In the resolutely good will one might hope to find evidence of a faith more than temporary.

R. T. Kendall in his fine book *Calvin and English Calvinism to 1649* (1979)[13] explores in the England of Bunyan's century the developing pastoral response to Calvin's clear teaching about temporary faith. The *pièce de résistance* was Calvin's insistence that even the reprobate might have a calling of a sort, which meant that for a time they would be indistinguishable from the elect. To affirm this, of course, was to make problematic the whole matter of Christian assurance. 'I know that to attribute faith to the reprobate', admits Calvin, 'seems hard to some, when Paul declares it the result of election. Yet this difficulty is easily solved. For . . . experience shows that the reprobate are sometimes affected by almost the same feeling as the elect, so that even in their own judgment they do not in any way differ from the elect.'[14] The inverse, history would also show, was entirely too plausible to the believer: the elect one might

---

[12] Thomas Adams, *The White Devill, or The Hypocrite Uncased* (1613), p. 30.
[13] Oxford, 1979.
[14] Cit. by Kendall, *Calvin*, p. 23. The ref. is to *Institutes*, III. ii. 11.

discern that he did not in any way differ from the reprobate. Where was the touchstone for discrimination?

Kendall observes that Calvin seems not to have anticipated the dilemma for believers. 'Much less could he have known that a tradition would emerge that would incorporate his teaching and try to solve the problem it raises by a voluntaristic doctrine of faith.' The result is a vision of the church as utterly mixed, with elect and reprobate side by side in the way, with neither certain how to discern which was which. Perkins, following Calvin, is adamant in affirming that the visible church includes 'true beleevers and hypocrites, Elect and Reprobate, good and bad.'[15] Hence one is ever obliged to distinguish between how men appear to men, and how they appear to God. Perkins, indeed, allows for the reprobates' mimicking the elect in almost every virtue, insisting that yet the ineffectual calling will be manifest in the end. Even so, the reprobate's certainty of falling away is scarcely a consolation to the troubled wayfarer well short of his end, and the need for pastoral interpretation of the teaching is obvious.

Kendall traces out pastoral developments stretching from Perkins through Paul Baynes to Richard Sibbes, a process in which the will to be godly assumed ever greater importance. It should surprise no one that Sibbes, that master of encouragement who was instrumental in Richard Baxter's conversion, writing in the admonitory light of several generations of English Calvinist experience, moves quite beyond the notion of temporary faith. He never uses the phrase and in fact preaches a voluntarism, in which the determination that one does in fact will the good is an adequate assurance of election: 'And there is no other way to know whether the former work of the understanding and persuasion be effectual and to purpose or now [sic], but this; to know whether the will choose and cleave to good things, and whether our affections joy and delight in them.'[16]

Bunyan does not, to my knowledge, use the phrase 'temporary faith', but he readily acknowledges the reality of ineffectual calling. In *The Desires of the Righteous Granted* (1692) for example, he discusses hypocrisy in connection with the wealthy young man who came to enquire of Jesus about eternal life:

[15] Cit. by Kendall, *Calvin*, p. 59. The ref. is to William Perkins, *Workes*, 3 vols. (1608–9), i. 310.
[16] Cit. by Kendall, *Calvin*, p. 107. The ref. is to Sibbes, *Complete Works*, 7 vols. (Edinburgh, 1862–4), vii. 446. For Baynes and Sibbes see *DNB*, s.vv.

There is the hypocrite's desire. Now his desire seems to have life and spirit in it. . . . He comes running and kneeling, and asking, and that . . . in youth and health; and that is more than men merely natural do. But all to no purpose; he went as he came, without the thing desired.[17]

Though by grace he had been stirred beyond the purely 'natural', his impulse is inadequate, and he turns back.

The visible church with elect and reprobate members mixed as thoroughly as the wheat and tares of another parable by Jesus: surely this is the milieu of pilgrimage as we find it in the first part of *The Pilgrim's Progress*. The reprobates may not turn aside as promptly as the wealthy young man. Some mere formal hypocrites may endure as long as Ignorance, having reproduced, we suppose, the full complement of observances and victories associated with morality and churchmanship — only to be cast away at last. The challenge to know one's own heart is a forceful one.

Part II's treatment of false pilgrims is quite different from Part I's and the reason is not hard to find. While in the first part Bunyan is concerned to disturb the comfortable, ensuring a close examination of the reader's own calling, in the second part his concern is plainly to comfort the disturbed. After hearing old Honest's account of Mr Fearing, who 'had some doubts about his Interest in that Celestial Country', Christiana, Mercy, and Christiana's oldest son Matthew all testify to their own anxieties about election. So in Part II the cautions of Part I are curiously inverted. Whereas Mr Ignorance is damned, Mr Feeble-mind of Part II can dare to present himself as 'a very ignorant Christian-Man'.[18] Contrast the stern cross-examination of Ignorance with Great-heart's assurance to Feeble-mind:

You must needs go along with us; we will wait for you, we will lend you our help, we will deny our selves of some things, both *Opinionative* and *Practical*, for your sake; we will not enter into doubtful Disputations before you, we will be made all things to you, rather then you shall be left behind.[19]

Note that the substance of the self-denial Great-heart is willing to practise is, it appears, the pleasure of that sort of contending over signs which Christian enters into so lustily in his engagement with Ignorance.

[17] *Works*, i. 764.   [18] *PP*, p. 270.   [19] *PP*, pp. 270–1.

Mr Feeble-mind has many like him on the journey: besides Fearing there are Ready-to-hault, Despondencie, and Much-afraid (the last two having been captive in Doubting Castle). All have in common the doubting of election, and Bunyan's emphasis throughout Part II is upon the assurance which ends doubts. Significantly, one of the major exploits of Great-heart's band is the slaying of Giant Despair and the demolition of Doubting Castle! This stroke is much like that which comes late in *The Holy War* when all Election-Doubters, Vocation-Doubters, and Grace-Doubters who have troubled Man's soul are summarily tried and executed by Emanuel.

The stress upon assurance does not mean Part II is wholly without its hypocrites, but they are on several counts a singularly undisturbing lot. Mr Honest, for example, lists the sorts of pilgrims he has observed, and five of the six categories are failures. But his list remains abstractly general, and he includes in his listing those pilgrims who 'have promised nothing at first . . . that yet have proved very good Pilgrims'.[20] Then there is Mr Self-will, an antinomian who probably presents Bunyan's attitudes about the Ranters. But Self-will is a gross caricature. His pretending that he can practise all vices as well as virtues 'and that if he did both, he should be certainly saved' is so ludicrous as scarcely to constitute a remonstrance, let alone a threat. Mr Brisk is a bit more the Formal Hypocrite we met in sundry ways in Part I, but we do not see him as actual wayfarer, but rather as a distraction, albeit momentary, at the wayside.

True, Bunyan provides in Part II a lengthy retrospect upon By-ends who is only briefly mentioned in Part I. But the description here is not of the formal hypocrite, but rather of the gross sort intent upon deceiving others: 'A very arch Fellow, a downright Hypocrite; one that would be Religious, which way ever the World went, but so cunning, that he would be sure neither to lose, nor suffer for it', sums up Great-heart; 'But so far as I could learn, he came to an ill End with his *By-ends*'.[21]

In the false pilgrims of Part I, formal hypocrites most of them, Bunyan condemns those travellers who deceive others as well as themselves. As reprobates they are, to be sure, beyond help, but their example is a pointed prod to the reader to scrutinize the state of his own will. In Part II, though admittedly we get final words on the formalists of the earlier narrative—persons like Talkative, Mistrust,

[20] *PP*, pp. 257-8.   [21] *PP*, p. 273.

and Timorous—and though we meet the caricature Mr Self-will and learn more of the gross hypocrite By-ends, Bunyan's emphasis lies elsewhere. His intent, one infers, is to draw in those only too ready to cast themselves as the Timorous or Mistrust of Part I and persuade them that they are, rather, the Fearing and Much-afraid of Part II, whose inheritance is in Heaven with others more readily assured of their election.

In explicating the difference between Parts I and II, one must notice another probable cause, beyond the discussed shift of emphasis from Bunyan's disturbing the comfortable to his comforting the disturbed. The evidence is modest but engaging that in his last years Bunyan, like William Perkins before him, developed a more accommodating and tolerant frame of mind.[22] In his last sermon, while still insisting that he is no free-willer, he is also pleading for concord among the brethren. 'If you are the children of God, live together lovingly; if the world quarrel with you, it is no matter; but it is sad if you quarrel together. . . . '[23] Plainly there is a time for the excruciating distinctions between pilgrim and pilgrim which *The Pilgrim's Progress* Part I lays out at length; but there is also a time for peacemaking and the discovery of common ground. *The Pilgrim's Progress*, Part II, the last in the sequence of Bunyan's great allegories, is also the most conspicuously eirenic of the lot. If it is not mellowing that we witness on Bunyan's part, it is at least his redressing the balance between opprobrium and approval as they are displayed toward fellow Christians.

---

[22] It is possible that in the opening scene of *The Holy War* we have further evidence of a softening rigour. Bunyan's narrator describes a walk through 'that famous *Continent* of *Universe*; a very large and spacious Countrey it is. It lieth between the two Poles, and just amidst the four points of the Heavens. It is a place *well* watered, and richly adorned with Hills and Valleys, bravely situate; and for the most part (at least where I was) very fruitful, also well peopled, and a very sweet Air.' The pedestrian observer is plainly sensitive to the amenities of this paradisial landscape. But this is not paradise, as we learn shortly. 'The people are not all of one complexion, nor yet of one Language, mode, or way of Religion; but differ as much as ('tis said) do the Planets themselves. Some are right, and some are wrong, even as it happeneth to be in lesser Regions' (*HW*, p. 7). This is the language of accommodation, prior to moral stricture or judgement. The perspective is one able to savour the world for what it is in its immediacy and heterogeneity, apart from what it may be, ultimately, in the divine plan. Indeed, the narrator assures us he would have continued in such a detachment had he not been called to something higher. 'Yea I had (to be sure) even lived and died a Native among them, (so was I taken with them and their doings) had not my Master sent for me home to his House, there to do business for him and to over-see business done.'

[23] *Works*, ii. 758.

Providence and the Reprobate

While election is that mystery of the divine will with which the two parts of *The Pilgrim's Progress* are centrally concerned, the mystery featured in *The Life and Death of Mr Badman* is that of providence. Calvinist tradition affirmed the universal scope of providence, even though the conviction that all was indeed the will of God in no way made clear *how* any particular event expressed that will. If anything, such a conviction made theodicy the more vexatious. In *Mr Badman* Bunyan poses this problem artfully, in terms of the life as well as the surprising death of his title character.

All is providence, Calvin had insisted; 'Nothing happens fortuitously'.[24] A. Mitchell Hunter, summarizing this resolute line of argument in Calvin, says 'It is obvious that contingency of any description is absolutely excluded from a system based on this fundamental idea of God's relation to the world. There is no possible place for anything to which can be applied the terms accident or chance.[25] God's providence, says William Perkins, 'ordereth all things and directeth them to good ends. And it must be extended to the very least thing that it is in heaven or earth. . . . '[26] George Abbot, speaking of the wind God sent to dry up the gourd that sheltered Jonah, observes:

For these and other meteors, are his creatures made by him: his subjects that live under him: his messengers sent from him to punish or to helpe, to execute his will. . . . The wind and the tempest depend not on chance, or any blind fortune, but on the sovereign power of the Almightie Creatour.[27]

This confidence was not, however, easily translated into the actual interpretation of phenomena. Says Thomas Adams, 'It is a true rule even in good workes: *finibus non officius, discernanda sunt virtutes a vitius*: vertues are discerned from vices not by their offices, but by their ends or intents.'[28] The difficulty with intents, of course, is that they are not readily accessible, and 'end' in the sense of outcome rather than informing purpose is often no more practical a guide.

---

[24] See n. 1 above.
[25] A. Mitchell Hunter, *The Teaching of Calvin*, 2nd edn., rev. (Westwood, NJ, 1950), p. 137. [26] Perkins, *Workes*, i. 155.
[27] George Abbot, *An Exposition Upon the Prophet Jonah* (1613), p. 45. For Abbot see *DNB*, s.v. [28] Adams, *White Devill*, p. 4.

Adams admits 'neither the outward form, no nor (often) the event, is a sure rule to measure the action by: the eleven Tribes went twice by Gods speciall word and warrant against the Benjamites, yet in both assaults received the overthrow.'[29]

Bunyan is no less honest in admitting the difficulties in interpreting events. 'Now there are providences of two sorts,' he says, 'seemingly good, and seemingly bad.' All is appearance, betraying the impetuous observer. Providences usually, concedes Bunyan, 'as Jacob did, when he blessed the sons of Joseph, cross hands; and lay the blessing where *we* would not.'[30] The appeal to Joseph epitomizes the impossibility of reading appearances apart from special access to the divine mind.

Such honesty, one might think, would be expressed in grave caution in the practice of the reading of providence. In fact, caution is usually set aside in crediting blessings to the godly and misfortune to the ungodly, and in this regard *Mr Badman* is, on first reading, as culpable as any tract of the time. Yet the pattern we are to notice is that, throughout, Badman is not reliably judged as others of like crimes generally were, and, most notable of all, he makes a good death, one quite different from what Attentive and, we suppose, most of Bunyan's readers would have expected. It is in the closing pages of the narrative that Bunyan makes his central point: while one may from social and pastoral necessity make all manner of interim judgements upon providence, it is finally only in the sanctuary, with its access to another order of truth altogether, that the final picture comes into (or returns to) focus.

I now review the evidence for the claim that throughout his life Badman is not judged as other wicked persons were. Badman's earliest vice, we learn, is lying, and he is a master at it. Attentive is quick to ask for the providential interpretation: 'Can you not give one some example of God's judgments upon liars?' And Wiseman is happy to mention Saphira [*sic, for Ananias*] and his wife.[31] Shortly we learn that Badman is wondrously adept at swearing, and again Attentive asks for the providential framing of the vice: 'But

---

[29] Adams, *White Devill*, p. 4.
[30] *Works*, ii. 11. This reference is to *The Saints' Knowledge of Christ's Love*, but Bunyan invokes the illustration again in Part II of *The Pilgrim's Progress*. Feeble-mind, marvelling at his deliverance when Not-Right was slain, sings: '*That very* Providence, *whose Face is* Death, / *Doth ofttimes, to the lowly,* Life *bequeath.* / *I taken was, he did escape and flee,* / *Hands Crost, gives Death to him, and Life to me*' (*PP*, p. 269).
[31] *Works*, iii. 598.

I wonder, since cursing and swearing are such evils in the eyes of God, that he doth not make some examples to others, for their committing such wickedness.' To this request Wiseman supplies the grisly details of three tales of sudden death following upon fits of profanity. And Attentive, not to be outdone, has his own grim tale of the half-fool Edward whose curses on his inciting father are answered 'through the righteous judgment of God'.[32]

Before long we learn of Badman's knavery in deceiving a godly woman so as to win her as his wife. Again, Attentive asks the leading question: 'Can you give me no examples of God's wrath upon men that have acted this tragical wicked deed of Mr. Badman.' And Wiseman is able to oblige with the biblical story of Hamor and Shechem, as well as a more immediate episode of one 'not far off from our town' who did not for very long enjoy a godly wife won by errant hypocrisy, since 'his horse threw him to the ground, where he was found dead at break of day; frightfully and lamentably mangled with his fall, and besmeared with his own blood.'[33]

In all of these cases, however, the tales of judgement have an ironic edge. They conclude discussion of a particular evil of Badman with biblical and popular illustrations of how such vices have been 'judged' in the past; yet Badman himself remains unjudged. The cumulative weight of Badman's apparent escapes from judgement finally breaks in upon Attentive, as he suffers the anguish of learning how Badman's godly wife suffered with him. 'Certainly some wonderful judgment of God must attend and overtake such wicked men as these.' And Wiseman takes the inevitable first line of defence against the seeming misfiring of justice: 'You may be sure that they shall have judgment to the full, for all these things, when the day of judgment is come.'[34]

Still, the precariousness of all reading of providence has been posed without any very satifactory resolution. The disparity between deed and judgement in Badman's life is constantly being heightened in Bunyan's narrative by the juxtaposing of the judgement upon others with the escape of the specimen rogue Badman. This pattern has its perfecting in the surprise which Wiseman eventually springs upon Attentive. Badman makes a 'good' death, that is, one without pain, terror, or other apparent judgement. When Attentive presses for the circumstances of his death, he explains that 'there is such an opinion as this among the ignorant, that if a man dies, as they call it, like

[32] *Works*, iii. 604–5.   [33] *Works*, iii. 620.   [34] *Works*, iii. 619.

a lamb, that is, quietly, and without the consternation of mind that others show in their death, they conclude, and that beyond all doubt, that such a one is gone to heaven, and is certainly escaped the wrath to come.'[35]

Wiseman's approach is to make a virtue of necessity, and before Bunyan is through his marshalling of arguments we are hearing this extraordinary witness to the counter-apparent: 'that a sinful life and a quiet death annexed to it is the ready, the open, the beaten, the common highway to hell: there is no surer sign of damnation than for a man to die quietly after a sinful life'.[36] To the objection that here is a death wholly without judgement displayed, Bunyan declares that it is in fact 'a Judgment of God upon his wicked beholder'.[37] Because, that is, the wicked spectator is apt to be hardened in his wickedness, God lays upon him the negative providence of a nudge onward on his course.

This is a *tour de force* of sorts, though some readers will surely dismiss it as sophistry. Judgement concealed, we are asked to believe, is at the same time the clearest judgement upon the careless. Yet the latter judgement, too, is quite opaque to any but the eyes of faith. All such so-called judgements draw their meaning from their end, that final disposition beyond death when God, like Milton's Jove, 'judges lastly on each deed'.

This is not to say that the Christian interpreter is wholly without recourse in divining the sense of the reprobate's life as it is being lived before him. Bunyan takes a traditional Calvinist line in discerning import in the very disorder of such a life, a disorder to be traced to the reprobate's own unwillingness or inability to read the providence in affairs. Aptly enough, the characterizing design of Badman's life is its lack of design, its departure from that Gospel order which is the sign of the spirit's hand in ordering the believer's life. Moses represented for us in the person of Esau, Calvin points out, 'what kind of men all the reprobates are, who, being left to their own disposition, are not governed by the Spirit of God'.[38] The clearest providence in the life of the believer is that ordering hand which shapes all to one end. The elect, Calvin insists, 'are renewed by the Holy Spirit, that they may be the workmanship of God, created unto good works'.

---

[35] *Works*, iii. 659.   [36] *Works*, iii. 663.   [37] *Works*, iii. 664.
[38] *Calvin's Commentaries, The Pentateuch* (Grand Rapids, Mich., n.d.), p. 247. This statement is part of Calvin's commentary upon Gen. 25: 29.

Man as he comes into the world, Bunyan had noticed in his exposition on the opening chapters of Genesis, 'abides a confused lump, an unclean thing; a creature without New Testament order'.[39] The thought is developed also by Thomas Goodwin: '[S]ince the fall, our hearts of themselves are nothing but *darknesse*. . . . The Apostle compareth this native darknesse of our hearts unto that *Chaos*, and lumpe of *darknesse* which at the first creation *covered the face of the deepe*.'[40] In the unregenerate this lumpishness goes unremedied. The disorder, for the Calvinist, represents the only corner of God's creation where his will might be said not to be wholly efficacious. 'As for evil instruments', William Perkins allows, 'hee [*God*] worketh by them onely, and not in them; because he holds back his grace from them; and leaves them to themselves, to put in practise the corruption of their owne hearts'.[41] Perkins, it is true, qualifies the extreme determinism of Calvin at this point, but the qualification is one which appears to have found favour in Bunyan's milieu. Richard Baxter says 'Mans not believing, not knowing, not loving, not obeying, not desiring, trusting, fearing, &c. being the far greatest part of the *sins* of his life, we see by this are not at all of God'.[42]

So the chaos of the reprobate's life, manifest in the vagaries of impulse, vice, and expedience, is the plainest sign of the absence of that ordering Spirit who makes the elect life a shaped pilgrimage or battle of certain outcome. Hell, according to that text from Job which Chaucer's Parson expounded at length, is altogether a place of disorder, and if Christian's life occasionally realized anticipations of the heavenly felicity, as on the Delectable Mountains, and in Beulah Land, Badman's life is throughout characterized by the adventitiousness of Hell.[43]

Certainly the narrative strategy of *Mr Badman* bears this out. While Christian's journey is, for all its detours and lapses, ever being

---

[39] *Works*, ii. 418.
[40] Thomas Goodwin, *A Childe of Light Walking in Darknesse* (1636), p. 30. For Goodwin see *DNB*, s.v.   [41] Perkins, *Workes*, i. 157.
[42] *Richard Baxter's Catholick Theologie* (1675), p. 61.
[43] The crucial difference between Badman and the false pilgrims of *The Pilgrim's Progress* is that the latter are reprobates who enjoy at least temporary faith, the short-term grace of the ineffectual calling. Grace creates order in the life, even if only for a time, and Bunyan allegorizes this in their conformity to the way. But Badman it is who truly deserves the name Graceless which Christian bore for a time; his life is unmitigated disorder.

pressed into order by Evangelist, by the providence of a clear path, and by Christian's instructed conscience, Badman's life is the *ad hoc* choice writ large. Evil is disintegrative, and its pursuit a protracted lapsing into chaos. Wiseman's own narrative focus is constantly being lost, with Attentive calling him back to some hoped-for continuity and consecutiveness, though this is never to be provided. Even the supposed apt close, as we noticed earlier, is not to be; Badman's quiet death is no more a plain evidence of a providence at work than is any of his earlier misdeeds which goes unjudged.

I commented above on the voluntarism which informs the reading of the signs of election in Bunyan's time. To will the will of God was taken to be an evidence of election. An interesting counterpart to this can be noticed in the reading of providence. For to see in one's life and world, by willing to see it, the diverse demonstration of an ordering providence, was to find (and co-operate in producing) that New Testament order which marked election.

When, well along in his narrative, Bunyan offers his reader what his marginal note calls a 'general character' of his central figure, the précis focuses upon two primary deficiencies in Badman. This reprobate refuses to read the divine will either in history or in Scripture. He refuses, in a word, all possible purchase upon meaning in his world. Here is the heart of the indictment:

Instead of honouring God, and of giving glory to him for any of his mercies, or under any of his good providences toward him, for God is good to all, and lets his sun shine, and his rain fall upon the unthankful and unholy, he would ascribe the glory to other causes. If they were mercies, he would ascribe them, if the open face of the providence did not give him the lie, to his own wit, labour, care, industry, cunning, or the like. If they were crosses, he would ascribe them, or count them the offspring of fortune, ill luck, chance, the ill management of matters, the ill will of neighbours, or to his wife's being religious, and spending, as he called it, too much time in reading, praying, or the like. It was not in his way to acknowledge God, that is, graciously, or his hand in things.[44]

This refusal to see providence at work in the world—Badman's 'general character'—is the chief evidence for his lack of ordering grace; his life abundantly confirms that contingency he insists upon seeing about him. And it is Wiseman the Puritan elder who finally

[44] *Works*, iii. 646.

articulates the truth about providence to which the narrative has been leading. The ability to discern providence which he and Attentive share, but which Badman so grievously lacks, is in fact the divine gift of an ordering faith. The ambiguity is never wrung out of events. The discernment of judgements moves from will to event, rather than from event to will. One exercises the will of the elect in so reading events; nothing in events coerces him. On the penultimate page of the narrative, Wiseman determines the bedrock of the matter: 'only the godly that are in the world have a sanctuary to go to, where the oracle and Word of God is, by which his judgments, and a reason of many of them are made known to, and understood by them.'[45] He had earlier referred to David's mystification by the eventualities of this life, to have his vision clarified only when he retreated into the Sanctuary of God: 'Then I saw, that thou has "set them [*the wicked*] in slippery places", and "thou castedst them down to destruction." '[46] The insight comes in communion with God, 'but not without great painfulness. . . . so deep, so hard and so difficult did he find it, rightly to come to a determination in this matter.' The providential will remains mysterious, as mysterious as God's will in election. Ever in tension is the pastoral impulse to locate threat and promise in history, and the honest recognition that all such interpretation is suspect.

What goes unquestioned in *Mr Badman*, as in *The Pilgrim's Progress*, is the assurance that God Himself is to be known as summoning, self-disclosing will—that, and the conviction that the disposition of one's own will may be fixed in the choosing of ends.

[45] Works, iii. 664–5.   [46] Works, iii. 664.

10

'With the eyes of my understanding': Bunyan, Experience, and Acts of Interpretation

BY VINCENT NEWEY

Introduction

THE salient principles of experimental religion are nowhere more obviously put than by the character Talkative, who speaks, for example, of the value of godly conversation, 'the necessity of the New-birth, the insufficiency of our works, the need of Christ's righteousness', the 'great promises & consolations of the Gospel', 'the need of faith, and the necessity of a work of Grace in [the] Soul'.[1] But Talkative himself represents, of course, the type of the mere opinionative believer regularly condemned in Puritan discourse.[2] Impeccable though his doctrines are, they have no place in his heart or actions. As the clear-sighted Christian puts it, 'all he hath lieth in his *tongue*'. 'Lieth' is one of Bunyan's puns: Talkative's fine words, we soon learn, veil an 'ugly' and unclean life.

On two levels then, that of Talkative's statements abstractly considered as well as the satire against the superficial and false professor, the episode foregrounds the Puritan's habitual elevation of interior events and the condition of the inner man, 'heartwork', as the true centre, grounds, and measure of religious being. Beyond

---

[1] *PP*, p. 76. No refs. are given for brief quotations or citations where a preceding nearby ref. clearly indicates their position in the text of *The Pilgrim's Progress*.
[2] See, e.g., Richard Baxter's observation that 'It was never the will of God that bare *speculation* should be the end of his Revelations, or of our *belief*' (*Directions for Weak Christians* (1669)), and Thomas Adams's aphorism, 'One steppe of our feet, is worth ten words of our tongues' (*Works*, 1630); quoted in *The Pilgrim's Progress*, ed. N. H. Keeble (Oxford, 1984), p. 272.

this, however, it brings into focus another, less familiar dimension of Bunyan's Puritan ontology—the individual's constant involvement in acts of interpretation and decipherment. Whatever the pros and cons of the 'realist' or mimetic approach to Bunyan stemming from Coleridge's view of his characters 'as real persons',[3] it remains that Talkative exists for Christian and Faithful, as he does for us, as a text to be read and understood. Faithful, naïve and unschooled, is 'beguiled' by Talkative's suave rhetoric, but Christian, armed with the pilgrim's most potent weapons, memory and the Word, has no difficulty in getting the meaning right. He recalls that Talkative is the 'sorry fellow', the son of Saywell, and then discloses the true significance of his words, which is in fact their emptiness, for *'Saying, if it be alone, is but a dead Carkass'* and *'the Kingdom of God is not in word, but in power'*. Talkative is at bottom an *exemplum* whose import is, in a circular process, determined and then unlocked by biblical concept.

This is a very straightforward instance of what is, in Puritanism generally and Bunyan in particular, a varied, complex, and far-reaching preoccupation, some aspects of which I shall explore in this essay. For Isaac Ambrose, whose *Prima, Media, & Ultima* is a repository of shared attitudes, interpretation, in the form of self-scrutiny and the scrutiny of others in relation to the Word, becomes virtually synonymous with the best of experience itself:

When I mark how true every part of God's Word is, how all the Doctrines, Threatnings and Promises contained therein, are daily verified in others, and in my own self, and so improve or make use of them to my own Spiritual advantage, this I call *Experience*.[4]

And *Grace Abounding*, on which I shall concentrate, is the apogee of a tradition where the habit of self-scrutiny made the introspective conversion document, the presentation of one's life as a text, a requirement for church membership: 'Every one to be *admitted*, gives out some *experimental* Evidences of the work of *grace* upon his *soul* . . . whereby he (or she) is *convinced* that he is *regenerate*'.[5] It

---

[3] See *Coleridge on the Seventeenth Century*, ed. Roberta Florence Brinkley (New York, 1968), p. 475. This approach reaches its apogee in F. R. Leavis's influential afterword to the *Signet Classics* edition of *The Pilgrim's Progress* (New York and London, 1964); repr. in *Casebook*, pp. 204-20.

[4] Isaac Ambrose, *Prima, Media, & Ultima* (1654), ii. 164.

[5] John Rogers, *Obel or Beth-shemesh, A Tabernacle for the Sun* (1653), p. 354.

should be said at once, however, that, judging by Bunyan, these references, like the Talkative episode, delineate ideal rather than characteristic situations: contemplation and *'practical subjection in Faith . . . to the power of the word'*[6] do not usually yield such perfect spiritual advantage or conviction; whether in his consideration of his 'own self' in his spiritual autobiography or in the events of Christian's pilgrimage, interpretative process is most often a strenuous and problematic affair, fraught with uncertainty, danger, and the consequences of error. We tend to think of religious experience as a state of privilege, knowing, and being in the right, but, as we shall see, in Bunyan we are much more aware of desperation, blindness, and mis-taking. These are conditions which the Christian protagonist must strive to transcend but which are also fundamental to the dynamics of his existence and of the works that most powerfully portray it.

Grace Abounding: The Mistakings of the Convert

Grace Abounding belongs to a well-documented genre. It conforms broadly to the standard pattern of the conversion narrative as it emerged among the radical sects before and during the Civil War: that is, in Roger Sharrock's convenient outline, early providential mercies, unregenerate life, calling, and conversion, often followd by a vocation to preach and an account of the ministry.[7] It manifests that dual motivation, didactic and autodidactic, which Bunyan's near-contemporary, Thomas Halyburton, offers as the rationale of spiritual autobiography:

. . . if I can recount the Lord's gracious conduct toward me, and the state of matters both before and under the Lord's special dealings with me, in a way that shall tend to the conviction, consolation, and edification of the reader; and so arrange . . . the work in the several stages of its advancement, and in its final results; it may, at least, be a great use to my own confirmation.[8]

---

[6] *PP*, p. 83.   [7] Introduction to *GA*, pp. xxvii–xxxiii.
[8] *Memoirs of the Revd Thomas Halyburton* [1674-1712], *Professor of Divinity in the University of St Andrews* (Princeton, 1833), p. 57. For a useful general account of the motives and form of Puritan spiritual autobiography (though Bunyan is surprisingly omitted from the copious examples), see G. A. Starr, *Defoe and Spiritual Autobiography* (Princeton, 1965), pp. 3–50. For Halyburton see *DNB*, s.v.

The same twofold gain of encouraging others and stabilizing the individual present through an appeal to the evidences of the past is immediately evoked in Bunyan's preface, where he recalls '*the great grace that* God *extended to such a Wretch*' and, assuming the role of a father addressing his '*dear Children*', hopes that his readers may be '*put in remembrance of what he hath done for their Souls*'.[9] We are prepared for a text where the affirmation of divine interposition will both confirm a sense of personal identity and, through the very rehearsal of shared concepts of the shape of private experience, nourish the corporate life of the Church community.

But that is not quite the text we get, at least after the series of early deliverances—Bunyan is preserved from drowning, from death by a bullet, from an adder's sting, and from the sin of bell-ringing—which represent the most obvious evidences of election, of God's 'special dealings', in the Puritan repertoire.[10] Reading *Grace Abounding* is like travelling in a mighty maze whose plan is far from clear, and where at every turn we meet some new and puzzling psychodrama suggesting not so much providential design as solitary struggle in a spectacular universe of the mind's own making. The raw, specific intensity of these psychodramas makes Barrett John Mandel's complaint of Bunyan's 'basic unoriginality' irrelevant and bears out, rather, Sharrock's belief in its 'uniqueness' of 'psychological penetration'.[11] Here, for comparison, is the Scot, James Fraser, whose *Memoirs* (1670) have recently been paired with *Grace Abounding* in a discussion of the 'double conversion' narrative (a subject we shall come to in due course):

> There would come a wave of the Spirit that would overflow largely, but after that a little ebb; and then, when I had little expected, there would come a wave that would set me as far forward as ever again: and then a little decay, and then a recovery . . .[12]

This delineates the workings of the S/spirit from a distance, the metaphor of undulation threading its way through the syntax so as

---

[9] *GA*, pp. 2-3.   [10] *GA*, §§ 12-13, 33-4.
[11] Barrett John Mandel, 'Bunyan and the Autobiographer's Artistic Purpose', *Criticism*, 10 (1968), 225-7; Sharrock in *GA*, p. xxxii.
[12] 'Memoirs of the Revd. James Fraser of Brea, Minister of the Gospel at Culross, Written by Himself', *Select Biographies*, ed. W. K. Tweedie (Edinburgh, 1847), ii. 134-5. Fraser and Bunyan are compared (and insufficiently contrasted) in Anne Hawkins, 'The Double-conversion in Bunyan's *Grace Abounding*', *Philological Quarterly*, 61 (1982), 268-9. For Fraser see *DNB*, s.v.

to fuse 'outer' and 'inner', influence and interior motions, in a generalized account of gradual, delayed upraising. It is as if Fraser is conscious first of a configuration of experience, which he then applies in relation to himself. Bunyan, on the other hand, realizes all the immediate sensation of a violent assault and relentless oscillation: '. . . my peace would be in and out sometimes twenty times a day: Comfort now, and Trouble presently; Peace now, and before I could go a furlong, as full of Fear and Guilt as ever heart could hold'.[13] Comfort itself becomes a physical presence, strangely hostile in its unaccountable penetration and withdrawal; in the extremeness of 'twenty times a day', the abrupt syntactical units, and the swift interchange of 'in/out' and 'now/presently' chronological sequence (which is very conspicuous in Fraser's adverbial structures of 'after . . . then . . . then') is subsumed in repetition, a virtual stasis, signifying an arrestment of the power to act and have continuous being; the usurpation of the will to break out (to 'go a furlong') by heart-bursting Fear and Guilt has the vividness of a painful nightmare.

Turmoil and dereliction abound in *Grace Abounding*. Richard Baxter, reminding us of Halyburton's rationale and the encouraging words of Bunyan's preface, advises the convert to recall 'all the progress of [*God's*] *Spirit* in his workings on thy soul';[14] but Bunyan, though assuming God's omnipotence, focuses primarily upon the self, and the self seemingly in perpetual crisis, breeding situations of confinement and conflict. Emotions, as we have seen, become fierce adversaries that cannot be negotiated with. Elsewhere we read of how he was able to resist the compulsion to deny Christ only by thoughts of leaping 'with my head downward, into some Muckhil-hole or other'.[15] On another occasion (beside which the sometimes quoted analogue, the Quaker John Crook's 'I thought every Man or Woman to be in a better Condition than my self', signifies at most a mild case of ahedonia) he enters a weird oneiric dimension, experiencing the world as a field of absolutely hostile forces where 'the very stones in the street, and tiles upon the houses, did bend themselves against me . . . to banish me out of the World . . . because I had sinned against the Saviour'.[16]

---

[13] *GA*, § 205.
[14] Richard Baxter, *The Saints Everlasting Rest*, 4th edn. (London, 1653), Part 4, pp. 187-90.   [15] *GA*, § 103.
[16] *A Short History of the Life of John Crook* (1706), p. 145; *GA*, § 187. Cf. Anna Trapnel's analogous but faintly realized sense of the spiritual dangers that lurk

Such moments are, of course, Bunyan's version of the soul-trouble which was everywhere a recognized ingredient of the Puritan conversion process, and which Luther, with whom Bunyan always felt a special kinship, emphasized, when formulating the Protestant tradition of self-analysis, as 'bitterness and anguish of spirit' necessarily arising from doubt and man's unregenerate nature.[17] But Bunyan, in interpreting his life in the given terms, made himself the protagonist in a singularly powerful and densely textured drama of calling, vulnerability, and ineradicable sinfulness. It is a drama constituted, on one level, from blindness, mistakes, and wrong moves. We remember, for example, the famous 'game of Cat' episode, where the young Bunyan, playing with his friends in the street, is visited by 'a voice . . . from Heaven' asking him to choose between Heaven or Hell.[18] He 'looked up to Heaven, and was as if I had with the eyes of my understanding, seen the Lord Jesus looking down upon me, as being very hotly displeased'. Yet he chooses Hell: he resolves that *'it was now too late for me . . . for Christ would not forgive me, nor pardon my transgressions'*, and, deciding he had as good be damned for many sins as for few, makes haste to fill his belly with their 'sweetness' lest he should die before he has his 'desire'. The visitation thus occasions a misreading which defers, indeed challenges, the ends it theoretically promotes: the sign, Christ's threatening displeasure, which, understood rightly, should have admonished the sinner and set him on the way to the *telos* of redeemed selfhood in Christ, prompts instead the conviction that it was 'too late', and a desperate embrace of worldly appetite. This is an early episode, but the same pattern of mis-taking and the deferral of predicted ends is repeated over and over again in *Grace Abounding*—not least, as we shall see, in the 'unpardonable sin' episode, to which the nightmare experiences of violent emotions and accusing presences belong.

---

after conversion: 'dark misty clouds will arise upon our spirits . . . Obscurity after the shining of Gospel light is terriblyer to bear, then that darkness before a freedom' (*A Legacy for Saints* (1654), p. 19).

[17] Luther, *A Commentarie upon the Epistle of S. Paul to the Galatians*; see John R. Knott, jun., *The Sword of the Spirit: Puritan Responses to the Bible* (Chicago, 1980), chap. 6, which contains a valuable discussion of the relationship of Luther's commentary to *Grace Abounding*, and also remarks by Paul Delany, *British Autobiography in the Seventeenth Century* (1969), pp. 33-6.

[18] GA, §§ 22-6.

We are aware, however, of two Bunyans in *Grace Abounding*, the recreated self of the past (the protagonist) and the authorial self of the present (the narrator–teacher), who defines the despair of salvation and gourmet pursuit of sin issuing from the vision of a 'hotly displeased' Christ as a 'temptation of the Devil'. The contrast between the two selves, the unknowing and the enlightened, indicates another reading of the text, as a drama of maturation, of learning to 'see' correctly. Then, just afterwards, a third perspective is generated, when Bunyan recounts the dream in which he saw the poor people of the Bedford congregation 'set on the Sunny side of some high Mountain, there refreshing themselves with the pleasant beams of the Sun', but immediately experienced also the difficulty of gaining access to that sunny side through a 'very strait, and narrow' gap in a surrounding wall: 'I was well nigh quite beat out by striving to get in: at last, with great striving, me thought I at first did get in my head, and after that, by a side-ling striving, my shoulders, and my whole body; then I was exceeding glad . . . '[19] This projects the essence of conversion experience as it is made manifest in *Grace Abounding*. The idea of conversion as rebirth is spectacularly revivified in the imagery, or rather imagining, of the actual process of being born: for Bunyan there is no flash of light such as visits St Paul on the road to Damascus, nor the turning of a sharply demarcated corner into a new dimension taken by St Augustine in the garden in the *locus classicus* of *crisis* conversion, but a prolonged effort to emerge, a 'great striving'.[20] It is important to note, moreover, that 'the happy and blessed condition' of those who 'enter into life', basking passively in the glory of the Sun/Son, is available to the Bunyan of *Grace Abounding* only in isolated periods of exceeding gladness, and is in *The Pilgrim's Progress* as it were relocated in the Celestial City altogether beyond the confines of this world. This side the ideal repose of Heaven, the striving is without end.

These three ingredients, mistaking (which in retrospect becomes temptation or sinful error), learning, and striving, are constants in Bunyan's reconstruction of his past, and dominate those interactions

---

[19] *GA*, § 54.
[20] Cf. William James's comment on the garden episode in the *Confessions*, where the voice, '*sume, lege*', led Augustine on to an encounter with the text, 'not in chambering and wantonness', which 'laid the inner storm to rest forever': *The Varieties of Religious Experience* (1902; repr. Harmondsworth, 1982), p. 171.

with the Word which form by far the greatest part of his recorded history. Coming to the Word is a crucial stage on the Puritan soteriological journey, and for the young Bunyan the path seems plain ahead as he feels 'a great bending in my mind to a continual meditating' on Scripture: 'I began to look into the Bible with new eyes, and read as I never did before'.[21] A measure of spiritual progress, and also its means, this 'new' capacity for perceiving truth, comfort, and direction stands over against the 'blind, ignorant' state of his unregenerate self before his acquaintance with the Bedford Church.[22] Alertness to the 'teachings of God in his Word' leads him, for example, to recognize the errors of the Quakers (one of which, Bunyan thought, was a belief that the Scriptures were not the Word of God); and about the same time he learns under the tutelage of pastor Gifford to seek the 'reality' of the Word, being brought to a conviction of the Resurrection, the Second Coming, and—a particular pillar of Puritan doctrine—the need for Christ's imputed righteousness.[23]

But there is a dark side to the relationship between the Puritan convert and the Word, amply signalized by the prayer, *'Lord leave me not to my own blindness'*, which Bunyan had uttered when puzzled and tempted by the texts of the antinomian sect, the Ranters.[24] Though one might improve one's competence in interpreting the Bible (and U. Milo Kaufmann identifies several manuals for doing just that),[25] absolute self-reliance was out of the question; God alone is infallible. 'Our duty, indeed, is attentively to hear God speaking to us', Calvin announces; and Thomas Adams declares that 'All right and sober exposition is of God': but the Puritan Arthur Hildersham's parenthesis concedes the insecurity endemic to such a stance when he remarks (italics mine) that 'we certainly (*if the fault be not in ourselves*) find cleere, and certain direction in the Word'.[26] What is for Hildersham an aside occupies the centre in *Grace Abounding*, which constantly dramatizes the implications of a situation where the Word carries incontestable weight and the individual cannot

---

[21] *GA*, § 46.   [22] *GA*, § 41.   [23] *GA*, §§ 117–28.
[24] *GA*, §§ 44–5.
[25] Kaufmann, chap. 2, *passim*.
[26] Calvin, *Commentaries on the First Book of Moses Called Genesis*, trans. Revd. John King (Edinburgh, 1847), i. 265; Thomas Adams, *A Commentary or, Exposition upon the Divine Second Epistle Generall* (London, 1633), p. 366; Arthur Hildersham, CLII *Lectures Upon Psalme* LI (London, 1635), p. 381.

embrace either the idea of manifold, indeterminate meaning or a confident faith in the efficacy of subjective reasoning.

The period of the protagonist's early doubts about his election affords an obvious case in point.[27] Bunyan, looking back, had glossed the Wall that divided the 'happy' Christians from the world in his dream as the Word itself, but walls can shut out as well as protect, and here the text from Romans, '*It is neither in him that willeth, nor in him that runneth, but in God that sheweth mercy*', presents the youthful Bunyan with a terrible impasse by raising thoughts of whether he is, or is not, among the chosen: 'I could not tell what to do'. With that stifling physical weight characteristic of his sense of the Word's might in opposition, it 'trample[s]' on all his desires of Heaven. The recovery comes, with the help of another 'sentence', '... *did ever any trust in God and were confounded?*', and after much strenuous searching for its corroboration, when he understands that the original text is really an injunction *not* to worry but to leave all in God's hands. He has fallen victim to what Calvin saw as at once the most common and the most perilous of faults:

For there is scarcely a mind in which the thought does not sometimes arise, Whence your salvation but from the election of God? But what proof have you of your election? When once this thought has taken possession of any individual, it keeps him perpetually miserable, subjects him to dire torment, or throws him into a state of complete stupor.[28]

Bunyan issues a similar caveat himself in *The Heavenly Footman* (1698): 'if thou be *prying overmuch into Gods Secret Decrees* . . . thou mayest stumble and fall . . . to [*thine*] eternal overthrow'.[29] The proper condition of the believer is one of confiding uncertainty, such as this episode proclaims in the reversal from one kind of blindness, self-centred, anxious, to another kind of blindness, God-centred, grounded in faith. Yet warnings like Calvin's cut two ways, conceding even more strongly than Hildersham's aside the mind's continuing vulnerability to its own natural impulses: and when at the end of the episode Bunyan says that the word of comfort 'doth still, at times, shine before my face' he too leaves space for further

---

[27] GA, §§ 57-65.
[28] Calvin, *Institutes* (Florida, n.d.), Book III, chap. xxiv, pp. 515-16.
[29] Misc. Wks., v. 156. Cf. *The Jerusalem Sinner Saved, Works*, i. 102.

trials, down to and including the present. Although lessons are learnt, the struggle must continue, for in nature mistakes are inevitable.

The turmoil of the 'election' episode is repeated in intenser form in the episode of 'the unpardonable sin'. Psychologically understood, the compulsion to 'sell and part with this most blessed Christ, to exchange him . . . for any thing' represents the self's subconscious bid for autonomous being, for freedom from the authority of Other.[30] In Puritan ontology, however, with its imperious model of dependency and unnegotiable birthright bond, it is interpretable only as self-destructive temptation. The very thought of such apostasy casts Bunyan into a living hell of bodily stasis and paroxysms of resistance, which William James saw as 'a typical case of the psychopathic temperament, sensitive of conscience to a diseased degree': 'I could neither eat my food, stoop for a pin, chop a stick'; 'my very Body also would be put into action or motion, by way of pushing or thrusting with my hands or elbows . . . I will not, I will not, I will not'.[31] When he finally yields—'*Let him go if he will*'—it is a consent to the demonic, bringing, not freedom or release, but the affliction of 'guilt and fearful despair', which takes the form above all of an assault by verbal automatisms, mostly texts from the Bible that come in half-hallucinatory shape to haunt and buffet him. The text from Hebrews about Esau selling *his* birthright, after which '*he found no place of repentance, though he sought it carefully with tears*', becomes the locus of his obsessive guilt and his especial tormentor, resounding in his soul like 'Fetters of brass', flying in his face like lightning, blocking out all 'relief' from other places in Scripture.[32] Nowhere does the Puritan apprehension of the active might and indisputable truth of the Word have severer repercussions, as the protagonist then contemplates the Gospel in a bitter travesty of the principle that 'if the heart be sanctified, it ordinarily distils holy, sweet, and useful Meditations out of all objects' (Isaac Ambrose), comparing himself with the archetypal apostates, David, Peter, and Judas, and finding himself 'nearer to Judas'.[33] Every word reflects and confirms the conviction that the promise of salvation is 'not to me'. So great is his desperation that he wishes

---

[30] GA, § 133.
[31] James, *Varieties of Religious Experience*, p. 157; GA, §§ 135, 137.
[32] GA, § 145.
[33] Ambrose, *Prima, Media, & Ultima*, ii. 68-9; GA, §§ 151-71.

the offending texts 'out of the Book'; but this, like the original covert desire to break free from Authority, is impossible: *'the Scriptures cannot be broken'.*[34]

The nature of Bunyan's recovery deserves close attention, for it makes prominent the part that the individual must ultimately play in stabilizing his spiritual existence. God does not send answers to the distressed soul but hints or clues, signs that must be applied to advantage in acts of 'useful Meditation'. At a crucial moment the sentence *'My grace is sufficient'* darts in upon the protagonist, being described by Bunyan both as having 'arms' open to receive him and as a 'place', 'so wide, that it could not onely inclose me, but many more beside'.[35] There is no real contradiction in this mixed metaphor but rather that conjunction of sent help and self-help that is characteristic of Bunyan's understanding of positive experiential situations: the space created by the 'arms' of grace is at once an available resting-place and, recalling the 'place of repentance' sought by yet denied to Esau, an abode which has to be worked for. As Robert Wickens's comment on concordances, 'barren and rocky, yet . . . able to show the discoveries of the whole land of Canaan', suggests, the route to a place/word of comfort lies often across the roughest territory;[36] and in the present episode the mind claws its way to equilibrium by painful slow degrees, gradually establishing reciprocity with, and mastery over, the Word which previously 'would shut him out'. Movement to-and-fro and up-and-down, motor and sensory, by which Bunyan habitually delineates the topography of soul-trouble (he 'did so tug' with Satan for possession of an encouraging text, his 'soul did hang as in a pair of Scales again') is breached by a forwards thrust of intellect and emotion as he learns to 'apply the whole sentence' and finds in it a largeness and largesse: 'O me-thought that every word was a mighty word unto me; as *my*, and *grace*, and *sufficient*, and *for thee*; they were then, and sometimes are still, far bigger than others be'.[37] Most strikingly, in an event that gives an alternative meaning to the phrase *'arms* of grace', he sets the text about grace at the throat of the Esau text, making his mind a battleground:

---

[34] GA, § 209. [35] GA, § 204.
[36] Robert Wickens, *A Compleat and Perfect Concordance* (1655), dedicatory epistle.
[37] GA, §§ 206, 207.

> ... I had a longing mind that they might come both together upon me; yea, I desired of God they might.
>
> Well, about two or three dayes after, so they did indeed; they boulted both upon me at a time, and did work and struggle strangly in me for a while; at last, that about *Esaus* birthright began to wax weak, and withdraw, and vanish; and this about the sufficiency of Grace prevailed, with peace and joy.[38]

This does not in fact decide the issue, but it does clear a way to a necessary wide-awake assessment in which Bunyan himself enters the field against the hostile texts, 'to read them, and consider them, and to weigh their scope and tendence'.[39] He brings even the Esau text over to the right side, discovering in *it* a place of comfort, for Esau's sin was different from his own, not a 'hasty thought' but one 'after some deliberation'. 'My sin was not the sin in this place intended': what he finally unearths is a mistake, and also the power to correct it, for 'thus to understand . . . was not against but according to other Scriptures'. The greatest of 'great striving' for Bunyan lies in the sphere of interpretation; the mind which from a single error weaves a net of near-deadly misconceptions itself undoes that net through an ability to 'read', 'consider', and 'weigh'.

At this point in *Grace Abounding* we become unusually aware of a linear, or developmental, structure, and of the author's hand in its making. The mighty maze, it seems, begins at last to unwind towards a significant close. The account of how the young Bunyan was able to reconstitute the meaning of the offending texts in a correct and benign form indicates a crucial historical advance in the command both of Truth and the strategies of self-stabilization, and there follows an even more notable affirmation of progress in the crossing of a threshold from understanding to exaltation, a transcendent apprehension of Christ's glory and his own share in it. Passing in a field one day, he was visited by the words, *Thy righteousness is in Heaven*: 'withall, I saw with the eyes of my Soul Jesus Christ at God's right hand'.[40] He saw for the first time 'a whole Christ':

> 'Twas glorious to me to see his exaltation . . . Now I could look from myself to him, and should reckon that all those Graces of God that now were green in me, were like those crack'd-Groats . . . that rich men carry in their Purses, when their Gold is in their Trunks at home: O I saw my Gold was

---

[38] *GA*, §§ 212-13.   [39] *GA*, § 222.   [40] *GA*, § 229.

in my Trunk at home! . . . Now Christ was all; all my Wisdom, all my Righteousness, all my Sanctification, and all my Redemption.

Further, the Lord did also lead me into the mystery of Union with this Son of God . . .[41]

The text plots a precise psychological movement within the determining ambit of Puritan dogma: where Bunyan had thought to 'sell' Christ for worldly goods he now finds in Christ all his 'Gold'; where there had been a desire to 'part with him' there is now recognition of the 'mystery of Union' between self and Other; there is a new concept of 'home', which is no longer in the 'arms' of the Word of Promise but in the Redeemer himself and 'in heaven'; to see 'with the eyes of my Soul' is to break through to a superior level of perception, a state of faith beyond both the need for mediating texts or signs and the dangers of misunderstanding. Here if anywhere in *Grace Abounding* is the climax of a conversion process, and the expression of the Puritan autobiographer's edifying and self-confirming organization of past experience. The event distributes order over what has gone before, making the alienation of the 'unpardonable sin' episode the prelude to a richer unity, and extending such earlier, brief intimations of salvation as in the vision of 'many golden Seals' which prompts desire for the 'communion of him, whose Head was crowned with Thorns, whose Face was spit upon, and Body broken, and Soul made an offering for my sins'.[42]

Anne Hawkins, who to my mind offers the most persuasive reading of *Grace Abounding* as a conversion narrative, sees in these experiences of Christ crucified and Christ risen the salient landmarks in Bunyan's reiteration of a dyadic, or two-stage, process of regeneration grounded in the Calvinist precepts of 'justification' (through Christ's imputed righteousness) and 'sanctification'.[43] Calvin had himself spoken of a twofold 'participation in Christ', for 'if we truly partake of his death, our old man is crucified by its power . . . If we are partakers of his resurrection, we are raised by it to a newness of life'; and Bunyan, in *Solomon's Temple Spiritualized* (1688), talks similarly of an incremental ascent through mortification of the flesh to vivification of the spirit, 'That [*stairway*] by which we turn from nature to grace, and that by which we turn from the

---

[41] *GA*, §§ 232-3.
[42] *GA*, § 128.
[43] Hawkins, 'The Double-conversion Narrative in *Grace Abounding*', pp. 265-7.

imperfections which attend a state of grace, to glory . . . for true repentance stopeth not at the reception of grace; for that is but a going up these Stairs to the middle chambers'.[44] The 'golden seals' episode represents the turning 'from nature to grace', the later 'exaltation' the turning 'from grace to glory'. In the changed posture of the Saviour we register the changed psyche of the autobiographical persona, the suffering Christ imaging forth the mind of the youthful hero, burdened by guilt, at the beginning of his soteriological journey, the resurrected Christ indicating a newly vivified Bunyan.

This reading of *Grace Abounding*, which elaborates William James's seminal account of the *lysis* or gradual mode of conversion, is a valuable counter to the confusion that has arisen among the critics who, under the influence of the more typical Pauline *crisis* model, have sought a single dramatic point of transformation in Bunyan's spiritual history.[45] But it leads Anne Hawkins finally into the same false position as that she opposes, for she assigns to the 'exaltation' episode the status of a *terminus*, a conclusive 'liberation from guilt, a certitude which can affirm the self only by looking beyond it'.[46] There are configurations of spiritual progress in *Grace Abounding* but no such closure in 'liberation' or 'certitude'. It is interesting that right at the end of the main body of the text, before the added sections on his ministry and imprisonment, Bunyan should introduce a recollection very like the 'grace to glory' episode, describing how once, under 'a great cloud of darkness', 'loyns . . . broken' and 'hands and feet . . . bound with chains', he had been surprised by the words '*I must go to Jesus*', which lead him to remember and experience 'wonderful glory' in the text from Hebrews (12: 22-4), '*Ye are come to mount Zion, to the City of the Living God, the heavenly Jerusalem* . . .'[47]

---

[44] Calvin, *Institutes*, quoted in Hawkins, 'The Double-conversion Narrative', p. 265; Bunyan, *Solomon's Temple Spiritualized* (1688), in *Works*, iii. 482.

[45] See James, *Varieties of Religious Experience*, p. 183: 'The older medicine used to speak of two ways, *lysis* and *crisis*, one gradual, the other abrupt, in which one might recover from a bodily disease. In the spiritual realm there are also two ways, one gradual, the other sudden, in which inner unification may occur. Tolstoy and Bunyan may again serve us as examples . . . ' As I shall argue, however, there is in fact no 'inner unification' in Bunyan. Hawkins, 'The Double-conversion Narrative', p. 263, cites several examples of '*crisis*' interpretation of Bunyan's conversion, where the location of the turning-point ranges from the encounter with the Bedford women (Margaret Bottrall) to the battle between the texts about Esau and the sufficiency of grace (Dean Ebner).

[46] Hawkins, 'The Double-conversion Narrative', p. 267.

[47] GA, §§ 261-2.

The effect of this is to override the conclusiveness of the earlier event, not only by suggesting the attainment of a higher level of exaltation in which (as Richard Sibbes puts it) Heaven itself is known 'in our affections before we be there in our bodies',[48] but also by emphasizing that all exaltation is a state of mind that comes and goes. Vivification of the spirit is for Bunyan no absolute change but a glimpse of glory occurring intermittently and shadowed by its own inevitable passing. He chooses in fact to concede (and Hawkins to ignore) the provisionality of 'joy, and peace, and triumph', saying of the Christ risen episode 'I lived, for some time, very sweetly', and of the one about Mount Sion 'this great glory did not continue upon me until the morning'. When he finally remarks of the latter, 'These words also have oft since this time been great refreshment to my Spirit', he points the still-continuing need for 'refreshment'—but also the value of his golden hours, which, through memory, bear consoling witness to the potency of the Word, God's grace, and a personal capacity for making successful trial of the 'wonderful glory' that is given.

If *Grace Abounding* ended there, it could be said to conclude, if not in certitude, then at least in comforting thoughts. But it doesn't end there, and in the accounts of Bunyan's ministry and imprisonment we are plunged once more into a world of turmoil, conflict, and struggle. Anne Hawkins, striking a not unfamiliar critical attitude, sweeps these sections aside as the produce of an 'exhausted' Bunyan,[49] but in reality they contain some of Bunyan's most vigorous writing and very specifically challenge any reading of his life in terms of transformation, advancement by stages, or wholeness. Impressions of a movement from 'nature to grace' or 'grace to glory' are subsumed in evidences of conflict between the natural and the spiritual man, and between self and God: 'I have gone full of guilt and terrour even to the Pulpit-Door, and there it hath been taken off . . . and then immediately, even before I could get down the Pulpit-Stairs, have been as bad as I was before'; still worse, 'Sometimes again, when I have been preaching, I have been violently assaulted with thoughts of blasphemy, and strongly tempted to speak them with my mouth before the Congregation . . . so

---

[48] Richard Sibbes, *Light from Heaven* (London, 1638), p. 194. Cf. *PP*, p. 161: 'And now were these two men, as 'twere, in Heaven, before they came at it'.

[49] Hawkins, 'The Double-conversion Narrative', p. 262.

blinded, and so estranged from the things I have been speaking . . . as if my head had been in a bag all the time of the *exercise*.'⁵⁰ This is moving because it insists that, whatever has happened outwardly, *in essence* nothing has changed since those early days when Bunyan had felt the urge to worship 'a Bush, a Bull, a Besom, or the like', or to declare the Scriptures 'a Fable and cunning story', or to sell Christ.⁵¹ The 'old man' never has been crucified in him; with a frankness that makes nonsense of the popular idea of Puritan self-righteousness, he confesses to a split existence and personality as the mouthpiece of God, the mediator-receptacle of His Word, whose feelings do not naturally accord with the demands of his calling and in whom blindness, estrangement, and even blasphemous defiance hover like demons.

Grace Abounding thus becomes in the final analysis the history, not of a two-stage liberation, but of a twofold burden—the burden of an inescapable commitment and the burden of irrepressible natural inclinations. William James's phrase, the 'hue of resolution',⁵² catches admirably the characteristic texture of Bunyan's emotional response to the world and his existence in it, but that response intensifies at times in his recorded experience into the effort of hanging on by the last thread of courage and will. During his imprisonment, his calling demanded at once the greatest sacrifice of and the fiercest resistance to the promptings of nature:

> the parting with my Wife and poor Children hath oft been to me in this place as the pulling the flesh from my bones . . . especially my poor blind Child, who lay nearer my heart than all I had besides . . . Thou must be beaten, must beg, suffer hunger, cold, nakedness . . . yet thought I, I must do it, I must do it.⁵³

Grace Abounding comes more than ever to life as a human drama at such moments. Though he sees the pull of worldly ties as an infirmity, a temptation not 'to live upon God that is invisible', yet Bunyan cleaves with tremendous honesty to their irreducible claims and the pain of necessary renunciation: 'I must do it, I must do it'. Just as the action had earlier been fuelled by mistakes, so now it is fired by the realization of those natural instincts that must be overridden in the service of Faith and vocation. The realization is

---

⁵⁰ GA, §§ 277, 293.   ⁵¹ GA, §§ 108, 96.
⁵² James, *Varieties of Religious Experience*, p. 188.
⁵³ GA, §§ 327–8.

ubiquitous but not always explicit: it extends even to that strangest of all Bunyan's additions to the text, his self-defence against charges of fornication with Agnes Beaumont, where, in his insistent protestations of innocence — 'I seldom so much as touch a woman's hand', 'I know not whether there be a woman breathing . . . except my wife'[54] — we read no bland dismissal of 'the flesh' but a knowledge of what it is to be tempted and to resist. As the text draws to a close, the battle between nature and calling takes on a truly heroic swell as Bunyan describes his trial, when a young prisoner, in the face of fear of death at the gallows (which again involves a mistake, for the relevant law did not in fact prescribe execution):

> I was bound, but he [God] was free: yea it was my dutie to stand to his Word, whether he would ever look upon me or no, or save me at the last . . . if God doth not come in, thought I, I will leap off the Ladder even blindfold into Eternitie, sink or swim, come heaven, come hell; Lord Jesus, if thou wilt catch me, do; if not, I will venture for thy Name.[55]

The bonds of the believer who may not 'chuse whether I would hold my profession or no', blindness on the question of whether salvation will come or not: these, not liberty or ecstasy, are Bunyan's last perception of the way of Faith. Their embrace and celebration of the resolve to venture on though there may be no return provides a stirring ending, but hardly a conclusive one.

Significantly, Bunyan appends a formal Conclusion in which nothing whatsoever is concluded. Conflating his present self with all his past selves, he lists the several 'abominations' found 'to this day . . . in my heart', not least inclinings 'to question the being of God, and the truth of his Gospel'. That he should know these things, and oppose to them the several supports of self-help and sent help, culminating in a looking 'to God, through Christ, to help me, and carry me through this world', signifies the growth of strategic awareness that has taken place during composition of the work, the reading, considering, and weighing of the evidences of past trials and triumphs; but this itself projects, more in hope than certainty (' I hope I know something of these things', says Bunyan when referring to 'goodly' experience), a future that will continue the battles of former times, in which the only permanent aspect of conversion is its incompleteness.

[54] *GA*, §§ 309–16.   [55] *GA*, § 337.

Grace Abounding: Self-affirmation and Self-abnegation

This concentration on the continuum of experience, as strong at the end as in earlier parts of the text, has significant implications for the status of *Grace Abounding* within the tradition of religious autobiography, and as a precursor of the autobiographical novel. Robert Bell and William C. Spengemann have both recently identified in the work a radical modification of standard confessional writing stemming from St Augustine's *Confessions*, with Spengemann talking, for instance, of Bunyan's new 'novelistic density and bustle' and, more suggestively, of a shift of emphasis from 'the truth that life illustrates to the life that embodies truth'.[56] We have only to compare the famous pear-stealing episode from the *Confessions* with Bunyan's counterpart, the game of cat, to remind ourselves how far in Bunyan the static design of known truth, *mythos*, has yielded the centre of focus to the dynamic process of experience itself:

> . . . it was our habit to carry on our games in the streets till very late. We carried off an immense load of pears, not to eat, for we barely tasted them before throwing them to the hogs. Our only pleasure in doing it was that it was forbidden. Such was my heart, O God, such was my heart . . .[57]

As Robert Bell observes, Augustine 'sharply delineates a "self" before and after conversion':[58] 'such was my heart, O God'. Writing from a 'redeemed' perspective and seeing himself as re-enacting the sacred drama of the Fall, he appropriates the personal past to the eternal pattern of human sin and divine grace, unconcerned with any precise exploration of consciousness or circumstantial detail. In Bunyan, on the other hand, the event is keenly particularized ('having struck it one blow from the hole . . . '); the perspective of the time is given minute attention, especially, as we have seen, in the protagonist's 'conclusion', after the vision of a hotly displeased Jesus, 'that it was now too late for me to look after Heaven', so that the stress falls, not on any emblem of absolute depravity or love of the forbidden, but, more sympathetically, upon mental activity and the individual's

---

[56] Robert Bell, 'Metamorphoses of Spiritual Autobiography', *ELH* 44 (1977), 108–26; William C. Spengemann, *The Forms of Autobiography: Episodes in the History of a Literary Genre* (New Haven, 1980), esp. pp. 44–51.

[57] St Augustine, *The Confessions*, trans. F. J. Sheed (New York, 1942), pp. 26–7.

[58] Bell, 'Metamorphoses', p. 110. My argument is at this point indebted to certain details of Bell's illuminating article.

capacity for making mistakes (and therefore also for learning to know better); and thirdly Bunyan is much more present in his text and conscious of his role as its maker, expressing in his protestation 'before God, I lye not, neither do I feign this sort of speech' a mixture of confidence in his own authority and an uneasy sense of the limitations of human perception, of the still-persisting danger of creating misguided or false meanings.

This last point is an important one, for the psychodrama of *Grace Abounding* extends finally to the consciousness of the author-narrator himself, who is poised indeterminately between the postures of self-affirmation and self-abnegation, thus repeating at another level the tension between nature and faith that dominates so many of the historical episodes and Bunyan's assessment of his condition in the Conclusion. In the section on his ministry Bunyan is much exercised about the question of glorifying self: 'shall I be proud because I am a sounding Brass?'[59] The inevitably negative answer, 'He hath cause also to walk humbly with God, and be little in his own eyes', is a resounding acknowledgement of the Order and Providence superior and unaccountable to man. That the issue should be raised at all, however, suggests that he was perhaps himself conscious of the way his text, in Felicity Nussbaum's words, asserts ' a self that proselytized and witnessed for his God, but also . . . competed with the Scriptures for authority'.[60] *Grace Abounding* 'competes' with Truth, the authority of God and the Word, not only because Bunyan makes himself the hero of the work, or because it makes the self the centre of attention, valorizing the excitements of inward experience and situating God and the Word themselves as concepts within an individual consciousness (the Word never exists here as a privileged marginal gloss), but also because it declares itself as the form one man has uniquely given to his life. Bunyan holds powerfully to a world view that assumes that all things are ordered from without, yet in writing an autobiography bears witness to what James Olney terms 'the vital impulse to order that has always caused man to create and that, in the end, determines both the nature and the form of what he creates'.[61] *Grace Abounding* presents in the end a paradox: though

---

[59] GA, § 300.
[60] Felicity A. Nussbaum, ' "By These Words I Was Sustained": Bunyan's *Grace Abounding*', ELH 49 (1982), 32–3.
[61] James Olney, *Metaphors of Self: The Meaning of Autobiography* (Princeton, 1972), p. 3.

distrusting subjective interpretation and making, seeing them as a source of error, hostile to faith, malign opposites of God's meaning resident in the Word, Bunyan was so far their exponent as to leave the world a book for all time, equating truth not only with the events of a personal life but with that which is personally created in the act of inscription.

The Pilgrim's Progress: The Irresolution of Vulnerability

The writing of *Grace Abounding* was for Bunyan a great seminal experience: there is hardly an ingredient in his two other major works, *The Pilgrim's Progress* and *The Holy War*, which did not originate in the earlier text. Roger Sharrock's well-known article tracks down many of the parallels with *The Pilgrim's Progress*, at least where these involve the theology of 'conversion'—so that, for example, the Slough of Despond reiterates Bunyan's first bout of despair in the 'miry bog that shook as I did but stir'.[62] There is so much that might be added to the list. A positive link emerges, for instance, in the fact that Christian's story of Little-faith's assault and battery at the hands of Faint-heart, Mistrust, and Guilt is followed by a disquisition on the text about Esau selling his birthright, which views the text as benign and distinguishes Little-faith's case from Esau's on the grounds that the former, though sorely pressed, held on to his 'jewels' of 'saving faith'.[63] Little-faith is the self of the 'unpardonable sin' episode seen with detachment and transformed into the 'hero' of a brief parabolic allegory (while the man in the iron cage at the Interpreter's House is that self foreclosed at the point of imagined 'despite to the spirit of grace' and transformed into a cautionary spectacle). Christian eventually tells Hopeful that he too has been 'engaged' like Little-faith, and that the future is uncertain since all is 'as God would have it' and no man 'can tell what in the combat attends us'. I have argued elsewhere that this acceptance of the precariousness of the believer's condition signals Christian's advance from natural anxiety to spiritual wisdom and the status of enlightened interpreter,[64] but the whole episode also characterizes

---

[62] Roger Sharrock, 'Spiritual Autobiography in *The Pilgrim's Progress*', *RES* 24 (1948), 102–20.

[63] *PP*, pp. 128–9.

[64] 'Bunyan and the Confines of the Mind', in Newey, pp. 35–6.

Bunyan's own achieved movement from the raw self-consciousness of *Grace Abounding* to a more controlled and objective viewpoint — to the anthropomorphic allegorical method in which, for most readers, he displays the full extent of his insight and creative genius. The materials of the precursor text are at once recapitulated and refashioned.

It cannot be my purpose here to explore that refashioning in great detail. One of its salient effects, however, is the more certain and deliberate foregrounding of spiritual, as opposed to natural, 'seeing' and 'doing'. I am not thinking simply of Christian's reliance upon the efficacy of the Word (which recalls of course such episodes as the young Bunyan's discovery of the liberating power of the text about the sufficiency of grace), though this is of manifest importance, and boldy underlined in Apollyon's defeat, not by the *s*word, but by words: '*Christian* nimbly reached out his hand for his Sword, and caught it, saying, *Rejoyce not against me, O mine Enemy!* . . . and with that, gave him a deadly thrust'.[65] I have in mind, rather, the wider embrace of seeing by the light of Faith and with 'the eyes of the soul', which emerges variously as the determining principle of the work, and which represents an exfoliation of the comparatively rare moments of unclouded faith in *Grace Abounding*. Evangelist's instruction to Christian and Faithful, as they enter Vanity Fair, is to 'believe stedfastly concerning things that are invisible. Let nothing on this side the other world get within you'.[66] This premise inheres positively in Christian's dedication to the 'way' of Christ's 'I am the way' and negatively in the many erring pilgrims who walk by the light of their own reason, desires, or imagination, and thus in darkness. Atheist (a good example of how *The Pilgrim's Progress* separates out and gives independent life to facets of the divided self of *Grace Abounding*), asked about the Celestial City, jeers, 'There is no such place as you Dream of, in all this World'.[67] Precisely: that place is 'in the world to come', and no dream. Or there is Ignorance, the man 'wise in his own conceit', who falsely identifies the way to the Celestial City with that which is visible, measurable, and pleasing to the eye, 'a fine, plesant, green Lane, that comes down from our Countrey the next way into it'.[68] The people of Vanity Fair do not even so much as look beyond their world of vain conceit, but sit

---

[65] *PP*, pp. 59–60.
[66] *PP*, pp. 86–7.
[67] *PP*, p. 135.
[68] *PP*, p. 124.

there hatching carnal plots: 'They therefore brought him out, to do with him according to their Law; and first they Scourged him, then they Buffetted him, then they Lanced his flesh . . . Thus came *Faithful* to his end'. The sequential syntax mirrors their confinement to a this-worldly order of action and events. But there is another plot, another 'end', which leads suddenly upwards, for 'a Chariot and a couple of Horses' come to take Faithful '(so soon as his adversaries had dispatched him) . . . the nearest way to the Cœlestial Gate'.[69] Placed in parenthesis, the designs of men become subordinate to, and ironically serve, the designs of Providence; and the reader of *The Pilgrim's Progress* is manœuvred into a position where he must himself renounce the interest of this-worldly narrative and truth for those of Truth—must read according to a belief in 'things that are invisible'. Thus in this text the conflict between 'nature' and 'spirit' is carried also into the sphere of rhetorical persuasion, and we ourselves are made protagonists in a drama of blindness and enlightenment.

It might seem from this affirmation of providential design and intervention, and from what I have said of the Little-faith episode, where everything is 'as God would have it', that the ontology of *The Pilgrim's Progress* situates the individual in a position where he must simply await the outcome of events, participating passively in the unfolding of his destiny. There is something in this, but by no means all; for, as in *Grace Abounding*, there can be no escape from doubt, error, and other infirmities, or from the responsibility of transcending them. Though the *telos*, or presupposed and governing focus, of Christian's journey, and therefore of the work that embodies it, is the repose of spiritual fulfilment, the *dynamis*, or source of action, is the deferral of that end by abiding pressures from within the self. The erring pilgrims, Atheist, Ignorance, and the rest, are not the only ones to make mistakes. Christian, though not like them the victim of irredeemable illusion, remains nevertheless vulnerable to comparable misconceptions. The mental strife of the 'unpardonable sin' and other episodes in *Grace Abounding*— generated in 'fault', sustained by false reasoning and the shadow side of imagination, provisionally resolved through sent help and the strategies of meditation—recur in the great experiential episodes of *The Pilgrim's Progress*, with the difference that biblical texts are now

[69] *PP*, p. 97.

invariably supportive and memory replaces wrestlings with the Word as the chief source of stability. There is no better example than Doubting Castle. Christian falls into the clutches of Giant Despair because he makes the same mistake that he has just avoided when resisting the temptation of Demas, 'son of Judas', to leave the Way for the silver mines of Lucre Hill (selling Christ for the things of this world), and then shown himself apparently above when being able to 'pick out the meaning' of the cautionary monument of the Pillar of Salt.[70] Letting 'this side of the other world' get within him—that is, following the promptings of nature, acting autonomously—he follows a plan of his own: "Tis according to my wish . . . here is the easiest going'.[71] Despair itself is the projection of guilt: 'they knew themselves in a fault', and the Giant *therefore* drove them before him', beating them 'so they were not able to help themselves', as the guilt-infected texts had beaten Bunyan in the earlier work.[72] Stanley Fish and U. Milo Kaufmann see Christian's release, which comes when he discovers the 'key of promise' in his bosom, as an act of faith discontinuous with the mental processes that have taken place in the dungeon;[73] but it is not really so, for it is the culmination of a discourse in which arrestive psychic energies are countered through the agency of memory, as Hopeful, Christian's worthier self, reminds his 'brother' that God *'may cause that* Giant Despair *may die'* and urges him to recall *'how valiant thou hast been heretofore'*. Christian finally escapes because he remembers the Promise outlined long ago by Evangelist: 'All manner of sin and blasphemies shall be forgiven unto men; be not faithless, but believing'.[74]

The Pilgrim's Progress is no more a straightforward account of the progressive stages of salvation than *Grace Abounding* is of the stages of conversion. In both texts diachronic sequence is subsumed in a synchronic insistence on repeated dramas of infirmity and strength, deviation from and recovery of the Way of Faith. Anyone who has read the book carefully will know that the mental topography of Doubting Castle, the configuration of precariousness and great striving inherited from *Grace Abounding*, is re-enacted even at the

---

[70] *PP*, pp. 107–8. [71] *PP*, p. 111. [72] *PP*, pp. 113–14.
[73] Stanley E. Fish, *Self-consuming Artifacts* (1972; repr. Berkeley and Los Angeles, 1974), pp. 257–8; Kaufmann, p. 198. For a detailed discussion of this point and the configurations of mental process that constitute the great experiential episodes of *The Pilgrim's Progress*, see Newey, pp. 22 ff. [74] *PP*, pp. 115–16, 22.

River of Death, where Christian counters desperate thoughts of 'the sins that he had committed' (and not simply fear of death) by an appeal to memory ('call to mind that which heretofore you have received of his goodness'), the Bible, and Christ's image ('Oh I see him again!').[75] When Worldly-Wiseman, early on, presses Christian to avoid *'the dangers that thou wilt in this way run thy self into'*[76] his words pose a double threat, not only the temptation of 'formalist' religion but also the extinction of *The Pilgrim's Progress* itself, which everywhere depends upon Christian running *himself* into dangers and fighting his way out.

This cyclical structure is of course broken with Christian's entry into the Celestial City, where we move into a situation of closure unprecedented, though not unprophesied, in *Grace Abounding*. The intimations of 'wonderful glory' in the City of the living God with which the conversion narrative had ended now expand in a sustained envisioning of the 'other world' in which 'difficulty, because of the infirmity of [*the*] flesh' has passed away, exaltation is habitual as the soul is 'swallowed up' with sights of the Holy One, texts (*Blessed are they that do his commandments . . .*) require no interpretation or application but simply declare the site of an inalienable repose. But this closure is in the event Christian's alone, not Bunyan's, or ours, or that of the narrator who is our fellow: 'I looked in after them; and behold, the City shone like the Sun . . . And after that, they shut up the Gates: which when I had seen, I wished myself among them'.[77] This image of impossible desire and felt exclusion is only one of the ways in which Bunyan relinquishes the satisfaction of celebratory and authoritative completion, pushing the focus back with peculiar force upon this-worldly perspectives and consciousness, upon uncertainty, undecidability, a sense of incompleteness. The damnation of Ignorance, on which the spotlight finally falls, introduces an alternative ending:

> When he was come up to the Gate, he looked up to the writing that was above; and then began to knock . . . Then they asked him for his Certificate . . . So he fumbled in his bosom for one, and found none . . . Then they took him up, and carried him through the air to the door that I saw in the side of the Hill, and put him in there. Then I saw that there was a way to Hell, even from the Gates of Heaven, as well as from the City of *Destruction*.[78]

[75] *PP*, pp. 157–8. [76] *PP*, p. 19.
[77] *PP*, p. 162. [78] *PP*, pp. 162–3.

Much critical effort has gone into explaining the theological grounds on which Ignorance is justly condemned to Hell—the rightful fate of a 'hypocrite'.[79] That, it seems to me, is at best narrow labour, and one which misses the patent complexity and richness of Bunyan's representation of the event, which prompts us irresistibly to a set of mixed reactions. Certainly, Ignorance is of the 'reprobate' and suffers the inevitable consequence; and certainly there is in the text a didactic intent, a caution to be watchful and not vain-confident. Yet none of this precludes sympathy for Ignorance's misunderstanding of the words above the Gate, his misconceived hope, his fumbling helplessness—nor shock at the nature of the last reckoning. The Shining Ones judge Ignorance in absolute terms, and find him wanting by the strict rules of dogmatic faith; but that is their, or rather God's, unquestionable privilege, and is a model of response ultimately unavailable to us in the state of nature. The reader cannot but see something of himself in Ignorance, his human errors and vulnerability writ large; we cannot help things 'this side the other world' getting within us, for we are *of* the world of nature. We saw earlier how in the Vanity Fair episode Bunyan subordinates the claims of truth (man's plots) to those of Truth (God's plots). This hierarchy is preserved and promulgated throughout *The Pilgrim's Progress*: Ignorance's plan, after all, fails before God's. Yet in the final analysis *The Pilgrim's Progress* is paradoxical, and subverts Truth, in the same way as *Grace Abounding*, for the absolutes it upholds are inscribed in an overall structure of indeterminacy that on various levels calls them in question: by, that is, giving spectacular imaginative realization to the theoretically negative positions or points of view (Worldly-Wiseman's, say, as well as Ignorance's), thus upgrading them to the status of potential alternatives; by involving us in double readings of the same event, as when in witnessing the destruction of Ignorance though we may wish ourselves entirely on the side of the angels we find ourselves, in our humanity, their rivals; by centralizing self and processes of the mind, Christian's, ours, the dreamer–narrator's; by manifesting Truth itself as a matter of how things are seen, of commitment, right and wrong choices, going this

---

[79] See, e.g., Maurice Hussey, 'Bunyan's "Mr Ignorance"', *MLR* 44 (1949), 483–9, which limits the passage to a sweeping of 'the last devil . . . into Hell'. Hussey's reading is continued, albeit with less strict condemnation of Ignorance, by Paula R. Backscheider: *A Being More Intense: A Study of the Prose Works of Bunyan, Swift, and Defoe* (New York, 1984), pp. 118–19.

way or that; and finally by referring us to the value of writing, the authority, satisfactions, and very existence of John Bunyan's own book. For what matters in that last sentence about Heaven and Hell is not any doctrine *per se*, the belief in a scheme of salvation and damnation, but its impact in the mind and imagination of the seeing 'I' — or rather the impact of Bunyan's text, since what the 'I' sees is nothing more nor less than the bifurcation of the way that has already been effected in his alternate endings, Christian's glory, Ignorance's tragedy. *The Pilgrim's Progress* comes to rest, self-reflexively, in an awareness of the one true certainty of its own being and the experience it offers.

The Holy War: The Resolution of Abstraction

In *The Holy War* Bunyan returns once more to the materials of *Grace Abounding*, but to wholly different effect, applying a spare, impersonal allegorical method that throws weight firmly upon the force and presentation of doctrine. It operates in a manner akin to the sermon, and to Scripture itself, communicating inviolable truths, fixed meanings. The double conversion narrative reappears in Diabolus's two occupations of Mansoul and Emanuel's two victories over him ("'Tis not grace received, but grace improved, that preserves the soul from temporal dangers' is Bunyan's gloss as the second fall begins), but its experiential content is reformulated in a series of set speeches and brief tableaux. Of the latter, we may note accounts both of the workings of sin and the receipt of grace abounding:

Now were the Townsmen strangely altered; they were as men stricken with a panick fear: they ran through the Streets of the Town of *Mansoul* crying out, help, help . . .

Yea, my Lord *Wilbewill* swounded out-right, but the Prince stept to him, put his everlasting arms under him, imbraced him, kissed him, and bid him be of good cheer . . .[80]

Psychological events are exhibited from the outside, iconographically, with the human interest limited to a plain, and effective, appeal to the average visualizing imagination which reminds us of the 'homely' allegories of Part II of *The Pilgrim's Progress*. More characteristically, however, the drama of sin and grace, nature, faith, and great striving,

---

[80] *HW*, pp. 40, 106.

is delineated in abstract terms, through the self-defining speeches of the 'characters', Incredulity, Hard-heart, Understanding, and the rest, and through the addresses of Diabolus and Emanuel. *The Holy War* is not so much a war, either inward or cosmic, or even of words, as a topography of concept, tenet, and instruction. Where the difficulties and stress of the way of Faith are acknowledged, they are a corporate, not individual, problem, and solutions are quickly given; we remember Bunyan's solitary struggles with the Word in *Grace Abounding* when we learn that it contains 'riddles', but Mansoul is a different world and Emanuel is there to explain them: 'Oh how they were lightned . . . they could not have thought that such rarities could have been couched in so few and such ordinary words'.[81] And so it is for the reader of *The Holy War*: he is the passive recipient of 'such rarities' as Bunyan unveils.

In the long concluding section of *The Holy War* the text passes all to Emanuel himself, in whose monumental words is inscribed that inner life of vulnerability and strength, bondage and mental fight, heroism, blind faith, which Bunyan had so powerfully expressed and brought into being through the protagonist-selves of his autobiography and *The Pilgrim's Progress*:

O my Mansoul, *should I slay all them within, many there be without that would bring thee into bondage . . . Thou must live upon my* Word. *Thou must believe . . . when I am from thee . . . Remember therefore, O my* Mansoul, *that thou art beloved of me; as I have therefore taught thee to watch, to fight, to pray . . . so now I command thee to believe my love is constant to thee . . . Hold fast till I come.*[82]

This is in a sense a starting-point, creating a future space for the same holy war, individual and now also collective, to be lived through over and over again, until the end of time. But it is also an ending: *The Holy War* has *its* resting-place in self-abnegation; a work in which Bunyan not only turns 'experience . . . to an universal advantage' (Isaac Ambrose) in a different way, translating it into dogma, but also finally withdraws his own presence, yielding all authority to the one true source of his creative vision and achievements in the realms of experience, making, and the word—Christ, the still small voice, *logos* itself. This is a fitting moment, replete with integrity; and its quiet, frugal sublimity is but one of the qualities of *The Holy War*

[81] *HW*, p. 116.   [82] *HW*, pp. 249–50.

I am unable on this occasion to pursue.[83] Yet in our fallen world, where the immediate stir of nature is inevitably more real than the distant harmonies of faith, Bunyan's last epic cannot but forfeit the precedence it claims; it stands in Bunyan's corpus as *Paradise Regained* stands to *Paradise Lost*, or *The Excursion* to *The Prelude*, a solid monument to what has gone so richly before.

[83] Knott, *The Sword of the Spirit*, pp. 153–63 develops an effective reassessment of Bunyan's inventive use of biblical materials and epic-dramatic form. For some recent suggestive comments on Bunyan's 'ambitious design', see Backscheider, *A Being More Intense*, pp. 71–5.

11

Glossing and Glozing: Bunyan and Allegory

BY VALENTINE CUNNINGHAM

BUNYAN's texts have a marked taste for meditating on the meat of the Word and on the word as comestible stuff. Their appetite whetted by constant biblical talk of God as host, provider, cook, and quartermaster, they keep on greedily contemplating the biblical promise that the Lord will grant nourishment, eatables, and drinkables, variously raw and cooked, to pilgrims. In Part II of *The Pilgrim's Progress* Innkeeper Gaius and his cook Taste-that-which-is-good lay on a whole six-course meal for Christiana and her boys. The affair starts with an Old Testament meat course of 'heave-shoulder' and 'wave-breast', washed down with a New Testament bottle of blood-red wine and (for the lads) milk 'well-crumbed', followed by a pudding of honey and butter and a two-part dessert of apples and nuts.[1] All of which makes a very tasty dish, wholly garnered from biblical sources, for interpreters of Bunyan's allegory to get their teeth into. Mine Host himself—a conflation of the Gaius in whose house the Corinthian church met (1 Corinthians 1: 14 and Romans 16: 23: 'Gaius mine host, and of the whole church') and the 'wellbeloved Gaius' of the third epistle of John (who would bring Christians 'forward on their journey after a godly sort'), and so a type of the caring pastor and Bible teacher—is not slow, in the fashion of Bunyan's self-interpreting text, with his own explications of the feast he's provided ('Drink freely, this is the Juice of the true Vine, that makes glad the Heart of God and Man', and so on).[2] And until recently it would have seemed clearly to be implied that with the aid of Gaius and his interpretative allies in the text, the marginal

---

[1] *PP*, pp. 259, 261–2.   [2] *PP*, p. 262.

pointings running alongside it, backed up by centuries of assumptions about the legibility, not to say logocentricity of the Judaeo-Christian Scriptures, readers could themselves sit down with Christiana and her group and enjoy a nourishing bout of edifying interpretation, indulging themselves in a hermeneutic experience that promised positive instruction and spiritual gain for believing readers and also more mundane pleromas, secular satisfaction of sense and meaning, for the non-believing reader. Nowadays, however, before any reader can make a meal of Bunyan's meals, he or she is compelled to partake of something fishier. For Stanley Fish's dedicated subversions have strikingly challenged any casual assumption about the simplicities of reading Bunyan's re-readings of the Scriptures and of the Christian and Christiana way. The Bunyanesque menu now comes with as it were a compulsory Fish course for starters. 'The illusory nature of the pilgrim's progress is a large part of Bunyan's point, and the reader's awareness of the problematics of the narrative is essential to this intention, which is nothing less than the disqualification of his work as a vehicle of the insight it pretends to convey'.[3] Fish's intervention argues that *The Pilgrim's Progress* is not going to wait for any reader to get conventional satisfactions out of consuming it; it has already eaten itself up.

Fish's talk of intentions is undoubtedly a mistake. At any rate his chapter on *The Pilgrim's Progress* in *Self-consuming Artifacts* does not effect a convincing alliance between Fish's credible argument that Bunyan intended his text to act out warnings against casual readings of Word and word, simple ideas about progress and the way, and Fish's much more contentious faith in the intentionality of this (and any other text) as a self-subverting textual system. It's more usual for deconstructionists to prefer that intentions be left out of their argument except in the most metaphoric of senses which would grant a sub-conscious to texts. Deconstructionist readings are more commonly and properly supposed to be readings against the grain of a text's overt directions and 'intentions'. But still, intentionality aside, the question of textual self-subversion, of *mise en abîme*, is seriously levelled at Bunyan, and must be taken seriously. And the question strikes particularly deeply right into the heart of the Bunyanesque matter, into that fundamental place in Bunyan's

---

[3] 'Progress in *The Pilgrim's Progress*', in Stanley E. Fish, *Self-consuming Artifacts* (1972; repr. Berkeley and Los Angeles, 1974), pp. 224–5.

thinking and practice, the location where Fish himself curiously declined to pursue his allegations, namely into the nature of allegory itself ('allegory (I do not use the word in my chapter on *The Pilgrim's Progress*)').[4] For in the current climate (or tank) of prevailing Fishy opinion, the question naturally arises as to how far the deconstructive logics now being applied to allegory may be applicable to Bunyan. And then, of course, comes the next and analogous question: how far are we to heed the now well-advertised deconstructive logics of the marginal gloss?

The post-modernist argument is that allegory is always double reading. It exists in the juxtaposition and superimposition of different senses, readings, stories. And while a univocity and equality of the separate senses is sought for, allegory never wholly shrugs off the divisiveness that comes from the dividedness of attention it incites — that invitation to the reader to keep two levels of reference continually in mind. And in this bifurcation of the reader's attention, this constant two-ness of reference, the conceptual life of allegory resembles the physically endorsed textual doubleness that the use of marginal glosses imposes: that text:margin/margin:text situation and problematic that confronts the reader on every page of *The Pilgrim's Progress* and on numerous other Bunyan pages as well. The questions busily arising from a text girded about with marginal glosses focus the question of allegory and other belated, marginal textual activities such as prefaces, footnotes, supplements, indexes, commentaries, in an obvious and immediate form. Glosses, like allegories — which are extended, fictionalized glosses indulged in the margins so to say of some anterior or precedent text, story, historical situation, moral case — undermine the idea of textual monodicity, the authorizing status of texts as original, authoritative, final, necessary and self-sufficient source and guarantor of meaning. Glosses, like allegories, undermine logocentricity. Under the busy accumulations of the gloss's accusing presence the prime text inevitably sheds some or all of its claim to the power of sole origination of meaning, its very primeness. The real practical question of where the reader should look first, at text or at margin, is an emblem of the conceptual dilemma glosses plunge one into. And, of course, once the act of supplementation begins, there seems little reason for it ever to stop. And it doesn't stop, certainly not in the

---

[4] Fish, *Self-consuming Artifacts*, p. xi.

case of what we can call the classic glossable texts. The first step into glossing, like the first step into the rereading known as allegory, usually proves a *felix culpa*, an inviting fall into the joys of Midrash, that endless, exfoliating process of comment upon comment, reinterpretation layered upon reinterpretation, a licensed game of commentary that resists closure, defies certainty, and puts off conclusion. Midrash gets interpretation on to a busy unstoppable escalator of interpretative opportunism, an activity flushed with the prodigality of the free imaginative rein it sanctions, unperturbed by the undecidability of texts that it promotes and seems decided on. So that glossing inevitably takes on the air of glozing: that misleading task of giving a shine to texts without regard to questions of truth. No wonder Edgar Allan Poe declared that 'nonsense' was 'the essential sense of the Marginal Note'.[5] And as gloss slides into gloze, allegorizing elides into allegorizing *out of* or *away*, an activity in which the idea of any original sense is rubbed right out, explained away. So it's no wonder either that Walter Benjamin should have thought that allegories were a ruinous way of thinking: 'Allegorien sind im Reiche der Gedanken was Ruinen im Reiche der Dinge'.[6] Allegorical explanations could easily be read as darkening further the very conceits, the dark conceits, whose lightening they're commonly supposed to lead to. It comes as no surprise at all, given such reflections, that allegory, the marginal gloss, the activity of religious and secular Midrash, should now be taken as symptomatic of deconstructive textuality *per se*—instructive emblems of a totalizing post-modernist hermeneutics whose essence is felt to be widely valent across the whole canon of classic and not-so-classic texts.

But Bunyan? How much does all this touch him? On the face of it, the eager logocentrism of Bunyan's Protestant and Puritan hermeneutic looks pretty well armoured against the subverting Midrashic logics of allegory and gloss as they've been recently

---

[5] Lawrence Lipking, 'The marginal Gloss: Notes and Asides on Poe, Valery, "The Ancient Mariner", The Ordeal of the Margin, *Storiella as She is Syung*, Versions of Versions of Leornado, and the Plight of Modern Criticism', *Critical Inquiry*, 3 (1977), 609–55.

[6] Walter Benjamin, *Ursprung des deutschen Trauerspiels* (Frankfurt-on-Main, 1963), p. 197. (Mis)quoted by J. Hillis Miller in 'The Two Allegories', in Morton W. Bloomfield (ed.), *Allegory, Myth, and Symbol*, Harvard English Studies, 9 (Cambridge, Mass., 1981), pp. 355–70.

interpreted.[7] The 'staple of allegory is personification', as Samuel Levin has put it.[8] And that traditional view is most pertinent to Bunyan's activity as an allegorist. The rhetorical function allegory traditionally draws on most is prosopopoeia, the activity of making present in a discourse things, concepts, people normally characterized by invisibility, abstraction, absence, the lack of personality or presence.[9] Prosopopoeia is a textual practice of old-fashioned presenting that, just as it was the rhetorical device that sanctioned the presence on stage and in the poem of ancient deities, is in the case of Christian writers like Bunyan a recipe for the practice of the presence of God, a method for actualizing the Christianly transcendent. Bunyan's characters are a demonstration that the biblical text out of which they arise in such an impressively steady stream is a living, life-imparting word, precisely the 'lively oracles' of God. They demonstrate that the Scriptures are a text that has always had presence and can go on manifesting this presence in the lived experience of the receptive reader. The Word, the *logos* of Scripture became a person, Jesus Christ; and the Scriptural words are, or can become, living persons too.

When Bunyan's *Grace Abounding* focuses on the power of the biblical words it does so in a series of prosopopoeias. The Word and the words run, wax strong, wax warm; they make the narrator look up and they fall in upon him; they make a joyful sound in his soul; they follow him; they sound loud within him, call strongly and loudly to him; they seize his soul, lay sin at his door, come rolling into his mind, run in his mind, clap him on the back, 'justle' his fear and doubt. 'That piece of a sentence darted in upon men, *My grace is sufficient*'.[10] The Word seemed to have 'arms of grace so wide, that it could not onely inclose me, but many more besides.[11] The personality the text assumes is not, obviously, always benign. In

---

[7] See not only Lipking and Miller just cited (nn. 5, 6), but also Terence Cave, *The Cornucopian Text: Problems of Writing in the French Renaissance* (Oxford, 1979), and numerous of the contributors to Geoffrey H. Hartman and Sanford Budick (eds.), *Midrash and Literature* (New Haven, 1986).

[8] Samuel R. Levin, 'Allegorical Language', in Bloomfield (ed.), *Allegory, Myth, and Symbol*, pp. 23–38.

[9] For some useful thoughts on prosopopoeia see J. Hillis Miller, 'Catachresis, Prosopopoeia, and the Pathetic Fallacy: The Rhetoric of Ruskin', in Roland Hagenbüchle and Laura Skandera (eds.), *Poetry and Epistemology, Turning-points in the History of Poetic Knowledge*, Papers from the International Poetry Symposium Eichstätt 1983, *Eichstätter Beitrage*, vol. 20, *Abteilung Sprache und Literatur*, 6 (Regensbur, 1986), pp. 398–407. [10] GA, § 204. [11] GA, § 204.

A Few Sighs from Hell (1658) the Scripture even turns piercer, wounder, and killer: believers have been 'killed by the authority of the holy Scriptures; struck stark dead in a spiritual sense by the holy Scriptures . . . *The letter killeth*; the letter strikes men dead'.[12] But always the effectuality of the word is felt to consist in its assumption of personality, its likeness to the incarnated logos—a powerful presence demonstrated nowhere more tellingly in Bunyan's *œuvre* than in *Come, & Welcome, to Jesus Christ* (1678), where what Bunyan calls the absoluteness of the biblical promises and in particular the promise of his chosen text, 'All that the Father giveth me, shall come to me; and him that cometh to me, I will in no wise cast out' (John 6: 37), is especially demonstrated as the promissory words *shall come* turn into a character whose name is Shall-come. 'Why, *Shall-come* answered all this . . .'; '*Shall-come, can raise them from this Death*'; '*shall-come* puts forth itself . . . for comeing to Jesus Christ'. The mere verb rises into a Proper Noun. A character in the Christian drama is baptized and christened in an act of grammatical resurrection that reflects and also enacts Bunyan's faith, the faith of the text he's engaged on, that the Bible has power and presence because of the presence in it of the Word: '*shall-come*, is the Word of God: therefore *shall-come* must be fulfilled'.[13] In just this fashion Taste-that-which-is-good and all the rest of Bunyan's memorable cast in *The Pilgrim's Progress* got their names. It's a hermeneutic assumption and narrative practice whose propriety gets special endorsement in the case of By-ends. Like all his kinsfolk a deceiving Fair-speaker, By-ends will not at first own up to any name. He refuses to name himself and when he is named by Christian he still disowns and distances his name, calling it a mere nickname got from his enemies. Christian, however, fears that '*this name belongs to you more properly then you are willing we should think it doth*'.[14] All Bunyan's acts of Proper Naming are, it's implied, like this one, proper names, completely sanctioned by Scripture and truth.

And this confident claim of the Bunyan texts to know the person of the biblical Word and all the implied personalities of the Scriptural words is only one of the most obvious manifestations of the Puritan faith in the legibility of Scripture. Diabolus wallows in a black pit of language ('he has a language, proper to himself, and it is the

---

[12] *Misc. Wks.*, i. 353.   [13] *Misc. Wks.*, viii. 278.   [14] *PP*, p. 100.

language of the infernal cave, or black pit').[15] The jurymen of Vanity Fair have the darkened understandings of their Foreman Mr Blind-man and their colleague Mr Hate-light. But the true pilgrim rejoices in the spangling and shining, the sunlight of biblical truth. This claim about the illuminating readability of Scripture is made, of course, most tellingly in Bunyan's verse Apology prefixed to Part I of *The Pilgrim's Progress*. In this powerful bout of hermeneutic theorizing Bunyan justifies his allegorical method with reference to the Bible's own use of parables, dark sayings, 'Types, Shadows and Metaphors'. Bunyan's allegories are offered as readable signs, stories, fictionalizings of Christian truth because they're modelled on biblical examples which are held to function with a ready legibility. Christ was the personification of that readability, the meaning of the figures and types in person. He and the New Testament writers had little trouble seeing through the Old Testament's shadowy forms and figures. Moses was, in the words of a favourite Puritan metaphor for the legibility of Scripture taken from St Paul, both unveilable and unveiled:

As in the Creation darkness went before light . . . and Moses covered with a vaile stood before the people; Even so, in the detection of the glorious worke of man's redemption, mysticall promises went before mercifull performance, darke shadowes were the forerunners of that bright substance, obscure types were harbingers to the glorious anti-type, the Messiah, who coming after Levi's law with its figurative and vailed ceremonies, was the resemblance, painting and pointing out that cleere Lampe and Lambe of God, the express Image and ingraven Character of the Father.[16]

And Christ, the substance and presence within even the obscurest parts of Scripture, is exhibited as the New Testament explicates the Old and as both are expounded and unfolded in turn by the diligent interpreter. Meaning is to be uncovered, unveiled (*'Put by the Curtains, look within my Vail/Turn up my Metaphors'* as the Conclusion to Part I of *The Pilgrim's Progress* exhorts):[17] Christ is to be discovered, disclosed within the interpreter's imitative allegories,

---

[15] *HW*, p. 72.
[16] William Guild, *Moses Unvailed, or those Figures which Served Unto the Patterne and shaddow of Heavenly Things, Pointing Out the Messiah Christ Jesus, Briefly Explained* (1626), quoted by Mason I. Lowance, jun., in *The Language of Canaan: Metaphor and Symbol in New England from the Puritans to the Transcendentalists* (Cambridge, Mass., 1980), p. 33.
[17] *PP*, p. 164.

as he was within the figural occlusions and hermeticisms of the curtained discretions of the biblical text. The veil of both sanctums, the biblical figures' and Bunyan's, can be penetrated as they both all at once conceal and reveal the person of the Christ who was exposed in that tearing of the Jewish temple veil, the revelation of the mysteries veiled in his 'flesh' and within the figurativeness of the Old Covenant, as described in the biblical book of Hebrews. As Bunyan put it in *The Doctrine of the Law and Grace Unfolded* (1659):

Therefore I say, these words are rather to discover, that the time was come to change the dispensation, to take away the type and bring in the substance, and so manifesting that more clearly which before lay hid in dark sayings and figures. And this is usuall with God to speak in this manner.[18]

Meanings once wrapped up can be unwrapped.[19] So the Interpreter is never stuck for the sense of any of the emblematic tableaux and dramas that he shows to pilgrims staying at his House. Christian and Hopeful may be foxed at first by the strangeness of the pillar of salt that was once Lot's wife ('they stood looking, and looking upon it, but could not for a time tell what they should make thereof'). Indeed, Hopeful ('no Scholar') goes on having trouble picking out the meaning for himself. But Christian is learned and schooled enough to make out the text *Remember Lot's wife* after just 'a little laying of Letters together'. To be sure the pair of pilgrim interpreters never shed all of their amazement, for this is truly an 'amazing sight'; but their combined effort in hermeneutics brings them both to proper conclusions: 'they both concluded, that . . .'; 'And it is most rationally to be concluded that . . .[20]

(It's tempting, hereabouts, to associate Hopeful's shortage of scholarship with the lack of Greek that Bunyan got taunted with in *A Relation of the Imprisonment* (1765). It's inviting too to take Bunyan's interest in the shadowy underground where figural meanings lie, his delight in the obscure places of undercover biblical significance that's being drawn from humble imagery of domestic,

---

[18] *Misc. Wks.*, ii. 93.
[19] 'No marvel, therefore, if when he treateth of the New-Covenant, in which the Lord Jesus is wrapped, and presented in a Word of Promise to the World . . .', *Light for Them that Sit in Darkness, Misc. Wks.*, viii. 63; cf. '*What if my Gold be wrapped up in Ore*', Conclusion, *PP*, p. 164.
[20] *PP*, pp. 108–9.

rural, and working-class life, to which you need to 'stoop' for a full sense of God's revelation (*'he rather stoops, / And seeks to find out what by pins and loops, / By Calves, and Sheep; by Heifers, and by Rams; / By Birds and Herbs, and by the blood of Lambs, / God speaketh to him'*),[21] to see all this as being linked with Bunyan's proudly repeated role as tinker interpreter,[22] poor tradesman preacher,[23] and labouring-man pilgrim[24] in a fraternity of what *A Relation* calls 'the foolish, and the base',[25] humble readers greatly at odds with unstooping and therefore deluded gentlemen readers like Worldly-Wiseman and *A Relation*'s villains, Dr Lindale and Justice Kelynge.)

The true Christian is never, then, going to stay locked up in a cage of daunting and opaque meanings, with those modernist victims of a lapsing hermeneutic, the post-office clerk straining to make sense of her customer's tantalizingly telegraphic messages in Henry James's *nouvelle* 'In the Cage', or T. S. Eliot's blind interpreters and muted, fragmented speakers in *The Waste Land*—whose section now known as 'A Game of Chess' was originally entitled 'In the Cage'. The man Christian is shown in an iron cage at the Interpreter's House is an emblem of the despairing reading that shuts you 'out of all the Promises' and interferes in any fruitful encounter with Shall-come. The caged man is in the case of the narrator of *Grace Abounding* during those times when the offered encouragements of the Word fail to reassure. When for his part Christian recalls the Key called Promise that he has all the time in his bosom he and Hopeful speedily get away from Doubting-Castle, Giant Despair, and that awful Lady Macbeth of faltering, locked-up hermeneutes, the Giant's sadistic spouse Mrs Diffidence.[26]

There will be, in other words, on this view of reading, no utterly insoluble riddles, no rebuses that go on puzzling endlessly. '*Would'st thou read Riddles, and their Explanation?*' the Apology to Part I of *The Pilgrim's Progress* enquires.[27] If so, Bunyan's text will offer a

---

[21] *PP*, p. 4.
[22] 'Aiming 'tis like at me, because I was a Tinker'; 'If any man have received a gift of tinkering, as thou hast done, let him follow his tinkering' (*GA*, pp. 108, 117–18).
[23] Christ 'goes not . . . to the schools of learning, to fetch out his Gospel Preachers, but to the trades, and those most contemptible too', I.G.'s Preface to *A Few Sighs from Hell, Misc. Wks.*, i. 244.
[24] 'sleep is sweet to the Labouring man', *PP*, p. 136.
[25] *GA*, p. 111. [26] *PP*, pp. 114, 117, 118. [27] *PP*, p. 7.

consolingly explicatory practice. The legibility and utterability of the biblical words and names will be like the prompt solubility implied for the rebus or anagram of Bunyan's own scarcely veiled name in the 'Advertisement to the Reader' at the end of *The Holy War*:

> Witness my name, if Anagram'd to thee,
> The Letters make, *Nu hony in a B*.[28]

And this confidence comes about in particular because of Bunyan's Puritan faith in the univocity of Scripture. The Word is not divided against itself. Comment, allegorical explanation, and expansion, exposition may all come belatedly after the texts they seek to illuminate, but this alterity is only in the same relation to the biblical original as one biblical text succeeding another or the New Testament following on from the Old. The unity of Scripture will never be interfered with if the belated explicators act faithfully. The narrator of *Grace Abounding* is mightily perturbed by the apparently contradictory signals Scripture gives off. He oscillates between 'comfort' and 'torment'. He is variously in 'diverse frames of Spirit'. It's a discomfiting diversity incited by the apparently opposing 'nature of the several Scriptures that came in upon my mind; if this of Grace, then I was quiet; if that of *Esau*, then tormented. Lord, thought I, if both these Scriptures would meet in my heart at once, I wonder which of them would get the better of me'.[29] Eventually, though, he comes to realize that 'the Word of the Law and Wrath must give place to the Word of Life and Grace' and '*That the Scriptures could . . . agree in the salvation of my Soul*'.[30] Diversity yields to unity, just as the Old Testament types converge in all their variousness in the one Christ. 'For all the Types and shadows of the Saviour, are virtually so many Promises . . . for as God spake at sundry times to the Fathers, so also in divers manners, Prophetically, Providentially, Typically, and all of the Messias.'[31] There are on this view no substantive differences across the biblical play of figures. In using the figurative method Bunyan is only, then, collaborating with this true and final oneness of Christological meaning that persists for all the overt diversity of allegorical practices. Which was the widespread assumption of Puritan hermeneutes. William Perkins, for instance, in *The Arte of Prophesying* (1592): 'There is only one sense, and

---

[28] *HW*, p. 251.
[29] *GA*, § 212.
[30] *GA*, §§ 214, 228.
[31] *Misc. Wks.*, viii. 60.

the same is the litteral. An allegorie is onely a certain manner of uttering the same sense. The Anagoge and Tropologie are waies, whereby the sense may be applied.'[32] And along just the lines of these assumptions the marginal gloss is thought of simply complementing the shining work performed by the illuminated and illuminating practices of the true hermeneutes and allegorists—the company of preacherly and teacherly shining ones clustered about the biblical text. These interpreters do not believe their glosses are a gloze. Rather they're a work of glazing, the installation of windows giving on to the text and providing helpful views into it that, in the manner of allegory in the Perkins passage just quoted, confirms biblical univocity and doesn't at all subtract from it, subvert it, or supplant it. The textual activity going on in Bunyan's margins is offered, in fact, as a set of keys to the mysteries being enunciated by the text, an open window on to the figures and allegories that the text trades in. It's a key that possesses a good deal of the character of that promissory key Christian used to unlock the prison of despairing misinterpretation. As the lines 'To the Reader' have it at the beginning of *The Holy War*:

> Nor do thou go to work without my Key,
> (In mysteries men soon do lose their way)
> And also turn it right if thou wouldst know
> My riddle, and wouldst with my heifer plow.
> It lies there in the window, fare thee well . . .[33]

And the margin, in a proud metatextual moment, glosses '*the window*' as 'The margent'.

Turn it right: Misinterpreters and misinterpreting come, naturally, from the left. They are sinister workers doing sinister work. Hypocrisie and Formalist, for instance, who eschew the wicket gate and the laws and ordinances of Christ and who 'walk by the rude working of your fancies', came 'tumbling over the Wall, on the left hand of the narrow way'.[34] They are left-handed readers, agents of the Satan who, father of glozing, reads things backwards ('Satan reads all backwards' observes the margin in the matter of Diabolus's 'sugared' words.)[35] These are all bad interpreters, and bad interpreters operate not with but against the text, alongside and beyond it. Their way of reading puts their interpretations among the fictions that the damned soul

---

[32] Quoted in Kaufmann, p. 35.   [33] *HW*, p. 5.
[34] *PP*, pp. 39 ff.   [35] *HW*, p. 193.

prefers to the living Word: 'the Scriptures thought I, what are they? a dead letter, a little ink and paper, of three or four shillings price. Alas, what is the Scripture, give me a ballad, a Newsbook, *George on horseback*, or *Bevis* of *Southampton*, give me some book that teaches curious arts, that tells of old fables'. This is the reading matter of those 'carnal Priests' who 'tickle the ears of their hearers with vain Philosophy and deceit . . . who nuzzle up your people in ignorance with *Aristotle, Plato*, and the rest of the heathenish Philosophers'. Devotion to these texts places readers in the *besides* and *beyond* place, the place of the devil's lying marginalia and illicit supplementation and subversion: where 'the blind world do slight the authority of Scripture':

because they give ear to the devil, who through his subtilty casteth false evasions, and corrupt interpretations on them, rendring them not so point blank the minde of God, and a rule for direction to poor souls, perswading them, that they must give ear and way to something else besides and beyond that . . .[36]

The devil's marginalia are certainly glozes. They comprise a set of delusive margins for readers. They are an interpreter's equivalent of By-Path Meadow, that misleading, distracting place where alternative and false readers and readings lurk with the likes of By-ends and other people who have duplicitously forked tongues, such as Mr Facing-bothways, Mr Two-tongues, Mr Turn-away the Apostate, and Demas who has turned aside to the Hill Lucre 'a little off the Road'.[37] For Christian and Hopeful to go into By-Path Meadow and take that deceptive marginal route that runs 'along by the way side'[38] was to behave illegally, to commit an act of trespass, an overstepping of legitimate bounds. Giant Despair then had a legalist's right to lock them up in Doubting-Castle, the prison of the despairing misreader.

Bunyan's opposition to marginal alterity as devilish, his resistance to the idea of validly alternative readings, to a hermeneutic of diversity such as his extended trade in margins and allegory might be thought to condone, could not be clearer. On the face of it, the idea of Midrashic openness could not be further from what Bunyan's texts purport to believe in. What these writings wish to keep proving is a notion of figurative reading and writing not as some Benjaminesque ruin or failure, as repetition of the original darkness of conceits, a

[36] *Misc. Wks.*, i. 333, 345–6.   [37] *PP*, p. 106.   [38] *PP*, p. 112.

plunge into a version of the modernist abysm of meaning, but rather as success, enlightenment, pleroma, true and presentable meaning. In other words, Bunyan's writing reaches out for the successful outcome that is traditionally ascribed to his work: 'this agreeable, edifying, and succinct mode of expression', as the Preface to the French translation of *The Pilgrim's Progress* had it in 1685, whereby 'divine truths may penetrate to the inmost heart'.[39]

And yet; and yet . . . What goes on in Bunyan's texts frequently turns out to be somewhat less simple than Bunyan's repeated arguments and practices would persuade us to be the case. At times, in fact, these writings seem to be running rather along the byways and collapsing into the ditches and quags of an ur-post-modernist hermeneutic almost as much as managing to keep on the main way, the route announced as the only way by Bunyan's graphic polemics.

If Moses be unveiled, one is driven to ask, to what extent is the veil removed and for whom? It's a striking fact about one's reading of *Grace abounding*, for example, that the terrible aspects of the narrator's readings in Scripture remain intensely memorable. He may resolve them but they remain unforgettable for us. Not dissimilarly, the incarceration in Doubting Castle is possibly the most unforgettable episode in *The Pilgrim's Progress*. This particular story of caging registers a haunting, lingering fear of *The Pilgrim's Progress* that the promises are always potentially missable, misreadable, about to be become null and void, that they might simply be absent when you most want them to be present. And this terrifying prospect remains in place from start to finish of Christian's walk. Puritan theology might be strong on the irresistibility of grace and the perseverance of the saints but Bunyan never allows any lulled sense of security to take over completely. The Word, the promises, prove rather slippery sources of consolation. Steps across the initiating Slough of Dispond do indeed exist, and they are the Word, the Promises. But 'stepping besides', loosing your footing, is always possible— Christian himself steps 'besides'—because when the weather changes (and this being an English story, the presumption is that the weather will always keep changing), filth is spewed out of the mire and so the steps 'are hardly seen'.[40] And even at the end of the journey,

---

[39] From the Preface to *Voyage d'un Chrestien vers l'Éternité . . . nouvellement traduit en François. Avec Figures* (Amsterdam, 1685), as trans. by Roger Sharrock in *Casebook*, p. 45.   [40] *PP*, p. 16.

with heaven ever so near, the River of Death has a terrible way of rising tantalizingly, testing the pilgrim's already tried (and proven) faith. Even at this very last moment Christian succumbs to the horror of dying and loses his memory, unable to recall any of the much bruited consolations of the Word, plunging into an awful enactment of some penitential Psalms: 'I sink in deep Water, the Billows go over my head, all his Waves go over me, *Selah*.'[41] At any time, then, Christian himself is liable to join the ranks of those travellers who have the appearance of being on the same road as the true believer but who are really not in the same orthodox way at all—all those sad missers of the promises whom we and Christian meet, the deluded striders along byways, the ones who supposed they had ears to hear the Word but who found out in the end that they had been mishearing it all along.

And when, alerted by this gaggle of deluded encumberers of the pilgrim way, one starts looking closely at Bunyan's repeated assurances about the legibility and gracious personality of the Word, it becomes rapidly obvious that no Bunyan text comes totally heedless of the experiential and tormenting fact that many serious readers of the Bible were actually fumbling the promises, misreading them in part or whole, and even missing them entirely. 'The Scriptures I say, they are able to give a man perfect instruction into any of the things of God necessary to faith and godliness', *but only* 'if he have but an honest heart, seriously to weigh and ponder the several things contained in them.'[42] The conditional clause is always present; it's what gives the pilgrim way its perpetual nail-biting suspense. 'Coming sinner, what promise thou findest in the word of Christ, strain it whither thou canst, so thou dost not corrupt it, and his Blood and Merits will answer all, what the word saith, or any true Consequence that is drawn there-from, that we may boldly venture upon . . .'[43] Christian is on a venture. The word *venture*, with its variant *venturous*, occurs several times in *The Pilgrim's Progress*,[44] and this venture, like the travels of Robinson Crusoe (whose author also uses the word to describe that journey) is an adventure, a gamble, a risk-taking matter, an *enjeu*, in which heaven can be lost or won. And the essence of this venture is that it is an adventure or voyage of interpretation in which the Word must be strained and consequences

[41] *PP*, p. 157.
[42] *Misc. Wks.*, i. 324–5.
[43] *Misc. Wks.*, viii. 297.
[44] See, e.g., *PP*, pp. 43, 48, 56.

drawn from it. And the risk to be taken is that in that effort of straining the Word might be corrupted and wrong consequences might be drawn from it. In which case all one's ventured capital, the stake put down in a hermeneutic version of the Pascalian wager, would be squandered and lost. Which is what so many of the characters Christian meets have had happen to them, and what Bunyan's narrative holds out as a perpetual source of terror to Christian. Talkative is just one of these losing gamblers. He believes he has discovered what a work of grace is and that he has cracked the 'Gospel Mysteries'. But his is a 'false discovery'. There is, as the margin puts it, '*Knowledge and knowledge.*'[45] Awingly, an interpretable text is also a misinterpretable one. As Bunyan warns his own readers:

> take heed
> Of mis-interpreting: for that, instead
> Of doing good, will but thyself abuse:
> By mis-interpreting evil insues.[46]

All in all, it begins to look as if Bunyan's texts suspect that Moses might remain veiled, as St Paul suggested he did for Jews in 2 Corinthians 3, and that once unveiled, or at least partly unveiled, the veil could slip back into place. Take an arresting passage in *Come, & Welcome, to Jesus Christ* (1678):

Indeed, the Carnal Man sayes (at least) in his Heart, Isa. 53. 1,2,3. There is no Form or Comliness in Christ, and when he shall see him, there is no Beauty that he should desire him; *But he lies*: This he speaks, as having never seen him. But they that stand in his House, and look upon him through the Glass of his Word, by the Help of his Holy Spirit, they will tell you other things. *But we*, say they, *all with open Face beholding, as in a Glass, the Glory of the Lord, are changed into the same Image, from Glory to Glory*, 2 Cor. 3. 17,18. They see Glory in his Person, Glory in his Undertakings, Glory in the Merit of his Blood, and Glory in the Perfection of his Righteousness; yea, Heart-affecting, Heart-sweetening, and Heart-changing Glory!

Indeed, his Glory is veiled, and cannot be seen, but as discovered by the Father (*Matth*. 11. 27). It is veiled with Flesh, with Meanness of Descent from the Flesh, and with that Ignominy and Shame that attended him in the Flesh; but they can, in God's Light, see through these things, they shall see Glory in him; yea, such Glory, as will draw, and pull their Hearts unto him.[47]

---

[45] *PP*, pp. 81, 82.   [46] *PP*, p. 164.   [47] *Misc. Wks.*, viii. 289–90.

It is a startling enough suggestion from Bunyan that the words of Scripture can constitute a lie. Clearly Old Testament Isaiah comes rather heavily veiled and needs somewhat drastic straining. But it is also arresting that after the passionate affirmation of the Glory of the Christ in the Word, the next paragraph should resume 'Indeed, his Glory is veiled . . . veiled with Flesh'. The veil of discovery, it seems, is only going to be lifted for some readers. *See through* even suggests that the process of trying to see is a tricky one; it almost implies treachery on the part of the veiled text, a wilful deceptiveness that has somehow to be *seen through*. But then, the hermeneutic difficulty hereabouts is the result of what Bunyan cannot bring himself to state too openly, namely the divine limitedness of the atonement and the gloomy reverse side of unconditional election to salvation. Many readers won't ever see the point, however hard they strain at it.

And some of the readers fortunate to have been elected to enlightenment will not see clearly all the time. Mysteries will remain. When the Pauline passage about the unveiling of Moses is referred to in *The Pilgrim's Progress* it is still in need of, and getting, an interpretative massage: 'But . . . the reflections of the Sun upon the City (for the City was pure Gold), was so extreamly glorious, that they could not, as yet, with open face behold it, but through an *Instrument* made for that purpose.'[48] 'With open Face beholding, as in a glass' (or mirror) is not at all the same as 'they could not, as yet, with open face behold it, but through an instrument made for that purpose'. The pilgrims' need for the eclipsing intervention of some optical instrument for looking at the sun-bright City hooks back on to earlier moments of occluded, eclipsed sight: the invitation to view the Delectable Mountains, but only 'if the day be clear'; and that gazing at the Celestial City gates from The Hill Clear through the shepherds' perspective glass, when the pilgrims' hands shook so much that they 'could not look stedily through the Glass' and only 'thought they saw something like the Gate, and also some of the Glory of the place'.[49] After that particular unsteady vision the travellers sang '*Thus by the* Shepherds, *Secrets are reveal'd*'. But in truth a good deal of secretiveness had actually stayed unrevealed. Bunyan's striking negation of 2 Corinthians 3 ('they could not . . . with open face behold') leans, perhaps knowingly, towards that other

[48] *PP*, p. 156.   [49] *PP*, pp. 54, 123.

Pauline statement about visions in a glass—in 1 Corinthians 13: 'For now we see through a glass, darkly': *Videmus nunc per speculum in aenigmate*: now we see in a mirror in an enigma. No doubt Bunyan's Latin was as shaky as his Greek and he was unaware of the Vulgate text. But what he was in effect advertising was the occasional enigmatic darkness, the remnants of riddle, even on the illuminated Christian walk: he was indicating the hermetic character even of the enlightening Word and an enlightening hermeneutic approach to it.

Some texts would remain hard nuts; some riddles would go on proving difficult to open. When the men Gaius, Honest, and Greatheart sit over their dessert course, cracking hard Scriptural nuts and opening out the meaning of riddles, their efforts are shown amply to succeed. This part of their feast makes an emblem of Bunyan's positive faith in the legibility of the text. Indeed Honest's claim that one particular riddle 'is a hard one, hard to expound, and harder to practise', reads as only a token hesitation, an excessively modest show of interpretative reluctance from an unpushy man. He has no trouble expounding that enigma. But Gaius's rhymed pronouncement:

> *Hard* Texts *are* Nuts (*I will not call them* Cheaters,)
> *Whose* Shells *do keep their* Kirnels *from the* Eaters[50]

in verses which cheer up the eagerly interpretative group ('Then were they very Merry') does at least raise the less cheering possibility that some hard nuts *are* cheaters. At least it is allowed that some readers would so label them. And even Bunyan, busy resolver of contradiction and enigma, cannot erase all the rebus elements of the Word. Nor can the generations of commentators on his texts. The words in parenthesis in the lines '*Men (as high as Trees) will write / Dialoguewise*'[51] are taken to suggest some author's name in rebus form; but this rebus remains, as the Whalley/Sharrock notes put it, 'obscure'. And the obscurity is instructive.

Evangelist is a busy discoverer of meanings to Christian, but even he can't escape entirely the mysteries of Scripture. Legality, as he tells it, 'is the Son of the Bond woman which now is, and is in Bondage with her children, and is in a mystery this Mount Sinai, which thou hast feared will fall on thy head'.[52] The declared meaning of the allegory is still, then, a mystery. Even the certainties

---

[50] *PP*, p. 263.   [51] *PP*, p. 6.   [52] *PP*, p. 23.

about final destinations that generally characterize *The Pilgrim's Progress* admit of occasional uncertainties. What happened to By-ends and his chums? 'Now whether they fell into the Pit, by looking over the brink thereof, or whether they went down to dig, or whether they was smothered in the bottom, by the damps that commonly arise, of these things I am not certain'. Occasionally Christian will lay claim to honest ignorance: 'for ought I know', he'll say. 'For ought I know', he and Hopeful would have 'been made our selves a spectacle for those that shall come after to behold', had they gone over to keep Demas company. 'You have spoken, for ought I know, the true Gospel sense of those Texts', Christian tells Faithful, who has just interpreted some Mosaic distinctions about clean and unclean beasts with special reference to Talkative. They are just the distinctions that the narrator of *Grace Abounding* says he was 'also made . . . to see'; and he too knew he was involved in a process of speculative reading: 'I *thought* that signified . . .' (The *Everyman's Library* edition's version of § 71, 'I was *almost* made . . . to see', looks, alas, like a misprint).[53]

The key Promise serves its turn very well. It will open 'any Lock in *Doubting-Castle*': the margin affirms Christian's 'perswasion'. But this did not prevent the lock in the final gate going '*damnable* hard': that gate, 'as it opened, made such a creaking, that it waked *Giant Despair*'.[54] On occasion the interpretative door will be articulated about a squeaky hinge. Some figures, even inviting biblical ones, will protest at the work they're being made to do. To be sure the protest is not as warningly loud as the squeaking of the hinge in *Tristram Shandy*, nor yet does it denote as problematic and deterring a hermeneutic space as the Derrida-an *brisure*, but still a warning note of some sort is sounding. The sealed roll that Christian carries and reads in, his evidence, the assurance of life, the certificate to heaven, can get lost and become, for the time being, effectively a sealed-up roll. Just so, the written note the Shepherds give to Christian, a set of directions for the journey, can get forgotten and stay shut ineffectually away, unread. And Bunyan's text is sometimes as lost for words as Christian is occasionally bereft of his roll or forgetful of his note. The Fiend of Part II of *The Pilgrim's Progress* remains as indescribable, as unspeakably evil, as anything at the modernistic heart of Conrad's darkness. Words simply collapse under the effort of seeking to know this evil one:

[53] *PP*, pp. 108, 109, 80; *GA*, § 71.   [54] *PP*, p. 118.

and then *Christiana* said, Methinks I see something yonder upon the Road before us, a thing of a shape such as I have not seen. Then said *Joseph*, Mother, what is it? An ugly thing, Child; an ugly thing, said she. But Mother, what is it like, said he? 'Tis like I cannot tell.[55]

And the ending of *The Pilgrim's Progress*, never, of course, as defeated or sceptical as the modern period's downbeat refusals of closure, none the less accepts silence ('what I here am silent about')[56] as a contingent if not absolutely necessary part of any retelling of the Christian story. The 'Conclusion' of *The Pilgrim's Progress* proved inconclusive. Part II followed, and it eschews a 'Conclusion'.

Doubt can hover, then, even in the triumphalist interpretative margin that Bunyan's work stations itself in. It can inhabit even Bunyan's margins. However decided they are they never shed the infection of undecidedability hovering about the uncertain origins of many of them. Did Bunyan pen them all? No editor can tell. It's only apt then that an occasional marginal note will indicate very clearly that the wayward, bifurcating, undoing logics of the margin as enacted in recent writing (such as *Finnegans Wake* where marginal activity is the mark of interpretative difficulty and the refusal or failure of closure) are sometimes not too far from Bunyan's own glossing activities. In *The Doctrine of the Law and Grace Unfolded* (1659) Bunyan dwells with characteristic verve on the glorious readability of Adam as a figure of Christ and on Christ as typified and foreshadowed in Adam. But this typically confident moment is spectacularly reversed by the marginal gloss's quite stunningly subversive reminder of continuing enigma in the figurative relation of the first and second Adam and the chronological siting of the First and Second Covenants that the main text is so confidently busy with: 'Yet the second *Adam* was before the first and also the second Covenant before the first. This is a Riddle.'[57] Suddenly, at such a moment, a whole set of hermeneutic beliefs and practices wobbles disconcertingly. Some dark conceits, and the whole art of interpreting them, are, it seems, going to remain matters of darkness, of riddle. But then, margins, glosses, allegories, even ones like Bunyan's so devotedly aimed at propping rather than contradicting the texts they refer to, will perhaps always have an undermining effect. For the sceptic's naughty question will poke itself through: if Scriptural

[55] *PP*, p. 241.   [56] *PP*, p. 311.   [57] *Misc. Wks.*, ii. 94.

meanings are so very clear, how come they need this massive heaping up of margin upon margin, explanation upon explanation, figure upon figure, allegory upon allegory?

In any case, the result of piling up so much text about text, and metatext about metatext, is a prodigal expansion, or implosion, into explanation that looks increasingly belated, and as it moves more and more away from its supposed original and authoritative source texts looks increasingly like mere fiction. Certainly glozing looks as if it's obtained a curious foothold when St Paul is negatived, Isaiah is proved a liar and misprizer, and Jeremiah is shown to need parenthetical modifying in the matter of the Valley of the Shadow of Death: 'The Prophet *Jeremiah* thus describes it, *A Wilderness, a Land of desarts, and of Pits, a Land of drought, and of the shadow of death, a Land that no Man* (but a Christian) *passeth through, and where no man dwelt*'.[58]

That Bunyan seeks to wrest back margins and marginalia from the glozing hands of Satan, By-ends, and Giant Despair is obvious from the rhetoric of godly margents that *The Pilgrim's Progress* deploys. The meadows on the margins of The River of the Water of Life are the good marginal place of which By-Path-Meadow is offered as the wicked travesty. The delighting country of Beulah is marginal to the Celestial City — 'upon the Borders of Heaven'. There are some byways which are actually on the true way (Christian and Hopeful talk with the good shepherds leaning on their staves, 'as is common with weary Pilgrims, when they stand to talk with any by the way'.)[59] But this propaganda for margins, like the insistence in *The Holy War* that the margent is a mere window into the text, cannot entirely rebut the presumption that the kind of reading and rereading going on is not just simply secondary and juxtapositive but is also alternative, divisive reading. This notion was, after all, not unknown in Protestant circles in Bunyan's time. The translators of the Authorized Version of the Bible, for example, knew that alterity of meaning was what their margins were promoting and they welcomed the resultant loosening of textual univocity and monodic authority with an enthusiasm that should at least give our current anti-logocentrists some pause in their ready pronouncements on the alleged certainties of traditional Christian hermeneutics:

[58] *PP*, p. 61.   [59] *PP*, pp. 155, 119.

it hath pleased God in his diuine prouidence, heere and there to scatter wordes and sentences of that difficultie and doubtfulnesse . . . that fearfulnesse would better beseeme vs then confidnce, and if we resolue, to resolue upon modestie with *S. Augustine* . . . it is better to make doubt of those things which are secret, then to strive about those that are vncertaine . . . Now in such a case, doth not a margine do well to admonish the Reader to seeke further, and not to conclude or dogmatize vpon this or that peremptorily? . . . so diuersitie of signification and sense in the margine, where the text is not so cleare, must needes doe good, yea, is necessary as we are perswaded . . . They that are wise, had rather haue their judgements at libertie in differences of readings, then to be captivated to one, when it may be the other.[60]

Liberal as the Preface to the 1611 translation sounds, and is, its authors would of course have mightily resented the charge that a practice of marginal difference of opinion — the essence of the *via media* — might license any notion that such exegetical manœuvring amounted to a kind of fictionalizing. They did after all believe that the Bible's textual 'difficultie and doubtfulnesse' obtained only in matters of small theological moment. And Bunyan would have agreed. But among some observers it was readily recognized that the marginal practice of allegorical interpretation often led well beyond what Scripture might be thought of as overtly licensing. Erasmus, for example, objected that allegorizing often outdid what Christ's use of parable and St Paul's allegorical rereadings of the Old Testament sanctioned, running commentary headlong into fanciful narration and really rather independent fiction. Upon the authorized fiction of the Prodigal Son, for instance, the allegorizers would prodigally build their own endless and distortive affictions:

inventing (*affingens*) the journey of the son as he sets out and returns, as if he now eats in the tavern a pudding made of tongues, now passes by a water-mill, now does this, that or the other; to such confected fairy-tales (*confictas naenias*) the theologian deflected (*detorquebat*) the words of the prophets and Gospels.[61]

---

[60] 'The Translators to the Reader', Authorized Version of the Bible (1611), in *Records of the English Bible: The Documents Relating to the Translation and Publication of the Bible in English, 1525–1611*, ed. Alfred W. Pollard (1911), pp. 372, 373.

[61] Quoted in Cave, *Cornucopian Text*, p. 88. The whole of Cave's discussion in his chap. 3, 'Interpretation', is most stimulating and very pertinent to the case of Bunyan (and others).

Erasmus resistance to such prodigality is akin to Bunyan's resistance to 'painted By-paths'. In *The Heavenly Footman* (1698), those invented, fictionalized pilgrim alternatives are said to be the corrupted opposite to 'the plain way to the Kingdom of Heaven'.[62] Walking that painted By-path or margin was indulging in personal reading and invention, personal 'chalking out', making up a theologically unsound picture, story, fiction of your own. In *Come, & Welcome to Jesus Christ* (1678) Bunyan suggests that one cause of despair to coming sinners is precisely this 'chalking out': 'Fears that Christ will not Receive thee, *may arise from thine own Folly, in Inventing; yea, in thy Chalking out to God a way to bring thee Home to Jesus Christ*'. God, Bunyan suggests, is probably drawing these fearers along a different way from the one they've invented for themselves and then 'because they come not the Way of their own Chalking out, therefore they are at a loss'.[63]

But, of course, chalking out is what Bunyan himself does:

> This Book it chaulketh out before thine eyes
> The man that seeks the everlasting Prize.[64]

Inventing is exactly what Bunyan's sermons and *The Holy War* and *The Pilgrim's Progress* are good at. Rich, even prodigal invention, is what Bunyan goes in for, not least (and as instructively as ironically) in the case of biblical stories of the wickedly rich and prodigal. There's the fetchingly free vein Bunyan allows himself in his rereading of the story of Dives and Lazarus. The version of Dives and Lazarus in *The Pilgrim's Progress*, the drama of the two children Passion and Patience at the Interpreter's house, might seem expansively free and fictionalized enough.[65] But compared with what happens in *A Few Sighs from Hell* (1658) it looks remarkably chaste. In the graphic rewriting of *A Few Sighs* there are extended speculations about states of mind and what happens next ('*Lazarus* it may be, might have . . .'). Vivid reconstitutings of the speech of the damned proceed almost as an extensive series of short stories, a whole set of little fictions. And, notably, these fictions get their authorization rather jauntily from (where else?) a margin which defies the reader to enquire how the narrating sermonizer can possibly know what went on in Hell and in the silent interstices of Christ's narrative:

---

[62] *Misc. Wks.*, v. 156. [63] *Misc. Wks.*, viii. 354.
[64] *PP*, p. 6. [65] *PP*, pp. 30–1.

'This language is sometimes heard at the gallows, but for ought I can learn, it is more to be heard in hell'.[66] There's precious little restraint and little poverty of affiction there. Just so, and even more revealingly, there is utter prodigality in Bunyan's rereading and rewriting of the story of the Prodigal Son in *Come, & Welcome to Jesus Christ* (1678). It comes, again with a kind of defiance, only a few pages before the attack on the folly of inventing just quoted.

Bunyan is eager to reread the story of the Prodigal as one more version of the Christian of *The Pilgrim's Progress* and of the narrator of *Grace Abounding*. The Prodigal is read as a coming sinner on the pattern they would make famous. This means that the Prodigal has to be shown as subject to their kind of despondency and sinkings of mind on his way back to his Father. There appears to be no evidence of this in the Bible's version of this return. But Bunyan sets about showing and proving it with great verve. Kisses in Scripture, he declares, were 'often used to remove Doubts and Fears', so in Christ's story the Father's kissing of his prodigal child must be taken to mean that this coming sinner had his own sloughs of despondency to wade across. Invention once begun then runs wild:

'Tis true, as I said, at first setting out, he spake heartily, as sometimes Sinners also do in their beginning to come to Jesus Christ: But might not he, yea, in all probability he had (between the first step he took, and the last, by which he accomplished that journey), many a thought, both this way and that; as whether his Father would receive him, or no? As thus; I said, *I would go to my Father*: but how, if when I come at him, he should ask me, *Where I have all this while bin*; What must I say then? Also, if he asks me, *What is become of the portion of Goods that he gave me*; What shall I say then? If he asks me, *Who have bin my Companions*; What shall I say then? If he also shall ask me, *What hath bin my Preferment in all the time of mine absence from him*; What shall I say then? Yea, and if he ask me, *Why I came home no sooner*; What shall I say then? Thus, I say, might he reason with himself; And being Conscious to himself, that he could give but a bad Answer to any of these Interogatories; no marvel, if he stood in need first of all, *of a Kiss* from his Fathers Lips. For, had he answered the first, in Truth he must say, *I have bin a haunter of Taverns, and Alehouses*; and as for my Portion, *I spent it in Riotous Living*; my Companions, *were Whores, and Drabs*: As for my preferment, the highest was, *that I became a Hoggard*: and as for my not coming home till now, *Could I have made shift to have staid abroad any longer, I had not lain at thy Feet for Mercy now.*

[66] *Misc. Wks.*, i. 304, 311.

I say, these things considered, and considering again, how prone poor man is, to give way, when truly awakned, to despondings, and heart-misgiveings; no marvel if he did sink in his mind, between the time of his first setting out, and that of his coming to his Father.[67]

This makes a most impressively supple piece of suppositious and inventive rereading, and one that rises, as is the wont with Bunyan, to the condition of impressive fiction. It comes as small surprise that the progress of this piece of interpretative adventurism should be dynamized by the use of just those modal auxiliary verbs (*might*, *should*, *shall*) that Tristram Shandy's father recommended as the way to keep even the unlikeliest of fictions (the one about the white bear) ticking along nicely. The whole passage takes a happy dive, with its subject the Prodigal, into the byways of invention and fiction—'many a thought, both this way and that'—in an exercise of speculative characterization evidently delighted by the prodigal hermeneutic sport to be got in the biblical margin.

But however delightful this rereading game, and however effective such graphic rewriting of biblical stories might have been in getting the hold preachers sought to achieve over the minds of their hearers, such a passage scarcely keeps at bay the kind of criticism and fears enunciated only a small clutch of pages later, the worry that supplementation (or gloss, or allegory) tends to the hermeneutically illicit and textually subversive, running quite counter to Bunyan's own stricter intentions as a reader and expounder of Scripture, his more orthodox claims and wishes in the business of interpretation. The instructive proximity and relevance of this particularly exuberant bout of biblical rereading to all of Bunyan's rereadings—and of course to the whole current debate about Christian logocentrism—cannot however be evaded in any simple way. With Bunyan himself being so prodigal, the likes of Stanley Fish can hardly be accused of being all that outlandish.[68]

---

[67] *Misc. Wks.*, viii. 342.

[68] Cf. Cave, *Cornucopian Text*, p. 88 n. 17, on the Prodigal narrative and 'the ambivalence of a fiction which enacts in its own structure a deviant "prodigality" in order to fulfil its narrative destiny of a triumphant conversion and homecoming'.

12

'Of him thousands daily Sing and talk': Bunyan and his Reputation

BY N. H. KEEBLE

The Seventeenth-century Bunyan

IT took the congregation of John Gifford's Bedford Church only a few months to realize that their new member, John Bunyan, was possessed of unusual gifts. In *Grace Abounding* Bunyan writes that 'after I had been about five or six years awakened . . . some of the most able among the Saints with us . . . did perceive that God had counted me worthy to understand something of his Will in his holy and blessed word, and had given me utterance in some measure to express, what I saw'.[1] This characteristically casual dating seems to refer to 1654-5. We know that Bunyan's 'awakening' commenced soon after, and in part as a consequence of, his first marriage, but the date of that marriage is itself uncertain. Bunyan himself says only that 'Presently after' leaving the army (in 1646) he 'changed [*his*] condition into a married state'. The baptism in July 1650 of his first child, the blind daughter Mary, suggests this 'change' occurred in 1648-9. Elsewhere, Bunyan writes that he was finally 'set . . . down . . . blessedly in the Truth of the Doctrine of Jesus Christ' 'just before the men called Quakers came into the Countrey', an apparent reference to the mission from the North which brought William Dewsbury and George Fox to Bedfordshire in 1654 and 1655 respectively. By 1654, Bunyan had been received into Gifford's Church.[2]

---

[1] *GA*, § 265.
[2] Brown, pp. 52, 56, 87, 91, 105-6, 222; *GA*, §§ 15, 17; *Misc. Wks.*, ii. 157; William Braithwaite, *The Beginnings of Quakerism*, 2nd edn., rev. Henry J. Cadbury (1955; repr. York, 1981), pp. 175, 185; *The Journal of George Fox*, ed. John L. Nickalls (1952; repr. 1975), pp. 207-8. See also above, pp. 3-4, 9-10.

It was probably the encouragement of the Church to take a fuller part in its worship and ministry which prompted Bunyan's removal from Elstow to Bedford in 1655. Invited to 'discover my Gift amongst them', and, 'when some of them did go into the Countrey to teach', to 'go with them', Bunyan initially, 'with much weakness and infirmity', confined himself to the private exhortation and admonition of the converted. Soon, however, 'being still desired by the Church', he was 'more particularly called forth, and appointed to a more ordinary and publick preaching the Word' both to 'them that believed' and to 'those who had not yet received the faith' of the Gospel.[3] An entry later inserted in the early pages of the Church's records reads 'Mr Bunyan began to preach some time in the year 1656'. By August 1657, he was so 'taken off by the preaching of the Gospell' that the Church agreed, he 'being otherwise imployed', to suspend his 'tryall . . . to exercise the office of deacon'. John Burton had succeeded Gifford as the Church's pastor three years before, but in 1659 it was nevertheless as 'Bunyan's people' that the congregation was known to Quakers.[4]

Bunyan himself they knew as their adversary. The beginning of his ministry coincided with their own first missionary successes in southern England and, as Professor Sharrock has observed, 'Baptists had good cause to be alarmed at [*their*] progress, for the Quakers were their rivals for the allegiance of the common people'. Bunyan's evangelism necessarily and immediately brought him into conflict with Quaker converts: as early as April 1656 he took part, with Burton and other Bedford Church members, in the first of a series of disputations with them. Such disputes eventuated in Bunyan's first two publications *Some Gospel-Truths Opened* (1656) and its *Vindication* (1657) against the strictures of Edward Burrough's *The True Faith of the Gospel of Peace Contended For* (1656). Bunyan acquitted himself with sufficient pugnacity and cogency to attract the animadversions of Fox himself in his *The Great Mistery of the Great Whore Unfolded* (1659).[5]

Bunyan's religious and literary vocations were thus of an age. A committed and zealous evangelism marked both: 'My great desire

---

[3] GA, §§ 266–8; Brown, pp. 91–2.
[4] *Minutes*, pp. 21, 28; Brown, p. 119; GA, p. xxii. See also above, p. 10.
[5] Sharrock, p. 36; *Misc. Wks.*, i. xxi–xxx; Brown, pp. 106–9; Edward Burrough, *Truth (the Strongest of All) Witnessed Forth* (1657), pp. 53–5 (included in Burrough's collected works, *The Memorable Works of a Son of Thunder and Consolation* (1672), pp. 275–309 (pp. 304–5); *The True Faith* occupies pp. 136–52).

in fulfilling my Ministry, was, to get into the darkest places in the *Countrey*, even amongst those people that were furthest off of profession . . . because I found my spirit leaned most after awakening and converting'. How great an influence he consequently and quickly came to wield is implicitly demonstrated by the treatment of him at the Restoration. His arrest in November 1660, so soon after the King's return, while the restored regime was still in the process of regaining control of the country and well before the re-establishment of the episcopal Church of England by the Act of Uniformity (1662), suggests that his was a voice too loud to be permitted to continue sounding the strains of Interregnum Puritanism. The misrepresentations and slanders his sermons provoked ('It began . . . to be rumoured up and down among the People, that I was a Witch, a Jesuit, a highway-man, and the like') bear a similar witness to his ministerial authority and power as a preacher; so, too, does the sobriquet 'Bishop Bunyan' later bestowed upon him, 'though in jeering manner no doubt'.[6] We should expect partiality in the anonymous *Continuation* (1692) of *Grace Abounding*, usually attributed to the ejected London Congregational minister George Co[c]kayn[e] (or Cockin), a Bedfordshire man and Bunyan's friend, but it seems to have had good grounds to claim that 'the Seed of the Word (he all this while) sowed in the hearts of his Congregation, Watered with the Grace of God, brought forth in abundance, in bringing in Disciples to the Church'.[7] The Congregationalist leader and Cromwellian Vice-Chancellor of Oxford University, John Owen, is said to have confessed to Charles II that he would willingly sacrifice all his learning could he but preach like Bunyan.[8]

Meanwhile, the stock of Bunyan's literary reputation was not high. In prefatory epistles Burton, Richard Spensely (or Spencly, a deacon of the Bedford Church), John Child (another Bedford Church member, who later conformed) and 'I.G.' (probably John Gibbs, afterwards ejected vicar of Newport Pagnell) had sought to recommend the then unknown author of *Gospel-Truths*, the *Vindication* and

---

[6] *GA*, §§ 289, 307, p. 169.

[7] *GA*, p. 169. For Cokayne see *DNB* and *CR*, s.v. (and cf. *Minutes*, pp. 34, 66, 79, 87, 90), and for the attribution of the *Continuation* to him, *GA*, p. xlii, and Brown, pp. 378, 386–7.

[8] John Asty, 'Memoirs of the Life of John Owen', prefaced to *A Complete Collection of the Sermons of John Owen* (1721), p. xxx, and repeated in Peter Toon, *God's Statesman: The Life and Work of John Owen* (Exeter, 1971), p. 162.

A Few Sighs from Hell (1658). They were sensitive to the fact that Bunyan's 'outward condition, and former employment was mean, and his humane learning small', but nevertheless defended his claim on the attention of potential readers as 'one that hath acquaintance with God, and taught by his Spirit': 'this man is not chosen out of an earthly, but out of the heavenly University'.[9] From the earliest days of his ministry, Bunyan himself was made aware of his vulnerability as an ill-educated and vulgar intruder into the province of duly qualified theologians, scholars, and men of letters: 'When I went first to preach the Word abroad, the Doctors and Priests of the Countrey did open wide against me'. Rather than deny his ignorance, Bunyan, in the manner characteristic of radical Puritanism, defiantly asserted it as his strength. It is quite true that he 'never went to School to *Aristotle* or *Plato*, but was brought up at my fathers house, in a very mean condition', but, far from disqualifying him, this is precisely what qualifies him to be an author for it confers upon his writing not the second-hand authority of scholarship but the immediate authority of experience:

I never endeavoured to, nor durst make use of other men's lines . . . for I verily thought, and found by experience, that what was taught me by the Word and Spirit of Christ, could be spoken, maintained, and stood to, by the soundest and best established Conscience.

He writes, as he preaches, with 'experimental' (or, as we would say, 'experiential') authenticity: 'I preached what I felt, what I smartingly did feel'.[10]

This defence made as little impression upon the cultural and intellectual world of the Restoration as it did upon the judicial. At Bunyan's trial, his interrogators and judges harped constantly upon his low social status and his ignorance: they were outraged that this tinker ignorant of Greek should presume to know better than his betters.[11] This was a point of view which, as Bunyan's popularity increased during the 1670s and 1680s, found it hard to believe he *could* have written the allegories published over his name. More than once, Bunyan is at pains to defend the integrity and originality of his work, coming to assert its '*own native Language, which no man / now*

---

[9] *Misc. Wks.*, i. xxv–xxvi, 11, 243. For Gibbs see *CR*, s.v. and for his probable authorship of the preface, *Misc. Wks.*, i. 398.
[10] *GA*, §§ 276, 283, 285; *Misc. Wks.*, ii. 16.
[11] *GA*, pp. 108, 110–11, 117–18, 128.

useth', its very vulgarity, that is to say, as a mark of its authenticity.[12] That claim is from the preface to Part II of *The Pilgrim's Progress* (1684), where Bunyan distinguishes his own second part from the work of those such as T[homas] S[herman] who 'counterfeited' his pilgrim in *The Second Part of the Pilgrim's Progress* (1682).[13] Sherman's treatment endeavoured to bestow upon Bunyan's allegory due seriousness and literary decorum. Bunyan's refusal to follow Sherman in subscribing to sober and polite canons of taste is significant: it bespeaks a new confidence. The diffident author who had withheld Part I of *The Pilgrim's Progress* (1678) from publication for several years, and finally only printed it with a very defensive prefatory 'Apology', could, by 1682, describe the much more ambitious design of *The Holy War* (1682) with unapologetic confidence.[14]

For this increased trust in his literary instincts, Bunyan had good cause. Part I of *The Pilgrim's Progress* had proved an immediate and unprecedented bestseller. Sagacity hardly exaggerates when he exclaims that 'all our Countrey rings of' Christian, nor did Bunyan himself when he delightedly called attention to the book's popularity in the preface to Part II.[15] It went through three editions within the year of publication and had reached a thirteenth by Bunyan's death in 1688, going on to become by far the most popular work of seventeenth-century prose fiction.[16] It earned for its publisher, Nathaniel Ponder, the nickname 'Bunyan Ponder'. Not surprisingly, Ponder had to defend his copyright in so saleable a commodity against piracy, though with qualified success.[17] From the mid-1680s, ballads by 'J.B.' featuring 'Pilgrim' in their titles were on sale in London, and a brief chap-book version was put out in 1684. A steady stream of piratical and composite editions, supposititious works,

---

[12] *PP*, p. 168 (this point is made above, p. 85); *HW*, p. 251; *Misc. Wks.*, viii. 51.

[13] *PP*, pp. 338–9; Brown, p. 258.

[14] *PP*, pp. 1–7; *HW*, pp. 1–5. For the commonly received dating of the composition of *The Pilgrim's Progress* in the period 1666–72, see *PP*, pp. xxi–xxv and above, pp. 84–5. For a dissenting view, see above, p. 33.

[15] *PP*, pp. 169–70, 175.

[16] Donald Wing, *Short-title Catalogue of Books Printed in England . . . 1641–1700*, 2nd edn., 3 vols. (in progress) (New York, 1972–), B5557–5585; *PP*, pp. xxxvi–lxxiii; C. C. Mish, 'Bestsellers in Seventeenth-century Fiction', *Papers of the Bibliographical Society of America* 47 (1953), 358–9.

[17] F. M. Harrison, 'Nathaniel Ponder: The Publisher of *The Pilgrim's Progress*', *The Library*, 4th ser. 15 (1934), 268–74, 282–6; *PP*, pp. xlix, lxxiii–lxxiv; Brown, p. 444.

imitations, adaptations, and translations issued from the press in the last twenty years of the century.[18] These included Dutch and French translations in 1682 and 1685 respectively; the spurious Part III (1693), reprinted into the nineteenth century despite Ponder's immediate denunciation of it as a fraud;[19] *The Pilgrim's Progress from Quakerism to Christianity* (1698) by the lapsed Quaker Francis Bugg;[20] S.M.'s *The Heavenly Passenger: or the Pilgrim's Progress . . . Newly done into verse* (1687) and *The Pilgrim's Passage in Poesie* (1697) by 'Ager Scholae'.

The Augustan Bunyan

That odd pseudonym is informative: it implies an intention to improve Bunyan, to make him respectable. Amongst the literati of the early eighteenth century Bunyan's popularity was taken not as proof of his excellence but as confirmation of his vulgarity, and so of his inconsequentiality. He deserved his fame all right, but it was a kind of fame no cultivated person would seek. In a letter of 1709 Alexander Pope ironically contemplated the possibility that 'the Nosegays of Parnassus' might become as common as 'Bunyan's Sermons', and in the following year Joseph Addison cited Bunyan as evidence that anyone might gain a popular following, regardless of merit: 'I never yet knew an Author that had not his Admirers. *Bunyan* and [*Francis*] *Quarles* have pass'd through several Editions, and please as many Readers, as *Dryden* and [*John*] *Tillotson*.' It was a view to which the critic John Dennis subscribed: no one could suppose that Bunyan, however popular with 'The Rabble of the Nation' he might be, could '*please and gratify the Minds of Men of Quality and Education*'.[21] In just this spirit, the beau monde is to smile at Congreve's Lady Wishfort inviting Mrs Marwood to

---

[18] *PP*, pp. lxxiv–lxxxvii, 339; Harrison, pp. 75–6; Brown, p. 458; Margaret Spufford, *Small Books and Pleasant Histories* (1981), p. 198; *Works*, iii. 62–6.

[19] Brown, pp. 452–5, 456–7; Robert G. Collmer, 'The Reception of Bunyan's Works in the Netherlands', in Jan Van Dorsten (ed.), *Ten Studies in Anglo-Dutch Relations* (Leiden and London, 1974), pp. 173–4.

[20] For Bugg see *DNB*, s.v., and William C. Braithwaite, *The Second Period of Quakerism*, 2nd edn., rev. Henry J. Cadbury (1961; repr. York, 1979), pp. 487–8, 490, 704.

[21] Alexander Pope, *Correspondence*, ed. George Sherburn, 5 vols. (Oxford, 1956), i. 56–7; Joseph Addison, *The Whig-Examiner*, 2 (21 Sept. 1710), in *The Medleys and Whig-Examiners* (1712), p. 19; John Dennis, 'Of Simplicity in Poetical Compositions', in *The Critical Works*, ed. Edward Niles Hooker, 2 vols. (Baltimore, 1939–43), ii. 29–30.

entertain herself in the closet with 'Quarles and [William] Prynne, and [Jeremy Collier's] *Short View of the Stage*, with Bunyan's works'. The irony resides in the inappropriateness of this collection of Puritans and writers against drama gracing Lady Wishfort's shelves, their inability to supply 'entertainment' to the sophisticates of London society. They belong rather in the world of artisans and cottagers, enthusiasts and fanatical pedants, where the satirist Thomas Brown placed Bunyan in his *Letters from the Dead to the Living* (1702). It was through such lower-class characters that, in *The What D'Ye Call It* (1715), John Gay burlesqued the religious devotion *The Pilgrim's Progress* might arouse.[22] For them, the plainness of Bunyan's style might be appropriate: for Pope, it was akin to dullness. It would, wrote Edward Smith, 'profane heroick Songs', and was, opined Joseph Addison, quite incapable of the 'sublime'. Bunyan's was the work, wrote John Arbuthnot, of a Grub Street hack, fit only for 'Maids and Apprentices'.[23]

As the century wore on, there were occasional kinder comments. In a letter of 1743 the novelist Samuel Richardson, though he did not dissent from the received estimate of Bunyan's quality, nevertheless acknowledged his value for a particular kind of reader: 'Are all Men born to Taste?—No'; consequently, 'Bunyan may be of greater Use to the Multitude' than more refined writing. Thirty years later, Dr Johnson, with that clear-sightedness and independence of mind which marked his conservatism, made a different application of Bunyan's popularity: 'His "Pilgrim's Progress" has great merit, both for invention, imagination and the conduct of the story; and it has the best evidence of its merit, the general and continued approbation of mankind. Few books, I believe, have had a more extensive sale.'[24] However, though Dr Johnson could mention Bunyan in the same breath as Dante and Spenser, prevailing literary opinion in

---

[22] William Congreve, *The Way of the World*, ed. Brian Gibbons (1971), p. 50 (III. i. 55-9); Thomas Brown, *Works*, 8th edn., 4 vols. (1744), ii. 210; John Gay, *The What D'Ye Call It*, II. i. 22-30, in *The Poetical Works*, ed. G. C. Faber (New York, 1926; repr. 1969), p. 350 (excerpted in *Casebook*, p. 49).

[23] Alexander Pope, *Correspondence*, i. 426-7; Edward Smith, *A Poem on the Death of Mr John Philips* ([1708]), p. 8; Joseph Addison, *The Spectator*, ed. Donald F. Bond, 5 vols. (Oxford, 1965), iv. 365 (524 (31 Oct. 1712)); John Arbuthnot, *The History of John Bull*, ed. Alan W. Bower and Robert A. Erickson (Oxford, 1976), pp. 63, 92.

[24] Samuel Richardson, *Selected Letters*, ed. John Carroll (Oxford, 1964), p. 57; *Boswell's Life of Johnson*, ed. George Birkbeck Hill, rev. L. F. Powell, 6 vols. (Oxford, 1934-50), ii. 238 (and printed in *Casebook*, p. 51).

mid-century was of another mind. Edmund Burke contrasted Bunyan's 'degraded' style with that of Virgil and, in 1757, David Hume was unequivocally dismissive: regard for Bunyan was, he pronounced, proof merely of bad taste:

> Whoever would assert an equality of genius and elegance between [JOHN] OGILBY [or OGILVIE] and MILTON, or BUNYAN and ADDISON, would be thought to defend no less an extravagance, than if he had maintained a mole-hill to be as high as TENERIFFE, or a pond as extensive as the ocean. Though there may be found persons, who give the preference to the former authors; no one pays attention to such a taste; and we pronounce without scruple the sentiment of these pretended critics to be absurd and ridiculous.

As late as 1784, the far more sympathetic William Cowper was still sensitive to the indiscretion of praising a writer in such poor standing as Bunyan:

> O thou whom, borne on Fancy's eager wing
> Back to the season of Life's happy spring,
> I pleased remember, and, while memory yet
> Holds fast her office here, can ne'er forget;
> Ingenious dreamer, in whose well-told tale
> Sweet fiction and sweet truth alike prevail;
> Whose humorous vein, strong sense, and simple style
> May teach the gayest, make the gravest smile;
> Witty, and well employed, and, like thy Lord,
> Speaking in parables His slighted word;
> I name thee not lest so despised a name
> Should move a sneer at thy deserved fame,
> Yet, e'en in transitory life's late day
> That mingles all my brown with silver gray,
> Revere the man whose PILGRIM marks the road,
> And guides the PROGRESS of the soul to God.[25]

The Evangelical Bunyan

Cowper's recognition of Bunyan's literary merit is, if not quite unprecedented in fact (witness Dr Johnson, and examples cited

---

[25] Edmund Burke, *A Philosophical Inquiry into . . . the Sublime*, ed. J. T. Boulton (1958), p. 21; David Hume, 'Of the Standard of Taste', in *The Philosophical Works*, ed. Thomas Hill Green and Thomas Hodge Grose, 4 vols. (1882; repr. 1964), iii. 269; William Cowper, *Tirocinium*, ll. 131–46, in *The Poems*, ed. J. C. Bailey (1905), p. 370. For Ogilvie, now more completely forgotten than ever Bunyan was, see *DNB*, s.v.

below), certainly unprecedented in its sympathetic responsiveness and generosity. His praise for the 'well-told' fiction which had hitherto provoked derision and for the 'simple style' which so affronted Augustan taste heralds the Romantic reappraisal of Bunyan. Cowper is, however, equally appreciative of Bunyan's edifying didacticism. In this, he was very far from unique. Throughout the eighteenth century, Bunyan's reputation ran in two channels which rarely converged. While from one quarter there came dismissive and patronizing comment, from another issued testimony of a very different order. It had been above all as an exemplary Christian, one who 'went about doing good', 'in imitation of his great Lord and Master', that Cokayne had commemorated Bunyan in his *Continuation of Mr Bunyan's Life*. He did recognize in Bunyan a 'painful and industrious Author' who had furnished 'the World with sundry good books', but the merit he had in mind was moral and spiritual, not aesthetic or imaginative.[26] When, on the title-page, Charles Doe's 1692 edition of Bunyan's *Works* described its author as 'that Eminent Servant of Christ' and its contents as his 'Christian Ministerial Labours', it was justifying its publication in similar terms.

The reputation of this Bunyan, the pastor, preacher, and practical theologian who counselled, encouraged, and enlightened through his writings, had never faded since the days of 'Bishop Bunyan'. In 1708 the French Protestant mystic Pierre Poiret included in his 'Catalogus Plurimorum Auctorum qui de rebus Mysticis aut Spiritualibus scripserunt', '*Bunnian, Joan* Anglus, egregius'.[27] Their reading of Bunyan contributed to the conversion or rededication of many who were, or would become, dissenting ministers.[28] Leaders of the Evangelical Revival and of Methodism were inspired by him, returned to him often, and recommended him constantly. Howel Harris was a devoted reader.[29] George Whitefield contributed a preface to the third edition of *The Works* (1767). John Wesley more than once read through *The Pilgrim's Progress* (and other Bunyan titles) on horseback, and himself abridged it in 1743. *The Holy War* was included in his 'Christian Library' in 1753. Methodist preachers

[26] *GA*, pp. 168, 171.
[27] *Petri Poireti Bibliotheca Mysticorum Selecta* (Amsterdam, 1708), p. 328.
[28] See, e.g., Walter Wilson, *The History and Antiquities of Dissenting Churches and Meeting-houses in London* . . ., 4 vols. (1808–14), iii. 307, 316, 464.
[29] Geoffrey F. Nuttall, *Howel Harris: The Last Enthusiast* (Cardiff, 1965) pp. 26, 63.

made frequent reference to Bunyan, who exerted a formative influence on their own autobiographies.[30]

It was this tradition which in 1775 produced the first annotated edition of a Bunyan title: *The Pilgrim's Progress Complete in Two Parts . . . To which is now first added, Practical and Expository Notes*. Its dedication to Selina (Hastings), Countess of Huntingdon, and its prefatory commendation by John Edwards, a dissenting minister in Leeds, sufficiently declare its ambience and intentions. The anonymous editor's notes are 'judicious, spiritual and evangelical'. He offers no historical or linguistic glosses. Apart from occasional comment on 'lively' or 'striking' passages, the literary quality of the work does not concern him. He seeks rather to elucidate what 'is worthy the attention of every believer' in a series of expository discourses intended, in the words of the title-page, 'to reform the Judgment, and warm the Heart'.[31] In this enterprise, he quickly had successors. The next year, the Evangelical curate of Olney and close friend of Cowper, John Newton, contributed notes to an edition of Part I of *The Pilgrim's Progress*. William Mason, a canon of York, wrote 'explanatory, experimental and practical' notes for both parts in 1778 and for *The Whole Works* in six volumes ([1784?-92?]). George Burder, a Congregationalist minister and a founder of both the Religious Tract Society and the British and Foreign Bible Society, contributed a life and 'explanatory and practical' notes to a 1786 edition of *The Pilgrim's Progress*. Editions of 1792 and 1795 were annotated, respectively, by John Bradford, a member of the Countess of Huntingdon's Connexion, and by the Evangelical divine Thomas Scott. The stream of reprints of these editions which carried Bunyan into the new century was swelled still further by the addition to Newton's Part I notes of those on Part II by the West Country

---

[30] John Wesley, *The Journal*, ed. Nehemiah Curnock, 8 vols. ([1909-16]), ii. 288, 312, 313; Michael R. Watts, *The Dissenters: From the Reformation to the French Revolution* (Oxford, 1978; repr. 1985), pp. 435-6; Isabel Rivers, '"Strangers and Pilgrims": Sources and Patterns of Methodist Narrative', in J. C. Hilson, M. B. Jones, and J. R. Watson (eds.), *Augustan Worlds* (Leicester, 1978), pp. 189-203 (esp. pp. 193, 194, 195). Isabel Rivers, 'Dissenting and Methodist Books of practical divinity', in Isabel Rivers (ed.), *Books and their Readers in Eighteenth-century England* (Leicester, 1982), pp. 145-59, discusses the purpose of Wesley's 'Christian Library' and the nature of his editing. See also ead., 'John Wesley and the Language of Scripture, Reason, and Experience', *Prose Studies*, 4 (1981), 261.

[31] John Bunyan, *The Pilgrims Progress Complete in Two Parts* (1775), pp. iv, 7. For Edwards and the Countess of Huntingdon see *DNB*, s.vv. and, for the Countess, also Watts, *Dissenters*, pp. 400-1, 447-8, 451-4.

clergyman Robert Hawker (1803); the edition of *Grace Abounding* as *The Life of John Bunyan . . . In which is exemplified the power of evangelical principles* (1809) by the Baptist minister Joseph Ivimey; Ivimey's 1821 edition of *The Pilgrim's Progress* (he published his own *Pilgrims of the Nineteenth Century* in 1827); and the introduction to an 1828 edition by the poet and hymnodist James Montgomery.[32] In 1830 came Robert Southey's edition, but that is another story.

The Romantic Bunyan

The Evangelical Revival ensured that Bunyan was amongst the most frequently printed and readily available of English authors, but it was insistently as a preacher rather than as a writer that it promoted him. The incentive behind the various editions it inspired is well summed up by Bradford:

> The peculiar excellency of the Pilgrim's Progress, and that which was my principal inducement for engaging in this publication, was the practical improvement which may be drawn from every character therein described, and from every occurrence therein related. Let this be remembered, that the true end of reading is a practical improvement of what we read. This likewise is the true end of preaching.[33]

This was to read Bunyan as he had wished to be read, but elsewhere a very different, and potentially inimical, response was gaining ground. By the time of Southey's 1830 edition, the Romantic revolution in taste and aesthetics had effected that fundamental revaluation of Bunyan's literary quality anticipated by Cowper.

There had been earlier anticipations. In 1741 an anonymous contributor to *The Gentleman's Magazine* had recognized that Bunyan's style was essential to what, despite its ill-repute, was a surpassing literary achievement. Bunyan's 'Expression', though 'homely', 'is at the same time so just and natural, and so exactly of a Piece with the Structure of his Tale, that, take it all together, there never was an Allegory better designed or better supported.' The essay

---

[32] All these men are noticed in *DNB*, s.vv. Hawker was the subject of an engraving by Blake, who himself illustrated scenes from *The Pilgrim's Progress*: see Geoffrey Keynes, *Engravings by William Blake: The Separate Plates* (Dublin, 1956), pp. 30, 85.

[33] John Bunyan, *The Pilgrim's Progress . . . With Notes by John Bradford* (1792), pp. ix–x.

took the line Dr Johnson would later adopt, but developed it into an explicit challenge to both the Classicism of the eighteenth century and to the Augustan distrust of inspiration and originality. Though 'The Wits may perhaps take Offence at the Respect I pay to this Religious Romance' of *The Pilgrim's Progress*, yet 'if we consider the universal good Reception it hath met with at home and abroad, we must either allow that it has Merit, or that ourselves and our Neighbours are void of Penetration and true Judgment.' Comparable works 'tho' written by learned and judicious Men, have yet met with an indifferent Reception' compared to Bunyan's. 'He hath therefore, according to the Rules, a Right to Fame', and his 'Example might incline Men unacquainted with any but their Mother Tongue, to undertake somewhat therein . . . in point of *Invention*, all Men are on a *Par*'. The essay concluded with the subversive hope that such men might aspire to excellence 'rather by striking out new Paths, than treading very circumspectly in the old ones'. Twenty-five years later, an article in the same journal on the occasion of the publication of *A Relation of the Imprisonment of Mr John Bunyan* (1765) similarly insisted that *The Pilgrim's Progress*, though it 'has been frequently the Witling's jest', is nevertheless 'As a work of imagination . . . certainly a work of original and uncommon genius'.[34]

Bunyan's reputation thus registers the 'pre-Romantic' phase of eighteenth-century taste: admiration for genius untutored in artistic decorum, and the perception of originality in work ignorant of literary tradition, appeal to critical criteria which would have counted for little with Dennis but which will count for a great deal with Coleridge. It was a shift which made some impression on eighteenth-century reference works. The notices of Bunyan in *Biographia Britannica* (1747–66), James Granger's *Biographical History of England* (1769), and the second edition of *Encyclopaedia Britannica* (1778) were exclusively biographical, but to the entry in Granger's second edition (1775) was appended an appreciation of Bunyan's literary quality. To his original observation that *The Pilgrim's Progress* was 'one of the most popular books ever published' Granger now added that it was also 'one of the most ingenious books in the English language.' He lauded Bunyan's 'original and poetic genius', claimed that 'Bunyan, who has been mentioned among the least and

---

[34] *The Gentleman's Magazine*, xi (1741), p. 488; xxxv (1765), pp. 168–9 (quoted more fully in *Casebook*, pp. 50–1).

lowest of our writers, and even ridiculed as a driveller . . . deserves a much higher rank', and conjectured that 'if he had been a master of numbers, he might have composed a poem worthy of Spencer' [*sic*]. Granger's apprehension that 'this opinion may be deemed paradoxical' was, however, well-founded. Although he had conceded the 'coarseness and vulgarity' of Bunyan's language, the editors of the second edition of *Biographia Britannica* (1778-93), who drew substantially on Granger, had 'some doubt' whether his encomium 'be not carried rather too far'.[35]

Before long, the doubt would be whether it was carried far enough. In their subjectivity, demotic sympathies, idealism, greater trust in the heart than the head, meditative bias, and endeavour imaginatively to transmute the perceived world, Puritanism and Romanticism have a number of points of contact,[36] one consequence of which was that a patronizing and dismissive tone no longer characterized literary comment on Bunyan. The 'Witling's jest' and Cowper's 'despised name' was, for the first time, treated as an equal by men of letters. The stylistically lamentable and vulgarly enthusiastic work belittled by eighteenth-century literati was by early nineteenth-century writers perceived to be the experimentally authentic and dramatically imaginative creation of inspired genius. This change in Bunyan's literary status is evident in the work of Sir Walter Scott, the first British author to allude to Bunyan throughout his *œuvre*. In his journal, Scott recalled Bunyan as one of the few reliefs to the 'gloom' and 'tedium' of the presbyterian sabbaths of his childhood; he referred to him repeatedly in his letters; he took from him epigraphs to the chapters of his novels; and *The Pilgrim's Progress* shapes the journey

---

[35] *Biographia Britannica . . . digested in the Manner of Mr Bayle's Historical and Critical Dictionary*, 6 vols. (1747-66), ii. 1028-9; James Granger, *A Biographical History of England*, 2 vols. (1769), ii. 247-8; *Encyclopaedia Britannica*, 2nd edn., 10 vols. (1778), ii. 1521-2; James Granger, *A Biographical History*, 2nd edn., 4 vols. (1775), iii. 348; Andrew Kippis and Joseph Towers (eds.), *Biographia Britannica*, 2nd edn., 5 vols. (1778-93), iii. 12-13.

[36] This point is made in various ways in: Richard E. Brantley, *Wordsworth's Natural Methodism* (New Haven, 1975), *passim*; Dayton Haskin, 'Baxter's Quest for Origins', *The Eighteenth Century*, 21 (1980), 145-61; N. H. Keeble, *Richard Baxter: Puritan Man of Letters* (Oxford, 1982), pp. 108-13; id., *The Literary Culture of Nonconformity* (Leicester, 1987), pp. 181-6, 283-4; Vincent Newey, 'Wordsworth, Bunyan, and the Puritan Mind', *ELH* 41 (1974), 212-32, and 'The Steadfast Self', in R. T. Davies and B. G. Beatty (eds.), *Literature of the Romantic Period* (Liverpool, 1976), pp. 43-7; R. Parker, *Coleridge's Meditative Art* (Ithaca, 1975), pp. 28-45.

South of Jeannie Deans.[37] Bunyan had a particular fascination for the imagination of William Blake. Charles Lamb was an appreciative reader, though he feared Southey's 'splendid edition of Bunyan's Pilgrim' would transform 'His cockle hat and staff . . . to a smart cockd beaver and a jemmy cane': 'the thought is enough to turn one's moral stomach . . . Nothing can be done for B but to reprint the old cuts in as homely but good a style as possible'.[38] There is some sentimentality in this view, but, clearly, it is Bunyan's very lack of sophistication which Lamb identifies as his distinctive merit. Familiar and appreciative references to Bunyan occur in the journals, letters, and essays of George Crabbe, Dorothy Wordsworth, Keats, Hazlitt, and Emerson.[39] This appreciation was given public acknowledgement in Southey's edition which, with the reviews and notice taken of it, established Bunyan as an English classic.

That the poet laureate should not feel it beneath his dignity to write a hundred-page introduction to *The Pilgrim's Progress* implicitly testified to Bunyan's new-found status. The testimony was, however, explicit as well as implicit. Southey asserted that the popular reputation Bunyan had long enjoyed had now been confirmed by scholarly and literary circles. It was an approbation he himself entirely endorsed. Although markedly unsympathetic to what Southey saw as the 'hypocrisy . . . and fanaticism' of seventeenth-century Nonconformity, his introduction hailed Bunyan as 'The Prince of all allegorists in prose' and commended his 'homespun style' as 'a clear stream of current English'.[40] This appreciative tone was

---

[37] John Gibson Lockhart, *The Life of Sir Walter Scott*, 10 vols. (Edinburgh, 1902–3), i. 27; *The Letters of Sir Walter Scott*, ed. H. J. C. Grierson, 12 vols. (1932–7), i. 54, ii. 210, 344, iii. 40, 446, iv. 494, vi. 142, x. 236, xi. 43, 393, 480; Sir Walter Scott, *The Heart of Midlothian* (1818), chaps. XXX–XXXI.

[38] Harold Bloom, *Blake's Apocalypse* (1963), pp. 37, 52, 195, 373, 412; *The Letters of Charles Lamb*, ed. E. V. Lucas, 3 vols. (1935), iii. 178.

[39] *The Life of George Crabbe by his Son*, introd. by Edmund Blunden (1947), p. 257; *Journals of Dorothy Wordsworth*, ed. E. de Selincourt, 2 vols. (1941), i. 105, 208; *The Complete Works of William Hazlitt*, ed. P. P. Howe, 21 vols. (1930–4), iii. 43, v. 13–14, 94; x. 229; xvii. 129, 377; *The Letters of John Keats*, ed. Maurice Forman, 4th edn. (1952), pp. 37, 420; *Journals of Ralph Waldo Emerson*, ed. Edward Waldo Emerson and Waldo Emerson Forbes, 10 vols. (1909–14), iv. 421. For Bunyan's influence on Thoreau, Melville, and Whitman, as well as Emerson, see Kenneth W. Cameron, 'Bunyan and the Writers of the American Renaissance', *American Transcendental Quarterly*, 13 (1972), 1–47.

[40] John Bunyan, *The Pilgrim's Progress. With A Life of John Bunyan by Robert Southey* (1830), pp. v–vi, xiv–xv, lvi, lxxxviii, xcvi. Passages from Southey's introd. are printed in *Casebook*, pp. 56–8.

maintained in reviews of the edition, most influentially by Scott (in *The Quarterly Review*) and by Macaulay (in *The Edinburgh Review*). For Scott, there was no longer any doubt that Bunyan stood comparison with Spenser; for Macaulay, as for Hazlitt, Bunyan surpassed Spenser as an allegorist in his 'strong human interest', and was, with Milton, one of the two greatest creative talents of the later seventeenth century. There was, wrote Josiah Conder in 1838, 'no longer any danger of moving a sneer by naming the Author of the Pilgrim's Progress'.[41]

Romantic insight into Bunyan culminated in Coleridge's marginalia. A note Henry Nelson Coleridge associated with Coleridge's 1818 lectures articulated what was to become a common conviction of Bunyan criticism: that Bunyan's innovative fictional technique is inexplicable save by reference to his own daemon; originality is his most striking literary characteristic. Coleridge perceives in Bunyan an inspired genius liberated from the constraints of, rather than indebted to, his religious tradition:

in that admirable Allegory, the first Part of Pilgrim's Progress, which delights every one, the interest is so great that spite of all the writer's attempts to force the allegoric purpose on the Reader's mind by his strange names — Old Stupidity of the Town of Honesty, &c. &c. — his piety was baffled by his genius, and the Bunyan of Parnassus had the better of the Bunyan of the Conventicle — and with the same illusion as we read any tale known to be fictitious, as a novel, — we go on with his characters as real persons, who had been nicknamed by their neighbours.[42]

In the summer of 1830 Coleridge annotated a copy of Southey's edition, and the following year an 1820 edition of Parts I–II with Mason's notes. Despite the 1818 note, Coleridge's chief interest in

---

[41] [Sir Walter Scott], '[Review of Southey edn.]', *The Quarterly Review*, 43, no. 86 (Oct. 1830), 469; [Thomas Babington Macaulay], '[Review of Southey edn.]', *The Edinburgh Review*, 54, no. 108 (Dec. 1831), 451–2, 461; Hazlitt, *Complete Works*, v. 43, xvi. 54; John Bunyan, *The Pilgrim's Progress . . . With explanatory notes by William Mason, and a life of the author by Josiah Conder* ([1838]), p. xi. For Conder see *DNB*, s.v. Scott's review is printed in part in *Casebook*, pp. 59–65, and in Ioan Williams (ed.), *Sir Walter Scott on Novelists and Fiction* (1968), pp. 399–406; Macaulay's review was included in the various editions of his *Essays*, where, as in ref. works and in *Casebook*, p. 77, it is misdated 1830.

[42] Roberta Florence Brinkley (ed.), *Coleridge on the Seventeenth Century* (1955; repr. New York, 1968), p. 475; *The Collected Works of Samuel Taylor Coleridge*, gen. ed. Kathleen Coburn, 16 vols. (in progress) (1969–   ), XII. i. (*Marginalia*, ed. George Whalley), 801.

both these later sets of marginalia (and particularly in the first) was theological rather than literary. He vigorously defended the ecclesiastical stand of Bunyan and the Nonconformists against Southey's strictures, championed enthusiasm as 'almost a Synonime of Genius', and, with reference to Christian's exposition of the true nature of faith in the Talkative episode, asserted 'All the Doctors of the Sorbonne could not have better stated the Gospel Medium between Pelagianism and Antinomian Solfidianism. . . . It is indeed Faith alone that saves us; but such a Faith, as cannot be alone'. *The Pilgrim's Progress* is 'incomparably the best SUMMA THEOLOGIAE *Evangelicae* ever produced by a writer not miraculously inspired'. Even as he wrote that, however, Coleridge expressed disappointment that Southey had confined his stylistic comment to the 'homespun' quality of Bunyan's writing: 'I can find nothing *homely* in it but a few phrases & single words. The Conversation between Faithful and Talkative is a model of unaffected correctness, dignity and rhythmical Flow'. Bunyan's 'lowest style of English' is no mere incompetence but a *style*, essential to 'the reality of the vision', whose authenticity compels our assent. For Coleridge, the affective power which makes *The Pilgrim's Progress* such a 'wonderful work' hence had a literary quite as much as a religious cause.[43]

The Victorian Bunyan

Bunyan was henceforth a recognized part of the English literary heritage upon whom writers might now draw as a matter of course and without apology. He is a ubiquitous presence in nineteenth-century fiction. Little Nell, Maggie Tulliver, Adam Bede, and Huckleberry Finn read him. Nathaniel Hawthorne draws on *The Pilgrim's Progress* in *The Celestial Railroad*, *The Scarlet Letter*, and *The Blithedale Romance*. Jane Eyre makes her way through the 'dreary wilderness' of this world; Bunyan is quoted directly in the preface to *The Professor*; *Villette* uses allegorical nomenclature in the manner of Bunyan. Thackeray's first major, and best known, novel is entitled *Vanity Fair*. *Oliver Twist* is subtitled 'The Parish Boy's Progress'; Dickens habitually gives to his characters representative and emblematic names; his London frequently merges into the City

---

[43] Coleridge, *Collected Works*, XII. i. 802, 803, 814, 816, 818; Brinkley (ed.), *Coleridge on the Seventeenth Century*, pp. 475, 476, 477.

of Destruction; Little Nell begins her novel lost in the city and ends it in death with her eyes set on heaven. Louisa M. Alcott's *Little Women* adapts its Preface from Bunyan, and takes both chapter headings and its theme from *The Pilgrim's Progress*. George Eliot's Silas Marner first appears as an isolated individual carrying a mysterious burden; Dorothea's predicament in Chapter LXXX of *Middlemarch* is described and defined in terms which recall Christian's; Maggie Tulliver passes through 'The Valley of Humiliation'. It is, indeed, entirely possible to read nineteenth-century novels (especially in their frequent *Bildungsroman* mutation) as rewritings of Bunyan which trace the progress of their (often outcast, miserable or neglected) protagonists through trial and adversity to spiritual maturity and happiness. *The* question facing them is, if not quite 'What shall I do to be saved?', at least 'What shall I do?'. Victorian writers of fiction conceived of the novel 'as a *scola cordis*': 'by adopting the types, analogues, and allegorical suggestions of the popular religious tradition ... [*they*] cast themselves firmly in that tradition of writing represented by Bunyan. Their plots are essentially his plot'.[44]

Bunyan's claim to literary eminence was meanwhile receiving increasingly assured articulation. George Cheever's *Lectures on The Pilgrim's Progress* ([*c*.1828]), which appears to have been the first complete book devoted to Bunyan, consisted of theological exposition and moral commentary, rather than literary criticism, but Cheever is nevertheless clearly aware that his author excelled as a writer.[45] This excellence merited his inclusion as the father of the English novel in Henry Hallam's *Introduction to the Literature of Europe* (1837–9).

---

[44] For most of these (and other) examples, and for this whole subject, see in particular Barry Qualls, *The Secular Pilgrims of Victorian Fiction* (Cambridge, 1982), *passim* (quotations from pp. 1, 6, 13), and also: Valentine Cunningham, *Everywhere Spoken Against: Dissent in the Victorian Novel* (Oxford, 1975), pp. 80, 160, 185, 257; Vincent Newey, 'Dorothea's Awakening: The Recall of Bunyan in *Middlemarch*', *N & Q* 31 (1984), 497–9; Robert Stainton, 'Hawthorne, Bunyan, and the American Romance', *PMLA* 71 (1956), 155–65; David E. Smith, *Bunyan in America* (Bloomington, 1966), pp. 47–102; Alexander Welsh, *The City of Dickens* (Oxford, 1971), pp. 58–9, 70, 129, 170.

[45] I have seen only an 1846 London edn. of Cheever's *Lectures*. It is not listed in the British Library catalogue. James F. Forrest and Richard L. Greaves, *John Bunyan: A Reference G ide* (Boston, 1982), 1844 (1), gives as its earliest notice a New York edn. of 1844. ne Borough of Bedford Public Library's *Catalogue of the John Bunyan Library (Frank Mott Harrison Collection)* (Bedford, 1938), p. 32, lists a London edn. with the conjectural date '*c*.1828'.

The bibliographical and historical accounts of English literature by Robert Chambers (1844), S. A. Allibone (1859), David Masson (1859), George L. Craik (1862), Hippolyte Taine (1863-4; Englished 1871), and Henry Morley (1873) prepared the way for John Froude's 1880 study in the 'English Men of Letters' series.[46] Unlike Coleridge, Froude had scant sympathy for Bunyan's enthusiasm or Calvinism, and none at all for the Evangelical reading of Bunyan ('The conventional phrases of Evangelical Christianity', a mere 'cant', 'ring untrue in the modern ear like a cracked bell'), but he was nevertheless committed, as Masson had been, to the Romantic view of Bunyan as 'a man of natural genius'. He believed Bunyan knew George Herbert, and 'perhaps' Spenser and Milton, but 'His real study was human life as he had seen it'. It was the realistic accuracy with which Bunyan depicted that life, rather than his religious understanding of it, which was the burden of Froude's appreciation of *Mr Badman* and Part I of *The Pilgrim's Progress* where 'we are among genuine human beings' (Part II Froude dismissed as 'a feeble reverberation of the first'). *The Holy War*, however, was, like *Paradise Lost*, vitiated by that 'unreality' which is inevitable when art treats the supernatural not as myth but as truth.[47] Many literary commentators would subsequently yield to this inclination to separate Bunyan's novelistic genius for the realistic presentation of incident, character, and conversation from the allegorical tenor of his fictions, and his fictions from his other works. Parnassus was preferred to the Conventicle.

The Conventicle, however, bulked larger in the work of men religiously sympathetic to Bunyan, who began to examine his texts and context with a new scholarly rigour. In 1838 Conder, knowing only the second edition of *The Pilgrim's Progress*, had, like Southey before him, been unsure when it first appeared. In 1847, however,

[46] Henry Hallam, *Introduction to the Literature of Europe*, 4 vols. (1837-9), i. 430, iv 552-4; Robert Chambers, *Cyclopaedia of English Literature*, 3rd edn., 2 vols. (1876), i. 412-16; S. A. Allibone, *A Critical Dictionary of English Literature*, 3 vols. (Philadelphia and London, 1859-71), i. 282-5; David Masson, *British Novelists and their Styles* (Cambridge, 1859), pp. 72-7; George L. Craik, *A Manual of English Literature* (1862), pp. 338-40 (dissenting from Macaulay's preference for Bunyan over Spenser); Hippolyte Taine, *History of English Literature*, 2 vols. (Edinburgh, 1871), i. 398-408 (associating Bunyan's sublimity with Homer's); Henry Morley, *A First Sketch of English Literature*, new edn. (1901), pp. 615-16, 662-4 (Bunyan's 'genius akin to that of the dramatist').

[47] J. A. Froude, *Bunyan* (1880), pp. 29, 55-61, 84, 85, 95-113, 114-20, 118, 171; Masson, *British Novelists*, p. 73.

George Offor was able to edit the first edition (though still known only in a unique copy) for the Hanserd Knollys Society. Offor went on to produce what would, for over a century, remain the standard edition of *The Works* (1852-3; second edition, 1860-2). Offor's introductions and notes kept the religious value of Bunyan squarely in view, but he tried to establish the course of Bunyan's literary career, provided details of its historical context (stressing the sufferings of Nonconformists), explicated the texts, and sought out the earliest known editions as his copy texts. In this, he was hampered by their availability. *A Book for Boys and Girls* (1686), for example, was known to him only in the considerably reduced form of the second edition (1701) and as the *Divine Emblems* of 1724. The first edition did not come to light until 1888.[48] Among the earliest scholarly editions based upon modern bibliographical and editorial principles were an 1879 edition of *Grace Abounding* and *The Pilgrim's Progress* by Edmund Venables (who wrote the Bunyan entry in the *Dictionary of National Biography*) and John Brown's 1887 edition of *The Pilgrim's Progress* which was based upon a collation of ten editions published during Bunyan's lifetime and included textual notes, linguistic glosses, and explication of historical allusions. It was John Brown, pastor of Bunyan Meeting from 1864 until 1903, who in 1885 produced what was to be the standard biography for the next century.[49]

Brown's work concluded a century of scholarly, historical, antiquarian, sometimes quixotic, as well as continuing Evangelical, interest in Bunyan. In James F. Forrest's and Richard L. Greaves's *John Bunyan: A Reference Guide* (1982), eighteen pages carry us from Bunyan's death to 1800, but 116 pages are needed to document material published between 1800 and 1900. A perennial interest was Bunyan's sources. Although in 1838 Conder, noting the primary source of *The Pilgrim's Progress* in Hebrews 11, had asked rhetorically 'Surely one need look no further for the original of Bunyan's allegory?', and Offor had given considerable space to a survey of possible sources and analogues to show that 'no sentence or idea was borrowed', the question of Bunyan's indebtedness continued to

---

[48] Bunyan, *Pilgrim's Progress* (1838), p. xlix; Bunyan, *Pilgrim's Progress* (1830), pp. lxxxiv-lxxxv; *Works*, iii. 746-7; *Misc. Wks.*, vi. 186-8; John Bunyan, *A Book for Boys and Girls*, fac. edn., with introd. by John Brown (1889), p. x; Brown, p. 343.

[49] Brown's biography went into a second edn. in 1886, a third in 1902, and a fourth in 1902; it was revised by Frank Mott Harrison in 1928.

exercise commentators throughout the century.⁵⁰ So, too, did Bunyan's Bedfordshire origins. Scott had first raised the possibility that the tinker was of gypsy stock. Brown's evidence that the family had been resident in Bedfordshire for generations and that Bunyan's father was its first member to be a tinker barely succeeded in ending an extraordinarily prolonged debate.⁵¹ Debate on Bunyan's personality had a more constructive issue. Hitherto, the hectic anxiety of his spiritual experience had either impressed Evangelical commentators as analogous to Paul's, as it had Charles Doe, or distressed literary commentators like Southey as morbidity and feverish disorder. While Offor averred 'The Christian dares not attribute [*Bunyan's*] intense feelings to a distempered brain', John Ruskin, in a letter of 1845 to his mother, had likened Bunyan's conversion experience to a bad bout of indigestion; he dismissed the 'morbid fancies' of *Grace Abounding* as 'pure insanity', 'the workings of a diseased mind'. The new science of psychology, however, offered a middle way of sympathetic understanding, most influentially in William James's *The Varieties of Religious Experience* (1902).⁵² And, finally, we may notice that it was apparently in the 1870s that Bunyan attracted his first Ph.D. student.⁵³

The Modern Bunyan

Although the Romantic Bunyan is still to be met with (he is, writes Walter Allen, 'a transcendent genius', 'as original as anything in literature can be'),⁵⁴ the twentieth century has by and large been less

---

⁵⁰ Bunyan, *Pilgrim's Progress* (1838), p. xii; John Bunyan, *The Pilgrim's Progress*, ed. George Offor (1847), p. vi; *Works*, ii. 29–54; Forrest and Greaves, *Guide*, 1858 (4, 5), 1860 (8, 10), 1868 (2), 1874 (37, 44), 1875 (13), 1899 (5), 1904 (10).

⁵¹ [Scott], '[Review of Southey edn.]', pp. 469–70. For the debate see, e.g., Forrest and Greaves, *Guide*, 1833 (1), 1859 (6–7, 9–10), 1866 (2), 1874 (34, 37), 1875 (14, 16, 17, 22), 1880 (10, 11), 1882 (2, 4, 10, 11), 1883 (8), 1886 (5, 9, 12, 13, 14, 15, 17, 18, 22), 1891 (1, 9); Brown, pp. 18–30.

⁵² Charles Doe, *The Struggler*, in Folio (1692), sig. 5T2ᵛ (*Works*, iii. 766); Bunyan, *Pilgrim's Progress* (1830), pp. viii, xxxii; *Works*, i, p. ix; John Ruskin, *The Works*, ed. E. T. Cook and Alexander Wedderburn, 39 vols. (1903–12), iv. 348–9; William James, *The Varieties of Religious Experience* (1902), pp. 157–9, 186–8. This psychological interest in Bunyan is documented in Richard L. Greaves, 'Bunyan through the Centuries: Some Reflections', *ES* 64 (1983), 116–17.

⁵³ Forrest and Greaves, *Guide*, 1877 (6).

⁵⁴ Walter Allen, *The English Novel* (Harmondsworth, 1958), p. 32.

impressed by the singularity of Bunyan's genius than by its capacity to give enduring literary expression to convictions, attitudes, and topoi which were far from peculiar to him. This inclination has been encouraged by the replotting of seventeenth-century history. Historiography (and most influentially the work of Christopher Hill) has rediscovered, and treats with a new respect and seriousness, the enthusiasts and radicals previously banished to the lunatic fringe. The 'English revolution' is now discerned not in the resistance of Puritans to episcopalians and Cavaliers but in the heterodox, antinomian, quasi-mystical, often quirky and bizarre, but sometimes acutely prescient, ideas of those 'anabaptist' sectarians and extremists who appalled Puritans quite as much as episcopalians for threatening all too literally to 'turn the world upside down' (Acts 17: 6).[55] William York Tindall's *John Bunyan: Mechanick Preacher* (1934) was the first study to set Bunyan in such a context, emphasizing not his uniqueness but his affinities with seventeenth-century enthusiasts. Such subsequent studies as Owen Watkins's *The Puritan Experience* recognize that Bunyan's theological and religious commitments reproduce in his writing the structural and thematic patterns of a multitude of less-well-known Puritan texts. Roger Sharrock's critical and biographical study *John Bunyan* (revised 1968) is throughout sensitivie to the significance of the ecclesiastical and historical context of Bunyan's writing.[56]

It is the modern contention that not only were the occasion, theme, and form of Bunyan's work historically conditioned in a peculiarly pressing way, but also his sensibility and imaginative habits of mind. William Haller's *The Rise of Puritanism* (1938) was one of the earliest works to appreciate that Puritanism was, *inter alia*, a literary movement with, in the words of Lawrence A. Sasek's title, a characteristic *Literary Temper* (1961). This temper grew out of the religious and devotional life of Puritanism. Geoffrey F. Nuttall's seminal *The Holy Spirit in Puritan Faith and Experience* (1946), which stressed the immediate and 'experimental', the 'enthusiastic',

---

[55] See, e.g., Christopher Hill, *The World Turned Upside Down* (1972; repr. Harmondsworth, 1975); id., *Milton and the English Revolution* (1977; repr. 1979); id., *The Experience of Defeat* (1984); J. F. McGregor and Barry Reay (eds.) *Radical Religion in the English Revolution* (Oxford, 1984); Richard L. Greaves, *Deliver Us From Evil: The Radical Underground in Britain, 1660–1663* (New York, 1986); Richard L. Greaves and R. Zaller (eds.), *A Biographical Dictionary of British Radicals in the Seventeenth Century*, 3 vols. (Brighton, 1982–4).

[56] For other representative studies on these lines, see bibliography below, pp. 266–8.

nature of the Puritan religious experience, opened the way to relate, rather than oppose, Conventicle and Parnassus, by pointing out that the inner certitude of the reality of the presence of the Holy Spirit was accompanied by a consciousness of the difficulty of describing and validating such a personal conviction to others.[57] The obligation which lay on the saints, nevertheless, to make the attempt in order to encourage and inspire others (witness, for example, the preface to *Grace Abounding*, or Hopeful's account of his spiritual history),[58] led not only to writing which was necessarily autobiographical but also to a 'plain' style which was not spare and austere but affective and inevitably metaphorical. The only available evidence was individual experience, and the only possible method by which to convey the authenticity of what was uniquely an individual's perception was analogical. The consequent Puritan contribution to the development of autobiography has been documented in a series of studies,[59] and its metaphorical confidence in an age increasingly distrustful of imagery has received appreciative recognition.[60] The biblical source of this symbolism is the subject of, among other studies, John R. Knott's *The Sword of the Spirit: Puritan Responses to the Bible* (1980). Its encouragement by typological exegesis has recently received a good deal of attention.[61] U. Milo Kaufmann's *The Pilgrim's Progress and Traditions in Puritan Meditation* (1966) has shown how equally formative for Bunyan's literary technique was Puritan spirituality: that Bunyan allegorized now appears an almost inevitable consequence of his Puritan cast of mind. An understanding of the workings of that mind has been immeasurably aided by the publication, under Roger Sharrock's general editorship, of the *Oxford English Texts* edition of Bunyan's complete works.[62]

---

[57] Geoffrey F. Nuttall, *The Holy Spirit in Puritan Faith and Experience*, 2nd edn. (Oxford, 1947), esp. pp. 7–8, 49–57, 134–49.

[58] *GA*, pp. 2–3; *PP*, pp. 136–44.

[59] e.g., William Haller, *The Rise of Puritanism* (New York, 1938), pp. 95–101; Kaufmann, pp. 196–216; N. H. Keeble, *Richard Baxter: Puritan Man of Letters* (Oxford, 1982), pp. 132–9; Sharrock, pp. 55–61; G. A. Starr, *Defoe and Spiritual Autobiography* (Princeton, 1965), pp. 3–50; William York Tindall, *John Bunyan: Mechanick Preacher* (New York, 1934), pp. 22–31; Owen Watkins, *The Puritan Experience* (1972), pp. 9–36 and *passim*.

[60] Harold Fisch, 'The Puritans and the Reform of Prose Style', *ELH* 19 (1952), 229–47; Roger Pooley, 'Language and Loyalty: Plain Style at the Restoration', *Literature and History*, 6 (1980), 2–18; Keeble, *Literary Culture of Nonconformity*, pp. 240–62.   [61] For representative studies, see bibliography below, pp. 268–9.

[62] For details, see the bibliography below, p. 265.

While the prose of Donne, Milton, and Dryden has been printed with comparable editorial care, this Oxford edition confers upon Bunyan a status unique amongst seventeenth-century writers whose major works are in prose.

The consequence of this contextualization of Bunyan has been not a reduction of his literary stature but a definition of it in terms of popular and religious culture. The 'vulgarity' deplored by the eighteenth century now marks Bunyan's as one of the few authentic literary voices to speak not from the educationally and socially privileged courtly circles of a London élite, but from the common and lower-class experience of English provincial life. Appreciations of this are more likely to invoke Langland and Dickens than Spenser.[63] In Leavisite terms, it is a quality which gives to Bunyan the precision, expressiveness, vitality, and moral integrity of which his artificiality and 'extreme remoteness' from living experience and speech deprived Milton.[64] More recently, the free play of current critical theories has begun to doubt the competence of Bunyan's authorial intention to circumscribe his meaning and of his texts to signify a transcendental signified. 'Reader response' criticism has found his allegories textually problematic rather than theologically confident, and, after the work of Stanley Fish, they qualify as suitable cases for deconstructive treatment.[65] But if Bunyan the literary gamester is about to succeed Bunyan 'the greatest imaginative writer of [*his*] age' who owes his pre-eminence to the inspiration of 'his spiritual experience, and . . . the habits of mind of the religious brotherhood and the social class to which he belonged',[66] *The Pilgrim's Progress* yet momentarily, after 300 years, holds its place as perhaps 'the last great expression of the folk tradition of the common people'.[67]

---

[63] See, e.g., L. D. Lerner, 'Bunyan and the Puritan Culture', *Cambridge Journal* 7 (1954), 241–2, and the essays by David Mills and S. J. Newman in Newey, pp. 154–81, 225–50.

[64] F. R. Leavis, *The Common Pursuit* (1952), pp. 204–10; id., 'Milton's Verse', in *Revaluation* (1936; repr. Harmondsworth, 1964), pp. 43, 45, 48–56.

[65] Stanley E. Fish, *Self-consuming Artifacts* (1972; repr. Berkeley and Los Angeles, 1974), pp. 224–64; Wolfgang Iser, *The Implied Reader* (1974), pp. 1–28; Dorothy Van Ghent, *The English Novel* (New York, 1953), pp. 21–32.

[66] James Sutherland, *English Literature of the Late Seventeenth Century* (Oxford, 1969), pp. 31, 316–17.

[67] R[oger] S[harrock], 'John Bunyan' in the *Micropaedia* of the *New Encyclopaedia Britannica*, 15th edn., rev., 32 vols. (Chicago, 1985), ii. 637. Cf. Roger Sharrock's essay in Newey, pp. 55–67.

Select Bibliography

1. Texts

The most fully annotated standard text of *The Pilgrim's Progress* is Roger Sharrock's revision (1960) of James Blanton Wharey's edition (1928). This inaugurated the Clarendon Press's *Oxford English Texts* edition of Bunyan's corpus which will, when complete, supersede George Offor's three volumes of *The Works of John Bunyan* (1852–3; repr. 1860–2). Under the general editorship of Roger Sharrock it comprises separate editions of *Grace Abounding to the Chief of Sinners* (1962), *The Holy War* (1980), *The Life and Death of Mr Badman* (forthcoming), and twelve volumes of *Miscellaneous Works* (1976–). This edition's texts of *The Pilgrim's Progress* and *Grace Abounding* were reprinted in a single volume, with a brief introduction, in the *Oxford Standard Authors* series (1966). Roger Sharrock introduces and lightly annotates a modernized text of *The Pilgrim's Progress* in the *Penguin English Library* series (1965) and there is fuller annotation and the old-spelling text from Sharrock's *Oxford English Texts* edition in the *World's Classics* series, edited by N. H. Keeble (1984). Useful earlier editions include that by Louis Martz (New York, 1949), an edition in *Signet Books*, with an afterword by F. R. Leavis (New York, 1964), and one by G. B. Harrison in the *Everyman's Library* (1954). *Everyman's Library* also includes Harrison's edition of *Grace Abounding* and *Mr. Badman* (1928). More recently, James F. Forrest has edited *The Holy War* (Toronto, 1967) and W. R. Owens *Grace Abounding* (Harmondsworth, 1987).

2. Bibliographies and Guides

The authoritative guide to Bunyan's publications is F. M. Harrison, *A Bibliography of the Works of John Bunyan*, supplement to *The Transactions of the Bibliographical Society*, 6 (1932), and to the secondary material, James F. Forrest and Richard L. Greaves, *John Bunyan: A Reference Guide* (Boston, 1982). Roger Sharrock surveys the secondary literature in *The English Novel: Select Bibliographical Guides*, edited by A. E. Dyson (1974). H. G. Tibbutt, *What They Said About John Bunyan* (Bedford, 1981) prints extracts ranging from the seventeenth century to the present day. Richard L. Greaves, 'Bunyan Through the Centuries: Some Reflections', *ES* 64 (1983) traces the history of Bunyan's reputation, and David E. Smith, *John Bunyan in America* (Bloomington, 1966) Bunyan's American influence. More specialized is Robert G. Collmer, 'The Reception of Bunyan's Works in the Netherlands', in Jan Van Dorsten (ed.), *Ten Studies in Anglo-Dutch Relations* (Leiden and Oxford, 1974) and J. B. H. Alblas, *Johannes Boekholt (1656-1693): The First Dutch Publisher of John Bunyan* (Nieuwkoop, 1987).

3. Biographies

The standard biography is John Brown, *John Bunyan (1628-1688): His Life, Times, and Work*, tercentenary edition, revised by Frank Mott Harrison (1928), who wrote his own *John Bunyan: A Story of His Life* (1928). Also biographical are: Monica Furlong, *Puritan's Progress* (1978); G. O. Griffith, *John Bunyan* (1937); G. B. Harrison, *John Bunyan: A Study in Personality* (1928); O. E. Winslow, *John Bunyan* (New York, 1961); Christopher Hill's forthcoming study (Oxford 1988). Bunyan sites and localities are illustrated and mapped in Joyce Godber, *John Bunyan of Bedfordshire* (Bedford, 1972).

4. Social Studies

A number of works of social history are relevant to Bunyan, and draw evidence from him. E. P. Thompson defines Bunyan's place in *The Making of the English Working Class* (1963). Jack Lindsay, *John Bunyan: Maker of Myths* (1937; repr. 1969) is a Marxist interpretation of the pressures which resulted in Bunyan's spiritual crisis and later imprisonment. The social world inhabited by Bunyan is described in Peter Laslett, *The World We Have Lost Further Explored*, third edition (1983) and Margaret Spufford, *Contrasting Communities* (Cambridge, 1975); its sustaining ideas in Richard B. Schlatter, *Social Ideas of Religious Leaders, 1660-1688* (1940); and its domestic and marital relations in: Laurence Stone, *The Family, Sex, and Marriage in England 1500-1800*, abridged edition (1979); Edward Shorter, *The Making of the Modern Family* (1975); and Edmund S. Morgan, *The Puritan Family*, revised edition (New York, 1966). Bunyan's own social and domestic thought is discussed in Maurice Hussey, 'Christian Conduct in Bunyan and Baxter', *BQ* 14 (1951).

5. Ecclesiastical Studies

The historical and ecclesiastical context of Bunyan's life is most readily learned from Michael R. Watts, *The Dissenters: From the Reformation to the French Revolution* (Oxford, 1978; repr. 1985) and Gerald R. Cragg, *Puritanism in the Period of the Great Persecution, 1660-1688* (Cambridge, 1957). *The Church Book of Bunyan Meeting*, edited in facsimile by G. B. Harrison (1928) may now be more easily read in H. G. Tibbutt (ed.), *The Minutes of the First Independent Church (now Bunyan Meeting) at Bedford, 1656-1766*, Publications of the Bedfordshire Historical Record Society 55 (Bedford, 1976). Tibbutt has written a history: *Bunyan Meeting Bedford*,

1650-1950 (Bedford, [1950]). For the Baptists, see B. R. White, *The English Baptists of the Seventeenth Century* (1983), and the older histories by A. C. Underwood (1947; repr. 1956) and W. H. Whitley, second edition (1932); for the Congregationalists, see R. Tudur Jones, *Congregationalism in England, 1662-1962* (1962). William York Tindall, *John Bunyan: Mechanick Preacher* (New York, 1934) relates Bunyan to mid-seventeenth-century radical Puritanism, as does Christopher Hill in the second appendix of his influential *The World Turned Upside Down* (1972; repr. Harmondsworth, 1975) and in 'John Bunyan and the English Revolution', in *The John Bunyan Lectures, 1978* (Bedford, 1978). For the current historiographical assessment of enthusiasm, see J. F. McGregor and B. Reay (eds.), *Radical Religion in the English Revolution* (Oxford, 1984). Geoffrey F. Nuttall has written on 'Church life in Bunyan's Bedfordshire', *BQ* 26 (1976) and Richard L. Greaves on 'John Bunyan and Nonconformity in the Midlands and East Anglia', *JURCHS* 1 (1976); 'John Bunyan's *Holy War* and London Nonconformity', *BQ* 26 (1975); and 'The Organizational Response of Nonconformity to Repression and Indulgence: The Case of Bedfordshire', *Church History*, 44 (1975). John R. Knott, jun., 'Bunyan and the Holy Community', *SP* 80 (1983) explores Bunyan's conception of Christian and church fellowship, with particular reference to Part II of *The Pilgrim's Progress*.

6. Religious and Theological Studies

The religious experience of Puritanism is best understood from Geoffrey F. Nuttall's *The Holy Spirit in Puritan Faith and Experience*, second edition (Oxford, 1947). Gordon Wakefield has written on *Puritan Devotion* (1957) and Gordon Rupp has insisted on the joy of faith in the Puritan tradition in 'A Devotion of Rapture in English Puritanism', in R. Buick Knox (ed.), *Reformation, Conformity, and Dissent: Essays in Honour of Geoffrey Nuttall* (1977). Both these studies draw on Bunyan, but in *The Pilgrim's Progress and Traditions in Puritan Meditation* (New Haven, 1966), U. Milo Kaufmann offers a sustained and illuminating reading of Bunyan in the light of Puritan hermeneutics and devotion. In a series of articles, Maurice Hussey explored Bunyan's indebtedness to Arthur Dent in particular and to Puritanism in general (*MLR* 44, nos. 1, 4 (1949); *Theology*, 52 (1949); *English*, 7 (1949); *Scrutiny*, 16 (1949); *Congregational Quarterly*, 28 (1950)). Roger Sharrock relates Bunyan to the Puritan tradition in 'Spiritual Autobiography in *The Pilgrim's Progress*', *RES* 24 (1948) and 'Personal Vision and Puritan Tradition in Bunyan', *The Hibbert Journal*, 56 (1957). L. D. Lerner writes on 'Bunyan and the Puritan Culture' in *Cambridge Journal*, 7 (1954) and N. H. Keeble discusses *The Pilgrim's Progress* as 'A Puritan Fiction' in *BQ* 28 (1980). Geoffrey F. Nuttall discloses the religious

'Heart of *The Pilgrim's Progress*' in Peter Brooks (ed.), *Reformation Principle and Practice: Essays in Honour of Arthur Geoffrey Dickens* (1980). The allegory is set in the wider Christian tradition in R. M. Frye, *God, Man, and Satan: Patterns of Christian Thought and Life in 'Paradise Lost' and 'The Pilgrim's Progress'* (Princeton, 1960). Richard L. Greaves, *John Bunyan* (Appleford, Berks., 1969) is an admirably lucid exposition of Bunyan's theology. It argues, *inter alia*, that Bunyan's acquaintance with Luther's work 'cast an indelible imprint upon his conception of Christianity': one aspect of Bunyan's relationship to Luther is explored in Dayton Haskin, 'Bunyan, Luther, and the Struggle with Belatedness in *Grace Abounding*', *University of Toronto Quarterly*, 1 (1980-1). In *Journal of the Warburg and Courtauld Institutes*, 44 (1981) Gordon Campbell traces the theological 'Sources of Bunyan's *Mapp*'. A. Richard Dutton, '"Interesting but tough": Reading *The Pilgrim's Progress*', *Studies in English Literature*, 18 (1978), explores the discrepancy between the universal appeal of *The Pilgrim's Progress* and what he sees as the exclusivity of its predestinarian theology. Seventeenth-centry theological issues are explicated with a wealth of learning in C. A. Patrides, *Milton and the Christian Tradition* (Oxford, 1966).

7. Biblical and Hermeneutical Studies

Exegetical habits of mind, Bunyan's way with Biblical texts, and their literary and imaginative resonance are discussed in: David P. Alpaugh, 'Emblem and Interpretation in *The Pilgrim's Progress*', *ELH* 33 (1966); Sacvan Bercovitch (ed.), *Typology in Early American Literature* (Amherst, 1972); Peter J. Carlton, 'Bunyan: Language, Convention, Authority', *ELH* 51 (1984); John S. Coolidge, *The Pauline Renaissance in England: Puritanism and the Bible* (Oxford, 1970); Peter M. Daly, *Literature in the Light of the Emblem* (Toronto, 1979); Dayton Haskin, 'The Burden of Interpretation in *The Pilgrim's Progress*', *SP* 79 (1982) and '*The Pilgrim's Progress* in the Context of Bunyan's Dialogue with the Radicals', *Harvard Theological Review*, 77 (1984); Balmer H. Kelly, 'Pilgrim Existence: A Consideration of the Bible in *The Pilgrim's Progress*', *Interpretation*, 26 (1972); John R. Knott, jun., *The Sword of the Spirit: Puritan Responses to the Bible* (Chicago, 1980); Paul J. Korshin, *Typologies in England, 1650-1820* (Princeton, 1982); Barbara K. Lewalski, 'Typological Symbolism and the "Progess of the Soul" in Seventeenth-century Literature', in Earl Miner (ed.), *Literary Uses of Typology from the Late Middle Ages to the Present Day* (Princeton, 1977); Mason I. Lowance, *The Language of Canaan* (Cambridge, Mass., 1980); Perry Miller, *The New England Mind: The Seventeenth Century* (1939; repr. Boston, 1963); Vincent Newey, 'Wordsworth, Bunyan, and the Puritan Mind', *ELH* 41 (1974); Roger Pooley, 'The Wilderness of the World', *BQ* 27 (1978); Maureen Quilligan, *The Language of Allegory* (Ithaca, 1979); Roger Sharrock,

'Bunyan and the English Emblem Writers', *RES* 21 (1945); Brainerd P. Stranahan, 'Bunyan's Special Talent: Biblical Texts as "Events" in *Grace Abounding* and *The Pilgrim's Progress*', *ELR* 11 (1981); id., 'Bunyan and the Epistle to the Hebrews', *SP* 79 (1982); Margaret Olofsun Thickstun, 'The Preface to Bunyan's *Grace Abounding* as Pauline Epistle', *N & Q* 230 (1985).

8. Studies of the Puritan Literary Tradition

The literary consequences of Puritanism are, in different ways, the subject of: Sacvan Bercovitch (ed.), *The American Puritan Imagination* (Cambridge, 1971); Patricia Caldwell, *The Puritan Conversion Narrative* (Cambridge, 1983); William Haller, *The Rise of Puritanism* (1938; repr. New York, 1957); N. H. Keeble, *The Literary Culture of Nonconformity in Later Seventeenth-century England* (Leicester, 1987); Kathrine Koller, 'The Puritan Preacher's Contribution to Fiction', *The Huntingdon Library Quarterly*, 11 (1948); David Leverenz, *The Language of Puritan Feeling* (New Brunswick, 1980); Lawrence A. Sasek, *The Literary Temper of the English Puritans* (Baton Rouge, 1961); and Owen Watkins, *The Puritan Experience* (1972). Harold Fisch, 'The Puritans and the Reform of Prose Style', *ELH* 19 (1952) documents the Puritan inclination towards stylistic plainness, and Roger Pooley, 'Language and Loyalty: Plain Style at the Restoration', *Literature and History*, 6 (1980) draws out the political and ecclesiastical implications of stylistic debates after 1660 and the unexpected generosity of the Nonconformist conception of 'plainness'. Joan Webber writes on 'Donne and Bunyan: The Style of Two Faiths' in her *The Eloquent 'I': Style and Self in Seventeenth-century Prose* (Madison, 1968).

9. Literary Histories

J. A. Froude's *Bunyan* in the *English Men of Letters* series (1880) has been superseded as an introduction to Bunyan's literary career by Roger Sharrock, *John Bunyan* (1954), rev. edn. (1968) and Henri Talon, *John Bunyan: The Man and his Works*, trans. Barbara Wall (1951). There are two more recent accounts, both by American scholars: E. Beatrice Batson, *John Bunyan: Allegory and Imagination* (1984) and Lynn Sadler, *John Bunyan* (Boston, 1979). Bunyan's work is related to different aspects of literary history in: Robert Adolph, *The Rise of Modern Prose Style* (Cambridge, Mass., 1968); Walter Allen, *The English Novel* (1954; repr. Harmondsworth, 1958); Richard C. Altick, *The English Common Reader* (Chicago, 1957); Paul Delany, *British Autobiography in the Seventeenth Century* (1969); Rosemary Freemand, *English Emblem Books* (1948); Frank Mott Harrison, 'Nathaniel Ponder: The Publisher of *The Pilgrim's Progress*', *The Library*, fourth series, 15 (1934); Arnold Kettle, *An Introduction to the English Novel*, second edition, 2 vols. (1967); Q. D. Leavis, *Fiction and the Reading Public* (1932; repr. 1965); G. R. Owst, *Literature and Pulpit in Medieval England*, second edition (Oxford, 1961); A. C. Partridge, *Tudor to Augustan English* (1969); Paschal Reeves, 'The Pilgrim's Progress as a Precursor of the Novel', *Georgia Review*, 20 (1966); Walter C. Spengemann, *The Forms of Autobiography: Episodes in the History of a Literary Genre* (New Haven, 1980); Margaret Spufford, *Small Books and Pleasant Histories* (1981); James Sutherland, *English Literature of the Late Seventeenth Century* (Oxford, 1969); E. M. W. Tillyard, *The English Epic and its Background* (1954); id., *The Epic Strain in the English Novel* (1958).

10. Critical Studies

There is a critical dimension to very many of the studies already cited, but, more particular, the thematic and artistic structure of *Grace Abounding* is discussed in: John M. Barrett, 'Bunyan and the Autobiographer's Artistic Purpose', *Criticism*, 10 (1968); Robert Bell, 'Metamorphoses of Spiritual Autobiography', *ELH* 44 (1977); Anne Hawkins, 'The Double-conversion in Bunyan's *Grace Abounding*', *Philological Quarterly*, 61 (1982); Felicity A. Nussbaum, '"By These Words I Was Sustained": Bunyan and *Grace Abounding*', *ELH* 49 (1982). Roger Sharrock, who has written on *The Pilgrim's Progress* in Arnold's *Studies in English Literature* series (1966), has collected together examples of earlier critical comment on Bunyan's allegory in *'The Pilgrim's Progress': A Casebook* (1976). Vincent Newey (ed.), *'The Pilgrim's Progress': Critical and Historical Views* (Liverpool, 1980) is a collection of original essays. Coleridge made some characteristically suggestive notes which have been printed in Roberta Florence Brinkley (ed.), *Coleridge on the Seventeenth Century* (1955; repr. New York, 1968), most of which appear, thoroughly annotated, in volume XII. i of Kathleen Coburn's edition of Coleridge's *Collected Works* (1969–): *Marginalia*, edited by George Whalley. There are appreciative essays by F. R. Leavis in *The Common Pursuit* (1952) and by Maurice Hussey in Boris Ford (ed.), *From Donne to Marvell* (Harmondsworth, 1956), and critical analyses of Bunyan's narrative and fictional techniques and effects in: Stanley E. Fish, *Self-consuming Artifacts* (1972; repr. Berkeley and Los Angeles, 1974); Wolfgang Iser, *The Implied Reader* (1974); and Dorothy Van Ghent, *The English Novel* (1953; repr. New York, 1961). John R. Knott, jun., 'Bunyan's Gospel Day', *ELR* 3 (1973) argues against Fish's contention that in *The Pilgrim's Progess* the notion of progress is subverted. Charles W. Baird, *John Bunyan: A Study in Narrative Technique* (New York, 1977) discountenances the view that Bunyan was an unconscious artist and an unthinking teller of tales.

Index

Note: Bunyan's works are indexed under their titles

Abbot, George 181
Acceptable Sacrifice, The 42
Adams, Thomas 175, 176, 181, 196
Addison, Joseph 246, 247, 248
Advocateship of Jesus Christ, The 42, 81, 90
Alcott, Louisa M. 257
allegory 219–21, 222–4, 226–7, 237
Allen, Walter 260
Allestree, Richard 46, 47, 57
Allibone, S. A. 258
Alsop, Benjamin 81
Ambrose, Isaac 190, 198, 215
Ambrosiaster 138
Ames, William 122, 141
Andrewes, Lancelot, Bp. of Winchester 93
Antichrist and His Ruin, Of 40, 41, 78, 162
Antinomianism 59, 67, 78, 256
Arbuthnot, John 247
Attaway, Mrs 39
Auerbach, Eric 98–9
Augustanism, and Bunyan's reputation 246–8
Augustine, St, Bp. of Hippo 83, 98–9, 138, 142, 146, 195, 206, 237

Bampfield, Francis 39
Baptism
  in Bunyan's thought 16, 17–18, 24, 35, 42, 126, 141–3
  controversies over 8, 9, 12, 17–18, 35, 141–3
Baptists 2, 6, 12, 17, 18, 22
Barlow, Thomas, Bp. of Lincoln 89
Barren Fig-Tree, The 162
Barrow, Isaac 49, 52, 95
Bauman, Richard 103
Baxter, Richard 12, 35, 62n, 74n, 79, 94, 177, 185, 193
Bayly, Lewis, Bp. of Bangor 4, 46, 47, 74
Baynes, Paul 177
Beaumont, Agnes 126, 205

Bedford, Independent Church at 4, 5, 6, 7, 8
Beerbohm, Max 133
Bell, Robert 206
Benjamin, Walter 220
Bernard of Clairvaux, St 83
Bernard, Richard 63n
Bible
  concordance to the 97, 140
  dramatization of the 155, 160–1
  Genevan version of the 138
  imaginative and figurative development of the 98, 161–70, 217–40
  King James version of the 98n, 99, 139, 236–7
  interpretation of the 137–8, 144, 158–9, 220–9
  literal understanding of the 154–5, 162
  as manual of godly living 156
  'mysteries' of the 161–3, 229–36
  'physical sense' of the force of the 157, 158, 193, 221
  religious significance of the 137–8, 139, 153–4
  'simplicity' of the 161, 162
  stylistic significance of the 97–101
  typological reading of the 162, 163–4
Biographia Britannica 252, 253
Blake, William 251n, 254
Bolton, Robert 174–5
Bonner, Edmund, Bp. of London 23
Book for Boys and Girls, A 42, 71, 72, 81, 90, 259
Boyle, Robert 98
Bradford, John 250, 251
Brontë, Charlotte 256
Brown, John 84, 259, 260
Brown, Thomas 247
Bugg, Francis 246
Bunyan, Elizabeth 3, 143
Bunyan, John, the life of
  family of 260
  social status of 244

Bunyan, John, the life of *(continued)*
  in Civil War 3
  first marriage of 3, 4, 241
  early spiritual experiences of 3–8
  and Gifford 1, 6–7, 8, 11, 12, 17, 19
  and Ranters 5, 15, 31, 113
  joins Bedford Church 8, 241
  and Bedfordshire church life 13–15, 113
  and Independents 1, 3, 12–15, 19
  and Quakers 12, 15–17, 31, 113, 242
  early ministry of 9–11, 242
  arrest of 11, 22, 153, 243
  trial of 23, 153–4, 244
  imprisonment of 22, 25, 26–7, 31, 83–4
  grounds of for nonconformity 21–5
  and Bedford church life after 1660 25, 30–1, 34, 41, 79, 84
  and controversies over baptism 8, 9, 12, 17–18, 35, 141–3
  political involvement of 28–9, 39–41, 77–80
  appointed pastor 1, 34
  and Nonconformist affairs 34–5, 38–9, 42
  second imprisonment of 37, 84
Bunyan, John, writings of
  adventure in the 116, 230
  autobiographical 3, 25, 29–30, 85
  Biblical inspiration of the 153–70
  Calvinism of the 18–19, 147, 151
  and censorship 76–7, 81, 82
  church fellowship in the 8, 12, 24, 43, 124–5
  conception of the church in the 8, 12, 18, 24, 35
  controversial 11, 15–17, 35, 39, 59–62, 103–5, 141–3, 154–5, 242
  defence of his ignorance in the 83, 139–40, 141, 162–3, 243–4
  dialogue form in the 101, 105–7
  early 15–16, 73, 75, 82, 103–5, 154–5, 242
  fictional developments in the 85, 238–40
  gender roles in the 39
  homiletic 10–11, 76, 160, 162
  metaphor and allegory in the 94, 161–70, 219–21, 222–4, 226–7, 237
  millenarian 25–6, 27–9, 78, 80
  and oral culture 74, 90, 108–9
  poetic 25–7, 109
  prefatory recommendations of the early 83, 243–4
  press supervision of the 87–8
  prison 25–30, 59–60, 83–4
  publishers of the 80–2
  revisions of the 63, 87, 88–9
  soteriological emphasis of the 146–50, 157
  style of the 91–2, 94–7, 98–110, 159, 161–2
  Trinitarianism of the 144–5
  'vulgarity' of the 244–5
Bunyan, John (son) 3
Bunyan, Joseph 143
Bunyan, Mary 3, 143, 241
Bunyan, Thomas 3
Burder, George 250
Burke, Edmund 248
Burnet, Gilbert, Bp. of Salisbury 48, 52 53
Burrough, Edward
  style of 104
  and controversy with Bunyan 73, 82, 103–5, 242
Burton, John 13, 14, 16, 83, 242, 243

Calvin, John 196
  on election 172, 176–7, 184, 197
  on predestination 146–7
  on Providence 171–2, 181
Calvinism 2, 18–19, 45, 48, 50, 59, 111, 112, 130–1, 135, 147, 174, 175
Cambridge Platonists 48n
Case of Conscience Resolved, A 39
Caussade, Jean-Pierre de 115
censorship 76–7, 81, 82
Chambers, Robert 258
Chandler, Ebenezer 142, 143
Charles II 28, 30, 40, 77
Cheever, George 257
Child, John 83, 243
Chillingworth, William 50, 137
Christian Behaviour 25, 68, 128, 156
Church
  Bunyan's conception of the 8, 18, 124–30
  criteria for membership of the 8–9, 24, 42–3, 126, 148
  fellowship 8, 12, 24, 43, 124–5
  Roman 132n, 137
Clarkson, Laurence 6

Index

Cobb, Ralph 78
Cockayne, George 13, 35, 84, 243, 249
Coleridge, Samuel Taylor 190, 252, 255-6
College, Stephen 40
Collier, Jeremy 247
Come, & Welcome, to Jesus Christ 37, 42, 83, 89, 160, 222, 231, 238, 239-40
Common Prayer, Book of 21, 22, 23, 80, 106, 129, 139, 154
Conder, Josiah 255, 258, 259
Confession of my Faith . . ., A 17, 21, 35, 142
Congregationalists 8, 12, 19, 22, 35
Congreve, William 246-7
Conventicles
  Elizabethan Act against 22
  Restoration Acts against 30
Cooper, Anthony Ashley, 1st. E. of Shaftesbury 81
Cooper, Thomas 34
Coppe, Abiezer 6
Coppin, Richard 6
Cowley, Abraham 98
Cowley, Matthias 82
Cowper, William 248-9, 250, 251
Coxe, Nehemiah 34
Crabbe, George 254
Craik, George L. 258
Cranfield, Beds. 13, 34
Croft, Herbert, Bp. of Hereford 94
Cromwell, Oliver 6, 13, 77, 78
Crook, John 193
Cudworth, Ralph 48n

Dante 114, 247
Danvers, Henry 17, 18, 35, 38
declaration of Indulgence (1672) 34
Declaration of Indulgence (1687) 43, 81
deconstruction 218
Defence of the Doctrine of Justification by Faith, A 36, 59-62, 77, 89
Delaune, Thomas 35
Denne, John 35, 38
Dennis, John 246, 252
Dent, Arthur 4, 46, 47, 74, 101, 173
Derwentdale Plot 29
Desires of the Righteous Granted, The 42, 72, 177
Dewsbury, William 241
Dickens, Charles 256-7, 263

Differences in Judgment about Water-Baptism 17, 35, 142, 143
Discourse Concerning the Pharisee and the Publican, A 38
Discourse of the Building . . . of the House of God, A 42
Doctrine of the Law and Grace Unfolded, The 31, 73, 75, 76, 83, 96, 100, 114, 122, 157, 224, 235
Doe, Charles 72, 81-2, 84, 88, 139, 249, 260
Donne, John 13, 34
Donne, John (poet) 93, 263
Draper, J. W. 173
Dryden, John 246, 263

Edwards, John 250
election 46, 47, 148-9, 171, 176-80
Eliot, George 257
Eliot, T. S. 225
Emerson, Ralph Waldo 254
Encyclopaedia Britannica 252
enthusiasm 256
Erasmus, Desiderius 237
Evangelical Revival 249-51
Everard, John 118
Exclusion Crisis 40
Exposition on . . . Genesis, An 41, 144-5, 164

Familists 15, 79
Fathers
  Church 50
  Desert 118, 120
  Greek 131
  Latin 141
Fenn(e), John 34, 77
Fenn(e), Samuel 25, 34
Ferrar, Nicholas 77
Few Sighs from Hell, A 31, 68, 72, 73, 76, 78, 82, 89, 109, 140, 141, 155, 161, 222, 238, 244
Fifth Monarchists 12-13, 27, 28, 77
Fish, Stanley 211, 218, 219, 240, 263
Forrest, James, F. 175, 259
Foster, William 139
Fowler, Edward, Bp. of Gloucester 36, 48, 49, 55-9, 60, 61, 77, 147
Fox, George 241, 242
Foxe, John 106, 107, 153
Fraser, James 192
Froude, John 258
Fulgentius, St, Bp. of Ruspe 146

Gammon, John 42
Gay, John 247
Gentleman's Magazine, The 251-2
Gibbs, John 13, 83, 243
Gibson, Richard 106
Gifford, John 83
  and founding of Bedford Church 7, 8
  and Bunyan 1, 6-7, 11, 12, 17, 19, 127, 196, 241
  on churchmanship 8
Glanvill, Joseph 48, 49
Good News for the Vilest of Men 42, 90, 122
Goodwin, Thomas 185
Gottschalk 146
Grace 45, 47, 50, 111, 114, 147
Grace Abounding 3, 25, 29-30, 31, 74, 75, 76, 81, 84, 103, 113, 120, 146, 157, 170, 214, 215, 221, 225, 229, 234, 251, 262
  additions to subsequent editions of 87, 88-9
  authorial presence in 195, 200-1, 207
  and autobiographical tradition 190-2, 194, 206
  casual dating in 3, 241
  doubts of election in 148, 149, 157, 158-9, 197-8
  endlessness of spiritual struggle in 195, 197-204
  episode of 'unpardonable sin' in 122-3, 198-200
  episode of the vision of the people of Bedford in 86, 159, 195
  inconclusiveness of 202-5
  and *Pilgrim's Progress* 85, 166, 168, 208-9, 211
  'psychodrama' and mistaking in 192-8, 207, 226
  as record of Bunyan's early experience 3-5, 9-10, 114
  self-scrutiny in 193-4
  style of 91, 109
Granger, James 252-3
Greatness of the Soul, The 38, 39, 95, 170
Greaves, Richard L. 78, 141, 259
Gregory the Great, St 119
Gregory of Nyssa, St 131
Griffith, George 35

Hall, Basil 2
Hallam, Henry 257

Haller, William 261
Halyburton, Thomas 191, 193
Hammond, Henry 50
Harris, Howel 249
Hastings, Selina, Ct. of Huntingdon 250
Hawker, Robert 251
Hawkins, Anne 200, 202, 203
Hawthorne, Nathaniel 256
Hayes, Simon 34
Hazlitt, William 254, 255
Heavenly Footman, The 116, 120, 197, 238
  date of composition of 31-2
hell 72, 73n, 112, 115, 185
Hierocles 59
Hilders(h)am, Arthur 196
Hill, Christopher 25, 76, 261
Herbert, George 77, 130, 132, 258
Hobbes, Thomas 72
Holcroft, Francis 36
Holy City, The 21, 25, 29, 35, 77, 78, 80, 84, 86, 162, 163, 164
Holy Life, A 38, 68, 69, 89, 156
Holy War, The 61n, 71, 79, 81, 85-6, 121-2, 129, 149, 161, 170, 179, 180n, 208, 226, 227, 236, 238, 245, 249, 258
  abstract and iconographical method of 214-16
  conscience in 61n, 122
  and contemporary political affairs 40
  Diabolus in 103, 222-3
  Holy Spirit in 122, 169
  style of 91, 98, 99, 102-3, 108-9, 110
Homer 150, 258n
House of the Forest of Lebanon, The 144, 164
How, Samuel 92-3, 141
Hugo, Victor 113
Hume, David 248
Hunter, A. Mitchell 181
Hussey, Maurice 173
Hyde, Edward, 1st. E. of Clarendon 84
hypocrisy 172-80

Ignatius of Antioch, St 125
Independents: see Congregationalists
Instruction for the Ignorant 37, 156
intentionality 218
Israel's Hope Encouraged 38
Ivimey, Joseph 251
I Will Pray with the Spirit 22-3, 77, 80, 83, 84, 129

Index

James II 41
James, Henry 225
James, William 198, 202, 204, 260
Jerusalem Sinner Saved, The: see *Good News for the Vilest of Men*
Jessey, Henry 13, 17, 35
John of the Cross, St 117–18
Johnson, Richard 74
Johnson, Samuel 247
Julian of Norwich 134
justification 46, 50, 59, 60–2, 67, 68–9, 94, 103, 114–15, 117, 128, 154
Justin Martyr, St 120

Kaufmann, U. Milo 196, 211, 262
Keach, Benjamin 39, 63n
Keats, John 254
Kelynge, Sir John 23, 106, 225
Kempis, Thomas à 45, 57
Kendall, R. T. 176
Kiffin, William 17, 35, 39
King, Daniel 39
Knollys, Hanserd 39
Knott, John R., jun. 262

Lamb, Charles 254
Lamb, Thomas 39
Langland, William 263
Larkin, George 81
Last Sermon 42, 149, 180
Latitudinarianism 45–62, 67–9
Leavis, F. R. 190n, 263
L'Estrange, Sir Roger 77
Levellers 5
Levin, Samuel 221
Lewis, C. S. 99
Life and Death of Mr Badman, The 38, 71, 74, 81, 85, 87, 149, 258
and the difficulty of interpreting Providence 171, 172, 181–7
Light for Them that Sit in Darkness 36, 137, 163
Lindall, William 225
logocentricity 218
London, Bunyan's connexions with 12–13, 35, 37, 38, 39, 42, 56
Lord's Supper, in Bunyan's thought 9, 16, 17, 125–6, 126–7
Lower Samsell, Beds. 22
Luther, Martin 87
influence of on Bunyan 7, 24, 74–5, 112, 158, 194

Macaulay, Thomas Babington, 1st. B. Macaulay 255
Maltby, W. R. 112
Man, William 34
Mandel, Barrett John 192
Mapp Shewing the Order . . . of Salvation and Damnation, A 90n, 141, 145
marginalia 219, 227–8, 235, 236–7
Marshall, Walter 130
Mason, William 250, 255
Masson, David 258
Methodism 249
Millenarianism 15–16, 25, 27–9, 78, 80
Milton, John 105, 144, 184, 216, 248, 255, 258, 263
Montgomery, James 251
Moralism: see Latitudinarianism
More, Stephen 42
Morley, Henry 258
Moxon, Joseph 87
Mueller, Janel M. 99–100

Newman, Dorman 81
Newport Pagnell, Bucks. 3, 13, 34, 79, 82, 83
Newton, John 250
Nonconformists 25, 27, 28, 29, 34, 35, 40, 41, 49, 50, 93, 254, 256, 258
Nonconformity, grounds for Bunyan's 21–5
Nussbaum, Felicity 207
Nuttall, Geoffrey, F. 261

Offor, George 259, 260
Ogilvie, John 248
Olney, James 207
One Thing is Needful 27
Owen, John 35, 56, 89, 94, 243
Owst, G. R. 160

Palmer, Anthony 35
Parker, Samuel, Bp. of Oxford 93–4
Patrick, Simon, Bp. of Ely 48, 49, 59
Paul, St 95, 99, 129, 138, 153, 195, 222, 231, 232, 233, 237, 260
influence of on Bunyan 4, 6, 98, 100, 101, 161
Paul, Thomas 35, 38
Peaceable Principles and True 35
Péguy, Charles 113
Penn, William 36
Perfectionism 119, 131

276 Index

Perkins, William 92, 122, 141, 159, 171-2, 177, 180, 185, 226-7
perseverance 117, 131-2, 174
Pertenhall, Beds. 13
Pilgrim's Progress, The 36, 38, 41, 71, 72, 74, 75, 76, 83, 86, 87, 88, 90, 110, 111, 112, 143, 146, 150, 151, 161, 170, 215, 238, 249, 250, 251, 252, 253, 254, 255, 256, 258, 259, 263
  Apology for Part I of 33, 164, 223, 245
  Atheist in 173, 175, 209
  Biblical inspiration of 164-5
  By-ends in 47, 63, 65-6, 85, 87, 105, 157, 173, 222, 228, 234
  Christian's flight in 149, 165
  Christian's progress in 131, 166-7, 208, 211
  date of composition of Part I of 32-3, 84-5
  Delectable Mountains in 166-7, 232
  Doubting Castle in 168, 179, 211, 225, 229, 234
  election and assurance in 171, 172, 176-80
  emphasis of Part II of 38, 39, 178-80, 214
  endlessness of spiritual struggle in 211-12
  Evangelist in 64, 100, 102, 165, 233
  Faithful in 106, 107, 190, 210
  Feeble-mind in 38
  Formalist and Hypocrisie in 172-3
  Gaius in 217, 233
  and *Grace Abounding* 85, 166, 168, 208-9, 211
  Great-heart in 127, 178
  and Hebrews 165, 259
  Hopeful in 63, 67, 120, 168, 224, 228, 262
  hypocrites in 174-6, 178-80
  Ignorance in 47, 63, 66-7, 114-15, 173, 175, 209, 212-13, 214
  inconclusiveness of 212-14, 235
  insecurity in 210-12
  inspired origin of 85
  Interpreter's House in 166, 167
  interpretative challenge and hermeneutics of 208-10, 217-40
  Little-faith in 208
  marginalia of 219-20
  memory in 167-8, 211, 212
  and oral culture 74, 90, 108-9
  Palace Beautiful in 125, 148, 166, 167
  Pliable in 149
  publication of Part I of 33, 37, 80-1, 84-5
  publication of Part II of 38
  revisions and additions to 63, 85
  River of Death in 133, 230
  spurious Part III of 246
  style of 98, 100, 101-2, 108
  success of Part I of 85, 245
  Talkative in 102, 105, 157, 179, 189-91, 231, 256
  trial scene in 106
  Vanity Fair in 63, 64-5, 106, 165, 209-10, 223
  vicissitudes in 117
  Worldly-Wiseman in 47, 63-4, 66, 87, 100, 101-2, 165, 212, 213
Poe, Edgar Allan 220
Poiret, Pierre 249
Ponder, Nathaniel 37, 80, 81, 83, 245, 246
Pope, Alexander 246, 247
Popish, Plot 37, 38
Powell, Vavasor 17, 74, 84, 89, 140
prayer 23, 80, 128-30, 154
Predestination 146-50
Presbyterians 2, 24
Prison Meditations 26-7, 90n
Prodigal Son, the 237, 239-40
Profitable Meditations 25-6, 31
Prosopopoeia 221
Providence 171, 181-7
Prynne, William 247
Puritanism 137
  and Bunyan 1-2, 18-19, 137, 155, 159
  importance of experimental religion in 189-90
  preference of for stylistic plainness 92-3
  radical 2, 5, 79

Quakers 2, 5, 31, 113, 116, 173
  Bunyan's controversies with the 12, 15-17, 79, 82, 103-5, 154-5, 242
Quarles, Francis 246, 247
Questions About . . . the Seventh-Day Sabbath 38-9

Ranters 2, 5-6, 15, 16, 17, 31, 79, 113, 116, 155, 179

Relation of the Imprisonment of Mr John Bunyan, A 105–6, 153, 170, 224, 225, 252
Reprobation Asserted 147
Restoration (1660) 21, 243
Resurrection of the Dead, The 27, 84
Revolution, English 261
Richardson, Samuel 247
Rogers, John 13
Romanticism 251–6
Royal Society 52
Ruskin, John 260

Sabbath 39
Sacraments: see Baptism; Lord's Supper
Salmon, Joseph 6
Sanders, Laurence 107
Sasek, Lawrence A. 261
Saved by Grace 37, 72
Scott, Thomas 250
Scott, Sir Walter 253–4, 255, 260
Seasonable Counsel: or, Advice to Sufferers 40, 79, 161
Sharrock, Roger 32, 38, 191, 192, 208, 242, 261, 262
Sherman, Thomas 245
Sibbes, Richard 177, 203
Simeon, Charles 131
Simpson, John 13, 17
sin 4, 10, 11, 120–2
  against the Holy Spirit 122–4
  original 138
Smith, Edward 247
Smith, Francis 81, 82, 83
Smith, John 59, 60
Smith, Thomas 139
Socinianism 144
Solomon's Temple Spiritualized 140, 162, 163–4, 201
Some Gospel-Truths Opened 15, 73, 75, 82, 83, 138, 162, 242
soteriology 46–7, 146–50, 157
South, Robert 95
Southey, Robert 251, 254–5, 256, 258
Spengemann, William C. 206
Spensely, Richard 77, 83, 243
Spenser, Edmund 170, 247, 253, 255, 258
Strait Gate, The 36–7, 42, 62n, 68
Stevington, Beds. 13, 34
style, prose
  Bible and 98
  Bible and Bunyan's 98–101

Bunyan's 91–2, 94–7, 103–7, 247, 248, 251, 254, 256
  colloquiality of Bunyan's 85, 101, 107–9
  Puritanism and plain 92–3
  Restoration debates about 50, 93–4, 97
  'Satanic rhetoric' 101–3

Taine, Hippolyte 258
Taylor, Jeremy, Bp. of Down & Connor 50, 57
Taylor, Thomas 34
Tertullian 142
Thackeray, William Makepeace 256
theology
  Biblical sources of Bunyan's 137–40
  covenant 141
  other sources of Bunyan's 141
  see: Calvinism, Election, Grace, Justification, Predestination, Perseverance, Righteousness, Soteriology, Trinitarianism, Works
Theophilus, St, Bp. of Antioch 144
Thomason, George 76
Tillotson, John, Abp. of Canterbury 246
  and latitudinarianism 49, 52, 53
  style of 95–7
Tindall, William York 261
Tombes, John 17, 35
Treatise of the Fear of God, A 38, 75, 81, 89
Trinitarianism 144–6
Tristram Shandy 234, 240
Tyndale, William 99, 100
typology 162, 163–4

Uniformity, Act of (1662) 21, 22, 52, 79, 243
Unitarianism 144

Venables, Edmund 259
Venner, Thomas 28, 78
Vindication of Some Gospel-Truths Opened, A 16, 73, 82, 83, 154, 242
Virgil 248

Waite, John 36
Water of Life, The 42, 81, 162
Watkins, Owen 261
Watson, Richard 56, 57
Wavel, Richard 39

Wesley, Charles 119
Wesley, John 131, 249
Wheeler, William 13, 15, 34
Whichcote, Benjamin 48–9, 51, 52
Whitaker, William 162
Whitefield, George 249
Whiteman, John 25
Whyte, Alexander 127
Wickens, Robert 199
Wilkins, John, Bp. of Chester 47, 48, 49, 52–5, 56, 59
Wills, Obadiah 35
Winstanley, Gerrard 73
Wood, Anthony à 72
Wordsworth, Dorothy 254
Wordsworth, William 86–7, 216
Work of Jesus Christ as an Advocate, The: see *Advocateship of Jesus Christ, The*
works 46–7, 50, 61, 68–9, 114–15
Wright, John 34
Wright, John, the elder 83
Wright, John, the younger 82, 83
Wright, M. 82